American Scots-Irish Research: Strategies and Sources in the Quest for Ulster-Scots Origins

By Dwight A. Radford

Getting Them Over the Water—An Irish Immigration Strategies Series

Copyright 2020 - June 2022 Printing
Dwight A. Radford
No part of this book may be reproduced in any form without permission in writing from the author or publisher except in brief quotations in articles or reviews.

Published by Family Roots Publishing Co., LLC
PO Box 1682
Orting, WA 98360-1682
WWW.FamilyRootsPublishing.com

Library of Congress Control Number: 2020942030

Paperback ISBN: 978-1-62859-280-1
eBook ISBN: 978-1-62859-281-8

Printed in the United States of America

Recommended Citation:
Radford, Dwight A., *American Scots-Irish Research: Strategies and Sources in the Quest for Ulster-Scots Origins.* Orting, WA: Family Roots Publishing Co., LLC, 2020.

Dedication

I dedicate this book to two of my good friends whose devoted assistance and donated time made this work possible. First, to Karen Meyn of Pennsylvania, who spent countless hours with the manuscript and questioning me so that the text would emerge as comprehensible as possible. Writing about and explaining genealogy is difficult, and she was on my right side throughout it all despite other commitments. Second, to Wade Hone of Utah, whose friendship over the last 30 years resulted in his creation of an amazing layout of graphics for the book. He was on my left side while withstanding daily interferences.

Both Karen and Wade are my inspiration for never allowing any circumstance to be a hindrance to friendship and love. They are indeed the best friends one could have. It has been my honor to be part of their lives.

Dwight Radford
West Valley City, Utah
United States

Abbreviations Referenced in Maps and Text

Scottish Shires/Counties

ABD= Aberdeen
ANS= Angus
ARL= Argyll
AYR= Ayr
BAN= Banff
BEW= Berwick
BUT= Bute
CAI= Caithness
CLK= Clackmannan
DFS= Dumfries
DNB= Dunbarton
ELN= East Lothian
FIF= Fife
INV= Inverness
KCD= Kincardine
KKD= Kirkudbright
KRS= Kinross
LKS= Lanark
MLN= Midlothian
MOR= Moray
NAI= Nairn
PEE= Peebles
PER= Perth
RFW= Renfrew
ROC= Ross and Cromarty
ROX= Roxburgh
SEL= Selkirk
STI= Stirling
SUT= Sutherland
WIG= Wigtown
WLN= West Lothian

Other

GENUKI=
Genealogy United Kingdom
and Ireland

IRE=
Republic of Ireland

MM=
Monthly Meeting (Quakers)

NARA=
National Archives and
Records Administration
(USA)

NI=
Northern Ireland

PRONI=
Public Record Office of
Northern Ireland

USA=
United States of America

Map/Image/Chart Reference List

Canada

Table of Contents

Scotland

Ulster

Connacht

Leinster

Munster

Foreword

By Wendy Elliott

"You're not alone" is a frequently used phrase to provide comfort, support, and understanding to another; these words also express encouragement. This phrase certainly works regarding the approaches Dwight Radford details for genealogists doing Scots-Irish research. All of us encounter a brick wall once in a while, and most of us need to follow our ancestors' paths from county to county, state to state, and across an ocean or sea to trace earlier generations. In this study, he discusses proven methods to avoid common hurdles and suggests records while explaining research strategies that may assist in providing a new breakthrough.

Working together is also the best approach to push through many genealogical quagmires. When we're bogged down, we may not realize the path to take, but others do. In this case, Radford—using thirty-plus years of experience as a professional genealogist—explains successful sources and methodologies for documenting Ulster Scots-Irish families. He reminds us that our ancestors were not alone; they lived among friends and family. When they moved to a new location, crossed a sea, or emigrated from their homeland, they didn't act alone. They worshiped together, made major decisions with input from friends and family, and rarely made difficult decisions on their own. Thus, he discusses research tactics to reconstruct and document neighborhoods and shows how using the records of many provides results that may help solve a lack of evidence for another.

Obviously, if you have Ulster Scots-Irish family, you know that no guidebook will provide instant answers, but Radford gives direction and discusses the availability, usefulness, and limitations of sources. He examines available records for the various groups and times and explains that with thorough research, these then can provide documentation of family members' moves. He reminds us not to think linearly, but to trace the generations both ways to find information. The evidence needed may not be recorded by members in our direct line, but records for their relatives—or even neighbors—may provide the sought-after details of who or where.

Perhaps, we need to remind ourselves that we are not alone; others have charted the paths that we need to follow to resolve our genealogical puzzles. Radford provides a delightful, short overview of United States history and discusses the records that resulted from these events. He reminds us that these events in our nation's past generated evidence we can use to pursue our families' histories.

Radford covers conventional "genealogical" resources such as church, military, vital, and immigrations records and includes topics such as wives' maiden names and typical migration patterns. He concentrates on the value of often neglected resources explaining how these may provide the documentation needed and suggests strategies for overcoming common problems. He discusses land and tax records and points out their value for genealogists. He addresses "unconventional" research methods and explains how the lack of records may result in relying on a Preponderance of Evidence to document the family history.

He provides a brief overview of each state's genealogical records with at least one bibliographical reference; he does the same for researching in the Canadian provinces. He acknowledges general websites, and for each section or topic, provides relevant sources.

The strength of Radford's work is in his Special Strategies section, where he charts new territory, explains the difficulties for Americans' use of Ulster records and guidebooks, and suggests strategies to resolve some of those problems. Then he gives a long overview of the Latter-day Saint history, genealogical interest explanation, members' migrations, proselytizing, and the resulting world's largest collection of historical and family history records. A third section discusses often overlooked Native American history, records, and connections with the Scots-Irish. He concludes these emphases with strategies for tracing the history of United Empire Loyalists and the records created in the Canadian provinces.

Reading Radford's work is enjoyable; he reminds even this tired and retired researcher of sources and strategies that are normally useful in solving genealogical research. His focus is on tracing Ulster Scots-Irish families' histories. His ideas will help us to discover some answers for our genealogical dilemmas. His work reminds us that we are not alone; genealogy is an addictive hobby, and we're all in this together.

Wendy Bebout Elliott, PhD

Professor Emerita of History, California State University, Fullerton
Past President of the Federation of Genealogical Societies
Distinguished Service from Utah Genealogical Association
Retired professional genealogist and author.

Introduction

By Dwight A. Radford

For more than thirty years, I have lived in Salt Lake City, working as a professional genealogist in the huge Family History Library. For my projects, I also have conducted extensive research at archives throughout the United States, Ireland, and Northern Ireland. Professional genealogists encounter almost every family history topic. Fortunately, during my decades of employment experience on others' genealogies, I have been able to explore techniques that do and do not result in breakthroughs in tracing lineages. In these pages, I have shared exactly how I, as a professional, would analyze and evaluate sources to develop plans to track ancestors from ethnic and cultural populations who had few early or complete records.

The Scots-Irish present the ultimate challenge in implementing unconventional research methods because of the scarceness of documentation for the group before immigration to the United States. The information herein is limited to Ulster, where most Scots-Irish were born, and mainly underscores records and strategies from the United States that will assist in proving or at least indicating the birthplace of an ancestor from that province.

The historic province of Ulster includes counties on both sides of the post-1921 border, which today separates Northern Ireland and the Republic of Ireland. They are Antrim (NI), Armagh (NI), Cavan (IRE), Donegal (IRE), Down (NI), Fermanagh (NI), Londonderry (Derry) (NI), Monaghan (IRE), and Tyrone (NI). The focus of this work is on non-Catholic families, because the majority of what is termed Scots-Irish or Ulster-Scots belonged to a denomination not of the Catholic tradition. Yet most people think of the Ulster-Scots as being Presbyterians, which is also a little narrow. Many came as Anglicans, Brethren (Plymouth) and Gospel Hall, Methodists, Moravians, Mormons, and Quakers. The people who did arrive as Presbyterians became unchurched for a couple of generations on the frontiers of the United States because few, if any, clergy or schools were in a number of areas. The Scots-Irish would convert to or reunite with the Presbyterian Church during the revivals on the frontiers, leaving the impression that they always had been Presbyterian.

While directing clients and communicating with other researchers over the years, I have learned how indispensable search tactics are in finding answers to investigations as difficult as those for the Scots-Irish and other groups. In addition to my freelance work for hire, I have spent countless hours as a professional consultant in one-to-one settings, and so I have witnessed how people undertake, correctly or incorrectly, complicated explorations. I also have been given substantial opportunities to converse with and accrue invaluable knowledge from many great researchers in the industry, who, during my formative genealogy career, impressed upon me the value of certain records, for instance, those for taxes and lands. That education also explains why I have chosen certain subjects to explain and have disregarded others, and although drawing attention to many of them,

I want to concentrate on strategies. When researchers know how to use documents effectively, even some with no apparent relevance can be helpful. Again, as the example, tax books do not have birthplaces, and so novices probably would not look at them. For seasoned researchers and as my mentors taught me, tax rolls can be a most important tool for discerning who is who, and where and when they were living.

I have observed researchers each spending years looking for a piece of paper stating where a person was born in Ulster. If one is found, it is remarkable, but in most cases, the pursuit is more complex. In the large majority of cases, the paper is nonexistent. What is required is not only identifying the immigrant but also tracing his or her life step by step for clues. It can be necessary to document the children and grandchildren of the immigrant in the hope that someone from a branch of the family preserved the knowledge of an Ulster birthplace. You may be the one who designs a new pattern of analysis that works for your family problem. The same tactic may not be successful for someone else's genealogy, but it will yield discoveries for you because of the circumstances in which your ancestors lived.

This is not a book for those seeking effortless answers. It is intended to disclose research strategies that perhaps have not been considered before. I ask that researchers not think in linear terms. If Scots-Irish research, especially in the eighteenth and early nineteenth centuries, were easy, the place of origin in Ulster would have been found long ago. Linear thinking, which seems to promote the notion of the existence of a document stating a place of birth when, in fact, it was never created, typically will hinder research and waste time. In most cases, an entry noting where someone was born in the 1700s is not in an archive in either Ireland or Northern Ireland. Therefore, it remains a United States research problem. The assertion is not that Irish sources cannot be used effectively but that records of births for documenting most Ulster-Scots during the 1700s are scarce. For 1800s immigrants, registers of birthplaces may be in Ulster. The same is true from the United States side of the research process, yet even that depends on the period, the sources, and the circumstances in which a family found itself.

Before the 1820s, the chance of finding an Ulster paper trail to where an immigrant was born is rare because the average Protestant church register began only in the 1820s or the 1830s, although that is not a universal fact. Every case can be an exception. After all, Quaker records date back to the 1600s and Moravian sources to the mid-1700s, and so in addressing and eventually solving the origins' question, research must be directed at several threads at the same time. It also means certain old family stories or stereotypes must be discarded while others must be adopted. Instead of direct evidence, reading between the lines and attentiveness to the preponderance of evidence are often all that can be accomplished and offered as proof. Thereupon, research becomes more of an art form instead of a hard science.

When a point needs to be stressed, the principle of repetition in the clarification of material is also employed over several of these chapters or within a single chapter. Thus, if a detail is missed in one area of the book, it can be picked up in another. Certain research procedures are really that significant, and they tie together various topics. A system, such as reconstructing and documenting an ancestor's neighborhood, may solve a research problem, and it is essential to repeat the technique in several places.

Another part of the strategies is not about reconstructing the immigrant's life but only about identifying him or her. Some researchers have not found their immigrant ancestors, and that becomes their main goal. Afterward, Ulster origins can be addressed.

Special Strategy Chapters

Several methods presented in this guide may seem unfamiliar or at least unusual. Consequently, more expansive information is provided in a kind of mini-research paper in the four "Special Strategy" chapters at the end of the book.

The first is "Using Ulster Records." Although marvelous books are on the market to teach researchers how to use the records of Ireland and specifically Ulster, they have their limitations. As a particular, they are usually written by genealogists in Ireland and Northern Ireland who are expertly familiar with the sources, but their approach assumes that researchers are ready to use them. Their books can help with immigration problems if the period is right, and they should not be overlooked. However, for families who immigrated before the 1820s and 1830s—the years when most churches began registering congregants—and especially for the tenant class, not many records of utility are in archives in either Ireland or Northern Ireland. Nineteenth century sources, often inventoried in the research guides, can still be utilized even if the ancestors emigrated in the eighteenth century. The "surname distribution" search mentioned in the "Using Ulster Records" chapter ties into additional information presented in the reference books produced in Ireland and Northern Ireland.

The second "Special Strategy" chapter, the Scots-Irish and Mormon connection, will be unfamiliar to most researchers and remains largely unexplored as a topic of its own. I discovered the odd relationship between the Mormons and the Scots-Irish when I moved to Utah and began a career in family history. The logic is straightforward and, once pondered, makes sense and can even be applied to Quaker and Moravian families. Even if an ancestor did not convert to Mormonism, a sibling might have done so in Ulster or, more likely, in England or Scotland. Many Scots-Irish had settled in Scotland and around Lancashire, England, by the 1830s and 1840s. There, the Mormon missionaries converted the scores of Scots-Irish Protestants who were already uprooted. The converts then were expected to immigrate into the Mormon colonies in the United States to help build Zion. Because of the Latter-day Saint emphasis on genealogy, the birthplace of a family from Ulster could have been preserved in its Mormon records. The accounts left behind by these converts can predate the beginning of most Protestant registers in Ulster and the founding of the Latter-day Saint movement itself, in 1830, making it a viable study. To hear researchers talk about discovering their "Mormon branch of the family" is not surprising.

The third "Special Strategy" chapter may seem unexpected to anyone who does not have a legend of a Native American ancestor somewhere in the family. The lore, whether true or not, is quite common, especially among people with roots in the southeastern United States. The historical relationship between the Southeast United States Native American tribes and the Scots-Irish and other Europeans is examined in numerous books. It may be that the origins of the family in Ulster lie in a record or book about a mixed-race family. Intermarriage, or at least having children, between the two groups was so frequent that by the time of removal, a good percentage of the Southeastern tribes had a large number of mixed-race (mixed-blood). In fact, many whites were on the Trail of Tears with their Indian wives and mixed-race children. The mixed-race families who were not removed stayed and intermarried with each other, the local white community, or the free color communities that riddled the South. Bi-racial and tri-racial backgrounds are complicated indeed, yet they generated written histories and genealogies. Using logic similar to the Mormon connection, even if your ancestor did not intermarry with a member of a tribe, a sibling might have.

The fourth "Special Strategy" chapter concentrates on the Ulster-Scots who became Loyalists and were exiled to what is now Canada. Among Americans, a common myth is that all Scots-Irish were loyal to the United States during the Revolutionary War. Perhaps the majority of them were. However, for those who were not, or for families who had split allegiances, entirely new sets of records are open for exploration. Because so many Canadians descend from Loyalists, they are accustomed to using those documents as primary sources in their research. Many Americans, though, especially the novices, may not be aware Loyalists existed. Keep in mind, such a large influx of Loyalists arrived in exile to Canada from the United States that several modern provinces owe their origins to that exodus.

As with the Mormons and Native Americans, a birthplace in Ulster preserved in the Loyalist branch of the family answers the most important question being asked. Where was the family from? Often, the problem is most difficult to solve from the United States perspective, but the Loyalists' records may have the locations. The incoming refugees often arrived in their new homes with only the clothes they wore. To accommodate so many people, the British had to begin organizing and interrogating them. The information collected frequently included birthplaces.

Also, just as the Americans have associations such as the National Society and the Daughters of the American Revolution, the Canadians have the United Empire Loyalists' Association of Canada that created still more material as descendants submitted their genealogies for society membership.

Use of Websites and Databases

Within each chapter is a listing of websites and particular databases. Unfortunately, one of the curses of writing in the modern age of technology is that website addresses can become obsolete the moment a book is published. To at least try to avoid the difficulty, the websites are mentioned in brief. State and local websites will alter. It is assumed that the titles of standard ones, such as Ancestry.com, FamilySearch.org, Findmypast.com, and MyHeritage.com, will remain constant, similar to books; therefore, they are presented in that format.

Currently, no organization alone can index everything, and so various organizations are cooperating to index and share databases and indexers. As a result, Ancestry.com and Findmypast.com may have identical databases as part of their subscription memberships, whereas the same one will be free on FamilySearch.org, which is a non-profit organization.

Chapter Topics

The material herein is not intended to cover all sources for all times and places. The chapters have been carefully chosen to reflect the starting places that are necessary to trace a family back, in order to at least identify the immigrant and not necessarily to find immigrant origins. Only after these sources are investigated can Ulster origins be examined. The search includes land and tax registers, although they typically have no reason to convey where someone was born. Others, such as naturalization and military, may state a birthplace in Ulster.

An area that is noticeably absent is a chapter on DNA, and for a deliberate reason. Even if a DNA match is found and the place in Ulster is indicated or identified, the paper trail still has to be undertaken to link to the DNA match and ancestor. Without the proper paperwork in place, the DNA findings are but the pot of gold at the end of the rainbow— with the rainbow missing.

Conclusions

I hope that the material in this book will help open new research areas for families who have been mired in their Scots-Irish lineages for years. It is not impossible research, but it cannot be judged by English, Scottish, or Welsh explorations, where parish registers can be hundreds of years old. Resolving a Scots-Irish predicament is hard work, but it can be rewarding if approached in a non-linear fashion. Linear thinking has A + B = C, which is not how this type of pursuit usually is performed. The approach is definitely unconventional: It is more A + B = C, but only by taking C and going back to A and B two or three times can results be obtained.

Dwight Radford
West Valley City, Utah
United States

Figure 1: Counties in the historical Ulster Province.

Chapter One

Who Were the Scots-Irish?

The majority of Scots-Irish came from the historical Ulster Province, the six counties that now comprise Northern Ireland (Antrim, Armagh, Down, Fermanagh, Londonderry, and Tyrone) and three in the Republic of Ireland (Cavan, Donegal, and Monaghan). What constitutes the Scots-Irish is complicated and depends on how broadly or narrowly a person defines the terms Scots-Irish, Irish, Scots, and British.

Traditionally, the ethnic group of Scots-Irish is generally thought of as Presbyterian and Scottish in origin, and although the categorization was mostly true in the 1600s, it is now somewhat incomplete because of intermarriages and church conversions in Ulster. An example of the obscuring of the traditional Scottish surname would be an immigrant who has a Welsh father named Jones and a Scot-Irish mother named Stewart, resulting in the immigration under the Welsh surname Jones. Jones, however, does not mean the person was not Scot-Irish. The same is true with religion. A Presbyterian and Catholic marrying in Ulster does not exclude the person and his or her descendants from being Scots-Irish even if they arrived in America as Roman Catholics, Anglicans, Methodists, Quakers, Mormons, Plymouth Brethren, Moravians, or nothing at all! Even though the focus of this book is mainly on Protestants, ancestors, regardless of their surnames or religions, could have been Scots-Irish.

The description Scots-Irish, or as some say "Scotch-Irish," is an American-created word for those who were designated Ulster-Scots. They were the families who flooded from Ulster into the American colonies. While they have been in America since the 1600s, five distinct waves came, each of which contained large numbers:

> 1717-1718, when a destructive drought killed crops, the linen industry was crippled, and rack-renting prevailed;
>
> 1725-1729, when continued rack-renting and poverty prompted such a massive departure that even the English Parliament became fearful of losing the Protestant majority in the area;
>
> 1740-1741, when a famine struck and letters from relatives living in America encouraged emigration;

1754-1755, a time of a disastrous drought;

1771-1775, when leases on the large estate of the Marquis of Donegal in County Antrim expired and the tenants couldn't afford to renew them.

The chapters presented herein mainly concern conducting research for the throngs of people who arrived in the American colonies from Ulster beginning in 1718, when a group followed their Presbyterian minister to the Massachusetts Bay Colony, founding Londonderry, New Hampshire. As part of the original migration, the immigrants came from the area in and around Aghadowey Parish, County Londonderry. That first wave is undemanding for seeking the Ulster origins of an immigrant because it is a well-documented, congregational migration. Be aware, though, that most lineages are not as effortless, and so the purpose of this book, *American Scots-Irish Research: Strategies and Sources in the Quest for Ulster-Scots Origins,* is to facilitate the tracing of the ancestors' origins. Even if family roots are found in the original Londonderry, New Hampshire, citizens, the lineage has to be verified in a process to connect with that settlement so that generations will not be missed between when an ancestor arrived in 1718 and when the descendants settled elsewhere a hundred years later.

What if the ancestors came from the American South to Ohio from, for instance, North Carolina by way of East Tennessee and then to Ohio? Likely, they were not of the New Hampshire group

because the migration pattern, from New Hampshire to Ohio, was totally dissimilar than it would have been from North Carolina through East Tennessee into Ohio. Lots of rugged mountains and various river systems distinguish a migration pattern out of New England from one out of the American South. Therefore, Scots-Irish research in the 1700s and early 1800s, especially on the frontiers of America, is more complex than many people realize.

All the immigration waves occurred before a substantial number of records began to be created in Ireland, and so locating an entry from an index of church registers is not probable. Research from the 1700s and early 1800s customarily remains a United States problem with few Irish records, if any, ever consulted.

Ulster-Scots Origins and Migrations

The Scots-Irish had their origins in the wars between England and Ireland. The infamous Flight of the Earls in 1607 usually is pinpointed as the pivotal event that gave rise to the distinct Ulster-Scots. In 1607, the Catholic Irish Earls were forced to leave Ulster with many of their people, fleeing to the European continent. By the end of the Nine Years' War in 1603, Ulster lay bare. The same year, the province—desolate, destitute, and accompanied by famine—was destroyed, and Ulster fell under control of the English government in Ireland. The Gaelic system that had governed Ulster for centuries ended.

With the old order gone, a plan was devised to resettle the land with loyal Protestants from Scotland, England, and

Primary Scottish Landlords in Ulster

Antrim
- Stewart
- MacDonnell
- Adair
- Colville
- Shaw
- Agnew
- Edmonstone
- Hamilton

Armagh
- Acheson
- Hamilton

Cavan
- Craig
- Acheson
- Bailie
- Hamilton

Donegal
- Cunningham
- Knox
- Leslie
- Murray
- Stewart

Down
- Hamilton
- Montgomery

Fermanagh
- Balfour
- Creighton
- Dunbar
- Hume

Londonderry (Derry)
- McClelland

Monaghan
- None

Tyrone
- Drummond
- Erskine
- Hamilton
- Richardson
- Stewart

Wales. The arrangement was in cooperation with the London Guilds, who would receive large tracts of land to manage and supply with settlers, infamously becoming known as the Londonderry Plantation. A tenant's landlord could certainly have been a London Guild Company, explaining its name on records, particularly those in County Londonderry.

Most of the incoming settlers were farmers from the Scottish Lowlands. The largest numbers would come from Ayrshire, Galloway, Lanarkshire, Renfrewshire, and along the border of England. Some did emigrate from the northern areas and even the Highlands, but they were not among the majority. The farmers were land tenants in Scotland, having gone to Ulster for a better life, only to continue to be tenant farmers under the English landlord system. The early Scots from the Lowlands and the border areas were poor, subsistence farmers. They were already desperately seeking better circumstances for themselves, and their immigrations to Ulster assisted in alleviating Scotland of them and their accompanying social issues.

Even before the Flight of the Earls in 1607, the Scots began arriving in Ulster, mainly to Counties Antrim and Down. The relocation was a private venture of fortune seekers. The massive state sponsored settlements, the first of which was to the Londonderry Plantation in 1609, were schemes that lasted until 1697; therefore, not all Scots came to Ulster at one time. Later migrants to Ulster or their children, did go to the American colonies, and in such circumstances, it is common to find that families have preserved the knowledge of Scottish origins in their histories. An estimated 200,000 Scots had immigrated to Ulster in those ninety-odd years.

As a result of the wars, along with increasing rents by the landlords, economic pressures, and local famines in Ulster, leaving was considered a viable option. While numbers of people arrived before the 1718 first wave to the American colonies, they were the minority. After 1718, groups would enter, and as additional land opened up, even more would come from Ulster. The city of Londonderry (Derry) was a major port of departure. The counts dropped during the years of the French and Indian Wars (1754 to 1763) and stopped abruptly during the American Revolution. By the time the Revolution had ended, upwards of 200,000 had immigrated to America.

What became the United States might have been a favored destination, yet as time progressed into the 1800s, it was not the only one. Ulster-Scots can be documented in all corners of the British Empire. Many would join, or at least follow, the British Army involved in the industries and businesses that accompanied its institutions. Ulster-Scots were numerous in Australia, British India, Canada, the Caribbean, New Zealand, South Africa, and all parts of the empire. They can even be documented in the United Kingdom, especially Scotland, and in Argentina and Chile.

Argentina and Chile were not part of the British Empire, but established Protestant churches served them in Argentina, although few Protestant churches or ministers were in Chile. Workers are in the Roman Catholic "dissenting registers." In other words, from the 1840s under

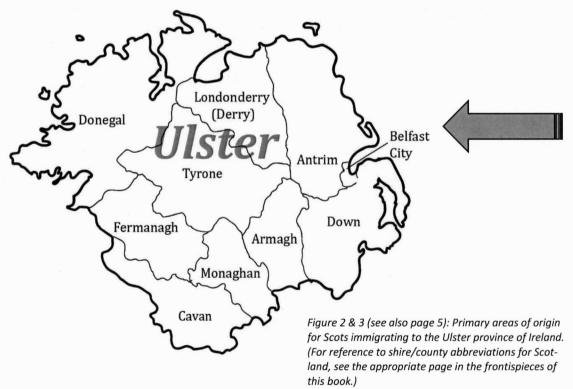

Figure 2 & 3 (see also page 5): Primary areas of origin for Scots immigrating to the Ulster province of Ireland. (For reference to shire/county abbreviations for Scotland, see the appropriate page in the frontispieces of this book.)

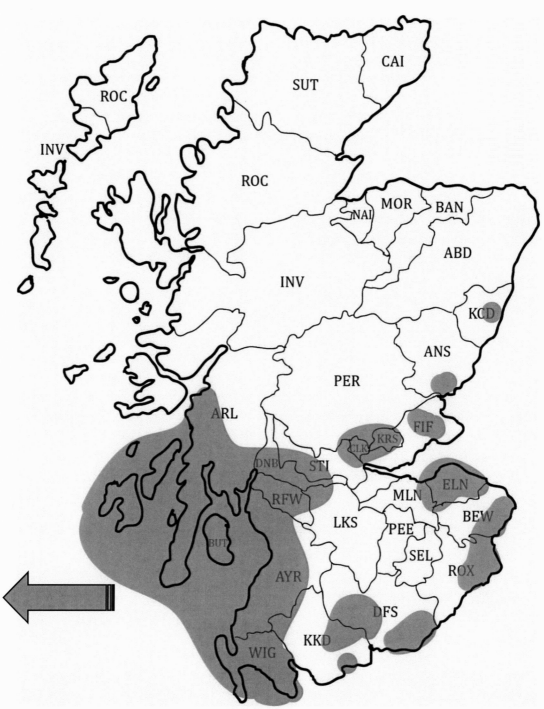

Chilean law, a Catholic priest could marry and baptize Presbyterians as Presbyterians but not as Catholics, called "according to their own rites." The incoming Ulster-Scots were buried in English cemeteries and were referred to as English, not as Scots or Ulster-Scots. Designated Protestant cemeteries are in Argentina,

and what came to be known as English cemeteries are scattered all along the coast of Chile.

Ulster-Scots also settled in the Netherlands, where they, as Protestants, were part of the Scottish Regiments who were stationed there. Both Scotland and the

Netherlands were Calvinist Protestants, a natural alliance. The soldiers married Dutch women, and their families are recorded in the Dutch Reformed Church registers.

In short, the migration of Ulster-Scots out of Ulster is more diverse and complex than most researchers realize. In regard to United States inquiries, the descendants of any of the worldwide Ulster migrants could have made their way to the United States. Consequently, United States search may lead somewhere else before it finds its way back to Ulster!

The Scotch-Irish Society of the United States of America promotes the history and culture of the Scots-Irish in America. On its website is an all-inclusive bibliography of published Scots-Irish books and articles compiled by Dr. Michael Montgomery. His list is a remarkable resource tool in itself and should be consulted for historical context.

Some excellent older and newer works are standard for the Scots-Irish. The older ones especially, written to accompany whatever topic is being addressed, can have lists of people. They are hidden lists, often forgotten, and can be a boon for the researcher. Among a select few books, considered to be time-honored among genealogists are:

Bolton, Charles Knowles. *Scotch Irish Pioneers in Ulster and America*. Boston, Massachusetts: Bacon and Brown, 1910.

Dickson, R. J. *Ulster Emigration to Colonial America, 1718-1785*. Belfast,

Northern Ireland: Ulster Historical Foundation, 2016.

Dunaway, W. F. *The Scotch-Irish of Colonial Pennsylvania*. Reprint. Baltimore, Maryland: Genealogical Publishing Co., Inc., 1985.

Fitzpatrick, F. *God's Frontiersmen: The Scots-Irish Epic*. London, England: Weidenfeld and Nicholson, 1989.

Ford, Henry Jones. *The Scotch-Irish in America*. Princeton, New Jersey: Princeton University Press, 1915.

Griffin, Patrick. *The People With No Name: Ireland's Ulster Scots, America's Scots Irish, and the Creation of a British Atlantic World, 1689-1764*. Princeton, New Jersey: Princeton University Press, 2001.

Hofstra, Warren R., ed. *Ulster to America: The Scots-Irish Migration Experience, 1680-1830*. Knoxville, Tennessee: University of Tennessee Press, 2011.

Leyburn, J. G. *The Scotch-Irish, A Social History. Chapel Hill, North Carolina:* University of North Carolina Press, 1962.

Marshall, William F., *Ulster Sails West: The Story of the Great Immigration from Ulster to North America*. Reprint. Baltimore, Maryland: Genealogical Publishing Co., 1977.

Montgomery, E. *The Scotch-Irish in America's History*. Belfast, Northern Ireland: Ulster-Scot Historical Foundation, 1965.

Webb, James. *Born Fighting: How the Scots-Irish Shaped America.* New York, New York: Broadway Books, 2004.

The Ulster-Scots Language (Ullans)

When the Scots-Irish entered the colonies and then the interior United States, survival took precedence over education in many areas. The types of records (or lack of them) in which an ancestor may be found are thereby affected. It was not exceptional for a Scot-Irish ancestor to have signed his or her name with an "X" on legal papers. Although the absence of literacy is not unusual on the frontiers of America, what is unique to the Scots-Irish is their accent.

Terms for the distinct accent among the isolated Scots-Irish population are various. One example is the "East Tennessee Twang," which is still definable. Today, accents are less problematic because most people are literate and spellings are standardized. To no small degree, the advent of nationwide television and radio programs have helped bring about a more uniform version of American English. Historically, however, the matter was not the same. Accents do affect what the records contain, and there are two main ways of looking at them.

In the first approach, if a family was illiterate, what they said for public documents was interpreted by someone else, such as a clerk or minister who could have been anywhere in a range from highly educated to only literate enough to be able to read and write. Hence, what was stated by the illiterate person and then written by the literate or semi-literate person can leave the family historian baffled. Regardless, the illiterate party was not the one writing, only speaking, and so some details are expected to have been lost in translation.

In the second approach, a literate or semi-literate family might have left behind a paper trail, such as wills, vital events in bibles, letters, and memories. If some of these are difficult to understand, think phonetically. What could the people have meant? If that does not help, perhaps it is time to consider the Ulster-Scots dialect and how it was transformed on the American frontier. For a legal record, the clerk or minister might not have cared whether the family members were literate or illiterate, but only that they could sign their names. Thus, the issues are the same as those in the first approach—that is, information was filtered through a second party.

Accents are particularly central to clarifying the censuses. Families might have been fluid on their surnames to the degree that McDonough became McDonner and McCurry became MacQuarry or just Cary—and they are the simple ones! Whether the fault was with the person giving the information or a civil servant, such as a census enumerator, may never be known. Recognize that the errors were habitual, and in determining how the name could have been written, it may be easier to read a county census one page at a time than to contend with the index.

Researchers often do not realize that the accents of the Scots-Irish in the United States originated as a distinct dialect in Ulster known as Ulster-Scots, or Ullans,

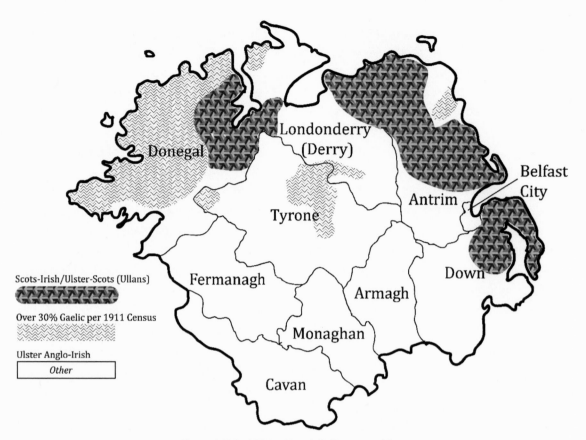

Figure 4: Select Ulster Linguistic Demographics.

concentrated mainly in certain areas of Counties Antrim, Down, and Donegal. Although it is not as common as it once was, it is still spoken by some in Ulster, with a current revival to preserve it.

The Ullans version of the Scots language is not only related to English but also to Dutch and Frisian. (Frisian is a West Germanic language spoken in the north of the Netherlands, mostly in Friesland Province.) Many words in both Scots and Ulster-Scots are shared with Danish and Norse. The Ulster-Scots Language Society, a registered non-sectarian charity in Northern Ireland, was formed in 1992 to encourage an interest in the Ullans language and literature as well as to protect and ensure both for future generations. The Society publishes several works and dictionaries for its purpose. For some,

whether Ullans is a dialect of Scots or a language in its own right continues to be debated.

Books and articles are available that might assist family research, although Ullans is a relatively unexplored topic among genealogists. The overall attention to it is somewhat new because the need to use it or lose it as a cultural marker has become evident. A few reference works are:

Fenton, James. *The Hamely Tongue: A Personal Record of Ulster-Scots in County Antrim.* 4th ed. Belfast, Northern Ireland: Ullans Press, 2014.

Montgomery, Michael. *From Ulster to America: The Scotch-Irish Heritage of*

American English. Belfast, Northern Ireland: Ullans Press, 2017.

Montgomery, Michael. 2006. "How Scotch-Irish is Your English?" *Journal of East Tennessee History* 77 (2006): 65-91. (In this article, Montgomery demonstrates the use of the dialect through examples of pronunciation, vocabulary, grammar, and immigrant letters from the 1700s. As scholars become more fascinated with the topic, more articles and websites no doubt will appear. The Ullans language is a subject that should be explored when documents are not clear or simply do not make sense. The language may explain why).

Robinson, Philip. Ulster-Scots: *A Grammar of the Traditional Written and Spoken Language*. 3rd ed. Belfast, Northern Ireland: Ullans Press, 2018.

Merely knowing that the issue of Ullans exists can revive and provide new possibilities in older reference works in the search for Ulster origins. One intriguing example, with many clues even exclusive of the birthplace in Ulster, is a short biography of Thomas Carr, a trader with the Muscogee (Creek) Nation:

> Thomas Carr (Creek). Scot "with the Irish dialect," trading at Cussetta, 1797; Hawkins in 1797 called him "an honest funny seaman;" last mentioned, 1824; said to be buried at Fort Mitchell, Alabama; father of Paddy, John (Tallassee Harjo), and Thomas (Don Martini's *The Southern Indians: A Biographical Guide to the Cherokee, Chickasaw, Choctaw, and Creek Indians, 1700-1907*. Ripley, Mississippi: [s.n.], 1993, p. 45).

The reference to Scot is to Scots-Irish, but more important is that he spoke "with the Irish dialect." Likely, the Ullans dialect was being indicated because his speaking with an Irish Gaelic one is not reasonable. Thomas Carr was a well-known Muscogee (Creek) Indian trader who married into the tribe, and his mixed-race descendants are in the thousands today.

Continuing with the foregoing example, a researcher not long ago, reading Thomas Carr's biographical sketch would have dismissed it as a typical accent of little significance. With the knowledge of Ullans, an investigation can advance another step. Concentrations of Ullans are known to be in the northern areas of Counties Donegal, Londonderry (Derry), Antrim, and Down. Also known is that as late as the time of Griffith's Primary Valuation (1847-1864), long after Thomas Carr had immigrated, the tax lists in those counties still carried the Carr surname. Because his small life history provides such a major clue, then what other records about Thomas Carr, Indian Trader, have been generated by historians, genealogists, descendants, and the Muscogee (Creek) over the decades? If a place of origin was not already known for Thomas Carr, the Ullans connection might have restricted it to the coastal areas of northern Ulster.

Scots or Scots-Irish

One research area that needs to be addressed when looking at the records or reading history books is whether the subject is a Scot or a Scot-Irish family. An essential consideration as research progresses is that beginning about 1609, the Scots and the Scots-Irish were separated. Although ties between Ulster and Scotland were historic and noteworthy, each culture had developed in its own way.

In United States research, it is customary to find Scots and Scots-Irish settling together. Having come from different places, they did not plan to do so, but they belonged to the same churches and social organizations. Even more convoluted is that they might have had the same last names, but they were not related to one another in any way.

"In United States research, it is customary to find Scots and Scots-Irish settling together. Having come from different places, they did not plan to do so, but they belonged to the same churches and social organizations. Even more convoluted is that they might have had the same last names, but they were not related to one another in any way."

Surnames from the Ulster Plantation Counties 1607 to 1633

The list below is adapted from Don Kelly's 1997 article "The Ulster Plantation (1605-1697)." He extracted the surnames from muster rolls and estate maps of 1607 through 1633 for Counties Antrim, Armagh, Cavan, Donegal, Down, Fermanagh, Londonderry (Derry), and Tyrone. The sources are cited in his article. The "Mac" and "Mc" names will be found after the "M" entries because they pose challenging spellings. The variations do not matter. If the pronunciation of a name is the same, it typically is the same.

Abercorn: Tyrone
Abercrombie: Down
Acheson: Armagh, Tyrone
Adair: Antrim, Donegal, Down
Adams: Down
Agnew: Antrim, Down
Aicken: Down
Alexander: Donegal
Allen: Armagh, Donegal, Down
Anderson: Cavan, Down, Londonderry (Derry), Tyrone
Andrews: Down, Londonderry (Derry), Tyrone
Archeson: Armagh
Arkles: Armagh
Arnett: Donegal, Tyrone

Aughmooty: Cavan
Bailie: Cavan, Down
Barber: Cavan
Barbour: Cavan
Barkley: Donegal, Tyrone
Barklie: Down
Barry: Donegal
Bauld: Donegal
Bayly: Down
Bean: Tyrone
Beatty: Down
Bell: Armagh
Black: Antrim, Donegal
Blackwood: Down
Blair: Antrim, Donegal, Down
Boyd: Antrim, Donegal, Down

Boyle: Donegal, Tyrone
Bozwell: Antrim
Brackley: Down
Bridger: Londonderry (Derry)
Brown: Antrim, Armagh, Donegal, Down, Tyrone
Bruce: Donegal
Bryce: Donegal
Buchanan: Donegal, Londonderry (Derry)
Burne: Donegal, Tyrone
Burns: Antrim
Buthill: Antrim
Cahoon: Londonderry (Derry)
Calte: Armagh
Calwell: Donegal
Campbell: Donegal
Carcott: Armagh
Carlile: Down
Carmichael: Down, Tyrone
Carothers: Armagh
Carr: Donegal, Down
Carslow: Tyrone
Carson: Down
Cathcart: Fermanagh, Down, Tyrone
Catherwood: Down
Cawder: Londonderry (Derry)
Chambers: Fermanagh, Down
Chermsides: Down
Cloggie: Donegal
Coch: Cavan
Colguhoun: Donegal
Colter: Londonderry (Derry)
Colville: Antrim, Tyrone
Coohoon: Donegal
Cooper: Down, Tyrone
Coulter: Londonderry (Derry)
Cowper: Down
Craig: Down, Tyrone
Cranston: Fermanagh
Crawford: Donegal, Fermanagh, Londonderry (Derry), Down
Crear: Down
Creighton: Cavan, Fermanagh
Creire (Greer): Tyrone
Crockett: Londonderry (Derry)
Crosby: Tyrone
Cummings: Down

Cunningham: Antrim, Armagh, Donegal, Down, Fermanagh, Londonderry (Derry)
Cutherbertson: Cavan
Danielston: Down
Davidson: Armagh, Down
Davyson: Cavan
Deans: Armagh, Cavan
Deinbone: Fermanagh
Demstar: Tyrone
Dewar: Antrim
Dick: Donegal, Down
Dickie: Antrim
Dickson: Down
Dobbin: Antrim
Dodds: Down
Doninge: Tyrone
Drum: Tyrone
Drummond: Down, Tyrone
Dufferin: Down
Dunbar: Antrim, Fermanagh, Down
Dunleath: Down
Dunlop: Antrim, Down
Dunne: Donegal
Dunsayer: Donegal
Dyke: Londonderry (Derry)
Echlin: Down
Edmonston: Antrim, Down
Edward: Londonderry (Derry)
Ekyn: Donegal
Elliot: Armagh, Fermanagh
Ellis: Antrim
Elpinstone: Tyrone
English: Londonderry (Derry)
Erving: Fermanagh
Ewart: Donegal
Fenton: Antrim
Ferguson: Armagh
Ferry: Tyrone
Fingleton: Tyrone
Finlay: Cavan
Flack: Armagh
Flemming: Donegal
Forecheade: Donegal
Forester: Londonderry (Derry)
Forsith: Down
Frazer: Down
Fullerton: Antrim, Londonderry (Derry), Donegal

Fulton: Donegal
Futhie: Antrim
Fyieff: Donegal
Gaate (Galt): Donegal
Galbreth: Donegal
Galloway: Down
Galt: Down
Galway: Down
Gamble: Armagh, Tyrone
Gelston: Down
Gemmil: Down
Gibb: Fermanagh
Gibbe: Tyrone
Gibson: Fermanagh, Tyrone
Gilmore: Armagh, Donegal
Glass: Donegal
Glen: Donegal, Down
Gordon: Donegal
Granger: Tyrone
Grant: Londonderry (Derry)
Granton: Armagh
Gray: Londonderry (Derry)
Greenshields: Down
Greer: Armagh, Fermanagh
Grier: Armagh
Grime: Tyrone
Grindall: Armagh
Gryme: Tyrone
Grynney: Donegal
Haldane: Antrim
Hall: Armagh, Donegal, Fermanagh
Hamill: Antrim
Hamilton: Antrim, Armagh, Cavan, Donegal, Down, Fermanagh, Tyrone
Handcock: Londonderry (Derry)
Hare: Down
Harper: Donegal, Down
Harvey: Down
Hatrick: Tyrone
Heigate: Fermanagh
Henderson: Tyrone
Hendrie: Tyrone
Henrison: Donegal
Henry: Donegal
Hexburn: Tyrone
Highgate: Tyrone
Hilton: Down
Hogg: Down

Holmes: Tyrone
Homes: Donegal
Hood: Donegal
Hope: Armagh
Howie: Down
Howson: Down
Huggins: Donegal
Hunter: Donegal, Down
Hutchins: Antrim, Donegal
Innes: Down
Irwin: Fermanagh
Johnson: Fermanagh
Johnston: Antrim, Armagh, Donegal, Londonderry (Derry)
Julius: Donegal, Down
Karns: Tyone
Keeland: Londonderry (Derry)
Keevet: Down
Kelly: Down
Kelso: Down
Kennedy: Antrim, Cavan, Donegal, Down, Tyrone
Kernes: Donegal
Kerr: Down
Kilpatrick: Donegal, Down
Kinnear: Antrim
Kirk: Armagh
Kirkpatrick: Antrim, Down
Knox: Donegal
Kyd: Antrim
Kyle: Down, Londonderry (Derry), Tyrone
Kylr: Down
Laderdeill: Antrim
Lainge: Fermanagh
Lawson: Tyrone
Laycock: Donegal
Leckey: Down
Leckit: Donegal
Leitch: Armagh, Donegal
Leslie: Donegal, Down
Lindsay: Donegal, Down, Fermanagh, Londonderry (Derry), Tyrone
Lloyd: Down
Lockhard: Donegal
Lodge: Donegal
Logan: Antrim, Down
Logy: Londonderry (Derry)
Lother: Cavan

Love: Tyrone	McAlexander: Londonderry (Derry)
Luke: Antrim	McAlison: Donegal
Lutfoot: Antrim	McAulay: Tyrone
Lynn: Tyrone	McAuld: Donegal
Lynne: Londonderry (Derry)	McBride: Down
Lyon: Londonderry (Derry)	McBurney: Down
Machell: Donegal	McCamuel: Donegal
Machen: Donegal	McCappin: Down
Mackclellane: Londonderry (Derry)	McCartney: Down
Mackerson: Tyrone	McCashin: Down
Mackleland: Londonderry (Derry)	McClairne: Donegal
Magee: Down	McCleery: Down
Magghee: Londonderry (Derry)	McClelland: Down
Martin: Donegal, Down	McComb: Down
Mathyson: Down	McCrae: Down
Maxwell: Antrim, Armagh, Donegal, Down, Londonderry (Derry), Tyrone	McCreaghan: Tyrone
Means: Tyrone	McCreedy: Down
Meen: Tyrone	McCrery: Tyrone
Melvin: Antrim	McCullagh: Cavan
Midell: Londonderry (Derry)	McCullen: Down
Millar: Antrim, Down, Tyrone	McCullough: Donegal, Tyrone
Miller: Cavan	McCurry: Down
Mitchell: Fermanagh	McDonnell: Down
Moffatt: Armagh	McDougall: Down
Moncreig: Londonderry (Derry)	McDowell: Down
Monett: Down	McErdy: Donegal
Moneypenny: Antrim, Down	McEwen: Down
Montgomery: Antrim, Fermanagh	McGarry: Down
Montgomery: Donegal, Down, Tyrone	McGee: Down, Tyrone
Moon: Down	McGifford: Down
Moore: Antrim, Donegal, Down, Londonderry (Derry)	McGoogan: Antrim
	McGowan: Tyrone
Moorhead: Donegal	McGunshenour: Tyrone
Morne: Tyrone	McIlcheny: Donegal
Morrison: Tyrone	McIlevrath: Down
Morrow: Tyrone	McIlmurry: Tyrone
Morton: Londonderry (Derry)	McIlveyne: Down
Mowlane: Down	McIntyre: Donegal, Tyrone
Muntreeth: Tyrone	McKaundy: Tyrone
Murdogh: Tyrone	McKay: Donegal, Down
Murduff: Tyrone	McKearne: Tyrone
Mure: Londonderry (Derry)	McKee: Down
Murray: Donegal, Down	McKernan: Armagh
Musgrave: Cavan	McKinney: Donegal
Macauley: Antrim	McKittrick: Tyrone
Macawley: Antrim	McKym: Donegal
Mackay: Antrim	McLarnan: Down
	McLean: Down

McLellan: Down
McLelland: Londonderry (Derry)
McLintagh: Donegal
McLoghery: Donegal
McLoran: Donegal
McLornan: Londonderry (Derry)
McMakene: Down
McMaster: Down
McMath: Donegal
McMillan: Down
McMullen: Down
McNabb: Down
McNaughton: Antrim
McNeile: Londonderry (Derry)
McNeill: Antrim
McPherdrish: Antrim
McRobert: Antrim
Nelson: Donegal
Nesbitt: Donegal, Down
Nevin: Down
Newburgh: Tyrone
Niven: Antrim
Nugent: Down
O'Greeve: Antrim
Orr: Donegal, Down
Palmer: Londonderry (Derry)
Parke: Tyrone
Parker: Armagh
Patoun: Donegal
Patrick Down
Patterson: Donegal, Down, Fermanagh, Londonderry (Derry), Tyrone
Patton: Donegal
Peacock: Down
Peebles: Down
Peere (Pery): Donegal
Polk: Londonderry (Derry)
Pollock: Down
Pont: Donegal
Pooke: Tyrone
Powr: Londonderry (Derry)
Price: Cavan
Pringle: Armagh, Tyrone
Purveyance: Donegal
Rae: Armagh, Cavan
Rankin: Donegal
Read: Down
Reade: Tyrone

Redgate: Londonderry (Derry)
Reid: Down
Reynolds: Down
Richardson: Tyrone
Ritchie: Antrim, Armagh, Donegal
Robb: Down
Robin: Donegal
Robinson: Tyrone
Robson: Donegal
Roger: Donegal
Ross: Antrim, Down
Rudd: Down
Russell: Londonderry (Derry)
Rutherford: Down
Saunderson: Tyrone
Sawyer: Donegal
Scott: Donegal, Down
Sempell: Donegal, Londonderry (Derry)
Semple: Donegal
Semple: Down
Seton: Down
Sharpe: Tyrne
Shaw: Antrim, Down
Shirloe: Armagh
Simpson: Donegal, Tyrone
Smelley: Donegal
Smellham: Fermanagh
Smith: Donegal
Smythe: Donegal, Tyrone
Somervell: Fermanagh
Spence: Donegal
Spier: Down
Spottiswood: Tyrone
Stanehouse: Down
Stanhouse: Down
Steele: Cavan
Stephenson: Donegal, Tyrone
Stevenson: Cavan
Stevenson: Donegal, Down
Stevin: Donegal
Steward: Tyrone
Stewart: Antrim, Cavan, Down, Donegal, Fermanagh, Tyrone
Sturgeon: Armagh
Sutherland: Donegal
Symington: Tyrone
Syne: Armagh
Tate: Cavan, Down

Taylor: Cavan	Wanchop: Down
Teyse (Tees): Donegal	Wardlaw: Down
Thomas: Londonderry (Derry)	Wardlow: Down
Thompson: Antrim, Donegal, Londonderry (Derry)	Watson: Armagh, Donegal, Down, Fermanagh
Thomson: Donegal, Down, Londonderry (Derry)	Weir: Fermanagh
	Welsh: Down
Todd: Antrim	Wilie: Tyrone
Trail: Down	Wilkie: Armagh
Trane: Antrim	Williamson: Down
Trimble: Armagh	Wilson: Armagh, Donegal, Down, Tyrone
Tullis: Antrim	Witherspoon: Donegal
Udney: Cavan	Wood: Donegal, Tyrone
Valantyne: Donegal	Wooley: Tyrone
Vance: Donegal	Wright: Tyrone
Waddell: Down	Wylie: Cavan, Down
Walker: Armagh, Down	Wyms: Down
Wallace: Antrim, Down, Tyrone	Young: Donegal, Down, Londonderry (Derry), Tyrone
Walshe: Armagh	

another in any way. As long as one is aware that not all Scottish sounding names in an area are necessarily from Ulster, research can proceed to categorize a community of immigrants.

As an illustration, while driving along the Antrim Coastal Road in Northern Ireland, it is possible to see Scotland from Ulster. It is that close. Naturally, as people began leaving Ulster, one of the places they would go was to Scotland, not because they had any known relatives there but that by the 1830s, many had already left for a better life in Scotland. There, they merged into their local Protestant congregations or Presbyterian parishes. They worked in the factories, mills, and heavy industries in the urban areas, as did anyone else looking for a job. The only clue that they were Ulster-Scots may be "Ireland" in the statistical column for birthplace in the 1841 census or spelled out in the censuses from 1851 forward. It was usual for the former

Ulster residents to move onward to the United States or elsewhere, and so it is wise to be alert about their relocations.

Moreover, Scots-Irish and Scots did intermarry. The custom was natural in the United States because people from the two ethnic groups owned farms near one another or were working and attending church together. However, when dealing with the period during which the censuses provide birthplaces, 1850 and afterward, the integration is a small issue when the places of birth were recorded correctly. The difficulty could arise if the immigrants died before 1850. If they did, the Scots or Scots-Irish question needs to be posed, and the research can be guided by the paper trail.

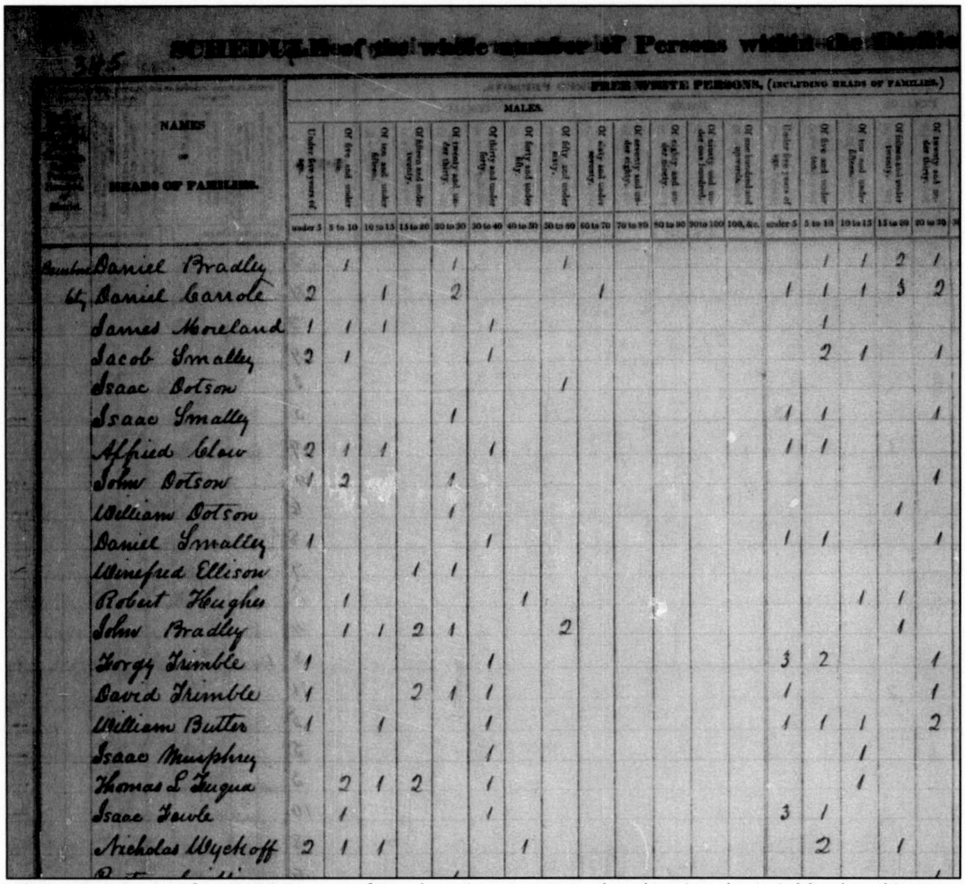
SCHEDULE of the whole number of Persons within the Division
FREE WHITE PERSONS, (INCLUDING HEADS OF FAMILIES.)
MALES.
NAMES of HEADS OF FAMILIES.
Daniel Bradley
Daniel Carrole
James Moreland
Jacob Smalley
Isaac Dotson
Isaac Smalley
Alfred Clow
John Dotson
William Dotson
Daniel Smalley
Winefred Ellison
Robert Hughes
John Bradley
George Trimble
David Trimble
William Butler
Isaac Murphrey
Thomas L Fuqua
Isaac Fowle
Nicholas Wyckoff

Figure 5: Snippet of an 1830 Census of Bourbon County, Kentucky, showing the neighborhood intact--as the enumerator went from house to house. (This work is in the public domain in the United States because it is a work prepared by an officer or employee of the United States Government as part of that person's official duties under the terms of Title 17, Chapter 1, Section 105 of the U.S. Code.)

Figure 6: An example of the 1800 census in Donegal, Westmoreland County, Pennsylvania, revealing the practice of some to rearrange households into alphabetical order by the first letter of their surname. (This work is in the public domain in the United States because it is a work prepared by an officer or employee of the United States Government as part of that person's official duties under the terms of Title 17, Chapter 1, Section 105 of the U.S. Code.)

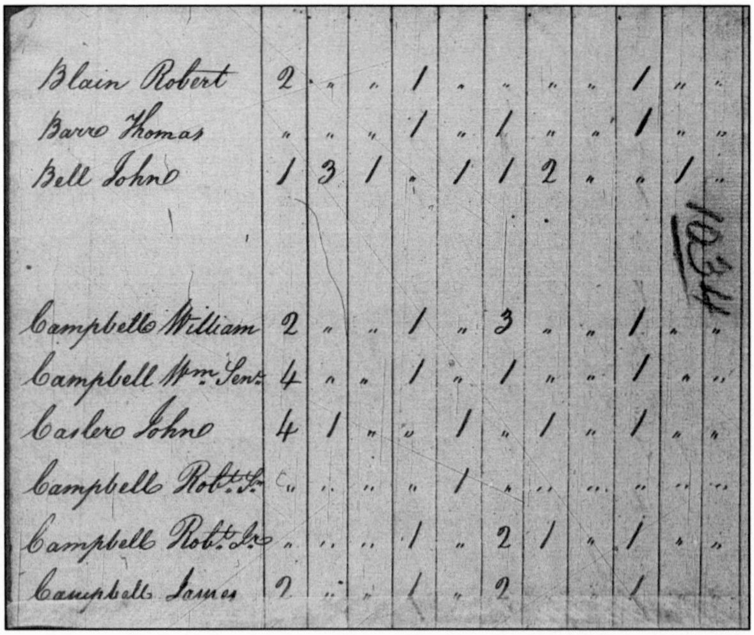
Blain Robert
Barro Thomas
Bell John
Campbell William
Campbell Wm. Senr.
Casler John
Campbell Robt. Jr.
Campbell Robt. Sr.
Campbell James

Chapter Two

Census Records to 1850

In Scots-Irish family research, the 1850 United States census is crucial because it was the first to record places of birth. In 1850, people born in Ulster in the 1770s or 1780s could be listed. In a minority of situations, the census enumerators were more specific and added places in Ulster where the persons were born. Nevertheless, the censuses almost always have Ireland alone, yet it is one of the first clues that the people being researched were the immigrants. The 1880 United States census is another key one because it was the first to ask where parents were born, providing good evidence about the generation of the immigrant.

Many researchers find it difficult to use the United States census reports from 1790 through 1840 because only heads of households were named, with statistics assigned for everyone else. Although the want of names can pose its own set of problems, the enumerations are essential pieces of the research. It is possible, at the least, to reconstruct who some of the statistics were in a household by using some of the following methods:

- Consult the 1850 census for the children of the head of household in, for example, 1840, and start determining whether ages match statistics.

- Identify marriages for the children in the family who were married before the 1850 census and then estimate daughters marrying at around 21 years of age and sons, at around 25 years old. The ages are guidelines only, but efforts have to start somewhere.

- Assuming the 1790-1840 censuses are not alphabetical with all A's being together and the "neighborhood" intact, find which younger people with the same surname are enumerated close to the head of household being researched. They could be older children with their own households. A general rule is that if the neighborhood is intact as the census taker found it (*compare figures 5 and 6 on the previous page*), the page before and the page after the one on which the ancestor was listed constitutes people living close by. Consider whether the age statistics of the younger people match the subjects in the earlier censuses.

- Find the ancestor's will, and if the children are listed, consult the censuses for which statistic could be which child. When the will lists the children in birth order, the comparison works well.

Cases where a statistic cannot be firmly tied to a name will no doubt arise. Remember that statistics could be nieces and nephews staying over on the enumeration day, or they could be farm hands, servants, or a household with two families living together. If a statistic cannot be identified, move on with the research process.

One idea incorporating the neighborhood strategy for census work is that some of those in the community might have had earlier connections to the ancestor. In effect, the tactic moves the group of them, including the ancestor, back to another place of settlement, which is significant. For instance, if an ancestor is found in the 1840 census in a county in Indiana and it is established that the ancestor was originally from Ohio, the ancestor likely went to that Indiana county because of knowing someone there who also traveled from Ohio. If the county in which the family was living in Ohio in 1830 cannot be proved, this approach will often provide the answer.

A solution may be as uncomplicated as comparing the Indiana neighborhood where the ancestor was residing with an online 1830 index for the Ohio census. If

a pattern emerges pointing to one specific county in Ohio that also includes the ancestral surname, the issue has been resolved. A group from that one county in Ohio settled in that one county in Indiana. The search can continue in Ohio in the same manner, taking an earlier group of people back to the eastern states. Gathering them in the East will not provide the birthplace in Ulster, but doing so is not the purpose of the search.

Continuing with the preceding example, the principle is to identify family members in a particular county in Ohio and begin the search for Ulster origins from there. Perhaps no other family members went to Indiana but as a young family, or even as a single young person, simply moved westward with friends. Once the Ohio connection is made, introduced are church records, military records, land grants, and, of course, more neighborhood research, any of which may disclose Ulster origins. If the immigrant was not in Ohio, continue to an earlier residence, for example, Maryland, and begin the process all over again. The immigrant still may be a couple of generations back.

In the neighborhood approach, the community of residents needs to be at least partly intact, as recorded by the census enumerator. If not, and it is alphabetical by first letter of the surname only and with a township listed, the same goal can be accomplished: The concept of a "neighborhood" is now expanded to include the geographical area of the township. This, of course, works well when reviewing states that have townships. The Midwest is an amazing place for the approach to be successful because they are federal-land states that were originally surveyed by township, section, and range, and so the physical township names and boundaries were built around them over time. The coordinates for land still exist today in surveys. Be aware that Ohio had several systems for dispersing land, but, eventually, they all came under the federal system.

In state-land states, such as Georgia, Kentucky, and Tennessee, a dissimilar approach has to be developed because they do not have townships. Nevertheless, if the census enumerator left the neighborhood intact, the same strategies can be employed, and nothing has changed. If the census taker designated a post office as the area, an historian can proceed with it as a "neighborhood." Otherwise, in state-land states, the neighborhood has to be reconstructed with land records to learn with whom an ancestor was associated, thereby ascertaining whether a migration pattern emerges.

Census Indexes

Online census indexes can be an amazing research tool. Keep in mind that not all entries were indexed correctly. When they are not or the original writing is exceptionally difficult to read, use wild cards in an online database search, even for the middle of the surname if needed. Think phonetically, especially in the southern United States, where literacy was an issue. If a surname, or something that sounds like it, cannot be found, study the images page by page for a name that is recognizable in the county or in a known area of the county.

With Scots-Irish surnames that begin with the Mc, be creative with online databases. Often the census worker would write M. Neil for McNeil. Does the search capability of the database handle the difficulty? If it picks up Neil, the problem is solved. Does it display Mac, Mc, Ma, and Muc? With the Mc names, a researcher cannot be too careful.

Moreover, surnames such as McCurry and McDonough can be a riddle in the census indexes with each having its own unpredictability. Aside from the Mc, Muc, Mac, or Ma dilemma, Curry can be Cary or Quarry with or without the Mc attached to it. Donough can be Donner, Dona, or even Donald or Donnell depending on the accent of the person speaking and what the census enumerator was hearing. In Scots-Irish research, especially in the southeastern United States, interpretation was a frequent challenge. Again, if a county is known before beginning the search, reading the census one page at a time may be easier than struggling with the index. Census images are widely available online. On Ancestry.com, digital images of the original counties can be viewed by any exact district or township.

Another way around faulty indexing is to find a published copy of the census that a genealogy society or individual has produced. The assumption is that if composed locally, the compilers knew the changeableness in the surnames and added some notations to them. Such works are indispensable and are widely available at archives and libraries with genealogy collections. USGenWeb.org is an excellent place to find links to genealogy societies that may have their constructed indexes already online. The USGenWeb.org can assist in identifying them, or county pages may host indexes.

Census Alternatives

When thinking in terms of the United States censuses from 1790 to 1850, be aware of compilations that can act as alternatives for missing enumerations. Not all early censuses survive. For instance, the first surviving United States census for New Jersey is 1830, and it is 1820 for Ohio. Therefore, census substitutes need to be found in order to locate people before moving them back in time.

The state of Tennessee is a perfect example of the need for census substitutes. Its first complete census for the entire state was 1830. Before that year, records are incomplete or were lost. For 1820, all of the censuses for the 22 counties in eastern Tennessee are missing. For 1810, the entire state, except for Rutherford County and part of Grainger County, is missing. There is nothing for 1790 (before statehood) and 1800. Consequently, at least before 1820, and definitely before 1810, some alternatives need to be found that can help reconstruct the population. Tennessee had a heavy Scots-Irish settlement between 1790 and 1830, and so the concept of locating other records is important.

One valuable compilation for reconstructing residents around 1810 is Charles A. Sherril's *The Reconstructed 1810 Census of Tennessee: 33,000 Long-Lost Records from Tax Lists, Court Minutes, Church records, Wills Deeds and Other sources* (2001). The author

collected a variety of sources and listed the people in alphabetical order. It is a major resource for Tennessee in 1810. The limitation is in the case of a burned county, from where few, if any, early courthouse archives can be drawn. However, the problem can be solved. A theoretical list of some, but certainly not all, census alternatives for pre-1830 Tennessee research documenting early residents could be assembled as follows:

Ancestry.com Tennessee, *Compiled Marriages, 1784-1825* [database-online]. Provo, Utah: Ancestry.com Operations Inc, 1997.

Chase, Marybelle W. *Records of the Cherokee Agency in Tennessee, 1801-1835*. Tulsa, Oklahoma: M. W. Chase, 1990.

Curtis, Mary Barnett. *Early East Tennessee Tax Lists*. Fort Worth, Texas: Arrow Print, 1964. (Note: This work covers the 22 counties of East Tennessee, for which no census exists before 1830.)

Dollarhide, William. *Tennessee Censuses & Substitute Name Lists, 1769-2008*. Orting, Washington: Family Roots Publishing Co., LLC, 2017.

Drake, Doug, Jack Masters and Bill Puryear. *Founding of the Cumberland Settlements: The First Atlas 1779-1804: Showing Who Came, How They Came, and Where They Put Down Roots*. Gallatin, Tennessee: Warioto Press, 2009.

Douthat, James L. *Fourth Survey Distr[i]ct of Tennessee, 1808-1810, John McClellan, Surveyor: Anderson, Bledsoe,*

Campbell, Knox, Overton, Rhea, and Roane Counties, Tennessee. Signal Mountain, Tennessee, 1988.

Douthat, James L., *Robert Armstrong's Survey Book of Cherokee Lands: Lands Granted From the Treaty of 27 February 1819*. Signal Mountain, Tennessee: Institute of Historic Research, 1993.

Griffey, Irene M. *Earliest Tennessee Land Records & Earliest Tennessee Land History*. Baltimore, Maryland: Clearfield Co., 2000.

Kegley, Mary B. *Soldiers of Fincastle County, Virginia, 1774*. Dublin, Virginia: M. B. Kegley, 1974. (Now southwest Virginia from Montgomery County west. Some of the men might have been living in the territory, which later became the State of Tennessee. Fincastle County was created in 1772 from Botetourt County but was dissolved in 1776 when the counties of Montgomery,

Washington, and Kentucky [now part of the state of Kentucky] were formed.)

Land Grants, 1775-1905, 1911. Nashville, Tennessee: Tennessee State Library and Archives, 1976. (Note: This is an alphabetical index to the land districts in Tennessee that dispersed grants, including North Carolina grants in Tennessee. The massive collection was digitized and is on *FamilySearch.org* and *Ancestry.com*.)

Masters, Jack and Bill Puryear. *Land Grant Genealogy... All of Rutherford, Williamson & Wilson Counties – Remainder of Davidson & Smith Counties – Portions of Cannon, Cheatham, DeKalb, Jackson, Putnam, Sumner & Trousdale Counties of Middle Tennessee*. Gallatin, Tennessee: Warioto Press, 2011.

Masters, Jack and Bill Puryear. *Land Grant Genealogy... All of Bedford, Dickson, Marshall & Maury Counties,*

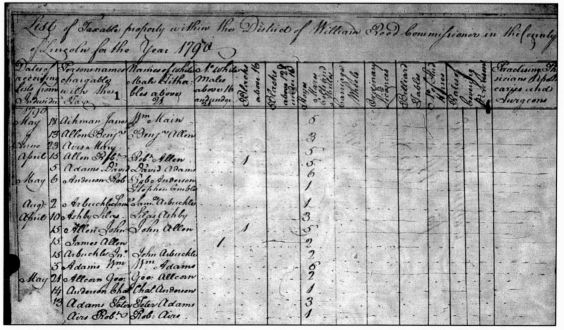

Figure 7: 1790 tax list for Lincoln County, Kentucky—an excellent census substitute for the missing 1790 census. (Image courtesy of Kentucky Historical Society, Frankfort, Kentucky.)

Remainder of Cheatham & Montgomery Counties, Majority of Hickman, Houston & Stewart Counties & Portions of Coffee, Giles, Humphreys & Lincoln Counties of Middle TN. Gallatin, Tennessee: Warioto Press, 2012.

McCown, Mary Hardin and Irma Bowman Kitzmiller. *The Wataugah Purchase, March 19, 1775 at Sycamore Shoals of Wataugah River: the Cherokee Indians to Charles Robertson, Trustee for the Wataugah Settlers, an Index of the Wataugah Purchase, the North Carolina Land Grants and Deeds Through 1782.* Johnson City, Tennessee: Overmountain Press, 1976.

McGhee, Lucy Kate. *Partial Census of 1787 to 1791 of Tennessee as Taken from the North Carolina Land Grants.* 3 vols. Washington, D. C.: L. K. McGhee, [196?].

Pruitt, Albert Bruce. *Corrections or Alterations to Land Grants in North Carolina (1714-1873) & Tennessee (1778-1796).* Whitakers, North Carolina: A. B. Pruitt, 2002.

Sherril, Charles A., *The Reconstructed 1810 Census of Tennessee: 33,000 Long-Lost Records from Tax Lists, Court Minutes, Church records, Wills Deeds and Other sources*, Mount Juliet, Tennessee: C. A. Sherrill, 2001.

Sistler, Byron and Barbara Sistler. *Index to Early Tennessee Tax Lists.* Evanston, Illinois: Byron Sistler & Associates, 1977. (Note: This includes county tax lists, petitions, voter lists, and newspaper lists, the earliest 1787 and the latest 1827.)

Sistler, Byron and Barbara Sistler. *Index to Tennessee Wills and Administrations, 1779-1861.* Nashville, Tennessee: Byron Sistler & Associates, 1990.

Sistler, Byron and Samuel Sistler. *Tennesseans in the War of 1812.* Nashville, Tennessee: Byron Sistler & Associates, 1992.

Willis, Laura. *Tenn. County, N.C., Early Deeds.* 2 vols. Melber, Kentucky: Simmons Historical Publications, 1994. (The area became Tennessee in 1796. It comprises what is today Montgomery County and parts of Dickson, Hickman, Houston, Humphrey, Robertson, and Stewart Counties. This work covers 1784-1797.)

Similar lists could be compiled for any state with missing census schedules. Once a listing of records that are available is made, regardless of the types, efforts can continue. If a census alternative is all that can be collected for research to progress, the situation must be acknowledged.

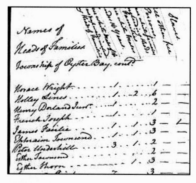

Figure 8: Sample of the 1790 Federal Census, Oyster Bay, New York. (This work is in the public domain in the United States because it is a work prepared by an officer or employee of the United States Government as part of that person's official duties under the terms of Title 17, Chapter 1, Section 105 of the U.S. Code.)

Chapter Three

Church Records

A good share of researchers shy away from church records, especially those from frontier churches and denominations. Their wariness is understandable because congregations moved, changed names, disbanded, split, united, and switched denominational loyalties, and so registers can still be with local congregations. The disarray tends to discourage researchers, rendering church records an underdeveloped topic, yet they can be rewarding when found and studied.

Although few reference books are on the market about the genealogical use of church registers, two are noteworthy. One is Harold A. Henderson and Sunny Jane Morton's *How to Find Your Family History in U.S. Church Records* (Baltimore, Maryland: Genealogical Publishing Co., 2019). It is peer-reviewed and explores only the major denominations.

The other is Holly T. Hansen, Arlene H. Eakle, Ruth E. Maness and James L. Tanner's *Discovering the Evidence in Church Records* (Morgan, Utah: Family History Expos, Inc., 2017), which also covers the major denominations.

Theology Creates Records

As a result of the general lack of emphasis placed on church records, understanding the records once they are found may be difficult. Here, a working knowledge of theology can be beneficial. Many books on the market outline the beliefs of a group or denomination, but in order to appreciate what the records reveal, consulting a theological guide is recommended so that the thinking behind the records can be analyzed. The books are in technical, introductory, historical, and dictionary formats.

An underlying theology creates the very records being researched, and so it is an important topic. Will theology determine where someone was born in Ulster? No, it will not. Instead, it is part of the holistic approach in documenting an ancestor. Theology can help in understanding how one becomes a member, is dismissed, or what it even means to be a member of a group, any of which can lead to other valuable discoveries.

The doctrine of baptism may be one of the best examples. Most traditional Christians and Christian-based denominations practice some form of baptism but for purposes that differ from one another. Some groups even perform rebaptism when uniting with the church. Why a rebaptism? That is where theology meets record keeping because the custom has an internal logic. Continuing with the example of baptism to demonstrate the reasoning, some key theological points to consider can include:

- Why do Presbyterians baptize entire families to create a "covenant family?"

- Why do Methodists allow sprinkling, pouring, or full submersion for baptism?

- Why do Baptists, as well as Disciples/Christians, practice believers' baptisms by full submersion, yet for dissimilar goals?

- Why do Quakers not baptize at all?

- Why do Mormons baptize the dead?

All have their own explanations understood by the believers. Baptisms also can assist in providing a basis for other records that might have been generated about church members during their lives. Will church baptisms, marriages, or burial records of members mention parents' names or places of birth? Sometimes they do, making these always essential sources to consult.

Many excellent contemporary one-volume books are on the market from which a foothold into logic, controversies, and attitudes can be obtained. Informative books include the following, with notations in parenthesis:

General Theology

Oden, Thomas C., *Classic Christianity: A Systematic Theology*. New York, New York: HarperOne, 2009. (An abridgment of a three-volume work.)

Thiselton, Anthony C., *Systematic Theology*. Grand Rapids, Michigan: William B. Eerdmans Publishing Company, 2015. (Thiselton is a Church of England scholar.)

Baptist and Baptist-Calvinistic

Akin, Daniel L., *A Theology for the Church*, rev. ed., Nashville, Tennessee; B&H Academic, 2014. (Written from a Southern Baptist Convention perspective.)

Garrett, James Leo, *Baptist Theology: A Four-Century Study*. Macon, Georgia: Mercer University Press, 2009. (A study in the development of Baptist theology from the differing perspectives.)

Geisler, Dr. Norman Geisler, *Systematic Theology: In One Volume*, Minneapolis, Minnesota: Bethany House, 2011. (Condensed from a four-volume work. A conservative Baptist-Calvinist perspective.)

Leonard, Bill J., *Baptist Questions, Baptist Answers: Exploring Christian Faith*. Louisville, Kentucky: Westminster John Knox Press, 2009. (An introductory text.)

Lewis, Gordon R. and Bruce A. Demarest, *Integrative Theology: Historical, Biblical, Systematic, Apologetic, Practical*. Grand Rapids, Michigan: Zondervan, 1996. (Written from a conservative Baptist position.)

Calvinism (Presbyterian/Reformed/ Congregational)

Beeke, Joel R. and Mark Jones, *A Puritan Theology: Doctrine for Life*. Grand Rapids, Michigan: Reformed Heritage Books, 2012. (An exceptional work in the study of Puritan and early modern Reformed theology.)

Bavinck, Herman, and John Bold, ed., *Reformed Dogmatics: Abridged in One Volume*. Grand Rapids, Michigan: Baker Academic, 2011. (An abridgment of the original translation of the four-volume Dutch work. A defining work on Reformed Church theology.)

Bloesch, Donald G., *Essentials of Evangelical Theology*. Peabody, Massachusetts: Hendrickson Publishers, Inc., 2006. (A broad approach to evangelicalism from a mild Reformed position. The author is a conservative voice in the United Church of Christ.)

Frame, John M. *Systematic Theology: An Introduction to Christian Beliefs*. Phillipsburg, New Jersey: P&R Publishing, 2013. (An abridgment of a four-volume work.)

Horton, Michael. *The Christian Faith: A Systematic Theology for Pilgrims on the Way*. Grand Rapids, Michigan: Zondervan, 2010. (The author is an associated minister in the United Reformed Church.)

Letham, Robert. *Systematic Theology*. Wheaton, Illinois: Crossway, 2019. (The author is a professor of Systematic and Historical Theology at Union School of Theology and a Presbyterian minister.)

McKim, Donald K., *Presbyterian Questions, Presbyterian Answers: Exploring Christian Faith*. Louisville, Kentucky: Westminster John Knox Press, 2003. (An introductory text.)

Reymond, Robert L., *A New Systematic Theology of the Christian Faith*, 2nd Ed. Rev. ed. Nashville, Tennessee: Thomas Nelson Inc., 1998. (Traditional Calvinist position. The author is an ordained minister in the Presbyterian Church in America.)

Evangelical (Fundamentalist)

Enns, Paul, *The Moody Handbook of Theology: Revised and Expanded*. Chicago, Illinois: Moody Press, 2008. (A popular work. The author is a conservative Baptist minister.)

Ryrie, Charles C., *Basic Theology: A Popular Systematic Guide to Understanding Biblical Truth*. Chicago, Illinois: Moody Press, 1986, 1999. (A popular work by a conservative theologian.)

Swindoll, Charles R. and Roy B. Zuck, eds. *Understanding Christian Theology*. Nashville, Tennessee: Thomas Nelson, Inc., 2003. (Previously published writings of some ten theologians. It is a major contribution to dispensational theological studies.)

Evangelical (General)

Bird, Michael F., *Evangelical Theology: A Biblical and Systematic Introduction*, Grand Rapids, Michigan: Zondervan, 2013. (The author is an Australian scholar.)

Erickson, Millard J., *Christian Theology*, 3rd ed. Grand Rapids, Michigan: Baker Academic, 2013. (One of the most popular evangelical systematic theologies today. Use alongside Grundem's work.)

Grundem, Wayne, *Systematic Theology: An Introduction to Biblical Doctrine*. Grand Rapids, Michigan: Zondervan, 2000. (One of the most popular evangelical systematic theologies today. Use alongside Erickson's work.)

Episcopal/Anglican

Booty, John E., *What Makes Us Episcopalians*, Harrisburg, Pennsylvania: Morehouse Publishing, 1982. (An introductory text.)

Holmes III, Urban T., *What is Anglicanism?* Harrisburg, Pennsylvania: Morehouse Publishing, 2003. (An introductory text.)

Ian s. Markham and C. K. Robertson, *Episcopal Questions, Episcopal Answers: Exploring Christian Faith*. Harrisburg, Pennsylvania: Morehouse Publishing, 2014. (An introductory text.)

Norman, Edward, *An Anglican Catechism*. London, England: Continuum, 2001.

Thomas, Owen C. and Ellen K. Wondra, *Introduction to Theology*, 3rd ed. Harrisburg, Pennsylvania: Morehouse Publishing, 2002.

Sykes, Stephen, *Unashamed Anglicanism*. Nashville, Tennessee: Abingdon Press, 1995.

Methodist

Campbell, Ted A., *Methodist Doctrine: The Essentials*. Nashville, Tennessee: Abingdon Press, 1999. (For use in the four largest Methodist denominations in the United States. An introductory text.)

Collins, Kenneth J. *John Wesley: A Theological Journey* (Nashville, Tennessee: Abingdon Press, 2003).

Collins, Kenneth J. and John H. Tyson. *Conversion in the Wesleyan Tradition* (Nashville, Tennessee: Abingdon Press, 2001).

Joyner, Jr., F. Belton, *United Methodist Questions, United Methodist Answers: Exploring Christian Faith*. Louisville, Kentucky: Westminster John Knox Press, 2007. (An introductory text.)

Maddox, Randy L., *Responsible Grace: John Wesley's Practical Theology*. Nashville, Tennessee: Kingwood Books, 1994.

Stokes, Mack B., *Major United Methodist Beliefs*, rev. ed., Nashville, Tennessee: Abingdon, 1989. (An introductory text.)

Moravian (United Brethren)

Crews, C. Daniel, *Confessing Our Unity in Christ: Historical and Theological Background to "The Ground of the Unity"* 2nd ed. Winston-Salem, North Carolina: Moravian Archives, 2000.

Crews, C. Daniel, *This We Most Certainly Believe: Thoughts on Moravian Theology*. Winston-Salem, North Carolina: Moravian Archives, 2005.

Freeman, Arthur Freeman, *An Ecumenical Theology of the Heart: The Theology*

of Count Nicholas Ludwig von Zinzen-
dorf. Bethlehem, Pennsylvania and Winston-Salem, North Carolina: Moravian
Church in America, 1999.

Quakers (Society of Friends)

Cooper, Willmer A. Cooper, *A Living
Faith: An Historical and Comparative
Study of Quaker Beliefs*, 2nd ed., Richmond, Indiana: Friends United Press,
2001.

Dandelion, Pink, *An Introduction to
Quakerism*. Cambridgeshire, England:
Cambridge University Press, 2007.

Scott, Janet, *What Canst Thou Say?: To-
wards a Quaker Theology*. London, England: Quaker Books, 1980.

Stone-Campbell Restoration Move-
ment

Brownlow, Leroy. *Why I am a Member
of the Church of Christ*. Fort Worth,
Texas: The Brownlow Corporation, 1945.
(A non-instrumental Church of Christ
perspective.)

Cottrell, Jack. *The Faith Once for All: Bible Doctrine for Today*. Joplin, Missouri:
College Press Publishing, 2002. (Exceptional conservative work from the Christian Church/Churches of Christ perspective.)

Turner, Rex A., Sr., Don Shackelford, ed.
*Biblical Theology: Fundamentals of the
Faith*. Rev. ed. 1989. Montgomery, Ala-
bama: Amridge University Press, 2010.
(Written from a non-instrumental
Church of Christ perspective.)

Williamson, Clark M. *Way of Blessing,
Way of Life: A Christian Theology*. St.

Louis, Missouri: Chalace Press, 1999.
(Written from a Christian Church (Disciples of Christ) perspective.)

General Research Strategies

A common perception about the religious lives of Scots-Irish ancestors in the
United States is that they were Presbyterians. As a place of beginning, the assumption is sound; however, it is more
complex. Many also arrived as Brethren
(Plymouth), Methodists, Quakers, Moravians, and Mormons. Others switched
faiths or dropped out.

Even if ancestors arrived as Presbyterians, they might not have remained Presbyterians. Entire segments of the populations were unchurched for a couple of
generations, especially on the frontiers
where churches and ministers were few
and far between, if they existed at all in
many localities! The situation evoked the
Great Awakening and Second Great
Awakening in American History. Escalat-
ing were massive revivals that were intended to gain converts, plant churches,
and establish schools on frontiers where
there were none. The revivalism of the
Great Awakenings altered the religious
landscape of America and set the stage
for the rise of a distinct American Evangelical movement.

The Great Awakening and the Second
Great Awakening

The Great Awakening started in the late
1720s, peaked in 1740, and continued to
some degree into the 1770s. It was a colonial movement that instigated the process wherein evangelicalism became a
dominant force in America, emphasizing
the need for conversion and acceptance

of Christ as a personal savior. It inundated Protestant churches and swept the colonies. One of the goals was to eliminate a formalistic worship style within Protestantism.

The Calvinistic churches (Congregational, Presbyterian, and Reformed) provided the core leaders during the Great Awakening. While revivalism extended into the northern and middle colonies, it grew more slowly in the southern colonies. The Baptists emerged as the predominant evangelical church in Virginia. The colonial Anglicans, mainly those aligning themselves with the growing Methodist element within their ranks, also prospered. After the Revolutionary War, though, these societies separated themselves from the newly formed Episcopal Church, creating the Methodist Episcopal Church.

The beginning of the Revolutionary War in 1775 officially brought an end to the Great Awakening. The Scots-Irish, chiefly within Presbyterianism, played a large role in spreading the fires of the Awakening.

The Second Great Awakening is better known in history than the original revival movement. It occurred in various locations throughout the United States between 1790 and 1830. Like the Great Awakening, it had both a corporate and an individual element to it. Not only did it emphasize the personal nature of salvation but also it underscored that a special divine blessing had been bestowed upon America by God. The preachers additionally stressed that individuals could reform both their own lives and society as a whole.

Figure 9: Methodist Camp Meeting representing the Second Great Awakening. Jacques Gérard Milbert (1766-1840). (1819 engraving-Public Domain. Library of Congress, Prints and Photographs Division (LC-USZ62-2497))

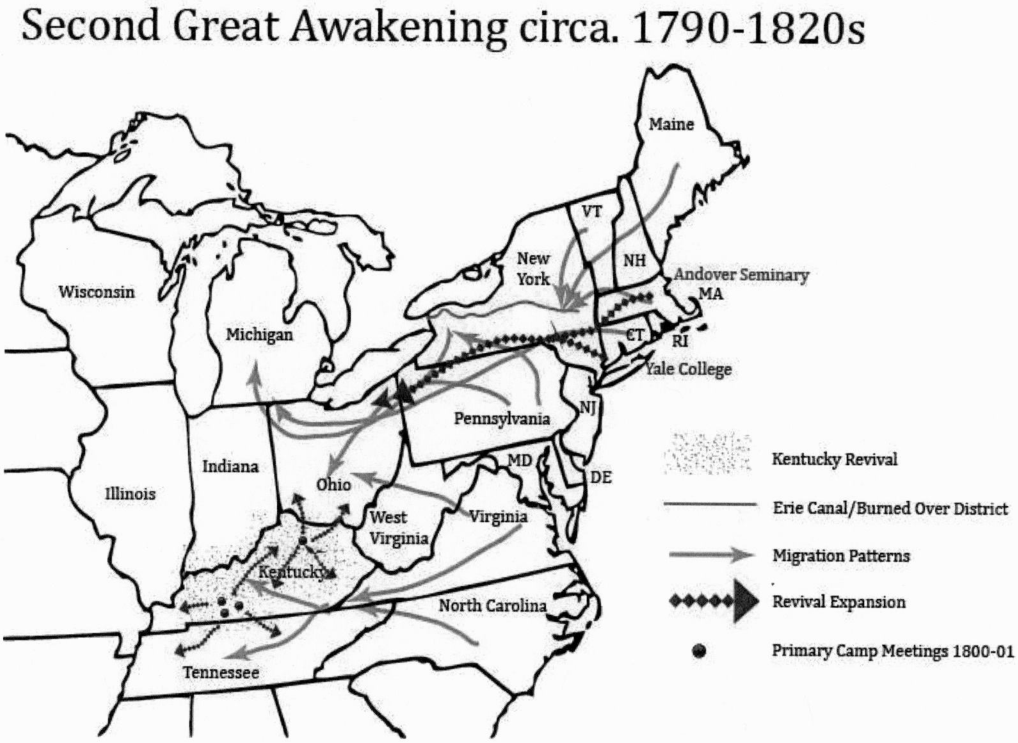

Second Great Awakening circa. 1790-1820s

Figure 10: Migration Effects from the Second Great Awakening.

As the revivals reached west and south of New England, the conservatism of the clergy seemed irrelevant on the frontier, where emotionalism replaced structure. One of the most famous of the frontier revivals was that held at Cane Ridge, Kentucky, in 1801. Over 10,000 people took part in the mass event, and it was symbolic of the changes occurring throughout the United States. As revivals sprang up in Tennessee, Kentucky, and southern Ohio, thousands of previously unchurched settlers became part of Protestant denominations.

The Second Great Awakening, too, gave rise to new expressions of American Protestantism, such as the Stone-Campbell Restoration Movement and its "Christians only" doctrine and the Cumberland Presbyterian Church in 1805, which divided Presbyterianism in Tennessee and Kentucky. The Methodist Church as well expanded widely on the frontier because it was at the forefront of the revivalism. Although the fires of the Second Great Awakening had dimmed by the 1830s, they ignited in Upstate New York, known as the "Burned-over District." Because of the revival fires, new and distinct religious movements such as Mormonism (1830), Adventism (1844), and Spiritualism (1848) continued to transform the American landscape. The Scots-Irish were heavily involved in the Second Great Awakening, furnishing the early leadership among the newly created Stone-Campbell Restoration Movement and the Cumberland Presbyterian Church.

The Assimilation of Scots-Irish into Their Community Church

Genealogists see history from the perspective of an individual family or community of families, which provides genealogists with a unique perspective that, when combined with the larger picture, can open novel avenues of research. For example, genealogists are well aware that tens of thousands of Scots-Irish traveled the same migration routes as did Swiss-Germanic families—westward and southward from Philadelphia. It was not unusual for Scots-Irish families to intermarry with the Swiss-Germanic Brethren families, who were historically called the Dunkers, Tunkers, or, officially, the German Baptist Brethren. It wasn't uncommon in diaries for the Brethren to write about the Scots-Irish people among whom they were settling. The logical result of the mixture of cultures was that many Scots-Irish families took on a distinctive Germanic characteristic over the years rather than a Scot-Irish one, and, therefore, a Brethren family may have been a Scot-Irish family.

In reverse, in the nineteenth century, large numbers of German Baptist Brethren converted to two American creations, the Stone-Campbell Restoration Movement (Disciples/Christians) and the Seventh-day Adventist Church. The Brethren lived among the Scots-Irish in places like Ohio, and the groups had conspicuous doctrinal similarities, which led to large numbers of Brethren conversions. At that point, the German Baptist Brethren families were integrated into Scots-Irish families by marriage and culture. To complicate the state of affairs even further, a Scot-Irish family absorbed into a Brethren family in the 1700s in Pennsylvania, Maryland, or Virginia might have been reabsorbed into a larger Scots-Irish society in Ohio upon uniting with the Stone-Campbell Restoration Movement.

The same occurred for the Scots-Irish living among Reformed and Congregational families, only in their case, the Reformed Church and the Congregational Church stood alongside the Presbyterians and French Huguenots as Calvinists. All originated in different parts of Europe. In areas of the country where the differences between these branches of Calvinism were of less importance, assimilation was a natural process. In colonial New England, the Congregational Church was the prevalent religion, and in the middle colonies, the Reformed Church was so. In this example, the Reformed Church originated from the Netherlands, and the Congregational Church was rooted in England. In America, both also found Scots-Irish Presbyterian Calvinists among their memberships.

Another often ignored aspect of assimilation is the Americans into Spanish territory, such as coastal Alabama, Mississippi, and Texas. In order to own land, a person had to be Roman Catholic. It is not unusual to discover that Scots-Irish settlers had married in a Catholic church or had their children baptized Catholic for the land motive, but they might not have practiced the religion. In some of the frontier areas, such as coastal Mississippi, the presence of priests was only sporadic, making it almost impossible to determine who was practicing Catholicism and who was not—that is, if parishes or missions even served the regions. As the areas were incorporated into the United States, the religious test was no longer applicable. In Spanish or Mexican America, do not be surprised to find a Scot-Irish ancestor, at least on paper, as Roman Catholic.

One feature of religion in America that is sometimes overlooked by genealogists but well documented by historians is the rise of American churches, with American concerns and worldviews. In many ways, these innovative churches and spiritual traditions rebelled against European Protestantism and progressed in their own directions. Some churches even went as far as losing their connections to European Protestantism altogether, choosing instead restorationist versions, hence bypassing Protestantism and Catholicism completely. They saw themselves as restoring doctrines and principles from the New Testament, if not actually reproducing the original version of Christianity itself as they read it into their New Testaments.

The restorationist theme was, and remains, a strong and potent part of the American view of religion, somewhat of an Americanization of Protestantism. These churches were concerned with American ideas of democracy, manifest destiny, capitalism, and individualism. American Christianity was highly anti-creedal and commonly highly suspicious of a professional clergy. The churches that developed were centered on Americans reading the Bible through American eyes. It is through these lenses that the destiny of America became intertwined with the biblical prophecies, with America being a chosen and blessed land. Not only did they see the United States as the chosen land but also Americans as the chosen people. When woven together with Calvinist doctrines arriving from Scotland, Ulster, England, Holland, and France, a whole new vision of Protestantism was born—an American version. In fact, in numerous American created denominations and groups, the concept of a Protestant Reformation was meaningless when a new vision replaced it.

Restorationist views can be found in the Baptists, Stone-Campbell Restoration Movement, Seventh-day Adventists, and, later, in the Pentecostal movement. Their concept of the Christian message perhaps found its strongest roots in the Mormons, who came to see America as the new Zion, with the chosen led by a modern prophet. In essence, they broke the monopoly that Protestantism had on the Bible by adding American scripture. In the Stone-Campbell Restoration Movement theology, the emphasis was built upon Christian unity as it sought to restore the first-century church of the New Testament on the frontier. In its view, it was reinstating an original Christianity that existed before the Roman Catholic tradition. With both the Roman Catholic Church and the Protestant Reformation being bypassed, neither was needed any longer.

Several excellent reference works can be used to understand the religious movements in American history. Some foremost ones are:

Barkun, Michael. *Crucible of the Millennium: The Burned-Over District of New York in the 1840s.* Syracuse, New York: Syracuse University Press, 1986.

Boles, John B. *The Great Revival: Beginnings of the Bible Belt.* Lexington, Kentucky: The University of Kentucky Press, 1972, 1996.

Conkin, Paul K. *American Originals: Homemade Varieties of Christianity.* Chapel Hill, North Carolina: The University of North Carolina Press, 1997.

Cross, Whitney R. *The Burned-Over District: The Social and Intellectual History of Enthusiastic Religion in Western New York, 1800-1850.* Ithaca, New York: Cornell University Press, 1950.

Hatch, Nathan O. *The Democratization of American Christianity.* New Haven, Connecticut: Yale University Press, 1989.

Hughes, Richard T. and C. Leonard Allen. *Illusions of Innocence: Protestant Primitivism in America, 1630-1875.* Abilene, Texas: Abilene Christian University Press, 2008.

Baptist Church

Baptist denominations historically baptized adults or mature children by full submersion. They do not christen infants, and in the Baptist tradition, baptism itself is not linked to a person's salvation, which is secured through faith and grace only. Baptisms might or might not have been recorded by the minister, but records of received members can be in the church minutes. Membership records kept by the local congregations usually do not include ages or parentages. The church minutes may note transfers of members from elsewhere, giving the names of the former Baptist congregations. If a person joined a Baptist church from a denomination that practiced infant baptism, there typically is not a record of the former denomination because infant baptism is not recognized by Baptists. A rebaptism by submersion would have taken place as a show of faith.

Although the Baptist Church was in Ireland, it was a minority religion. The vast majority of Scots-Irish who became Baptists did so after they immigrated.

In consequence of the lack of family information or birthplaces provided in Baptist records, which are typically in minute format, the use of the registers is to track a person back in time. By doing so, it can be determined with whom the family was associated and from where it came before joining that congregation. If a group of people are the founding members of a Baptist congregation in Alabama, they might have traveled together from North Carolina. It may be that within the core group, several members also had emigrated from Ulster to North Carolina and settled, thereby providing a principal strategy in working the family line backward.

It is important to realize there are many different kinds of Baptists, and each congregation acts as its own entity with the locals making decisions about beliefs and practices based upon their understanding of the Bible. A congregation could switch allegiances over time to one

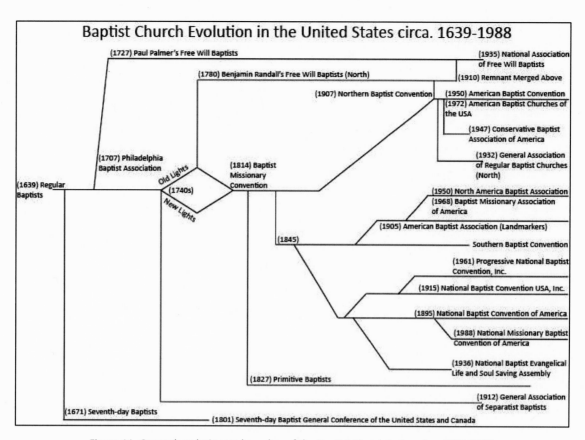

Figure 11: General evolutionary branches of the Baptist Church in America, 1639-1988.

of the several theological positions and to like-minded associations. Unless a congregation remains an independent Baptist, it tends to unite in conventions or conferences with other congregations that concur with it to accomplish business, such as funding missionaries and settling disputes. There are free-will Baptists, foot washing Baptists, General Baptists, Baptists who worship on Sunday, Baptists who worship on Saturday, Calvinist Baptists, Missionary Baptists, conservatives, right of conservatives, liberals, and independents. Expressions of the Baptist Church are even concentrated in certain areas, for instance, the United Baptist Church in Kentucky and Tennessee and the Baptist Church of Christ in Middle Tennessee. The largest Baptist

denomination in the United States today is the conservative-leaning Southern Baptist Convention, which is Baptist-Calvinistic in theology. For organizations such as a conference, convention, or association, another set of records was generated that may document ministers ordained, seminaries, obituaries, missionaries, or denominational business. Within these records, birthplaces in Ulster may be preserved. Many of the older issues of conference reports will be scanned on sites such as HathiTrust.org and Archive.org, among others. Denominational archives should also be consulted. Some mention of a Baptist ancestor in such localized denominational sources may be as easy as a click or an email away.

Determining to which Baptist denomination an ancestor belonged is the first step in searching for records. While some congregations still maintain their historic records, others have been deposited at libraries, for example, those of the Southern Baptist Historical Library and the American Baptist Historical Society. Still others may be found at local public and university libraries. Sometimes, historical works or journal articles were published about a certain congregation or early families within the congregation. The Family History Library has collections of Baptist records from the various branches.

Congregational Church

What developed into the Congregational Church arrived in the American colonies in the 1600s and became the leading faith of New England. It was the expression of Calvinism that was English in origin, and it reflected that culture. All others had to assimilate into that English-based background, including the incoming Ulster-Scots Presbyterians to New England. Finding an ancestor in the Congregational Church does not mean he or she was Congregationalist in Ulster, where the Congregational Church has always been a minority faith. What it indicates is that the person arrived as a Presbyterian and was served by the already established Congregational Church in the adopted community. The Congregational Church might have been the only church serving a community for a lot of years.

Historically, Congregationalism and Presbyterianism are similar, with the

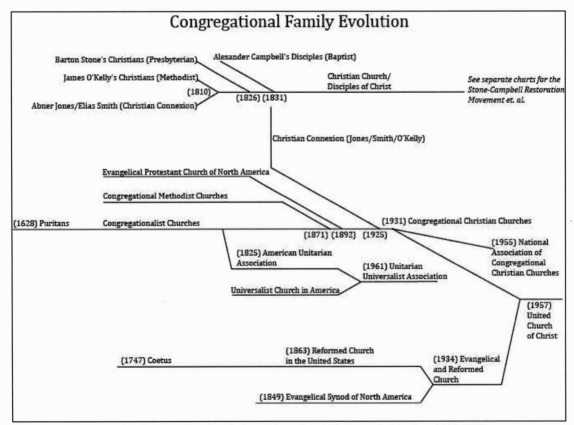

Figure 12: Congregational evolutionary branches and merges in America, 1628-1957.

differences being in non-theological matters. In fact, as an illustration, on the frontier, the Presbyterian Church and the Congregational Associations of New England consented to a plan in 1801 that allowed one denomination to call a pastor from the other denomination. The "Presbygational" agreement ensured that new churches could be staffed in the expanding areas of western New York State and further westward. Under the arrangement, Presbyterians and Congregationalists were a single denomination in Illinois, Indiana, Michigan, New York, Ohio, and Wisconsin. Many Presbyterian congregations rejected the union in 1838, and in 1852, it was discarded by the Congregational Church.

The Scots-Irish association with the Congregational Church was predominantly, although not exclusively, in New England. During the colonial era of New England, it was common for Scots-Irish to be married and have children christened by a Congregational minister. Afterward, if ministers from Ulster or Scotland came to the areas, Presbyterian Churches were set up apart from the Congregational Churches. Tensions often were present between the old-time, established Congregationalist families of English origin and the arriving Presbyterians in the congregation who were Scots-Irish or Scottish.

In a twist, as they progressed from New England Congregationalism, many former Congregational churches are now Unitarian Universalist congregations, affecting where records are stored today. The majority of Congregational churches

Congregational Churches in Ulster Prior to 1864

County	Civil Parish	Town	Formation
Antrim	Ballynure	Straid	1816
	Carnmoney	Ballycraigy	1805
	Carrickfergus	Carrickfergus	1816
	Shankill	Albertbridge, Belf.	1862
	Shankill	Donegall St., Belf.	1801
	Shankill	Rugby Ave., Belf.	1854
Armagh	Armagh	Armagh	1793
	Kilmore	Richhill	1800
	Newry	Newry	1820
Donegal	Donegal	Donegal	1833
Down	Bangor	Bangor	---
	Kilkeel	Kilkeel	---
Londonderry	Coleraine	Coleraine	1836
	Templemore	Londonderry	1821
Tyrone	Donaghenry	Donaghey	1860
	Donaghmore	Donaghmore	1834

are now affiliated with the mainstream Liberal Protestant denomination, the United Church of Christ. Because of their historical importance, most early Congregational Church registers, especially the vital records, have been published or indexed onto computer databases. Records are either microfilmed, digitized through FamilySearch.org, or are at the Congregational Library in Boston.

Conversely, if an ancestor did arrive in the United States as a Congregationalist, then by reason of the small denomination in Ireland, there is a chance of documenting the person in a church register, solving the question of Ulster origins. Locating where an ancestor was living based upon where the congregation was situated is also possible. By 1901, the census of Ireland listed only 10,000 Congregationalists. The table on the previous page shows where Congregational churches were located in Ulster before 1864. (The year 1864 was chosen as the cut-off year because it initiated the recording of births, all marriages, and deaths by the Irish government.) It has been adapted from Malcom Coles, *I Will Build My Church: The Story of the Congregational Union of Ireland* (Lisburn, Co. Antrim: Congregational Union of Ireland, 1979).

Websites such as RootsIreland.ie should be consulted to determine whether Congregational registers are currently indexed. Otherwise, the PRONI in Belfast is the repository for the Congregational Church in Ireland.

Episcopal Church

The impression that the Church of England was created by King Henry VIII so that he could divorce his wife is not entirely accurate because farther west the underpinnings for Anglicanism are much more complex. The Anglican tradition, of which the Episcopal Church is a member, views itself as a reformed Catholic Church. It splits the difference between Roman Catholicism and evangelicalism, being neither, yet it can resemble both. It is a theology that moves forward and reevaluates itself which has allowed movements such as Methodism to be embedded within the local parishes. The process still goes on today.

The Ulster-Scots association with the Episcopal Church is complex. Many from Ulster arrived as Anglicans, having intermarried with Anglican families in Ireland. The marriages were common because the Church of Ireland denomination was the state religion until 1871. For those associated with the Church of Ireland, they lost what made them Scots-Irish. Others became Episcopal (the Church of England in colonial times) upon immigrating because, in some colonies, it was the established church or even the only church. The Episcopal Church was strong in Colonial Maryland and Colonial Virginia. After the Revolutionary War, the Episcopal Church distanced itself from the Church of England and was more American in flavor. However, the further west the population moved, it was not a popular church and generally lacked clergy and parishes in the frontiers. At that point, families were unchurched or joined a new church when the revivals swept through vicinities.

Episcopal parish registers can be helpful. Sometimes, especially for prominent members, birthplaces and parents' names may be preserved in a record or in the church histories where a church was founded and wherein wealthy families in a community regularly associated. In these instances, the likelihood of finding birth information is good because literate families left records.

Episcopal records may still be with the local parish, deposited at the diocese, or microfilmed or digitized in places such as FamilySearch.org and Ancestry.com. The parish systems provided structures from which the local vestries acted as governing bodies and generated records, usually two main types. The parish registers consist of births/baptisms, marriages, and deaths/burials among those such as confirmations. The other is the vestry minutes, basically the business minutes and information about the parishioners. Birthplaces in Ulster may or may not be preserved in the parish registers or vestry minutes, which is why it is important to look.

The Episcopal Church in the U.S is organized by dioceses followed by parishes within each diocese. Often, a basic Internet search will locate a specific parish or diocesan office. If seeking parish registers that have not been indexed but that have been digitized through FamilySearch.org, and the name of the parish has not been identified, there are approaches. If the parish registers for an urban area are digitized, the straightforward tactic may be to examine all parishes for a select frame of years to document an ancestor. If a death date is

known, going through multiple parishes for the burial record for that date is a reasonable task. Customarily, the person's parish or the priest who performed the burial service is in the obituary. It is the same with marriage records. Frequently, county marriage records have the ministers' names, and city directories or a simple Internet hunt should reveal with which parishes ministers were affiliated.

Methodist Church

Various denominations over the centuries identified themselves as Methodists. They all trace their heritage back to John Wesley, a priest of the Church of England, and his brother Charles Wesley, who started Methodist societies in the 1740s in England and Ireland as supplementary study groups within Anglicanism. The Methodist societies acted in the role of a modern Sunday school, where ethics and Bible teachings could be discussed and explored. They revolutionized the Anglican tradition throughout the British Isles. Although the established church might not have always appreciated them and their spirited worship style, they were good for revitalizing parishes. It was not until 1817-1818 in Ireland that the Wesleyan Methodist Church separated from the Church of Ireland. To a lesser extent, Methodist societies were also in the Irish Presbyterian congregations.

From the 1760s onward, thousands of Irish Methodists immigrated to the American colonies, although technically they were still members of either the Church of Ireland or Presbyterian Church. They were instrumental in instituting

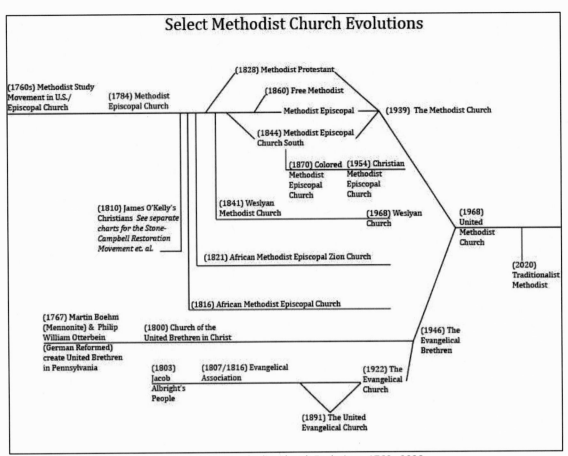

Figure 13: Select Methodist Church Evolutions, 1760s-2020.

Methodist societies throughout the eastern United States and Canada. Thus, it could be stated that the first Irish Methodist congregations were in North America, and not in Ireland, which was especially true in the colonies of New York and Maryland in the 1760s.

In the United States, the Methodist Episcopal Church was officially organized in 1784 in Baltimore. The Methodist Protestant Church was established in 1828, and the Methodist Episcopal Church South separated in 1844 from the Methodist Episcopal Church. The three American branches were united in 1939. In 1968, the United Methodist Church (the largest body of Methodists now in

the United States) was formed by the unification of the Methodist Church and the Evangelical United Brethren Church. The governing body of the United Methodist Church is the Annual Conference, within which are plentiful individual conferences covering particular geographical areas. The remaining three largest Methodist bodies in the United States are African American, testifying to the impact the faith had on the country.

The local churches generally kept records of membership, baptisms, marriages, and deaths. Marriage records sometimes indicate birthplaces, including specific ones in Ireland, as well as parents' names and witnesses. The records of membership were sometimes called class lists. The churches also kept registers of probationers, the individuals undergoing preparation for admissions to memberships. The membership or class lists indicate when members were admitted and from what denominations (if other than Methodist), as well as when members left. Class and probationer lists may have addresses within urban areas.

Further details about research may be found on the website of the General Commission on Archives and History. It has detailed information about how to locate records and what they contain. Some state archives also have micro-filmed Methodist church records. In addition, many are on microfilm or digitized at the FamilySearch.org, and Ancestry.com, as part of its website, has United Methodist Church registers from specific states.

Presbyterian Church

Various branches of the Presbyterian faith in North America have merged and divided throughout the years, confusing the reconstruction of history and identification of records. The majority of the Presbyterian congregations in the United States are now part of the more mainstream Presbyterian Church (USA) and the more conservative Presbyterian Church in America. There are a number of smaller groups, such as the Cumberland Presbyterian Church and the Associate Reformed Presbyterian Church, both of which were originally heavily Scots-Irish.

It was common for Ulster immigrants of Presbyterian heritage to join other denominations over the decades or not attend any churches. In either case, no records of the immigrant ancestors may be in early United States Presbyterian registers. No ministers or congregations were on the frontiers before the revivals, and the population was mostly un-churched. However, during times of revival, families were brought into the Presbyterian Church for the first time in a couple of generations. At that time, churches registered the names of those who were admitted by the session. Naturally, the very definition of what constituted the frontier was different in each decade!

Presbyterian registers vary in their content depending on the congregations. The registers may include records of birth/baptism, marriage, death/burial, session minutes, and communion rolls. If immigrant origins are preserved, it is usually in the session minutes, which were the business meeting records of the congregations. Mentioned in them may be transfers into the congregations from other locations and denominations or interviews for permissions to take communion. To be accepted into a congregation, an interview between the prospective communicant and the session was necessary. It is within the session minutes that the acceptance or rejection of the communicant was recorded.

One important research strategy for Presbyterian ancestors is the idea that a group of members from one Presbyterian congregation (or surrounding geographical area) in Ulster immigrated to the colonies following a minister. Such a congregational migration makes finding immigrant origins easier. Where the minister pastored in Ulster is usually where his congregants were living. For example, the first major migration of Scots-Irish immigrants to America was a group that came with Rev. James McGregor from Aghadowey parish, County Londonderry, to New England in 1718. They arrived at Boston, and many of them moved to New Hampshire, founding the town of Londonderry. It may be the best known of the congregational migrations, but it was by no means the only one. The Aghadowey Parish congregational migration has a bonus. Although the main Presbyterian baptismal registers for the congregation only began in 1855, a set of session minutes for the church from 1702 to 1765 does mention families before the emigration in 1718. The set of records is so important that a transcript of them is at the New England Historic Genealogical Society, and an index to them is on its AmericanAncestors.org website. They also have been digitized at PRONI.

When research has identified the immigrant and the first place the family settled, it must be asked if they were part of a congregational migration, requiring research into the local community of Scots-Irish for any patterns between the members and the minister. Irish Presbyterian ministers in Ireland have been documented and can be obtained from the fasti books, which are lists of ministers. They are on the website of the Presbyterian Historical Society of Ireland.

In the United States, a major repository of Presbyterian records of all types is at the Presbyterian Church (USA) Department of History in Philadelphia, collected from the various branches of Presbyterianism. The records are at the archive or through the Family History Library. Ancestry.com has a large collection from the Presbyterian Historical Society in the database "U.S., Presbyterian Church Records, 1701-1970."

Presbyterian congregations were part of a larger group of collective congregations known as the Presbytery, the local governing body that would settle disputes, offer resolutions on issues, conduct business, and hold conferences for meeting purposes. It generated another series of records outside the individual congregations. Presbytery meeting records can be published and be online at such sites as HathiTrust.org and Archive.org. They may also be deposited as state, local, and denominational archives. In addition, many published histories of presbyteries provide information on the ministers, those licensed by the presbytery, candidates for ministers, the ministers transferring into the presbytery from elsewhere, and any number of other topics specific to each locality. Whether birthplaces for any of the presbytery leaders or the ministers who have biographies will be preserved in such history books cannot be known in advance. Yet, if an ancestor was of the leadership level of church government, including ministers, the presbytery records and websites as well as the Presbyterian Historical Society will be important to consult.

The Presbyterian Historical Society website is valuable because it not only has information on individuals, such as ministers and missionaries, but also it holds

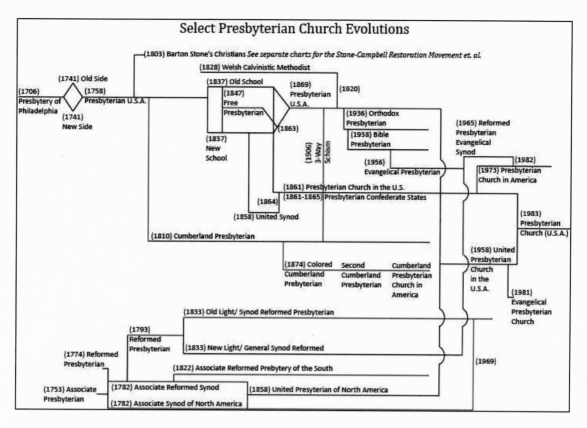

Figure 14: Presbyterian Church Evolutions in the United States, 1706-1983.

many of their papers. The catalog can be searched by locality, which will provide additional information on that specific congregation.

Society of Friends (Quakers)

The Religious Society of Friends, the members of which were commonly called Friends or Quakers, was formed in England in 1652 under the leadership of George Fox. The society came to Ireland soon afterward. Quakers from Ireland emigrated to a number of the American colonies, especially Maryland, New Jersey, Pennsylvania, Rhode Island, and Virginia. The largest migration was to the colony of Pennsylvania from 1682 to 1750. The Quaker influence in American history should not be underestimated. They were the true radicals of the 1600s

and 1700s because their beliefs and practices at that time were considered countercultural. By today's standards, their teachings are mild, but for their era, they were far ahead of typical thinking about complex social issues.

Quakers are not theologically based in the sense of traditional Protestant thinking. Therefore, a phase such as "Quaker Theology" must be used in general terms. Ideas and theological tenets come from a concept known as the Inward Light, also called the Inner Light. The Inward Light is a metaphor to express that all people have access to the inspiration of the Holy Spirit, which empowers individuals and groups, with no need for a clergy. Quakers understand that the Inward Light differs from conscience. The conscience is a developed awareness of the merits or the faults of an individual's conduct, intention, character, and sense of doing right. The Inward Light is a direct, unmediated experience with the Divine. In essence, it is a direct revelation.

Historically, the typical Quaker Meeting was based upon silence. No one spoke unless directed by the Inward Light. At that point, any man or woman could share promptings in an unedited format. If important, and judged to be true, the message was sent out far and wide. It was a call to action—the exact opposite from the professionally trained clergy of the day, all of whom were male and delivered their sermons in highly edited forms.

Today, the preceding paragraph is rather tame, if not boring. However, by the standards of the British Isles in the seventeenth and early eighteenth centuries, the ideas were heresy and dangerous. For people to not rely on a well-informed clergy, to expect their own inspirations, and to deliver those inspirations in unedited formats were incomprehensible. Moreover, that a woman was equal to a man in any arena simply made Quakers astonishing by the principles of the day because there was no frame of reference from which these new ideas could be judged. The strict Calvinists were horrified by the Quaker Inner Light, which they saw as outside the Bible. To the Calvinist mind, the Bible was the literal and final word of God, and all questions could be answered through the Bible because it constituted the mind and will of God. One's own inner promptings and revelations for guidance were not needed.

The Inward Light has allowed Quaker Thought to march forward with the times, giving the Quaker people a profound and progressive voice often decades or centuries ahead of the general culture in areas from women's rights to the abolition of slavery. Ideas originating from the Inward Light, once embedded within the general population, challenged both church and state and threw governments and churches into chaos.

The Friends gathered in meetings, known as Monthly Meetings, whose minutes are generally the most useful source for tracing Quaker families. Monthly Meetings were in turn organized into Quarterly Meetings. The Quarterly Meetings were arranged into several Yearly Meetings. Various splits have occurred in American Quakerism since 1828.

Albert Cook Myers in his *Immigration of the Irish Quakers into Pennsylvania, 1682-1750* (1902. Baltimore, Maryland: Genealogical Publishing Co., 1969, 1985, 1994) undertook a detailed study of the approximately 1,500 to 2,000 Irish Quaker immigrants who settled in Pennsylvania. Another book by Myers, *Quaker Arrivals at Philadelphia 1682-1750* (1902. Baltimore, Maryland: Genealogical Publishing Co., 1978), includes certificates of removal received at the Philadelphia Monthly Meeting from other meetings in America and from meetings in England and Ireland.

Quakers were good record keepers. They did not baptize, and so birth records were made instead. For immigrant research, the records of births, deaths and marriages, and minutes for members received by certificates are especially useful. Ellen Thomas Berry and David A. Berry's *Our Quaker Ancestors: Finding Them in Quaker Records* (Baltimore, Maryland: Genealogical Publishing Co., 1987) is a genealogical guide to tracing members of the Society of Friends. Thomas C. Hill's *Monthly Meetings in North America: An Index* (Cincinnati, Ohio: T. C. Hill, 1998) includes historical descriptions of each Yearly Meeting and Monthly Meeting and indicates where records of each meeting may be acquired.

William Wade Hinshaw's six-volume work *Encyclopedia of American Quaker Genealogy* (1936-1950. Baltimore, Maryland: Genealogical Publishing Co., 1969) has extracts from the minutes of Monthly Meetings in Georgia, Michigan, New Jersey, New York, North Carolina, Ohio, Pennsylvania, South Carolina, Tennessee, and Virginia. The books are on *Ancestry.com* in the database "U.S., Encyclopedia of American Quaker Genealogy, Vol. 1-VI, 1607-1943."

While numerous Quakers arrived as early as the 1600s in the colonies as Quakers, all might not have remained in the faith. It is common to find that an ancestor was disowned for some transgression against Quaker precepts. The early Friends were strict, and the smallest infractions led to enquiries and disownments. Disownments are typically in the Monthly Meeting records but also happened in Ireland as members were disowned and arrived in America as anything except Quakers. A clue to former Quaker roots may be discovered if an ancestor is found living among Quakers, either in or near a Quaker community. The Society of Friends was among the best record keepers of any denomination.

Stone-Campbell Restoration Movement

The Stone-Campbell Restoration Movement was a union of several strands of restorationist thinking on the American frontiers. In its early days, it had a heavy Scots-Irish membership. While rooted in the Second Great Awakening, or more specifically, the Cane Ridge Revival in Kentucky in 1801, it did not unify as a single strain of thought until the 1830s. It was originally composed of independent, like-minded congregations and remained a unified movement from 1832 to 1906.

The core thinking of the movement was that unity among Christians could be obtained if all churches would but discard man-made creeds and doctrines, following only what the New Testament taught. In this form of restorationism, the popular motto became "Where the Bible speaks, we speak. Where it is silent, we are silent." Another popular motto was "Christians only, but not the only Christians." They considered themselves non-denominational, and as the restored New Testament Church, they stood apart from the non-divine man-made churches.

In their thinking, they were not Catholic, Protestant, or Orthodox. Rather, their restoration of first-century Christianity bypassed them all. Their basic logic, which continues to this day, is that the

Roman Catholic Church was not the original Christianity but was an apostate version of the New Testament Church of the first century. To avoid denominationalism, the various independent congregations went by descriptions instead of names. The three used, usually at the same time, were Disciples of Christ, Christian Church, and Church of Christ.

By 1860, the movement was the fifth largest church body in the United States with some 200,000 members. It spread rapidly throughout the Midwest, the Southeast, and into Texas and what is now Oklahoma. It had a wide appeal. One teaching method was so plain that it was revolutionary and spoke directly to the common persons on the farms, whose concerns were more practical than mystical. The "Five Finger Principle,"

which acted as a visual while preaching, was merely counted on the hand to explain the salvation process. It was/is:

1. One confesses
2. Repents
3. Is baptized
4. Receives a remission of sins
5. Receives the Holy Ghost and eternal life.

This uncomplicated and rational approach to salvation appealed to countless thousands on the American frontiers because it respected the human mind for decisions. It attracted those who could not accept the emotional conversion experiences, which were preached so widely on the frontiers, and those confused by doctrinal requirements delivered by various denominations. The

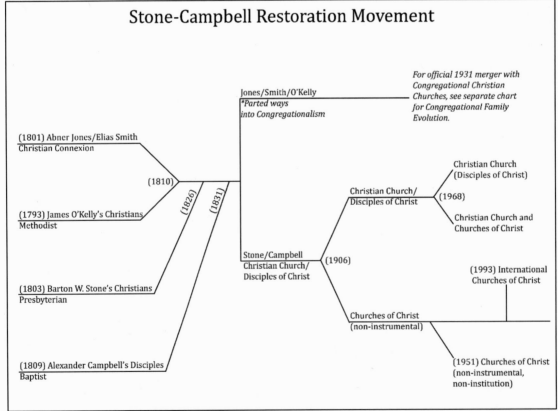

Figure 15: Stone-Campbell Restoration Movement, 1790s-1993.

message was clear: Humans are rational beings, the Bible is a rational book, and common people can understand it.

Like much of American Christianity, the Restoration Movement suffered from a liberal and conservative divide. By 1906, when the United States government was compiling a Religious Census of churches and memberships, it listed the obvious, a liberal Disciples of Christ and a conservative Church of Christ. The strength of the Disciples was in the Midwest, and the Church of Christ was in the Southeast into Arkansas, Oklahoma, and Texas. Issues of disagreement ranged from individual congregations banding together and cooperating in missionary efforts to instrumental music in worship being scriptural. Disagreements also included whether obtaining Christian unity meant an ecumenical approach with other denominations or whether the restoration congregations constituted the one true church with all others being false.

Some writers have argued that the divide had less to do with topics such as instrumental music in church than with the distribution of wealth. After the Civil War, the congregations in Ohio, for example, were installing stained glass windows and expensive organs while those in Tennessee lay in ruins. Regardless of the reason, the liberal-conservative divide and everything in between continues today.

At present, the Christian Church (Disciples of Christ) has an ecumenical approach with other denominations. It has gone beyond its Restoration Movement roots. The independent congregations are known as the Christian Church/ Churches of Christ; they are conservative evangelicals and grew out of the Disciples. Their congregations belong to a convention, which they organized in 1927. In the Midwest, these independent congregations can be called Christian Church or simply Church of Christ. In the Southeast, where the non-instrumental Church of Christ is strong, the Christian Church is almost always used.

The non-instrumental Church of Christ remains as independent congregations. Several million members from the three main groups are in the United States today.

The records for the restoration congregations, regardless of what they are called today, can be found in several places. Many are still with the local congregations. Others have been microfilmed or digitized through FamilySearch. The Disciples of Christ Historical Society in Bethany, West Virginia, collects for all branches of the Restoration Movement. Currently, they hold records for 23,000 congregations, 40,000 bibliographic files, and the personal papers of 35,000 members of the Disciples of Christ.

The Brown Library at Abilene Christian University, a non-instrumental Church of Christ institution, also has an archive that assembles a variety of records. The non-instrumental Church of Christ, the largest of the three branches of the movement, does not have an active program to gather congregational registers. A standard reference work covering all three branches is Douglas A. Foster, Paul M. Blowers, Anthony L. Dunnavant, and D. Newell William's *The Encyclopedia of the Stone-Campbell Movement* (Grand Rapids, Michigan: Wm. B. Eerdmans Publishing Col, 2005).

Moravian Meeting Places in Ulster		
County	Civil Parish	Congregation
Antrim	Ballinderry	Ballinderry
Antrim	Belfast City	Belfast
Antrim	Ahoghill	Gracehill
Cavan	Drumgoon	Cootehill
Down	Kilkeel	Kilkeel
Down	Hillsborough	Kilwarlin
Londonderry	Artrea	Gracefield

A typical register is in the form of minutes. Within the historical minutes will be records of believers' baptisms, which historically are linked to salvation, and church memberships. Registers may contain some marriages and deaths. The minutes will discuss congregational business and church disciplinary matters. There will be transfers in and out of the congregation. Early restoration periodicals may mention individual members and ministers. Where in Ulster a person was born would not be in the minutes because there was no reason to note it, although the periodicals might have, especially in an obituary. Nevertheless, they are all part of the process of moving backward in time toward the immigrant ancestor. Historically, the Stone-Campbell Restoration Movement was heavily Scots-Irish, and, therefore, is worth noticing, above all in the Midwest and Southeast.

Moravian (United Brethren)

The Moravian Church originated in Eastern Europe and was established in Ireland in 1746 through missionary efforts from England. The denomination had a few congregations in Ireland, from which many members immigrated to America. Numerous Moravians lived together in organized settlements, where they were self-sufficient. Ireland had one such town, Gracehill in County Antrim.

The number of Moravians in Ireland during the eighteenth and nineteenth centuries is uncertain, but some statistics do exist for specific years. There were 4,673 in 1824 and 5,000 in 1834. The strength of the Moravian Church was in Ulster with additional congregations in Dublin and Corofin, County Clare.

The Moravians recorded baptisms, marriages, and burials. Congregations kept Congregation Books that may have lists of members and their families and details on movements or emigration of church members. Some congregations composed diaries containing information on services held and absences of members, as well as arrivals, departures, and deaths of members. Nearly all of the Moravian records are at the PRONI in Belfast.

Unless people converted to the Moravians in the United States, the Moravian immigrants to America came from one of the aforementioned congregations. Moravian immigration to America took root in Pennsylvania and North Carolina.

The Moravians first entered America not as colonists but as missionaries to the Native Americans, among whom they opened missions as early as the 1730s. With communities established through their work, members immigrated, and the settlements grew. Among the immigrants were many Irish-born Moravians, although the Irish Moravians were a minority within the church as a whole because most were Germanic.

Most Moravian Church records of births/baptisms, marriages, and deaths will not have the birthplaces of the members. The record that is excellent for providing the information is called a "memoir." Memoirs are similar to eulogies. Before death, a person may have had a memoir written about his or her life and service to the church. If it was not created before death, the minister could have done so afterward.

Figure 16: James Fuller Queen's Central Moravian Church on Church Street in Bethlehem. (Image is from the Library of Congress. This work is in the public domain in its country of origin and other countries and areas where the copyright term is the author's life plus 100 years or fewer.)

Moravian immigrants of all nationalities first settled in Forsythe County, North Carolina, and the communities of Bethlehem, Nazareth, and Lititz, Pennsylvania. Records from the communities can indicate the members' congregations of origin.

The Moravian Archives in both Bethlehem and in Winston-Salem conduct genealogical research. Both repositories have gathered the birth/ baptisms, marriages, burials, minutes, and memoirs for the congregations in their respective areas.

The three major settlements of Moravian immigrants in Pennsylvania were Bethlehem and Nazareth in Northampton County and Lititz in Lancaster County. Immigrants would often settle in the area only to later migrate to other parts of the United States. Abstracts of the memoirs for their congregations were published and microfilmed as "burial" records and are available through the Family History Library. The "burial" records for the Bethlehem and Nazareth communities were published in *Gravestone Inscriptions in Moravian Graveyards in Nazareth and Bethlehem and Some Church records, 1742-1904* (digitized by Family-Search). The Lititz cemeteries have been transcribed in Abraham Reinke Beck's *The Moravian Graveyards of Lititz, Pa., 1744-1950* (digitized by FamilySearch) and in *Record of All the Interments on the Burial Grounds of the Moravian Congregation at Lititz, Lancaster County, from 1748-1820* (digitized by FamilySearch).

The memoirs for the Forsythe County congregations are at the Moravian Archives in Winston-Salem. The memoirs for non-Germanic people have been translated from the German. All of the North Carolina memoirs are indexed at the Archives. The index is completely cross-referenced for married women. Examples of Ulster born Moravians' Memoir cards are:

- Brietz, Margaret (nee Marrow). B. 02 Jan. 1829, Magherafelt, Derry Co., Ireland; d. 14 Jan. 1886, Salem; m. Charles G. Briety, 1857.

- Douthit, John (Sr.). b. 09 May 1709, Coolrain, Ireland; d. 22 Feb. 1784, Hope, NC; m. Mary Scott, 1738; 11 children.

- Mack, Mary (nee Grant). B. 01 Aug 1755, Ballinderry Co., Antrim, Ireland. Called to service in W.I [West Indies], 1799 & to marry Hanan. Trying trip, including capture by Irish rebels. M1. J. Hanan; m2. Jacob Mack.

Another source for immigrant origins is in the minutes of the North Carolina congregations. The minutes from 1752 to 1879 have been published in the series *Records of the Moravians in North Carolina* (Raleigh, North Carolina: Edwards and Broughton Printers, 1922-1969. 11 Volumes. Volumes 6-7 were reprinted by the North Carolina Department of Archives and History). They mention Irish families and sometimes the congregations in Ireland from where they came, and they are indexed. An example from the published church minutes is:

- November 8, 1826. John Spence, the journeyman tailor who is working for Br. Charles Levering, was formerly a Society Brother at Gracehill, Ireland. ("Salem Board Minutes," Volume VIII (1823-1837)), p. 3777).

Like Latter-day Saints and Quakers, the Moravians and their birthplaces in Ulster can be easier to trace than those of other denominations. All were good record keepers, and they tended to have colonies, towns, or communities where the majority of residents resided.

Chapter Four

Female Ancestors: Maiden Names

One of the major impediments in reconstructing a lineage is identifying a woman's birth—or maiden—name, affecting research to no small degree. The birth names of women can be an important tool in sorting through common Scots-Irish names. For example, even if every church and civil record in Ulster is indexed, the problem that still remains is whether adequate information exists to determine which family, if any, is the correct one. The dilemma is particularly true if birth dates seem to change with every record. When searching Irish databases such as RootsIreland.ie, knowing the name of an ancestor or even the father's name may not be enough. Obtaining the maiden name of a mother or a wife would quickly eliminate or substantiate the options.

If a couple married prior to immigrating to America, especially before the 1820s and 1830s, when most churches began recording congregants, verifying where they were living in Ulster may be challenging. With both the husband's surname and the wife's birth name, though, the two can be compared in the tax lists, for instance, Griffith's Primary Valuation, to discover whether they appear near each other geographically. Often, it is the only way to solve the difficult immigration obstacle. Accordingly, the identity of the wife is even more essential. The theory is that to have become acquainted, the man and woman must have been in the same general area. If their families were poor or were small farmers, they might not have owned a horse, which meant the future bride and groom were within a reasonable walking distance from each other—the exception being their meeting in the market town on market day. If so, it placed the young man and young woman some miles distant from each other.

If they married in America, a maiden name is still indispensable because a wife's family might have traveled with her husband's family from Ulster to America, leading back to relying on the Irish tax lists to distinguish where the two surnames intersect. Whether the ancestors emigrated a hundred years before Griffith's Primary Valuation (1847-1864) was taken in Ireland is of no concern. Logically, not all relatives with their surnames left Ireland, and so someone in the family, even if distant, was in the same parish or its vicinity. Griffith's is indexed and widely available online at sites such as Ancestry.com, Findmypast.com, and Askaboutireland.ie.

How to Identify Maiden Names

In contrast to circumstances in Ulster, where most people were tenant farmers, the immigrant might have actually owned something in America to bequeath when he or she died. Therefore, a will is valuable in locating a maiden name of an immigrant's wife. A search is fairly straightforward but does require published full-name indexes of counties' wills. Fortunately, they are becoming more widespread as genealogy societies and individuals index every name in the wills, producing the ultimate research tool. Look for the family names in the indexes and in other wills. Did they witness someone's will? Did they inherit something? All can identify family members and in-laws.

Since not everyone left a will, estate sales or administrations can be second best. Did the ancestors buy something at someone's estate sale? Were they appointed as administrators of any intestate probate? The clues can be a pathway to other records.

The same reasoning is applicable to the censuses. Based upon the idea that others in the neighborhood were designated as born in Ireland, who were the ancestors living close together in the neighborhood in the 1790 to 1850 United States censuses? The plan also is postulated upon the assumption that the pre-1850 "neighborhoods" were left intact by the enumerators instead of having been arranged in alphabetical formats. Perhaps most important is the

hope that your ancestors were living in the same neighborhood as their in-laws were.

The censuses tie into the deeds of a county. By consulting the deeds, it is often possible to reconstruct a "neighborhood" that was listed alphabetically by the census taker (reference *Chapter 2— Census Records to 1850* for more about this strategy). If an ancestor owned land, the strategy is to determine exactly with whom the ancestor was buying and selling, and those people will be of central significance (reference Chapter 5: Land records). Relatives often bought and sold real estate with one another or with in-laws. Reading about land sold for a small sum, such as one dollar, is customary. The amount was usually the filing fee, a key indication that either a close friendship or a family relationship was present.

Likewise, the neighbors mentioned as boundaries to properties being sold require attention. Who were they? Could they have been the in-laws? The witnesses to the deed transactions should be examined, too. Who were these people? All questions about persons on deeds are valid. With a core group of names in hand, the censuses, even if in alphabetical format, can be consulted again to learn the ages of the core people. If they lived long enough to be in the 1850 census, birthplaces can be assigned. Again, the plan is predicated on the hope that the ancestors lived in the same neighborhood as the yet-to-be identified in-laws.

Tracing the Siblings and Children of the Immigrant

Many people want to research only their direct lines and do not care about the immigrants' siblings or the children of the immigrants. The approach is narrow and most often will lead to obstacles in research. Necessary answers may be found by extending investigations to all the siblings or children of an immigrant. In documenting their lives, the goal is discovering the much-needed female maiden name. The approach multiplies the likelihood manyfold of finding the birth surname of a mother because the pool of family members being examined is enlarged. It's sort of a genealogy insurance policy.

Prime sources become sketchier as the search proceeds to earlier times. Certainly, 1700s document sources will differ from those in the 1800s. Marriage questions might have been asked during the 1800s for obituaries, death certificates, cemetery records, pension files, and even land grants. For the 1700s, strategies, as already noted, will usually associate an ancestor with potential in-laws.

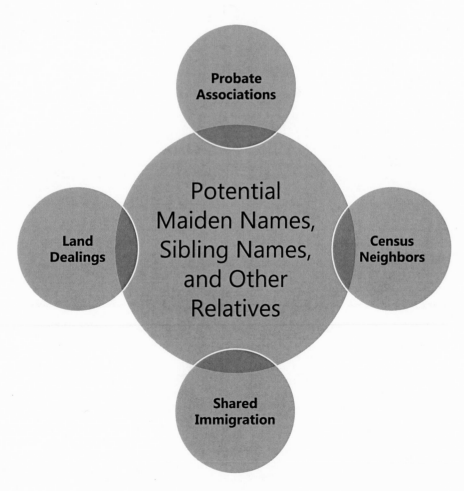

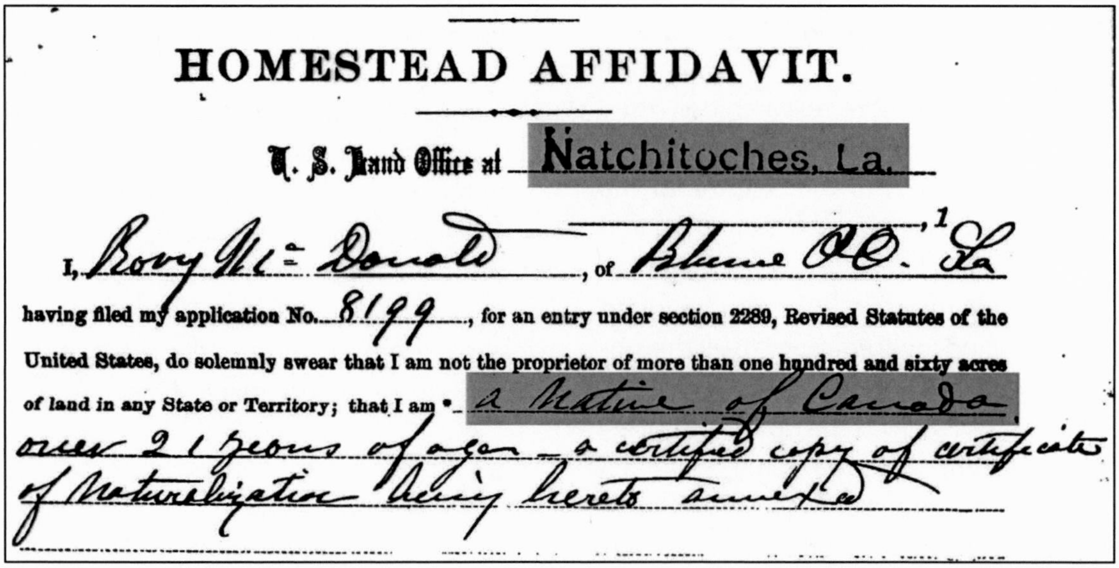

HOMESTEAD AFFIDAVIT.

U. S. Land Office at _Natchitoches, La._

I, _Rory Mc Donald_, of _Blume PO. La_[1]

having filed my application No. _8199_, for an entry under section 2289, Revised Statutes of the United States, do solemnly swear that I am not the proprietor of more than one hundred and sixty acres of land in any State or Territory; that I am * _a Native of Canada over 21 years of age a certified copy of certificate of Naturalization being hereto annexed_

Figure 17: Rory McDonald filed for a homestead in Louisiana but was born in Canada. Knowing where his naturalization was filed could lead to even more information. Homesteads are just one federal land program requiring individuals to prove their naturalization proceedings. See image below for a third location for which to search if Rory McDonald was your ancestor. (This work is in the public domain in the United States because it is a work prepared by an officer or employee of the United States Government as part of that person's official duties under the terms of Title 17, Chapter 1, Section 105 of the U.S. Code.)

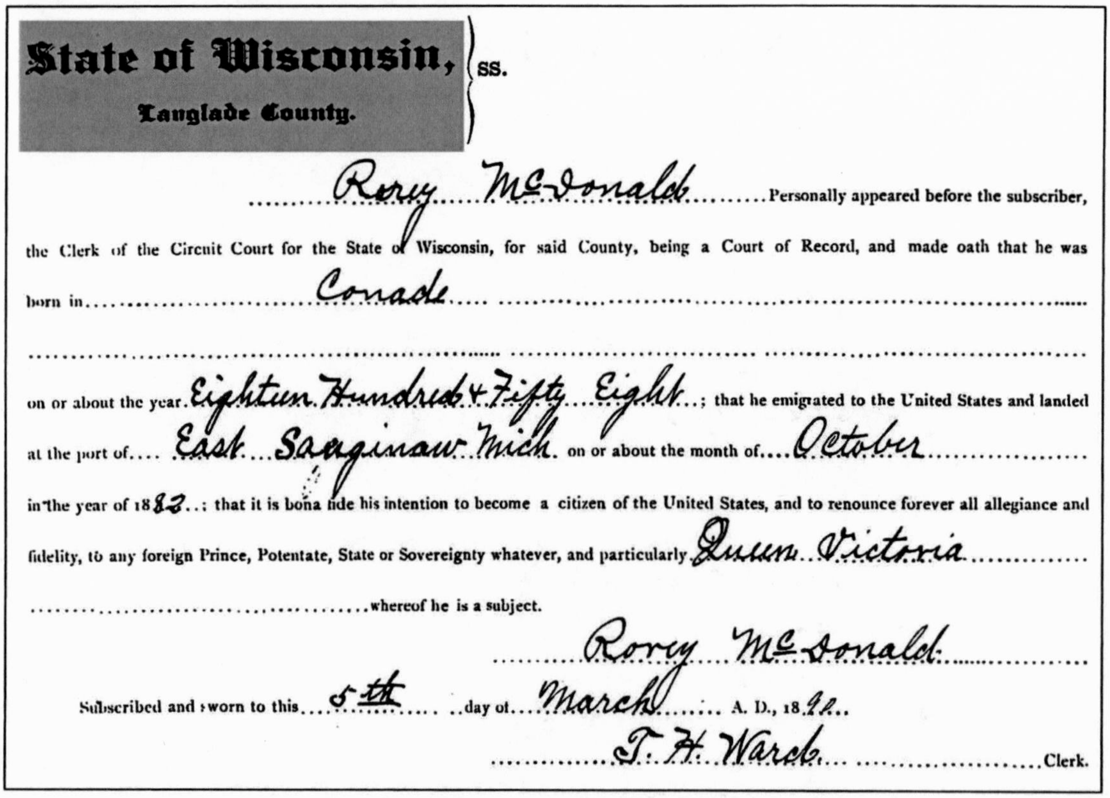

State of Wisconsin, ss.
Langlade County.

Rory McDonald Personally appeared before the subscriber, the Clerk of the Circuit Court for the State of Wisconsin, for said County, being a Court of Record, and made oath that he was born in _Conade_

on or about the year _Eighteen Hundred & Fifty Eight_; that he emigrated to the United States and landed at the port of _East Saaginaw Mich_ on or about the month of _October_ in the year of 18 _82_.; that it is bona fide his intention to become a citizen of the United States, and to renounce forever all allegiance and fidelity, to any foreign Prince, Potentate, State or Sovereignty whatever, and particularly _Queen Victoria_ whereof he is a subject.

Rory McDonald

Subscribed and sworn to this _5th_ day of _March_ A. D., 18 _22_

T. H. Ward Clerk.

Figure 18: Without examining this homestead file, a search for other residences in the United States for Rory or other potential family members may have never led to Langlade County, Wisconsin. (This work is in the public domain in the United States because it is a work prepared by an officer or employee of the United States Government as part of that person's official duties under the terms of Title 17, Chapter 1, Section 105 of the U.S. Code.)

Chapter Five

Land Records

Land records in the United States are one of the foundations of research. They can help determine from where in Ulster an immigrant originated but often not by directly stating a location. Some types do provide birthplaces, which may be found in grants or in papers associated with the government granting process. The vast majority of county legal deeds will have no reason to have birth facts, but they will disclose where the buyers (grantees) and sellers (grantors) were living at the dates of the purchases. The information concerning a person's first purchase of land in a county is vital because the residence of the buyer may have been out of state or in another county within the state, which is essential knowledge in documenting the life of someone backward in time.

United States property record research is a complicated topic. Reference books can be beneficial to anyone sorting through land laws and the various kinds of records. Of note are:

Greenwood, Val D. *The Researcher's Guide to American Genealogy*, 4th ed., Baltimore, Maryland: Genealogical Publishing Co., 2017. (Four chapters are dedicated completely or in part to land records, including: Government Land: Colonial and American," pp. 469-494; "Local Land Records," pp. 495-528; "Abstracting Probate and Land Records," pp. 529-546; and "Property Rights of Women a Consideration," pp. 575-584.)

Hatcher, Patricia Law. *Locating Your Roots: Discovering Your Ancestors Using Land Records*. Genealogical Publishing Co., Baltimore, Maryland, 2014.

Hansen, Holly T., James L. Tanner, and Arlene H. Eakle. *U.S. Land and Tax Records*. Morgan, Utah: Family History Expos, Inc., 2016.

Hone, E. Wade. *Land & Property Research in the United States*. Salt Lake City, Utah: Ancestry, 1997.

Luebking, Sandra Hargreaves. "Land Records." In *The Source: A Guidebook of American Genealogy*, 3rd ed., edited by Loretto Dennis Szucs and Sandra Hargreaves Luebking. Provo, Utah: Ancestry Publishing, 2006, pp. 431-498.

Creative strategies in land research can:

- Produce an approximate date of immigration
- Social status in the town
- Occupation
- Identify a spouse and release of dower rights
- Unveil relatives thru bordering properties/witnesses
- Reference naturalization information
- State places of previous origin
- Provide alternate residences
- Show date of death
- Include marriage information
- Allude to date of arrival into an area
- Allude to date of departure from an area
- Lead to other sources such as wills, etc.
- Reveal consistent association with others
- Enable segregation among common surnames

Developing a Research Strategy

Immigrants to America saw opportunities to own land in the 1700s. The prospect meant better lives than they had in Ulster, where the majority either rented or had leases to lands that were limited in ownerships to usually upper-class Protestants, who might or might not have lived in Ireland. For immigrants in the 1800s, circumstances might not have been much better because the common persons in Ireland did not begin to obtain properties until around 1900, when the government broke up the large estates. By the early 1800s the United States had spread beyond the coastal states, opening massive territories. As the first generation of immigrants was succeeded by the second and third, westward expansion was a certainty, and the Scots-Irish were at the forefront of frontier colonization.

Upstate New York and western Pennsylvania settlements led to more in the Midwest as the immigrants and their children and grandchildren either bought or were granted lands. Frontier areas in the western Carolinas, western Virginia, and then into Kentucky and Tennessee saw a flood of Scots-Irish migrating through the mountain passes, and with the removal of the Indian tribes in the first three decades of the nineteenth century, enormous tracts of native lands in Georgia, Alabama, Mississippi, Tennessee, and North Carolina could be obtained. Former tribal nations' regions were incorporated into the enlarging United States.

With so many properties available, families could purchase them if they had the means, creating documents about ancestors. Will land records convey where people were born? Sometimes one will, especially if it is for a later federal homestead. For state grants, the papers almost never will; however, that is not necessarily the reason for using these invaluable records. They are only a step toward the end goal of identifying the immigrants or from where in Ulster they came.

With the advent of various indexing projects, land records can be informative in new and inventive ways. When considering them as a source for tracking backward to the immigrant, several questions are suggested to formulate a viable research strategy:

- Did the ancestor actually own land? Remember, not all people owned land.

- What occupation did the ancestor have? Perhaps a blacksmith, merchant, or minister would not have a need to own land.

- Have the county or town deeds of the ancestor's place of residence been indexed? A quick check of a state archive, public library catalog, genealogy society, or the FamilySearch catalog will reveal whether they have been.

- What types of land records pertain to the ancestor's land? Knowing if the ancestor received a grant or bought land outright can promote a research strategy.

One instance from early New Hampshire records demonstrates how the inquiries can be utilized. The first large

group migration of Scots-Irish to colonial America was in 1718 from County Londonderry in and around Aghadowey Parish. Many of the group founded Londonderry, New Hampshire. Other immigrants from Ulster later joined the early immigrants. New Hampshire town records, including land transactions, have been indexed in a card file arranged by surnames, given names, and townships. The collection "Index to Early Town Records of New Hampshire (1639-1910)" in conjunction with the collection "Province Deeds and Probate Records (1623-1772)" can offer evidence about the early New Hampshire immigrants, but do not assume all incoming Scots-Irish after 1718 were from Aghadowey Parish, County Londonderry. It is solely a key consideration.

Although New Hampshire land records do not furnish immigrant origins, the collections can help answer certain questions. For example, when researching one of the early families in the Londonderry, New Hampshire environs, knowing the migration year is important. If the family was in the initial 1718 settlement, it was part of the organized group from the Aghadowey Parish area of County Londonderry. If the year was later, the family might have come from another part of Ulster, and research may not be so straightforward.

By documenting the family in land and town records, the following can often be determined:

- An approximate date of immigration
- Association with other families

- Social status in the town
- Occupation
- Movements from town to town

In resolving at least some of the aforementioned subjects, appropriate deductions can be made that eventually will facilitate and direct research in the Ulster records.

Accessing and Using Land Records

United States land records are filed and stored in a number of places, including county courthouses, state archives and libraries, the National Archives, and town halls. Massive collections of federal, colonial, and county land records are available online as they are being digitized on the FamilySearch.org website. In the case of the FamilySearch catalog, look under categories such as Alabama/Land and Property for digitized records constructed by the state. Then search under the county names, for instance, Alabama/Jackson/Land and Property, for records made by the county governments. If the records are digitized, camera images will be beside the entries, all of which can be searched online.

Some general principles may be used when examining United States land records. A major clue may lie in place name identification, that is, an immigrant might have named a tract of acreage after the old home in Ulster. In states such as Delaware, Maryland, and Pennsylvania, farms often had specific names by which they were identified in the county land deeds. Farm names such as Ballymena or Antrim may be clues about the origins of the first owner or the community.

If the ancestor's property was located in a community or township with an Irish name, determine when and by whom the township or community was named or whether a group from Ireland arrived together during the time. Deeds can be used to clarify how early the ancestor was in the locality as well as with whom the ancestor was associated. The families who initially settled a town might have been from the same area in Ireland. An ancestral family who arrived in later migrations to the community might or might not have been from one district in Ulster. If it was and the immigration was even decades after the initial settlement, people might have arrived through a chain migration in which they were joining relatives or friends. Regardless, they were from the same vicinity in Ulster, which solves the Ulster origins question.

One of the most successful strategies is presuming that immigrants from the same community in Ireland often emigrated together and settled together. Thus, if ancestors' origins cannot be found, research may fruitfully focus on those of neighbors. Deeds can contain names of the ancestors' neighbors as having boundaries to the properties being bought and sold or simply as witnesses to the transactions. Likewise, ancestors may be named in the deeds of the neighbors. By tracing the neighbors or the community in general, common patterns of origins may be found.

A variety of records—census, church, and tax, among others—can be used in conjunction with land records to reconstruct a neighborhood, for example, by comparing land records and tax records. The neighborhood begins to emerge by documenting persons who lived on the same watercourse, as in Kentucky, or in a township, as in Ohio. In addition, a model can be assembled by searching the place name indexes in published abstracts of land records for people who lived in the region that the ancestor did.

Maps, too, can assist in reconstructing neighborhoods, and many land-ownership maps are available for parts of the United States. They generally show property boundaries as well as the names of property owners for a specific period of time. For some counties, they have been published as historical atlases.

In the federal-land states, where the United States government granted the land during its initial dispersal, the Bureau of Land Management website Glore-cords.blm.gov (GLO = General Land Office) has a feature through which the lands bordering a particular person's grant can also be identified, hence reproducing all grants and persons in a neighborhood.

Figure 19: An example of land-ownership maps helping recreate neighborhoods and associations. (Image from Library of Congress, retrieved 1990s. This work is in the public domain in the United States because it is a work prepared by an officer or employee of the United States Government as part of that person's official duties under the terms of Title 17, Chapter 1, Section 105 of the U.S. Code.)

When immigrants or their descendants received grants from the various governments who owned the lands at the time, more related records were made. The British, French, Mexicans, and Spanish held lands in what was to become the United States, and the various governments kept reports. When the territories from California to Florida became part of the United States, the earlier residents had to prove their rights to them, creating additional records. These collections are known as Private Land Claims and are

Pre-U.S. Possessions — Private Land Claims

Spanish 1500s-1819

British 1600s-1783

French 1600s-1763, 1800-1803

Mexican 1821-1848

found under many jurisdictions in repository catalogs, even under the general United States/Land and Property heading. They will often have birthplaces and are occasionally indexed by genealogists or genealogy societies in the areas of the land claims because of their importance. English speaking Americans customarily migrated from the United States into what was then a foreign country to obtain lands. Scots-Irish Protestants migrated to Spanish Florida or Mississippi to purchase properties, which is why the Americans went to Mexican Texas to settle and spurred the secession of the Republic of Texas (1836 to 1846).

No matter the types of land records being used, common names are always a challenge, but the records can be implemented to sort through them. As an illustration, the search for a McDonald or Brown family in the 1700s from Ulster may be complicated by the county or township being already populated by unrelated McDonald families from Scotland or Brown families from England. Sometimes, that Ulster-Scots families had English surnames as a result of intermarriage with English families in Ulster is easy to forget. To circumvent the problem, land descriptions, including acreage and geographical features shown in an ancestral deed, may be used to separate the various families. A work about the strategy is Ge Lee Corley Hendrix's article "John Bond vs John Bond: Sorting Identities via Neighborhood Reconstruction" in *National Genealogical Society Quarterly* 79 (Dec 1991): 268-282. The common names are a predicament that almost all family historians will encounter.

In categorizing common names, the land records also can be employed in conjunction with tax records, which is especially true if the tax lists have more precise places where taxable lands were located, such as geographic features or watercourses. One family can be distinguished from another from the descriptions of the properties in the tax and land records.

State-Land States and Federal-Land States

The United States was divided into state-land states and federal-land states (also called public-land states). Most of the state-land states were east of the Mississippi River, and for them, primary jurisdiction over allocations rested with the

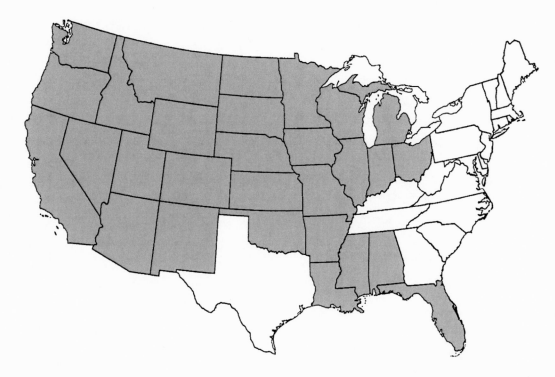

Figure 20: Federal-land States (Alaska and shaded), versus State-land States (Hawaii and unshaded).

states. For example, the Pennsylvania, Tennessee, and North Carolina grants were distributed under the system. Lands were divided into metes and bounds. Properties were disposed of through various grant programs as acreages became available for settlement.

In general, the records of initial land grants for the state-land states were filed

State-land States

20 States. The first time a piece of land was sold, it was dispersed by the state government.

Federal-land States

30 states. The first time a piece of land was sold, it was dispersed by the federal government.

Individual Lands

Once the sale had been made by the state or federal government, individuals bought and sold with one another, recorded as deeds in state, county, and town jurisdictions.

with the state. When a person sold the granted land following the initial grant, the transaction was filed with the county or town authorities.

The federal-land states were divided into townships, sections, and ranges. The sale of the lands opened millions of acres to homesteading and grants. The United States government generated documents for the transactions through land offices in each state and territory. Many Ulster immigrants and their descendants settled lands or applied for them in the federal-land states.

Some states constructed unique land records. Such records include the registrations of alien landowners in New York State and the grants of Donation Lands in Washington and Oregon. Both sets of records contain birthplaces in many cases.

Grants of State Lands

After the Revolutionary War, the newly formed states had the right to disperse

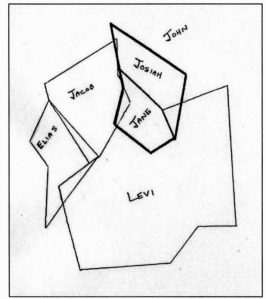

Figure 21: Example of metes and bounds lands--those found in state-land states.

properties in their respective states. Some states continued to grant bounty lands in territories they claimed outside the present-day boundaries of the states, as, for instance, Connecticut allotting grants in the Western Reserve (now northeast Ohio) and Virginia doing so in the Military District of Ohio as well as in Kentucky. North Carolina continued to give grants in what is now Tennessee. States granted lands mainly to produce revenue, fulfill bounty land obligations, and encourage settlement. The process for obtaining the property begot documents and was through several steps that involved the following:

1. An application was made for the grant and, if successful, a warrant was issued for a property survey.

2. The warrant provided the authorization for surveyors to mark, plat (draw), and record a formal description for the official title to ownership.

3. The survey was recorded with the local land office. The survey included neighbors' names. Some persons progressed as far as the warrant process and then moved on without completing the next stage, the patent.

4. When the survey was returned to the land office, a patent was issued. The patent was the owner's official title to the property, at which point, the property became part of the

private sector and could be sold by the owner.

The guideline was also used by speculators who would buy large tracts of land grants and proceed to sell them to incoming settlers. Thus, an ancestor will not appear in the grant records if the

process was already completed by the speculators.

The grant process varied from state to state, and the records may not directly convey where persons were previously living. Still, relationships among immigrants can be established from the records. Since most grants are indexed, family members who settled in the same area can be identified.

Grants in the Federal-Land States

In lands controlled and sold by the United States government, the grant plan was more uniform and yielded valuable information. Unlike the state-land states, the federal land sold by the United States government had restrictions placed on the sales. To purchase most types of grants, immigrants had to be naturalized or in the process of naturalization.

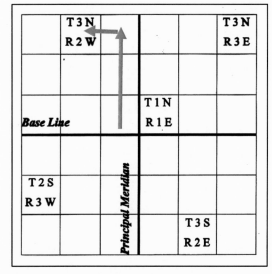

Figure 22: Example of township, range and section—those lands found in federal-land states.

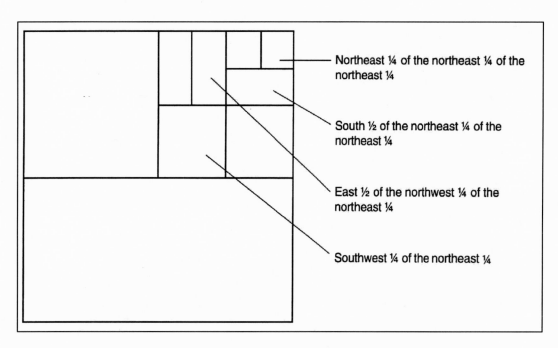

Figure 23: Each section inside the township and range description in federal-land states will have fractions within it.

The granting of federal lands began in 1797 with those in the West being sold from an office in New York City. An office was set up in Philadelphia in 1800, and by 1805, land offices were in Ohio and the Mississippi Territory. Early properties were sold at auction or through a credit system. The purchasing required the following steps:

1. A claim (application) was filed with the registrar at the land office.

2. If the application met the requirements, a warrant to survey the land was issued for a specific tract of land.

3. After completion of the registration, payment, surveys, and necessary proofs and testimonies, final certificate for a patent was issued.

4. Once the land had gone to the patent process, even if the applicant abandoned the process, the records for it were gathered into case files. The case files were sent to the General Land Office in Washington, D.C., now the Bureau of Land Management.

Some case files show birthplaces, naturalization information, and testimonials from friends and neighbors. As more country became available, much of it being that of former Native Americans, additional land offices were established in the states and territories. A state might have had several at one time. As fewer lands were offered through the patenting process, the offices were combined.

The Bureau of Land Management has indexed the claims that went to patent for the Glorecords website. In addition to its indexes, it provides scanned images of the patent records, but it does not include the case files, which are at the National Archives. The case files can be accessed by the legal description of the lands (township, range, and section).

Individual Land Sales

After lands had been purchased by grants, the owners could sell the properties on open markets. The process was the same whether they had been obtained through state or federal grants. Once the lands were in possession of individuals, the sales usually became county matters except in Alaska and Louisiana, which do not have counties (see access chart on the following page for additional exceptions). The properties retained the same legal descriptions that they did in the surveys during the grant process.

Through the careful study of individual land sales (also called private land sales), genealogical information can be found or inferred. Key details to be sought in the deeds include:

- residences of buyers and sellers
- information about deaths
- reconstructing neighborhoods
- witnesses' names
- dates recorded in the deeds
- study of a surname
- wealth and acreage

- personal property

On a deed, one date is for the day it was transacted and the other is for the day it was registered. The two are not necessarily the same. Sometimes, a sale was not officially recorded until years later. The delay in registration can throw off a search in the deed indexes, which means a search of buyers and sellers needs to be extended, sometimes even after the people have died.

Published Extractions of Land Deeds

If a book is indexed well, as many of them are, the indexes can be used to determine more than is stated in the records themselves. Some published books for county land deeds will have several indexes and can include personal, slave, and geographical names. Trying to make family connections by reading deeds using the microfilm or digitized versions of the originals can leave the impression that no connections can be made because the manuscripts typically have only a grantor (seller) and a grantee (buyer) index.

When a published book has an every-name index to records, in this case, to deeds, possibilities are increased. A published index may include every person mentioned in the deeds, including neighbors and witnesses to transactions. If so, peeling back the layers of the deeds for their real value is easy. People routinely settled among family, or if they were among friends, ancestors might have arrived with them from elsewhere. Family habitually bought and sold slaves among and with one another. Therefore, the names of the slaves might help determine relationships and associations. Family and friends frequently witnessed the transactions. If indexed in a book, all the people can be reconstructed or inferred by examining all the deeds in which an ancestor appears.

Other compilations and indexes are not strictly land related but do include such material. They often involve court records in which land matters ordinarily became court matters. One key work, in three volumes, is Lyman Chalkley's *Chronicles of the Scotch-Irish Settlement in Virginia: Extracted from the Original*

Accessing Land Deeds—Individual Lands

In most states, deeds are recorded and maintained on a county level. There were, however, exceptions to these jurisdictions:

- **Alabama:** Watch for multiple courthouses in the same county.

- **Connecticut:** Town level.

- **Massachusetts:** Watch for multiple courthouses in the same county.

- **New Hampshire:** Town level until 1769; county level thereafter.

- **Vermont:** Both town and county levels.

Court Records of Augusta County, 1754-1800 (1912. Baltimore, Maryland: Genealogical Publishing Co., Baltimore, Maryland, 1966). The composition should not be ignored because of its breadth. Although it comprises extractions of court records, it must be considered that Augusta County was much bigger in the past than it is today, and it also encompasses the Shenandoah Valley region, through which so many Scots-Irish settled or from where they emigrated. Families would continue from the Shenandoah Valley into the frontiers of Tennessee, Kentucky, the Midwest, and the Deep South.

In court record compilations, such as the aforementioned, all kinds of land matters are discussed. Consequently, they are standard genealogy sources for tracing groups from other parts of the United States back to geographical regions, maybe where one was a stop for a while for a group of people from Ulster, a temporary residence before they moved elsewhere.

Figure 24: State and federal military bounty lands—Revolutionary War through 1855.

Chapter Six

Lineage Societies

Numerous pedigrees have been compiled by persons wanting to join lineage fellowships, such as the National Society Daughters of the American Revolution or commonly called the DAR. The lineage, also known as hereditary, societies see themselves as educators, historians, and genealogists. They gather and preserve material as resources for future generations. As a result, it is not unusual for them to fund projects documenting specific facets of American history and culture. While the focuses of the hundreds of associations may differ, their bond is history and/or genealogy. For those centered on genealogy, memberships, whether open or by invitation-only, are dependent upon unbroken lineages from the applicants to ancestors who meet their requirements. The process of proving descent has created a mountain of historical material and is a valid genealogical research tool. The "Hereditary Society Community of the United States" is an umbrella organization, providing links through its website so that the various groups can have dialog with one another.

Standards of documentation required by the societies have changed and improved over the years. As with any genealogical material, the lineage collections are not always correct and must be tested. The societies themselves monitor applications, often with professional genealogists on their staffs, and many have indexed their pedigrees either in books or on their websites. Some suggestions for identifying societies that may be relevant to an immigrant ancestor are:

- Consider where and when an immigrant ancestor lived in the United States. The earlier the immigrant arrived, the more descendants he or she left in the United States. For example, if the ancestor was in Colonial America, there are many societies concentrating on the pre-1776 period to which descendants may have applied. State societies, such as the popular "First Families," are excellent choices for investigation.

- If the ancestor served in a war or conflict, target the various fellowships for military service. Ones devoted to the Revolutionary War and the War of 1812 are prime selections for explorations of Scots-Irish immigrants.

- Often, it is not necessary initially to contact the group because some have published pertinent information about the ancestors from applications. For example, the Society of the Descendants of the Colonial Clergy has issued biographies of colonial clergy in a series of books that provide birthplaces. If information is found in the volumes, copies of individual applications may be requested from the society.

- A second and often overlooked strategy can be used when considering hereditary societies. If a Scot-Irish ancestor married *into* a family whose lineage fits the original criteria for membership, he or she is still a valid link back into the society. Under the strategy, the Scot-Irish ancestor would not be the central figure of the search but would be a means to a part of the lineage of the applicant. Because Scots-Irish intermarried with most ethnic, religious, and cultural groups, not limiting the search is important.

Hereditary societies have been a part of American life since the colonial days. The first one, the Ancient and Honorable Artillery Company of Massachusetts, was founded in 1637. It is the third oldest chartered military society in the world and the oldest in the Western Hemisphere. Another old one with direct Scots-Irish connections is the upper-class Society of the Friendly Sons of Saint Patrick of the City of New York, founded in 1783. The Friendly Sons was a charitable association that was selective as far as class but did not discriminate on the basis of religion. In its early years, most of the membership was Presbyterian because most upper-class Irish merchants in New York belonged to that church, but Episcopalians, Quakers, and Roman Catholics were included as well.

Not all societies are technically concentrated on lineages. Their purposes may be history, education, preservation, and culture, with emphases on distinct sets of criteria. One such is the Scotch-Irish Society of the United States of America, whose goal is to promote the history and culture of the Scots-Irish in America. On its website is a bibliography of published Scots-Irish books, and the extensive listing is a resource tool in itself.

A sampling of the various societies, listed by dates they were founded, has been adapted below from the website "The Hereditary Society Community of the United States of America."

Societies with Potential for Scots-Irish Research

Founded	Society
1771	**Society of the Friendly Sons of Saint Patrick of Philadelphia**

Non-denominational charity society open to male citizens of Irish descent, lineage is not required.

Societies with Potential for Scots-Irish Research (cont.)

Founded   **Society**
1783   **Society of the Cincinnati**
Membership open to descendants of commissioned officers of the Continental Army and their French counterparts who served together in the American Revolution.

1814   **General Society of the War of 1812**
Membership is based upon any male over 21 who is a lineal descendant of one who served during the War of 1812 in the army, navy, revenue-marine, or privateer service of the United States.

1826   **Military Society of the War of 1812**
Members are male descendants of commissioned officers, aides de camp, and commanding officers of private armed vessels of the United States.

1850   **Society of California Pioneers**
The oldest historical organization west of the Mississippi. Membership is open to descendants of pioneers who arrived in California before January 1, 1850.

1863   **Society of the Order of the Southern Cross**
Membership is open to all male descendants (direct or collateral) of any honorably serving Confederate soldier, sailor, marine, or member of the civil government.

1876   **General Society Sons of the Revolution**
Membership open to men of lineal descendant of one who, as a military, naval, or marine officer, soldier, sailor, or marine in actual service under the authority of any of the thirteen Colonies or States or of the Continental Congress, and remaining always loyal to such authority, or a lineal descendant of one who signed the Declaration of Independence, or of one who, as a member of the Continental Congress or of the Congress of any of the Colonies or States, or as an official appointed by or under the authority of any such legislative bodies, actually assisted in the establishment of American Independence by services rendered during the War of the Revolution.

1881   **Sons of Union Veterans of the Civil War**
Membership open to any male who is directly descended from a Soldier, Sailor, Marine, or member of the Revenue Cutter Service (or directly descended from a brother, sister, half-brother, or half-sister of such Soldier, etc.) who was regularly mustered and served honorably in the service of, the Army, Navy, Marine Corps, or Revenue Cutter Service of the United States of America or in such state regiments called to active service and was subject to the orders of United States general officers between April 12, 1861, and April 9, 1865.

Societies with Potential for Scots-Irish Research (cont.)

Founded   **Society**
1883   **Auxiliary to Sons of Union Veterans of the Civil War**
Membership available to women who are lineal or collateral descendants of soldiers, sailors, or marines regularly mustered and honorably discharged from the Army, Navy, or Marine Corps of the United States during the War of the Rebellion 1861-1865. Daughters, granddaughters, great-granddaughters, as well as nieces, great-nieces, and legally adopted daughters qualify. Mothers, wives, widows, daughters, and legally adopted daughters of Sons of Union Veterans of the Civil War in good standing also qualify.

1884   **Sons and Daughters of Montana Pioneers**
Membership is open to any person descended from an ancestor who resided in Montana on or before December 31, 1868.

1885   **Daughters of Union Veterans of the Civil War 1861-1865**
Membership open to direct descendants of honorably discharged soldiers, sailors, and marines who served in the Union Army or Navy during the War of the Rebellion of 1861-1865.

1885   **Ladies of the Grand Army of the Republic**
Membership open to female descendants of honorably discharged Union soldiers, sailors, and marines of the Civil War, 1861 to 1865. Descendants of ex-army nurses of that War are also eligible for membership.

1889   **Scotch-Irish Society of the United States of America**
Membership open to those of Scotch-Irish descent. The Scotch-Irish Society and the Scotch-Irish Foundation consider that the term "Scotch-Irish" generically designates those persons who are descended in either the male or female line from an ancestor, or ancestors, who emigrated to America, directly or indirectly, from Ulster, and whose families, hailing from Scotland, Britain, France, and other places in Europe, had previously settled in Ulster about or after year 1600.

1889   **National Society of the Sons of the American Revolution**
Membership is open to males who are of lineal descendant of an ancestor who rendered active service in the cause of American independence as an officer, soldier, seaman, marine, militiaman, or Minuteman in the armed forces of the Continental Congress of any one of the several Colonies or States; or as a Signer of the Declaration of Independence; or as a member of a Committee of Safety or Correspondence; or as a member of any Continental, Provincial, or Colonial Congress or Legislature; or as a recognized patriot who performed actual service by overt acts of resistance to the authority of Great Britain.

Societies with Potential for Scots-Irish Research (cont.)

Founded   **Society**

1890   **National Society Daughters of the American Revolution**

Membership is open to women who can prove lineal, blood line descent from an ancestor who aided in achieving American independence. The National Society accepts service, with some exceptions, for the period between 19 April 1775 (Battle of Lexington) and 26 November 1783 (withdrawal of British Troops from New York) as follows: Signers of the Declaration of Independence, Military Service, certain types of Civil Service (under authority of Provisional or new State Governments), and certain types of Patriotic Service. Admission to membership in the NSDAR is either by invitation through a state chapter or unit overseas.

1891   **National Society of the Colonial Dames of America**

Membership is open to women who are lineal descendants of an ancestor who came to reside in an American Colony before 1750 and who rendered efficient service to his country before July 5, 1776. They include service as a Signer of the Declaration of Independence; the founding of either a Commonwealth or an institution that has survived and developed into importance; those who held an important position in a Colonial government; or by service, contributed to the founding of the United States of America.

1891   **Daughters of the Republic of Texas**

Membership is open to any woman who is a lineal descendant of a man or woman who rendered loyal service to Texas prior to the consummation of the Annexation Agreement of the Republic of Texas with the United States of America, February 19, 1846.

1892   **National Society United States Daughters of 1812**

Membership by invitation and is open to women who are of lineal descendants of an ancestor who, during the period of 1784-1815, rendered civil, military, naval service, or material aid to the U.S. Army or Navy, or who participated in the Lewis and Clark Expedition.

1893   **Sons of the Republic of Texas**

Membership is open to any man who is a direct descendant of an ancestor who was a resident and loyal citizen of Texas prior to its annexation into the Union.

1893   **General Society of Colonial Wars**

Membership is by invitation to males who are of lineal descent from a male or female ancestor who served as a military or naval officer, or as a soldier, sailor, or marine, or as a privateersman under authority of any of the Colonies that afterward formed the United States, or in the forces of Great Britain that participated with

Societies with Potential for Scots-Irish Research (cont.)

Founded   Society

those of the said Colonies, which afterward formed the United States, during the period from the settlement of Jamestown, May 13, 1607, to the battle of Lexington, April 19, 1775; or who held office in any of the colonies.

1894   Daughters of the Cincinnati

Membership is for women eighteen years of age or older who are lineally descended from an officer who was an Original Member, or would have been eligible to become an Original member, of the Society of the Cincinnati.

1894   United Daughters of the Confederacy

Membership is open to women 16 years old, or older, who are blood descendants, lineal or collateral, of men and women who served in the Army, Navy, or Civil Service of the Confederate States of America, or gave material aid to the cause.

1895   National Society of New England Women

Membership open to women descended from one or more ancestors born in New England prior to the signing of the Constitution of the United States in 1789, or in Nassau or Suffolk County, Long Island, before 1700.

1896   Sons of Confederate Veterans

Membership is open to all male descendants of any veteran who served in the Confederate armed forces. Membership can be obtained through either direct or collateral family lines.

1897   Minnesota Territorial Pioneers

Membership is based on tracing to the pioneers who settled in the Minnesota Territory before the state of Minnesota was admitted to the Union in 1858.

1898   National Society Daughters of Founders and Patriots of America

Membership open to women who are descended in an unbroken paternal line of either father or mother from an ancestor who settled in any of the Colonies now included in the United States of America during the period from the settlement of Jamestown, May 13, 1607, to May 13, 1687, and provided that in this unbroken line is an intermediate ancestor who, by personal service in a civil or military capacity, assisted in establishing American independence during the Revolutionary Period, 1775 to 1784.

1901   International Society Daughters of Utah Pioneers

Membership is open to any woman who is a lineal or legally adopted descendant of an ancestor who came to Utah before the completion of the railroad, May 10, 1869.

Societies with Potential for Scots-Irish Research (cont.)

Founded   **Society**

1901   **Sons and Daughters of Oregon Pioneers**
Membership open to descendants of the pioneers who arrived and settled in the Oregon Country, the present states of Oregon, Washington, Idaho, parts of Montana, and most of the Province of British Columbia before Oregon statehood in 1859.

1905   **Piscataqua Pioneers**
Membership is based on descent from one of the original settlers on either side of the Piscataqua River and its tributaries before 1775.

1912   **National Society Daughters of the Union 1861-1865**
Membership is open to any woman 18 years or older who is a direct lineal or collateral descendant of a man or woman who rendered military or civil service to the Union during 1861-1865.

1914   **United Empire Loyalists' Association of Canada**
Membership is open to anyone who can prove he or she has a Loyalist ancestor who meets the following criteria: (1) was, as of 19 April 1775, a man or woman who was a resident of the American Colonies and joined the Royal Standard before the Treaty of Separation of 1783, or otherwise demonstrated loyalty to the Crown, and settled in territory remaining under the rule of the Crown; or (2) a soldier who served in an American Loyalist Regiment and was disbanded in Canada; or (3) a member of the Six Nations of either the Grand River or the Bay of Quinte Reserve who is descended from one whose migration was similar to that of other Loyalists.

1916   **Society of Indiana Pioneers**
Regular Membership is open to men and women who can trace their lineage to one or more ancestors who lived within the present boundary of an Indiana county on or before December 31, 1840.

1920   **Daughters of the Pioneers of Washington**
Membership is open to female lineal descendants of pioneers who established residence in Washington Territory before 1870.

1921   **National Society Daughters of the American Colonists**
Membership is for women at least 18 years old who are lineal descendants of ancestors who rendered civil or military service in any of the colonies before July 4, 1776.

1932   **National Society Daughters of Colonial Wars**
Membership by invitation to any woman who is lineally descended in the male or female line from an ancestor who, from the time of the settlement of Jamestown, May 13, 1607, to the battle of Lexington, April 19, 1775.

Societies with Potential for Scots-Irish Research (cont.)

Founded   **Society**

1933   National Society Sons of Utah Pioneers
Membership is based upon descent from a Mormon ancestor who came to Utah as a pioneer before the completion of the transcontinental railroad in 1869.

1933   Society of the Descendants of the Colonial Clergy
Membership is based on descent from an ancestor who was a clergyman regularly ordained, installed, or settled over a Christian church within the thirteen colonies before July 4, 1776.

1962   Flagon and Trencher
No age restriction, male or female, and lineage must be traced back to a person who had a tavern, inn, ordinary, pub, or other hostelries. Membership is usually proven through a license granted by the local authorities before 4 July 1776 within the area that became the first 13 states. Brewers and distillers do not qualify unless they were licensed taverners or innkeepers.

1964   First Families of Ohio
Membership is through the Ohio Genealogical Society to those who are direct descendants of an individual who settled in Ohio before December 31, 1820.

1967   Order of the First Families of Mississippi 1699-1817
Membership is based on descent in a male or female line from a native or resident of the territory now included in the State of Mississippi between 1699, when the French established the settlement of Old Biloxi, and December 10, 1817, when Mississippi was admitted to the Union.

1974   Descendants of Whaling Masters
Membership is based upon descent from a whaling master.

1985   National Society Sons of Colonial New England
Membership is open to males 18 years old or more who can prove direct descent from a person who was born in one of the six New England colonies before July 4, 1776.

1988   Continental Society Daughters of Indian Wars
Membership by invitation to the direct lineal female descendants, at least 16 years old, either of Native or immigrant American ancestors who participated in any capacity in actual hostilities, one against the other, or in any other passive activity with each other, at any time during the period 1607-1900. Applicant must be a legal resident of the United States, Canada, or Mexico.

Societies with Potential for Scots-Irish Research (cont.)

Founded   **Society**

1989   **Descendants of Mexican War Veterans**

Membership is open to all persons who are: (1) lineal or collateral descendant of a U.S. veteran who rendered honorable service in the war with Mexico for any length of time between April 25, 1846, and August 2, 1848; (2) from a civilian employee of the U.S. armed forces who served during the Mexican War as a teamster, laundress, or steamboat hand; (3) from a veteran of General Zachary Taylor's "Army of Occupation" in Texas from July 1845 to April 1846; (4) from a veteran of Col. John Colonel Fremont's 1845-1846 expedition to California; or (5) from a California "Bear Flag Revolt" participant.

2000   **Alamo Defenders' Descendants Association**

Membership is open to lineal descendants of an Alamo defender, courier, scout, or non-combatant survivor; an indirect descendant of a defender, courier, scout, or non-combatant survivor; or interested individuals.

2004   **Guild of Colonial Artisans and Tradesmen 1607-1783**

Membership is open to men and women, 18 years or older, who are lineally descended from an artisan or tradesman who lived in the American Colonies from the founding of Jamestown, 13 May 1607, to the Treaty of Paris, signed 3 September 1783. Artisans and tradesmen are defined as those who made a living in the arts and those who crafted or traded items and/or were part of select Royal Guilds previously established in the Old World who continued their practices in the American Colonies.

2009   **First Settlers of the Shenandoah Valley**

Membership is by invitation and is open to men and women who trace their lineage to a qualifying first settler ancestor who resided in the Shenandoah Valley before 31 December 1799.

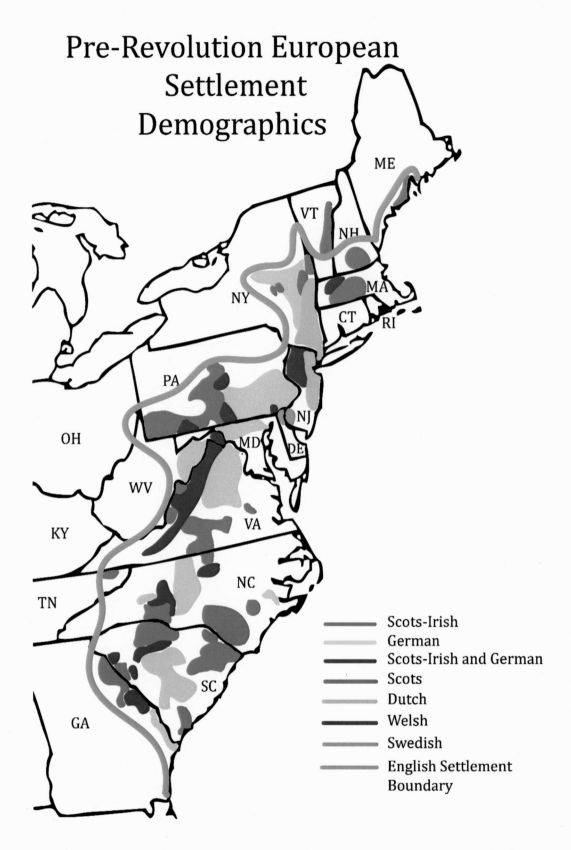

Figure 25: Pre-Revolution European settlement, the foundation from which migrations expanded.

Ulster

Chapter Seven

Migration Patterns

One of the most important questions that can be asked in research, especially for the colonial and frontier periods in America, is why the ancestors chose to settle where they did. A settlement pattern will assist in identifying from where in Ulster ancestors came. Main migrations were as follows:

- A ***group migration*** was common in the 1700s and 1800s as families settled collectively in an area. Chances are that at least part of the community had traveled together. The frontier was hostile, and people needed to protect and assist one another. Group migrations were also religious assemblages, for example, the Moravians, Mormons, Presbyterians, and Quakers.

- A ***congregational migration*** occurred when all or part of a Presbyterian flock followed its minister to America. If it is discovered that the ancestor's minister in America pastored in Ulster, his congregants could have lived in the same area in Ulster.

- A ***chain migration*** was common in the nineteenth century, in which case an ancestor might have followed a friend or a family member to America, and, in turn, was followed by another relative or friend. A chain migration from the same area of Ireland to a particular community in the United States can stretch over years, if not decades.

The earlier the person immigrated to America, the more important the reconstruction of his or her neighborhood of associates and friends will be. All might have arrived together from Ulster, and, therefore, identifying where at least some were residing also may isolate where an ancestor was. For instance, if all the ancestor's neighbors and associates are found to have been from County Antrim, a distinct possibility is that the ancestor was from there, too.

By the 1800s, the Scots-Irish were arriving through every American harbor. However, earlier in the 1700s, Baltimore, Boston, Charleston, New York, and especially Philadelphia were major ports of entry. Philadelphia provides an interesting study because from it, settlers could move west and into the Midwest as well as southward, all depending on when the settlers left the westbound main road from Philadelphia.

Colonial Scots-Irish
Settlement and Migration

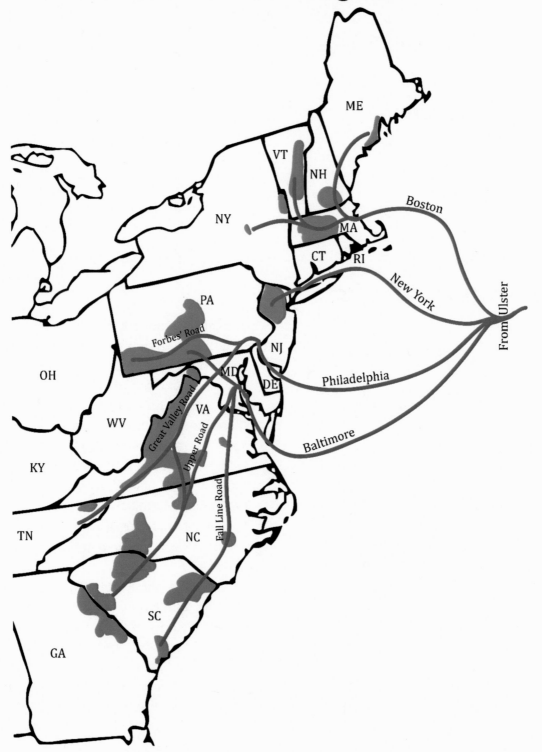

Figure 26: Scots-Irish settlement and migration according to colonial ports and roads.

Passenger arrival records are scarce before the United States government began keeping them in 1820, and so definite strategies have to be employed to reach back to that immigration point. Before 1820, researchers may never find records for the ports of entry. Because they are unavailable, developing a practical strategy around migration patterns is especially essential. If a pre-1820 passenger list is not found, move on and accept that it simply does not exist.

Do Not Make Assumptions

One issue in trying to link individuals back to the immigrants on databases is that often when the "Helpful Hints" or "Suggested Records" brings up entries, researchers automatically think those persons are their ancestors. The first question that should be asked is whether the clues even make sense.

As an illustration, if a man settled in Alabama in the 1830s and a "Helpful Hint" displays someone with that name arriving in Boston in the 1820s, is he or she the person being sought? The question is logical. Alabama does have the port of Mobile, and so, technically, a person could travel from Boston to Mobile—possible but in most cases, not probable. No direct routes were from Boston to Alabama, and so for people traveling by land at the time, the distance was long and over mountains. The explanation is that the search results are for two people with the same name. Confusing one person with another is frequent. With a little background study and reasoning, it would be determined that the migration from New England was westward into New York and, afterward, to the Midwest

of the country. An Alabama migration likely arose from the Middle States from Pennsylvania southward to Charleston or New Orleans. Remember, mountains are in the way, and the mountain passes funneled people through certain routes and not through others.

Study migration maps for knowledge of locations of waterways and roads through the mountain passes. They will assist in placing the information from the various databases into logical perspectives. Some of the Ulster-Scots names are just too common, leading to hasty decisions and linking people who should not be linked. A number of excellent migration maps can be found in the back of *The Handybook for Genealogists: United States of America*, 10th edition (Draper, Utah: Everton Publishers, 2002). Other standard works in the genealogy community are William Dollarhide's *Map Guide to American Migration Routes, 1735-1815* (Bountiful, Utah: Heritage Quest, 2000) and Beverly Whitaker's *Migration Patterns in the United States* (Toronto, Ontario: Heritage Productions, 2003).

Tracing the Neighborhood

In research, the goal automatically should not be to trace the immigrant but to trace *back* to the immigrant. The pursuit doubtless will be taken in steps, moving the ancestors through paper trails in reverse time decade by decade. If working from frontier areas to the populated coastal ones, each record must be viewed from its relevant geographical position.

When places of origin are unknown in the eastern states, finding a way to follow back the ancestors to locations is necessary. The plan typically encompasses identifying and tracking a group of people with whom the ancestors were associated on the frontier. The frontier was not safe, which is easy to forget. Native Americans were not happy with settlers coming onto their lands, but bandits were more than happy to see those same incoming, vulnerable settlers. The situation created one advantage for frontier research because almost always a group of people traveled with the ancestors for safety reasons. Who was this group?

The closer the group was to the immigrant ancestor's lifetime, the better the chances are that some of the people in it were also from Ulster and traveled with him or her. To find the emigration home in Ulster of the group is to find the home of the ancestor. If the people being traced are further removed from the generation of the ancestor, they might have been his or her children or grandchildren. The goal is still the same, to work back to the original group in an eastern area of the country. The method has not changed, but what will differ is not to find an Ulster location but to move this collection of friends and relatives to the East as a unit so that the Ulster origins' question can be explored.

Sometimes, a group, or part of an original one, continued to stay together throughout all kinds of circumstances. It was not uncommon for men who served in the same company in the Revolutionary War or the War of 1812 to have been from the same county in the East. At that point, when the young men wanted to move westward, they decided to go together. Occasionally, they even followed their captain to the frontier, which can make identification easy because so much has been written about veterans who settled in certain counties. In addition, the various military databases online, such as on FamilySearch.org, Fold3.com, or Ancestry.com, can help establish the patterns. Tracking a migration of the veterans of the War of 1812, as an example, may be as easy as finding the group in the 1820 census and then locating the group or at least the captain in the 1810 census in the East. The young men might not have been heads of households in 1810; instead, the ancestor might not have been the immigrant but perhaps a child or grandchild of the immigrant. Once identified in a county back East, the process of looking for the immigrant and Ulster origins starts over again.

Tracing Presbyterian Ministers as an Immigration Strategy

Of all the migration patterns, one that is particularly noteworthy is the migration of a congregation. An Ulster Presbyterian minister and at least part of his congregation leaving together and settling together as a group in America was not uncommon in the 1700s. If people are following their minister, the natural assumption is that they all lived within a short geographical distance from the church building in Ulster.

The average Presbyterian register in Ireland began in the 1820s or 1830s. With a few exceptions, early registers are rare, and thus there are no Presbyterian ones from which to document immigrants to America.

If documentation or a suspicion appears that an ancestor followed a minister out of Ulster, research should immediately focus on the minister and not the ancestor. The easiest way to do so is to identify the earliest period in which the immigrant was associated with a Presbyterian congregation and then determine

whether that minister pastored in Ulster. The strategy is valid and has been employed by researchers for decades. When considering tracing an Ulster minister, some basic principles need to be understood:

- Many different branches of Presbyterianism were in Ireland and still remain. The history of Presbyterianism on both sides of the

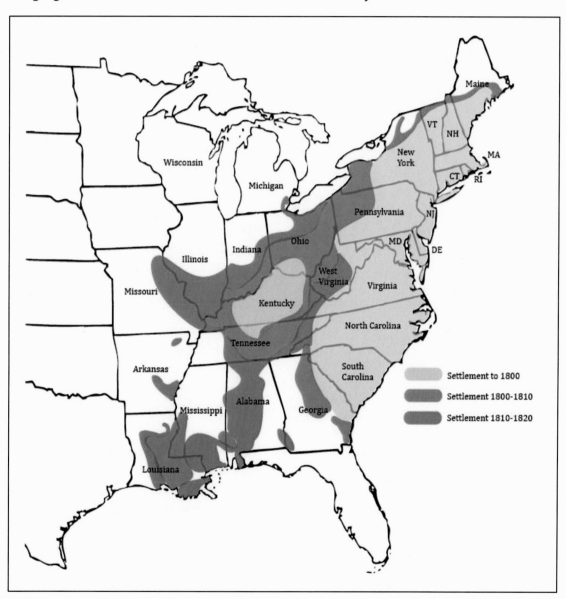

Figure 27: Westward expansion by decennial census.

Atlantic is one of division, merger, and division again, affecting what happened to records.

- Biographical lists of ministers are known as fasti books. They are important and are typically kept by Presbyterian denominations. The fasti books for Irish Presbyterians and American Presbyterians can be compared to determine when and where the minister pastored.

- Don't always assume a minister brought his congregation from Ireland, as it is only a place to begin the search.

- When studying fasti books in the United States, do not assume the minister in question ever had a congregation in Ireland. Remember, pastors were also trained in America and were actually Scottish and not Ulster-Scots. Be careful with this point in research.

- If a congregational migration is suspected, a reasonable conclusion is that an ancestral family lived within a short distance from where the minister pastored, which narrows a search to perhaps a radius of five miles at the very most. It also is logical that if congregants were on foot, not owning a horse, their geographical location to the Presbyterian Church was limited to walking distance, perhaps just a couple of miles. Even if they

owned a horse in Ulster, congregants likely still did not live far from the church building.

While searching for a minister, always remember that discovering a new congregational migration is a possibility. There is no complete list of congregational migrations from Ulster to America.

Ulster Presbyterian ministers were usually trained, and so records were kept. For many ministers, if not most, preparations took place in Scotland, especially before 1853, when the Presbyterian College was established in Belfast. Ministers' lists, or fasti books, sometimes state exactly when the ministers immigrated to America with their congregations. Not noted in the fasti books were members in chain migrations, that is, persons following others over a period. The same principle for tracing the chain of people applies but just not for all leaving at the same time. Sources for tracing ministers are:

Bailie, W.D. and L.S. Kirkpatrick, eds, *Fasti of Seceder Ministers Ordained or Installed in Ireland 1746-1948*. Belfast, Northern Ireland: Presbyterian Historical Society of Ireland, 2005.

Barkley, John M., *Fasti of the General Assembly of the Presbyterian Church in Ireland, 1840-1910*. Belfast: Presbyterian Historical Society, 1986-1987.

Loughridge, Adam, *Fasti of the Irish Reformed Presbyterian Church*. [S.l.]: Reformed Presbyterian Synod of Ireland and Presbyterian Historical Society, 1970.

Marshall, William F., *Ulster Sails West: The Story of the Great Immigration from Ulster to North America*. Reprint. Baltimore, Maryland: Genealogical Publishing Co., 1977.

McConnell, James and Samuel G. McConnell, *Fasti of the Irish Presbyterian Church*. Belfast, Northern Ireland: Presbyterian Historical Society, 1951.

Presbyterian Historical Society of Ireland, *A History of Congregations in the Presbyterian Church in Ireland, 1610-1982* (Belfast, Northern Ireland: Presbyterian Historical Society, 1982).

Stewart, Rev. David, *Fasti of the American Presbyterian Church: treating of ministers of Irish origin who labored in America during the eighteenth century* (Belfast, Northern Ireland: Bell and Logan, 1943).
Stewart, David, *The Seceders in Ireland with Annals of Their Congregations* (Belfast, Northern Ireland: Presbyterian Historical Society, 1950).

James McConnell and Samuel G. McConnell's book is especially important, although it does exclude dissenting Presbyterian ministers. The second part of this series is John M. Barkely's work, which also documents ministers in the main Presbyterian Church in Ireland.

Because of all the divisions and mergers within Irish and American Presbyterianism, chances are that the specific variants or denominations are not known ahead of time for colonial ancestors. If research does not reveal the minister in question in any of the compilations, it has to be considered that he was not a minister in Ireland.

Several of the pastors listed in the McConnell's volume mention Irish ministers going to the colonies, making his book a trove of information. Some stayed in one locality, others moved among different congregations in the colonies, and some returned to Ireland. One Irish minister who went to New England was Rev. Thomas Craghead, and his fasti entry is as follows:

> Craghead, Thomas; s. of Rev. Robert Craghead, Donoughmore and Derry; educ. Edin., M.A. (Edin.) 1691; lic. Laggan (Strabane) Pres. 1698; ord. (at Ballintra) Donegal and Castlederg, 6 July 1698; res. Donegal and retained Castlederg, 1710; res. 1715, granted testimonial to New England; ins. Freetown, Mass., 1715; res. 1723; ins. White Clay Creek, Delaware, 22 Sept. 1724; res. 1733; ins. Pequea, 31 Oct. 1733; res. Sept. 1736; ins. Hopewell, Oct. 1738. Died in the pulpit, April 1739.
>
> [Reff.: Mins. Of Derry Sub-Syn. 155; *Genealogical Memoir of the Craghead Family, 1658-1876*.]

Whether Rev. Craghead led or joined others from his congregation from Castlederg, County Tyrone, to Freetown, Massachusetts, requires a study of those congregants and their origins.

William F. Marshall's *Ulster Sails West: The Story of the Great Immigration from*

Ulster to North America is a classic history of the Scots-Irish. It contains a list, with some details, of ministers who came to America from Ulster.

A History of Congregations in the Presbyterian Church in Ireland, 1610-1982 has a brief history of each congregation with its succession of ministers, the dates when the congregations began, and whether they merged or closed. The Presbyterian Historical Society of Ireland published—and made available on its website—a supplement and index to the book in 1996, in which over 600 congregational histories have been brought up to date.

For denominations and movements outside the main church, works such as Loughridge's booklet on Reformed Presbyterian ministers can be helpful. Just one example from it reads:

> Gibson, William
> b. Knockbracken, Co. Down, July 1, 1753; s. Robert Gibson, and Susannah McWhir; ed. Glasgow University; grad. M.A. 1775; theological studies at Edinburgh; lic. Reformed Presbytery of I., May 19, 1781; ord. Kellswater and Cullybackey, April 171787; emig. To U.S.A. Oct., 1797; joined James McKinney and elders in constituting Refd. Pres. Of U.S.A. at Philadelphia, 1798; inst. Ryegate, Vermont, July 10, 1899 [sic]; res. 13th April, 1815; inst. Canonburg, Pa., Oct 13, 1817; res. May 27, 1826 (ill health); stated supply Paterson, N.J., Philadelphia, 1834-36; New York,

1836-1838; died Oct. 15, 1838; mar. Rebecca Mitchell, Londonderry; 5s. 4 d.; Mod. 1st Synod in U.S. in 1809.

> Cf. Howe, *"History of Pres. Church in S. Carolina,"* p. 698.

To complement all the Irish sources, one little known resource can be utilized. In 1943, Rev. David Stewart published *Fasti of the American Presbyterian Church: treating of ministers of Irish origin who labored in America during the eighteenth century,* containing records of 156 ministers who immigrated to America from Ulster. A copy can be found at the Presbyterian Historical Society of Ireland. Not all ministers in Stewart's biographical compilation, however, served a congregation in Ireland. Although Irish-born, they could have been trained in America, and, therefore, the work needs to be compared with all the Irish fasti books.

The Presbyterian Historical Society of Ireland is a main repository for information on Irish ministers, but it is not the only one. The Presbyterian Historical Society in Philadelphia collects records for all branches of Presbyterianism in the United States and includes details about immigrant pastors.

Ulster

Chapter Eight

Military Records

Military records are central to the search for immigrant origins because birthplaces in Ulster might have been preserved within various records generated about soldiers or potential soldiers. For the purpose of the Scots-Irish study, the early military records will be discussed in detail as they may help identify Ulster birthplaces during quite difficult times: the Colonial Period, the Revolutionary War, and the War of 1812.

Several books on the market, most dated, provide invaluable advice about accessing available sources. To complement these standard works, innumerable records in the immense U.S. military archives have been digitized and indexed on Ancestry.com, FamilySearch.com, and Fold3.com. Websites also have resources for a multitude of military papers from the state archives of soldiers' states, and they should be consulted. What is

important to remember is that military reporting is a vast topic with many records, often contradictory but within which birthplaces can be found. They are not to be ignored. Authoritative books on the market, useful even if dated, include:

Bockstruck, Lloyd DeWitt and Sandra Hargreaves Luebking. "Military Records." In *The Source: A Guidebook of American Genealogy*, 3rd ed., edited by Loretto Dennis Szucs and Sandra Hargreaves Luebking. Provo, Utah: Ancestry Publishing, 2006, pp. 431-498.

Greenwood, Val D. *The Researcher's Guide to American Genealogy*, 4th ed. Baltimore, Maryland: Genealogical Publishing Co., 2017, pp. 653-688 and 689-726.

Neagles, James C. *U.S. Military Records: A Guide to Federal & State Sources, Colonial America to the Present*. Provo, Utah: Ancestry Publishing ,1994.

Val D. Greenwood's book has two noteworthy chapters on military records, "Military Records: Colonial Wars and the American Revolution" (pp. 653-688) and "Military Records: After the Revolution" (pp. 689-726).

U.S. Army and local militia regiments can be confused. It is common to assume that a soldier served with a state regiment; however, his service also could have been with a federal regiment. In the latter case, the U.S. Army Enlistment records are a prime source for identifying birthplaces. They are on Ancestry.com, FamilySearch.org, and Fold3.com. The database on Ancestry.com is "U.S. Army, Register of Enlistments, 1798-1914," whereas on FamilySearch.org, it is titled "United States Register of Enlistments in the U.S. Army, 1798-1914." Both are from one source but are two different sets of indexing.

The records began in 1798 and vary in their content. Ireland alone may be entered in the birthplace columns, but on some of the same pages may be counties, such as Down, Ireland. Searching the database thus needs to be undertaken with care. If Down does not come up, try Ireland along with the soldier's name in the search. Where the men enlisted and/or their residence is also given can be used as a guide through common names. Always make sure the indexes being used have the birthplaces and not just the residences or enlistment seats.

1798). Even though he deserted in Pittsburgh, his birthplace is still noted. Chances are there is no surviving birth or christening record for him in County Tyrone. A second tier of questions is thereby raised. Who were the McSoleys in the area in and around Pittsburgh who could have been his parents or siblings? Were any McSoleys found in the Pittsburgh area also from County Tyrone? Did other McSoleys enlist in the U.S. Army? What exactly is Kilitar, County Tyrone? Is it a parish, a townland, or a minor, more localized place name? One entry alone broaches multiple layers of questions that research can now address.

In the discussions of the Colonial Period, Revolutionary War, and War of 1812, an extended bibliography of published sources and databases will be provided. They are drawn from the FamilySearch

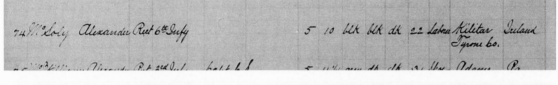
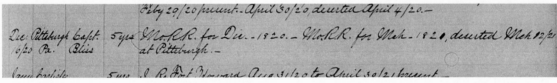

Figure 28: Snippet from U.S. Army Register of Enlistments, 1798-1914, revealing that Alexander McSoly was born in "Kilitar, Ireland, Tyrone Co." (This work is in the public domain in the United States because it is a work prepared by an officer or employee of the United States Government as part of that person's official duties under the terms of Title 17, Chapter 1, Section 105 of the U.S. Code.)

The places within counties where persons were born in Ireland are sometimes in the early records. For example, Alexander McSoly enlisted for five years as a private in the 6th U.S. Infantry on 6 December 1820 in Pittsburgh, Pennsylvania. His birthplace was noted as "Kilitar, Tyrone Co., Ireland." He was 22 years old (b.

catalog and from Ancestry.com. Although certainly not the only places published sources and databases can be found, they do afford a foundation from which to continue research. In the case of books, it is common for both FamilySearch.org and Ancestry.com to have built either databases or digital images

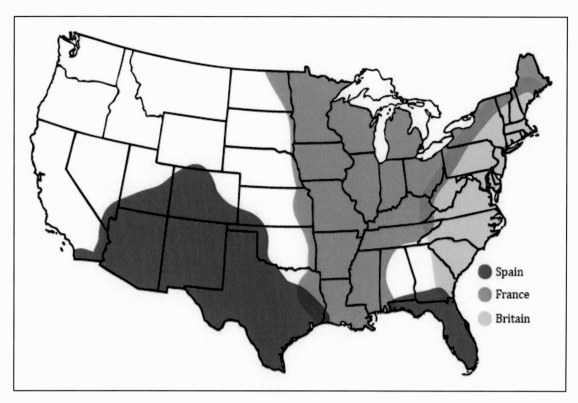

Figure 29: Pre-1776 sovereign possessions against the backdrop of present-day states. While Britain held the least land, they controlled most of the crucial seaport regions.

from books. Also referenced may be books on the same soldiers by a choice of authors, each of whom concentrates on one aspect of the soldiers' lives or deaths. One writer may list raw data, for example, the Revolutionary War soldiers buried in a particular state, while another may add biographical sketches of the soldiers. All the books and the sites should be checked for clues because of the dissimilar angles.

Books and databases are only the beginning of the search, which should be continued in primary records at state archives and at Fold3.com, where many U.S. National Archives digitized records may be found. The diversity of works cited in this chapter can be found at any number of local, state, and national libraries. Knowing that such volumes exist can unlock complex research problems,

leading to additional sources in the process. The Library of Congress and major libraries, one being the Allen County Public Library in Fort Wayne, Indiana, should not be overlooked either for foundational published sources.

Colonial Period (1718-1776)

In U.S. research, the Colonial Period is typically defined as that before 1776; however, technically, the Colonial Period was from 1607 to 1774. Before the creation of the United States in 1776, many Scots-Irish enlisted in English units within the individual colonies. The major waves of Scots-Irish arrived beginning in 1718, and so the period afterward is the focus of the discussion herein. Ulster-Scots certainly were in the American colonies before 1718 but their numbers were small compared to those after 1718.

Because the colonial period is crucial in documenting immigrants, the military records for the period are significant, so much so that it is common to find that historians and genealogists have already gone through the old records and extracted members of regiments. Concentrating mainly on the period 1718-1776, the following two wars are the foremost to explore for an Ulster-Scot soldier:

- King George's War (1744-1748)
- French and Indian War (1754-1763).

Briefly, King George's War (1744-1748) was the North American front of a larger war and was the third of four French and Indian wars. It took place mainly in the colonies of Massachusetts (which included modern Maine), New Hampshire (which included modern Vermont), New York, and Nova Scotia and was a conflict between France and Britain and their respective colonies. Tensions again broke out in what became known as the French and Indian War (1754-1763), in which the British colonies in North America fought New France (modern Quebec). Each country was supported by its European troops and its Native American allies. At the war's conclusion, France ceded most of its colonies in North America to either Britain or Spain, Great Britain became the dominant colonial power, and the all-important New France (Quebec) and Acadia (parts of modern eastern Quebec, Maritime provinces, and parts of Maine) were incorporated into British North America.

Most of the records kept for the 1744-1748 years consist mainly of rosters, rolls, and lists for men serving in the various units. They are indispensable but scattered, and so most of them have been published in journal articles and books or as databases.

The lists of officers and soldiers in the individual units often have places of births, which could be only Ireland or more exact locations, among which could be counties. Either way, they may be the earliest records in the colonies that inform researchers about the identities of immigrant ancestors. At that point, Ulster origins can be addressed.

Enlistment registers during the Colonial Period can have ages, occupations, and places of enlistments and births. The lists having only Ireland still can be helpful in associating ancestors with precise geographies and with other soldiers. In theory, each unit was raised from a specific county or a group of counties. The chances are high that some of the men who enlisted knew one another and were even neighbors. Hence, men from Ireland in the first generation in the colony who were listed alongside an ancestor might have been from the same place in Ulster—a valuable clue because finding from where the group originated will also identify from where the immigrant ancestor came.

One exceptional example is from the account of Capt. John Hasslet's Company in Pennsylvania, dated 21 May 1758. In this list, some men were recorded only as born in Ireland, but a significant number were registered with at least counties in Ireland and sometimes cities. There was also the odd entry that could raise the following questions:

> "AN ACCT. OF CAPT. JOHN HASSLET'S COMPA
> LAST PAST MAY 21ST, 1758." (a.)
>
> [Name, date of enlistment, where born, age, trade
> marks.]
>
> Captain—John Haslett, April 28, 1758.
> Lieut.—William Clinton, April 28, 1758.
> Ensign—Robert Bines, April 18, 1758.
>
> Privates.
>
> Aidley, John, May 8, Dublin, Ir., 23.
> Allen, John, May 14, Derry, Ir., 28, weaver.
> Allen, Peter, May 7, Chester, Penn'a, 22, saddler.
> Boggs, William, May 6, Chester, Penn'a, 40.
> Booth, Richard, May 10, Derby, Eng., 31, cordwainer.
> Brieslin, James, May 12, Chester, Penna., 17.
> Campbell, James, May 13, Antrim, Ir., 22, weaver.
> Campbell, Robert, May 11, Antrim, Ir., 22, laborer.
> Clark, James, May 15, Penn'a, 20.
> Collins, Thomas, May 13, Donegal, Ir., 22.
> Connelly, Bernard, May 17, Lowther, Ir., 20.
> Dick, Alexander, May 10, Lancaster, Penna., 18, black
> Donelly, Bernard, May 9, Ireland, 19.
> Kules, James, May 12, Tyrone, Ir., 22.
> Farquer, Hugh, May 9, Down, Ir., 26.
> Gallagher, Edward, May 12, Chester, Penna., 17.
> Gilmor, William, May 10, Kent, Del., 17, tailor.
> Hart, Hugh, May 22, Armagh, Ir., 23, labor.
> Harvey, Thomas, May 12, Chester, Penna., 17.
>
> Hennan, James, May 10, Armagh, Ir., 17.
> Holkins, William, May 9, Wiltshire, Eng., 22.
> Jenkins, Thomas, May 18, London, England, 38, watch-maker.
> Kennedy, Thomas, May 9, Monaghan, Ir., 24.
> Keysey, James, May 13, Meath, Ir., 21, weaver.
> Logan, Hugh, May 8, Scotland, 24.
> Lowry, David, May 13, Antrim, Ir., 31.
> McAfee, John, May 8, Chester, Penna., 21, laborer.
> McAllister, Patrick, May 9, Longford, Ir., 27, laborer.
> McCalla, James, May 16, Derry, Ir., 24—"a Scotchman."
> McCarty, Jeremiah, May 10, Scotland, 22, wig-maker.
> McClavren, John, May 10, Argyle, Scot., 20.
> McCluan, John, May 13, Armagh, Ir., 22, weaver.
> McClure, John, May 18, Antrim, Ir., 36—"well made, a good
>   woodsman."
> McHatten, Alexander, May 13, Derry, Ir., 20.
> McHatten, James, May 22, Derry, Ir., 23.
> McKeown, Felix, May 15, Cavan, Ir., 21, laborer.
> McMath, James, May 10, Monaghan, Ir., 17.
> Major, William, May 4, Ireland, 30.
> Mitchel, Robert, May 13, Tyrone, Ir., 22.
> Moore, James, May 6, Down, Ir., 22, fuller.
> Moore, William, May 10, Ireland, 20, weaver.
> Parks, James, May 15, Tyrone, Ir., 23.
> Purdey, Alexander, May 8, Scotland, 27, carpenter.
> Scott, William, May 8, Lancaster, Penna., 23, laborer.
> Smith, Gilbert, May 9, Argyle, Scot., 28.
> Thomas, James, May 8, Chester, Penna., 22, laborer.
> Walker, Hugh, May 10, Derry, Ir., 26.
> Weir [Weer], Hugh, May 10, Enniskillen, Ir., 28.
> Wharey, Samuel, May 10, Antrim, Ir., 22, laborer.
> White, Samuel, May 10, Chester, Penna., 26.
> White, James, May 8, Antrim, Ir., 24, weaver.

Figure 30: From Pennsylvania Archives, Fifth Series, Vol. 1, pp. 148-9, Company of Captain John Hasslet in 1758, including James McCalla (McCulla) of Derry, Ireland, "a Scotchman." (This work is in the public domain in its country of origin and other countries and areas where the copyright term is the author's life plus 80 years or fewer.)

- James McCulla, May 16, Derry, Ireland, 24 – "a Scotchman"

He enlisted in the year 1758, and although the assumption is that James McCulla was from either the county or city of Londonderry (Derry), Ireland, "a Scotchman" brings up additional possibilities. Based upon the fact that none of the other entries for Ulster-Scots stated "a Scotsman" (*Pennsylvania Archives*, Fifth Series, Volume 1 (1906), p. 149), the supposition is that McCulla was born in Scotland in 1734. Others from "Derry" (whether county or city unknown) in the example were:

- John Allen, age 28, weaver
- Alexander McHatten, age 20, no occupation listed
- James McHatten, age 23, no occupation listed
- Hugh Walker, age 26, no occupation listed

Did all these young men arrive together? Were they from the same parish in County Londonderry (Derry)? Did they know one another before enlisting in Capt. John Hasslet's Company in 1758? All are valid questions. Since likely no church records in Ulster can document the four men, a surname distribution survey using Griffith's Primary Valuation (1847-1864) will reveal whether the Allen, McCulla, McHatten, and Walker surnames remained in the same general area of the county a hundred years later. Too, concerning James McCulla, the "Scotchman," if more identifying information can be found about him from the U.S. records, it might be possible to find a birth or christening for him in Scotland around 1734.

Each schedule is unique, and the number of details about soldiers varies per listing. For those that provide the residences of the soldiers, either counties or towns, ascertain who was from the same place as the ancestor. Next, narrow that search by who was Scots-Irish and who was the immigrant. In places, such as New England, the investigation can often be done by comparing the list with an old town history containing family sketches. Is there a pattern to where the Scots-Irish were born? If so, they might have come together from Ulster or might have been acquainted in Ulster.

In situations in which the lists are basic, that is, with the names of the soldiers and their captains without further information, efforts may need to concentrate on the leaders of the units. The captains were more prominent, which means more records exist for them. When the residence of the leader of the unit is identified, logically he was in charge of young men from the area around his residence, which can include an assortment of towns or counties. The locale will help identify whether the person in the unit is indeed the ancestor, and if he is, the search can proceed to the others in the unit, all or any one of whom may be associated with him.

Substantial amounts of colonial military records have been transcribed and indexed or are in databases. Routinely, books are digitized and can be viewed online; large collections can be found on Ancestry.com and FamilySearch.org. Major compilations to demonstrate the types of works for the English colonies are:

Connecticut

Guertin, Iris Rose, comp. *Connecticut Soldiers, French and Indian War, 1755-62* [database on-line]. Provo. Utah: Ancestry.com Operations Inc, 2000.

Rolls of Connecticut Men in the French and Indian War, 1755-1762. Bowie, Maryland: Heritage Books Inc. 1993-1994. (These were taken from the *Collections of the Connecticut Historical Society*, volumes 9-10.)

Delaware

Penden, Jr., Henry C. *Colonial Delaware Soldiers and Sailors 1638-1776*. Westminster, Maryland: Family Line Publications, 1995.

Penden, Jr., Henry C. *Marylanders and Delawareans in the French and Indian War, 1756-1763*. Lewes, Delaware: Colonial Roots, 2004.

Public Archives Commission of Delaware, *Delaware Archives: Military Volume 1*. Wilmington, Delaware: Mercantile Printing Co., 1911.

Georgia

Clark, Murtie J. *Colonial Soldiers of the South, 1732-1774*. Baltimore, Maryland: Genealogical Publishing Co., 1983. (This is an Ancestry.com database.)

Kentucky

Kegley, Mary B. *Soldiers of Fincastle County, Virginia, 1774*. Dublin, Virginia: M. B. Kegley, 1974. (Now Southwest

Virginia from Montgomery County west. Some of the men might have been living in the territory that later became the State of Tennessee. Fincastle County was created in 1772 from Botetourt County but was dissolved in 1776 when the counties of Montgomery, Washington, and Kentucky [now part of the state of Kentucky].)

Maryland

Clark, Murtie J. *Colonial Soldiers of the South, 1732-1774*. Baltimore, Maryland: Genealogical Publishing Co., 1983. (This is an Ancestry.com database.)

Penden, Jr., Henry C. *Marylanders and Delawareans in the French and Indian War, 1756-1763*. Lewes, Delaware: Colonial Roots, 2004.

Peden, Henry C. *Colonial Maryland Soldiers and Sailors*, 1634-1734. Westminster, Maryland: Willow Bend Books, 2001.

Massachusetts

Donahue, Mary E. *Massachusetts Officers and Soldiers, 1702-1722: Queen Anne's War to Dummer's War*. Boston, Massachusetts: Society of Colonial Wars in the Commonwealth of Massachusetts, 1980.

Goss, K. David and Davis Zarowin. *Massachusetts Officers and Soldiers in the French and Indian Wars, 1755-1756*. Boston, Massachusetts: Society of Colonial Wars in the Commonwealth of Massachusetts, 1985.

MacKay, Robert E. *Massachusetts Soldiers in the French and Indian Wars, 1744-1755*. Boston, Massachusetts:

Society of Colonial Wars in the Commonwealth of Massachusetts, 1978.

Stachiw, Myron O. *Massachusetts Officers and Soldiers, 1723-1743: Dummer's War to the War of Jenkins' Ear*. Boston, Massachusetts: Society of Colonial Wars in the Commonwealth of Massachusetts, 1979.

Voye, Nancy S. *Massachusetts Officers in the French and Indian Wars, 1748-1763*. Boston, Massachusetts: Society of Colonial Wars in the Commonwealth of Massachusetts, 1975.

New York

Christoph, Florence. *Upstate New York in the 1760's, Tax Lists and Selected Militia Rolls of Old Albany County, 1760-1768*. Camden, Maine: Picton Press, 1992.

New York Colonial Muster Rolls 1664-1775, Volume 1. Reprint. Baltimore, Maryland: Clearfield Co., 1999. (This is a database on Ancestry.com.)

New York Colonial Muster Rolls 1664-1775, Volume II. Reprint. Baltimore, Maryland: Clearfield Co., 1999. (This is a database on Ancestry.com.)

New York Historical Society, *Muster Rolls of New York Provincial Troops*, 1755-1764. New York, New York: New York Historical Society, 1892.

North Carolina

Clark, Murtie J. *Colonial Soldiers of the South, 1732-1774*. Baltimore, Maryland: Genealogical Publishing Co., 1983. (This is an Ancestry.com database.)

North Carolina Militia Returns: 1754-1755, 1758, and 1767. Signal Mountain, Tennessee: Mountain Press, 2008.

Pennsylvania
Ancestry.com. *Pennsylvania, Published Archives Series, 1664-1902* [database on-line] Provo, Utah: Ancestry.com Operations, Inc. 2011.

Bradshaw, Audrey E. *Pennsylvania Soldiers in the Provincial Service, 1746-1759*. Ashland, Oregon: A. E. Bradshaw, 1985.

Officers and Soldiers in the Service of the Province of Pennsylvania 1744-1765. Harrisburg, Pennsylvania: Harrisburg Pub., state printer, 1906. (These were taken from *Pennsylvania Archives*, Fifth Series, Volume 1. There are also additional lists of officers and soldiers in *Pennsylvania Archives Series Two*, Part Two.)

Rhode Island
Ancestry.com. *The Muster Rolls of Three Companies Enlisted by the Colony of Rhode Island in May, 1746* [database on-line]. Provo, Utah: Ancestry.com Operations, Inc., 2005.

Ancestry.com. *Rhode Island in the Colonial Wars: A List of Rhode Island Soldiers & Sailors in King George's War, 1740-1748* [database on-line]. Provo, Utah: Ancestry.com Operations, Inc., 2005.

Ancestry.com. *Rhode Island Privateers in King George's War* [database on-line]. Provo, Utah: Ancestry.com Operations Inc, 2004.

Chapin, Howard M. *A List of Rhode Island Soldiers & Sailors in the Old French & Indian War 1755-1762*. Providence, Rhode Island: Rhode Island Historical Society, 1918.

Chapin, Howard M. *Rhode Island in the Colonial Wars: A List of Rhode Island Soldiers & Sailors in King George's War 1740-1748 and a List of Rhode Island Soldiers & Sailors in the Old French & Indian War 1755-1762*. Baltimore, Maryland: Genealogical Publishing Co., 1994.

Flint, James, ed. *Rhode Island Colonial Servicemen, 1740-62* [database on-line]. Provo, Utah: Ancestry.com Operations Inc., 1999.

Smith, Joseph Jencks. *Civil and Military List of Rhode Island*, 2 vols. Providence, Rhode Island: Preston and Rounds, 1900-1901. (Volume 2 includes Colonial Wars.)

South Carolina
Andrea, Leonardo. *South Carolina Colonial Soldiers and Patriots*. Columbia, South Carolina: R. L. Bryan, 1952.

Clark, Murtie J. *Colonial Soldiers of the South, 1732-1774*. Baltimore, Maryland: Genealogical Publishing Co., 1983. (This is an Ancestry.com database.)

Draine, Tony. *South Carolina Soldiers and Indian Traders, 1725-1730*. Columbia, South Carolina: Congaree Publications, 1986.

Tennessee
Kegley, Mary B. *Soldiers of Fincastle County, Virginia, 1774*. Dublin, Virginia:

M. B. Kegley, 1974. (Now Southwest Virginia from Montgomery County west. Some of the men might have been living in the territory that later became the State of Tennessee. Fincastle County was formed in 1772 from Botetourt County but was dissolved in 1776 when the counties of Montgomery, Washington, and Kentucky [now part of the state of Kentucky] were created.)

Virginia

Bentley, Elizabeth P. *Virginia Military Records: From the Virginia Magazine of History Biography, the William and Mary College Quarterly, and Tyler's Quarterly.* Baltimore, Maryland: Genealogical Publishing Co., 1983. (This is an Ancestry.com database.)

Bockstruck, Lloyd de Witt. *Virginia's Colonial Soldiers.* Baltimore, Maryland: Genealogical Publishing Co., 1988.

Clark, Murtie J. *Colonial Soldiers of the South, 1732-1774.* Baltimore, Maryland: Genealogical Publishing Co., 1983. (This is an Ancestry.com database.)

Crozier, William Armstrong. *Virginia Colonial Militia, 1651-1776.* Baltimore, Maryland: Southern Book Co., 1954. (This is an Ancestry.com database.)

Eckenrode, H. J. *List of the Colonial Soldiers of Virginia: Special Report of the Department of Archives and History for 1913.* Baltimore, Maryland: Genealogical Publishing Co. 1995, 1997. (This is an Ancestry.com database.)

Kegley, Mary B. *Soldiers of Fincastle County, Virginia, 1774.* Dublin, Virginia:

M. B. Kegley, 1974. (Now Southwest Virginia from Montgomery County west. Some of the men might have been living in the territory that later became the State of Tennessee. Fincastle County was formed in 1772 from Botetourt County but was dissolved in 1776 when the counties of Montgomery, Washington, and Kentucky [now part of the state of Kentucky] were created.)

West Virginia

Lewis, Virgil A. *The Soldiery of West Virginia.* Baltimore, Maryland: Clearfield Press, 1991, 1996, 1998. (This is an Ancestry.com database.)

Revolutionary War

In viewing the Revolutionary War as a resource in finding Ulster origins, the viewpoints of both sides must be considered: loyalty to the British and loyalty to the Americans. Although the present section focuses on the American side, it must be stated that Ulster origins also may be preserved for the Loyalists who were exiled to what is now Canada. Canadians who cannot identify Ulster origins from papers generated about their Loyalist ancestors may find answers by researching relatives who remained loyal to the American cause. The same is true for Americans: If they cannot find birthplaces in the American records, they need to look for possible Loyalist relatives in Canada. Such a holistic approach to the topic of identifying where someone was born in Ulster recommends two distinct avenues from which to approach the quest, doubling the chances of ultimately finding an answer. At the end of this book is a "Special Strategy" chapter on Loyalist research from the Canadian perspective.

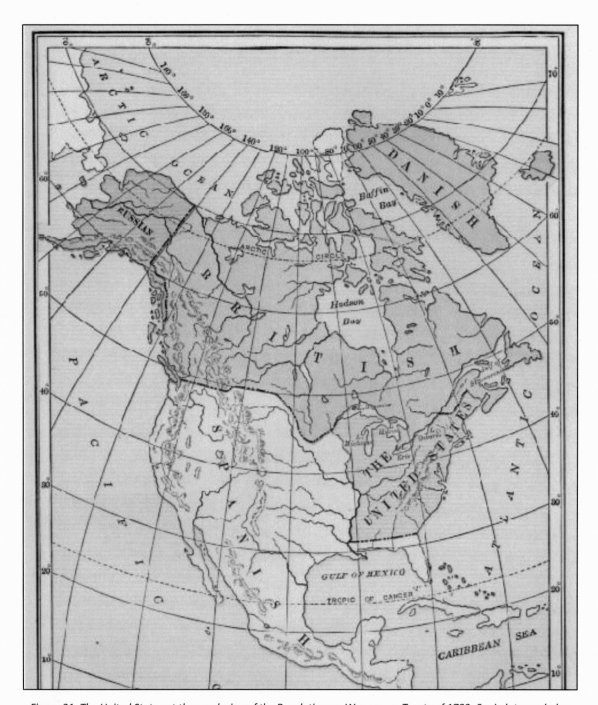

Figure 31: The United States at the conclusion of the Revolutionary War, as per Treaty of 1783. Spain later ceded a large tract to France, which the United States obtained from France under the terms of the Louisiana Purchase. From The History of the American People by Charles A. Beard, et. al., 1919. (Public domain, published before 1922.)

The roots of the American Revolution had been brewing as early as 1765 with the Stamp Act Congress, a revolt in which the colonists refused to recognize the authority of the British government to tax them without representation. The phrase "no taxation without representation" was thus provoked and is still heard today. Other events followed, including the infamous Boston Massacre of 1770. With the Boston Tea Party of 1773, the British closed the port of Boston and rescinded the Massachusetts Bay Colony's right to self-government. The other colonies rallied to the defense of Massachusetts and the Continental Congress of 1774. The colonies set up their own government to resist the British. Therein began the process of the Loyalists (Tories), who remained loyal to the Crown, separating from the Americans, leading to the colonists declaring the former colonies as independent states in 1776.

With the assistance of French allies, the Americans won the long and bloody war. With the Treaty of Paris, signed on 3 September 1783, the United States was recognized as an independent country. As a result of the Revolutionary War, the Americans took possession of the lands east of the Mississippi River and south of the Great Lakes. The British retained Canada, and Spain controlled Florida.

Because of the interest in the Revolutionary War in United States history, no shortage of records was created during the period or afterward. The Scots-Irish certainly played a vital role in the war, bequeathing a proud heritage to their descendants. The stories about an ancestor's involvement in the war could be exaggerated or incomplete, but the pride of participation elevated the veteran from being merely a pioneer or soldier to a hero and protector of all things righteous and good. Even if the myths may not be entirely accurate, they can be used to the advantage of the family historian. Moreover, if the soldier was the immigrant, the probability is good that something was written either during his life or during the life of his children and grandchildren that mentioned his

birthplace in Ulster, whether it is only a county in Ireland or an exact parish or townland within the parish.

Many records were produced along the way about soldiers, elevating them to larger-than-life national heroes. Certainly, records made during the lifetime of a soldier mentioning birthplaces are valuable. Enlistment or pension records may have the locations. Secondary records, in the possession of the descendants, need to be questioned a little further. They include genealogical sketches in old county histories, information found on the Internet and on databases, lineage society applications, and almost any such statements created after the soldiers died. A widow's pension may be doubted as well. The assumption is that she knew where her husband was born even if she met him after he immigrated. Nevertheless, as an extra layer of caution, it is essential to remember her age at the time of applying for the pension. Her memory might not have been clear—or she might have had no failing whatsoever in her mental acuity.

There are cases in which a veteran moved to the frontier, never received a pension, and died in relative obscurity, as did the majority of people in his community. If no record made during his lifetime has the birthplace, the records about his service may still solve the problem. They simply have to be used creatively, such as learning more about the other Irish-born in his regiment. Did they know one another in Ulster? Since the Ulster-Scots tended to immigrate as a group or as a Presbyterian congregation before the Revolutionary War, the others in the same regiment become important. In researching them, an emerging pattern, perhaps half being from County Antrim, can be meaningful and pursued further.

When approaching the potential service of an ancestor in the Revolutionary War, do not confuse men of the same name. Is the soldier found in the indexes and databases really the ancestor? Many researchers do not ask that question at the beginning of the search. Likewise, they do not notice the ages of the men. Using the year 1776 and 20 years of age as a guide, a soldier entering the war had to be born before 1756. The Revolutionary War lasted from 1775 to 1783; therefore, a reasonable age for an ancestor must fit into those years. While all this may seem obvious, it is one of the more common research mistakes. Always think in terms of what is logical and what is not.

Records generated about a soldier can be used in a variety of manners. Foremost is finding where the soldier was born in Ulster, but other strategies are equally as beneficial. Generally, relatives or friends from Ulster enlisted in the same unit, and so knowing with whom the ancestor served is an extended part of the research process. If the military and associated documents do not provide the birthplace, exploring the lives of other Ireland-born soldiers in the regiment may reveal it. If they were friends or family in Ireland, logically they were from the same county, a safe assumption unless the place of origin is on the border of another county. If that was the case, then the geography was perhaps five miles from where the ancestor was living.

The Revolutionary War has been a popular topic for researchers, and a great deal of biographical and genealogical material has been produced about it. Lineage societies, one of which is the National Society of the Daughters of the American Revolution, have added to the stockpile of biographical information. It is common to find those compilations, often through service records of states, burial sites, and "descendants of" Revolutionary War soldiers.

Numerous older collections, once on card indexes or locked in books, are now in databases online. The advantage of the databases is that the regiment name can be used as a search tool when a study of the men in a regiment is required, such as seeking relatives and friends from Ulster. Investigating soldiers by a particular surname in a state or geographical area is also possible. All the database features make the scrutiny much easier.

Some sources are basic to Revolutionary War research. The first is the service records themselves. Revolutionary War service records of enlistments are on Ancestry.com in the database "U.S. Compiled Revolutionary War Military Service Records, 1775-1784." Similar databases are also on FamilySearch.org and Fold3.com, among others. The information is basic because it was taken from card indexes at the National Archives, but the search engine allows the information to be narrowed to states and regiments. The manuscripts to the indexes should contain additional information. Frequently, birthplaces are disclosed, but simply Ireland is enough to determine whether the person being sought was the immigrant ancestor. To verify a pattern, research can proceed to others on the list born in Ireland.

An example of the abovementioned principle can be drawn from another important set of records that were compiled into a database as "U.S., Revolutionary War Rolls 1775-1784," also on Ancestry.com and the other websites. The originals are muster rolls, payrolls, and miscellaneous records. The muster rolls can be useful if they include ages and places of residence. The payrolls have little reason to give birthplaces, but like the service records, they have to be thought of as part of a larger research strategy. The payroll records are for the Continental Army and the state and special units that served with them, and so they are not complete listings of all who served. All kinds of possibilities unfold if muster rolls happen to state who in the regiments were born in Ireland. Did the Irish-born soldiers know one another in Ireland? When the muster rolls do not provide birth information, histories of the regiments would be helpful. Histories should state the geographical areas of the regiments' recruitments, and they may mention the soldiers and provide biographical sketches. Research can be taken to the next level if all that is known is the geography, for instance, the county from where the soldiers were recruited. Is there a pattern from that county or town of Ulster-Scots settlement? If so, is the pattern of immigration from an exact county in Ulster? A history book of the county or town may discuss this, even in passing.

Pension applications are excellent sources for documenting ancestors' lives and war service. Usually, research begins with one, with what is known about an ancestor and proceeding to what is not known. The record typically reveals where an ancestor lived, his address to where the pension payments might have been made. Land was also given to soldiers instead of financial pensions.

The largest collection in which to begin the quest for pension or bounty lands is the database "U.S., Revolutionary War Pension and Bounty-Land Warrants Application Files, 1800-1900." It includes applications for about 80,000 officers and enlisted men, and its database on Ancestry.com can be searched by names and by the places the veterans were living. The files themselves also are scanned on the database. Not all soldiers are listed, only those who applied for pensions or bounty lands. Worthwhile, too, are the rejected files, and they are National Archives documents that can be found online.

Widows' pensions can sometimes be just as informative as those for the veterans who submitted claims because widows had to prove they were married to veterans. In the applications for both veterans and widows, pages from family bibles or marriage certificates might have been included as proof. Valued features of the applications are that frequently veterans' birthplaces in Ulster were specified and family members could have been mentioned parenthetically.

One well known and respected published index to the pension files is Virgil

D. White's *Genealogical Abstracts of Revolutionary War Pension Files*, 4 vols (Waynesboro, Tennessee: National Historical Publishing Co., 1990-1992). If the search for relatives requires sorting through soldiers with the same surname, a work as good as White's can be educational. The few sentences in it can be enough to connect men who otherwise may be lost in a database format.

Unlike the Colonial Wars and the War of 1812, who served in the Revolutionary War has been of great interest over the years. No shortage of books has been published documenting the soldiers, whether they are biographical sketches or names of those receiving pensions or bounty lands. When studying the books, be attentive to what is presented as documentation, especially when it involves birthplaces. Some errors will be found, but a compiled biographical or historical presentation may hold some instructive clues for continuing research. Whether or not the soldier was the immigrant, enough information about him may be in a record that will lead back to the immigrant. After all, the children and grandchildren of the Scot-Irish immigrant were of the generation who served in the Revolutionary War.

Alabama

Ancestry.com. *Alabama, Revolutionary War Residents, 1776-1783* [database on-line]. Provo, Utah: Ancestry.com Operations, Inc., 2015.

Ancestry.com. *Revolutionary soldiers in Alabama* [database on-line]. Provo, Utah: Ancestry.com Operations Inc, 2005.

Drake, Betty. *Revolutionary War Soldiers, Patriots & Widows Who Resided in Alabama, Territory & State*. Hattiesburg, Mississippi: B. Drake, 2006.

Gandrud, Pauline Myra Jones and Desmond Walls Allen. *Alabama Soldiers: Revolution, War of 1812, and Indian Wars*. Hot Springs, Arkansas: B. J. 1975-2006.

Hageness, MariLee Beatty. *Revolutionary Patriots Who Resided in Alabama*. Anniston, Alabama: MLH Research, 1997.

Julich, Louise Milam. *Roster of Revolutionary Soldiers and Patriots in Alabama*. Montgomery, Alabama: Parchment Press, 1979.

Owen, Thomas M., comp. *Revolutionary Soldiers in Alabama*. Montgomery, Alabama: Brown Print Co., 1911.

Arkansas

Payne, Dorothy E. *Arkansas Pensioners, 1818-1900: Records of Some Arkansas Residents who Applied to the Federal Government for Benefits Arising from Service in Federal Military Organizations (Revolutionary War, War of 1812, Indian and Mexican Wars)*. Easley, South Carolina: Southern Historical Press, 1985.

Connecticut

Adjutants-General Office. *Record of Service of Connecticut Men in the I. War of the Revolution, II. War of 1812, III. Mexican War*. Hartford, Connecticut: Case, Lockwood & Brainard, 1889. (This is an Ancestry.com database.)

Rolls and Lists of Connecticut Men in the Revolution, 1775-1783. Hartford, Connecticut: Connecticut Historical Society, 1901. (This is from *Collections of the Connecticut Historical Society,* Volume 8 and is an Ancestry.com database.)

Delaware

Clark, Jr., Raymond B. *Index to Delawareans in the Index of Revolutionary War Pension Applications.* Arlington, Virginia, 1982.

Penden, Jr., Henry C. *Revolutionary Patriots of Delaware: Genealogical and Historical Information on Men and Women of Delaware who Served the American Cause During the War Against Great Britain, 1775-1783.* Westminster, Maryland: Family Line Publications, 1996.

Ward, Christopher L. *The Delaware Continentals, 1776-1783.* Wilmington, Delaware: Historical Society of Delaware, 1941.

Georgia

Arnold, H. Ross and H. Clifton Burnham. *Georgia Revolutionary War Soldiers Graves.* Athens, Georgia: Iberian Publishing Co., 1993.

Arnold, H. Ross. *Georgia Revolutionary Soldiers & Sailors, Patriots & Pioneers.* [Georgia]: Georgia Society, Sons of the American Revolutionary, 2001.

Carter, Mary. *Georgia Revolutionary Soldiers, Sailors, Patriots, & Descendants.* Albany, New York: Georgia Pioneers Publications, 1977.

Houston, Martha Lou. *600 Revolutionary Soldiers and Widows of Revolutionary Soldiers Living in Georgia in 1827-28.* Ann Arbor, Michigan: Edwards Bros. Lithoprinter, 1946.

Knight, Lucian Lamar. *Georgia's Roster of the Revolution.* 1920. Baltimore, Maryland: Genealogical Publishing Co., 1967.

McCall, Ettie Tidwell (Mrs. Howard H. McCall). *Roster of Revolutionary Soldiers in Georgia.* Baltimore, Maryland: Genealogical Publishing Co., 1968.

Payne, Dorothy E. *Georgia Pensioners.* McLean, Virginia: Sunbelt Pub. Co., 1985-.

Warren, Mary Bondurant. *Revolutionary Memoirs and Muster Rolls.* Athens, Georgia: Heritage Papers, 1994.

Illinois

Ancestry.com. *Web: Illinois, Databases of Illinois Veterans Index, 1775-1995* [database on-line]. Provo, Utah: Ancestry.com Operations, Inc., 2015.

Devanny, Mrs. John S. *Soldiers of the American Revolution Buried in Illinois: a Bicentennial Project of the Illinois State Genealogical Society.* Springfield, Illinois: Illinois State Genealogical Society, 1976.

"Illinois Soldier Burial Places, 1774-1974." Database. FamilySearch. http://FamilySearch.org: 14 June 2016. Illinois State Archives, Springfield.

Walker, Harriet J. *Revolutionary Soldiers Buried in Illinois*. Baltimore, Maryland: Genealogical Publishing Company, 1967. (This is an Ancestry.com database.)

Indiana

O'Byrne, Mrs. Roscoe C., ed. *Roster of Soldiers and Patriots of the American Revolution Buried in Indiana*. 3 vols. Brookville, Indiana: Daughters of the American Revolution. Indiana Society, 1938-1966. (This is an Ancestry.com database.)

Waters, Margaret R. *Revolutionary Soldiers Buried in Indiana (1949), with Supplement (1954)*. Baltimore, Maryland: Genealogical Publishing Co., 1970.

Wolfe, Barbara Schull. *Index to Revolutionary Soldiers of Indiana and Other Patriots*. Indianapolis, Indiana: Ye Olde Genealogie Shoppe, 1983.

Kentucky

Broglin, Jana Sloan, ed. *Kentucky Abstracts of Pensions: Revolutionary War, War of 1812 and Indian Wars*. Indianapolis, Indiana: Heritage House, 1999.

Burns, Annie Walker and Lucy Gates McGhee. *Record of Abstracts, Pension Papers, Pertaining to Soldiers of the Revolutionary War, War of 1812, and Indian Wars, Who Settled in Kentucky*, 7 vols. Washington, D.C.: A.W. Burns and L.G. McGee, [n.d.].

Burns, Annie Walker. *Revolutionary War Soldiers Who Settled and Lived in Kentucky Counties*. [S.l.]: A.W. B. Bell, 1935. (A version of this work has been

indexed by the Genealogical Society of Utah.)

Lindsay, Kennedy G. *Kentucky's Revolutionary War Pensioners, Under Acts 1818-1832*. Evansville, Indiana: Kenma Pub. Co., 1977.

Quisenberry, Anderson Chenault. *Revolutionary Soldiers in Kentucky*. Baltimore, Maryland: Genealogical Publishing Co., 1968.

Louisiana

DeVille, Winston. *Louisiana Soldiers in the American Revolution*. Ville Platte, Louisiana: Smith Books, 1991.

Pierce, Alycon Trubey. *Louisiana Revolutionary Records, Selected Final Pension Payment Vouchers, 1818-1864: Louisiana: New Orleans*. Athens, Georgia: Iberian Pub. Co., 1996.

Maine

Fisher, Carleton E. and Sue G. Fisher. *Soldiers, Sailors, and Patriots of the Revolutionary War, Maine*. Louisville, Kentucky: National Society of the Sons of the American Revolution, 1982.

Fisher, Carleton Edward. *Supplement to Soldiers, Sailors and Patriots of the Revolutionary War*. Rockport, Maine: Picton Press, 1998.

Flagg, Charles Allcott. *An Alphabetical Index of Revolutionary Pensioners Living in Maine*. Baltimore, Maryland: Genealogical Publishing Co., 1967.

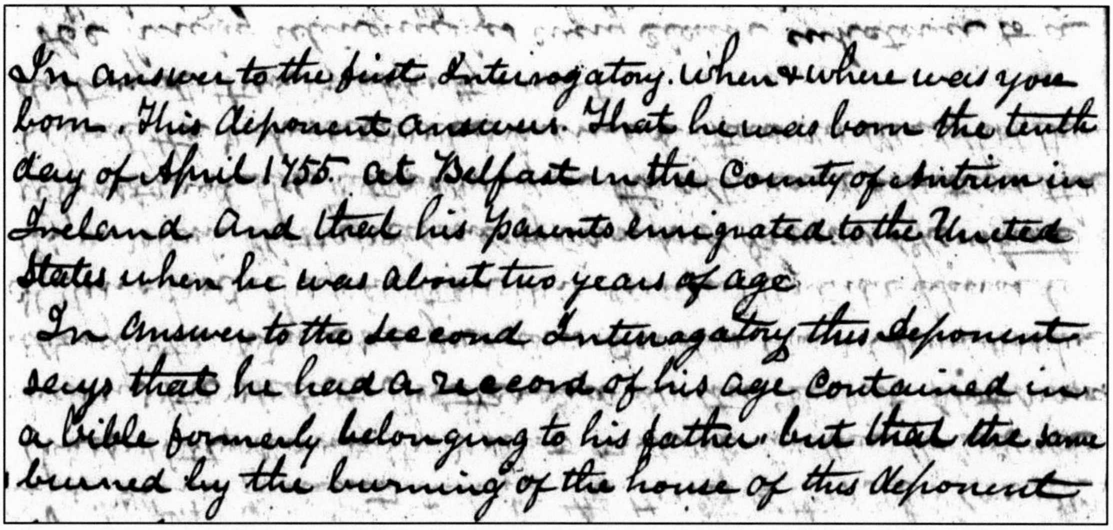
In answer to the first Interogatory. when & where was you born. This deponent answers. That he was born the tenth day of April 1755 at Belfast in the County of Antrim in Ireland And that his parents immigrated to the United States when he was about two years of age
In Answer to the second Interagatory this deponent says that he had a record of his age contained in a bible formerly belonging to his father but that the same burned by the burning of the house of this deponent

Figure 32: U.S. Revolutionary War Pension and Bounty-Land Warrant Application Files, 1800-1900, showing the birth date and place for Robert McClouchan as 10 April 1755 in Belfast, County Antrim, and that his parents immigrated to America when he was about two years old. (This work is in the public domain in the United States because it is a work prepared by an officer or employee of the United States Government as part of that person's official duties under the terms of Title 17, Chapter 1, Section 105 of the U.S. Code.)

Maine Old Cemetery Association. *M.O.C.A. Revolutionary War Solder Burial Place*. [S.l.: s.n.], 1987.

Maine Old Cemetery Association. *M.O.C.A. Revolutionary War Solders*. [S.l.: s.n.], 1986.

Maine Old Cemetery Association. *M.O.C.A. Revolutionary War Solders - Birth Places*. [S.l.: s.n.], 1987.

"Maine, Veterans Cemetery Records, 1676-1918." Database with images. FamilySearch. http://FamilySearch.org : 14 June 2016. State Archives, Augusta.

Maryland

Ancestry.com. *Maryland Revolutionary records* [database on-line]. Provo, Utah: Ancestry.com Operations Inc, 2005.

Clark, Raymond B. *Marylanders in the Index of Revolutionary War Pension Applications*. Arlington, Virginia: R. B. Clark, 1982.

McGhee, Mrs. Carl W. *Maryland Revolutionary War Pensioners, War of 1812 and Indian Wars*. Washington, D.C., C. W. McGhee, 1952.

Peden, Henry C. *Maryland Public Service Records, 1775-1783*. Westminster, Maryland: Willow Bend Books, 2002.

Massachusetts

Allen, Gardner Weld. *Massachusetts Privateers of the Revolution*. Boston, Massachusetts: Massachusetts Historical Society, 1927.

"Massachusetts, Revolutionary War, Index Cards to Muster Rolls, 1775-1783." Database with images. FamilySearch. http://FamilySearch.org : 9 April 2019. Massachusetts State Archives, Boston.

Secretary of the Commonwealth. *Massachusetts Soldiers and Sailors of the Revolutionary War: A Compilation from the Archives*. 17 vols. Boston, Massachusetts: Wright & Potter, 1896-1908.

Michigan

Silliman, Sue Imogene. *Michigan Military Records: The D.A.R. of Michigan Historical Collections: Records of the Revolutionary Soldiers Buried in Michigan; the Pensioners of Territorial Michigan; and the Soldiers of Michigan Awarded the "Medal of Honor; With an Added Forward by the Michigan Historical Commission."* Baltimore, Maryland: Genealogical Publishing Co., 1969.

Mississippi

Drake, Betty. *Revolutionary War Soldiers and Patriots Who Resided in Mississippi.* [S.l.]: B. Drake, 2004.

Pierce, Alcyon Trubey. *Selected Final Pension Payment Vouchers, 1818-1864: Mississippi: Natchez & Jackson.* Athens, Georgia: Iberian Pub. Co., 1997.

Missouri

Houts, Alice Kinyoun. *Revolutionary Soldiers Buried in Missouri.* Kansas City, Missouri: Houts, 1966.

McGhee, Lucy Kate. *Missouri Revolutionary Soldiers, War of 1812, and Indian Wars: Pension List.* Washington, D.C.: [s.n., 1957?].

New Hampshire

Batchellor, ed., Albert Stillman. *Miscellaneous Revolutionary Documents of New Hampshire: Including the Association Test, the Pension Rolls and Other Important Papers.* Manchester, New Hampshire: New Hampshire Historical Society, 1910.

Hammond, Isaac W. *The State of New Hampshire, Rolls of the Soldiers in the Revolutionary War, 1775, to May, 1777.* Concord, New Hampshire: New Hampshire State Legislature, 1885-1889.

Meyers, Frank C. *Composite Index to Volumes XIV Through XVII (Revolutionary War Rolls) of the New Hampshire State Papers.* Bowie, Maryland: Heritage Books, Inc., 1993.

New Jersey

Jackson, Ronald Vern. *Index to Military Men of New Jersey, 1775-1815.* Bountiful, Utah: Accelerated Indexing Systems, 1977.

New York

Ancestry.com. *New York, Pension Claims by Disabled Revolutionary War Veterans, 1779-1789* [database on-line]. Provo, Utah: Ancestry.com Operations, Inc., 2014.

Kelly, Arthur C. M. *New York Revolutionary War Pensioners in the 1840 Census.* Rhinebeck, New York: Kinship Books, 1995.

New York. Comptroller's Office. *New York in the Revolution as Colony and State: A Compilation of Documents and Records from the Office of the State Comptroller.* 2 vols. Albany, New York: J. B. Lyon Co, 1904-.

North Carolina

Burns, Annie Walker. *Abstract of Pensions of North Carolina Soldiers of the Revolution, War of 1812 & Indian Wars*, 15 vols. Washington, D.C.: A. W. Burns, [1960]. (This is an Ancestry.com database.)

Daughters of the American Revolution (North Carolina). *Roster of the Soldiers from North Carolina in the American Revolution: With an Appendix Containing a Collection of Miscellaneous Records*. [S.l.]: NCDAR,1932.

Haun, Weynette Parks. *North Carolina Revolutionary Army Accounts*. 17 vols. Durham, North Carolina: W. P. Haun, 1990-1999.

Kellam, Ida Brooks. *North Carolina, Revolutionary Army Accounts, Book W, No. 1, 1781-1783*. Wilmington, North Carolina: I. B. Kellam, 1960.

Maddox, Joseph T. and Mary Carter. *North Carolina Revolutionary Soldiers, Sailors, Patriots & Descendants*. 2 vols. Albany, Georgia: Georgia Pioneers Publications, [197?].

"North Carolina Revolutionary Pay Vouchers, 1779-1782." Database with images. FamilySearch. http://FamilySearch.org : 7 October 2016. Citing State Archives of North Carolina, Raleigh.

Roster of the Continental Line from North Carolina 1783. Signal Mountain, Tennessee: Mountain Press, 2004.

Snow, Carol Leonard. *Volunteer Revolutionary War Soldiers from North Carolina*. Toast, North Carolina: C & L Historical Publishing, 1993.

Speidel, Frederick G. *North Carolina Masons in the American Revolution*. [S.l.]: Oxford Orphanage, 1975.

Styles, Marshall L. *Western North Carolina's Revolutionary War Patriot Soldiers: A Collection of Their Records*. 20 vols. [S.l.]: M. L. Styles, 2010

Ohio

Dailey, Mrs. Orville D. *The Official Roster of the Soldiers of the American Revolution Buried in the State of Ohio*. 3 vols. Columbus, Ohio: F. J. Heer Print. Co., 1929-1959.

Michael, C. Richard, Norris Whittaker and Richard V. Moore. *Revolutionary War Patriots*. St. Clairsville, Ohio: Ebenezer Zane Chapter of the Sons of the American Revolution, 2000-.

A Reprint of Official Roster of the Soldiers of the American Revolution Buried in the State of Ohio: Volume 1, Published 1929 Together with Official Roster of the Soldiers of the American Revolution who Lived in the State of Ohio, Volume II, Published 1938. 2 vols. Mineral Ridge, Ohio: Ohio Genealogical Society, 1973.

Taylor, Mrs. George Ann Franklin. *Revolutionary War Pensioners Living in State of Ohio in 1840: Compiled and Indexed by County and Pensioner's Name*. Thomasville, Georgia: Mrs. George Ann Franklin Taylor, 1966.

Waldenmaier, Inez Raney. *Revolutionary War Pensioners Living in Ohio Before 1834*. Tulsa, Oklahoma: Inez Waldenmaier, 1983.

Pennsylvania

Ancestry.com. *Pennsylvania, Revolutionary War Battalions and Militia Index,*

1775-1783 [database on-line]. Provo, Utah: Ancestry.com Operations, Inc., 2012.

Ancestry.com. *Pennsylvania, Veterans Burial Cards, 1777-2012* [database on-line]. Provo, Utah: Ancestry.com Operations, Inc., 2010.

Closson, Bob and Mary, Richard Rush. *Register of Invalid Pensions, Revolutionary Service, 1789*. Apollo, Pennsylvania: Closson Press, 1981.

Egle, William Henry. *Muster Rolls of the Navy and Line, Militia and Rangers, 1775-1783, with List of Pensioners, 1818-1832*. Harrisburg, Pennsylvania: W. S. Ray, 1897.

Egle, William H. *State of the Accounts of the County Lieutenants During the War of the Revolution, 1777-1789*. 3 vols. Harrisburg, Pennsylvania: C. M. Busch, state printer, 1896.

Lemley, Marie Perrin. *Pennsylvania Migrations: "Here and There" Marriages, Revolutionary Soldiers, Tomb Records*. North Salt Lake, Utah: Heritage Quest, 1989.

McGhee, Lucy Kate. *Pennsylvania Pension Abstracts of Soldiers of the Revolutionary War, War of 1812, and Indian Wars*. Washington, D.C.: [L. K. McGhee, 1964].

Muster Rolls of the Pennsylvania Navy, 1776-1779. Harrisburg, Pennsylvania: Harrisburg Pub., State Printer, 1906.

Myers, Paul W. *Pennsylvania Soldiers of the Revolutionary War* (Living in States Other than PA). Apollo, Pennsylvania: Closson Press, 1987.

Williams, Mildred C. and Janet Brittingham. *Revolutionary War List of Pensioners: Abstracts of Pension Applications*. Newtown, Pennsylvania: Will-Britt Books, 1987.

Rhode Island
Chamberlain, Mildred M. *The Rhode Island 1777 Military Census*. Baltimore, Maryland: Genealogical Publishing Co., 1985.

Gunning, Kathryn McPherson. *Selected Final Pension Payment Vouchers 1818-1864: Rhode Island*. Westminster, Maryland: Willow Bend Books, 1999.

Murray, Thomas Hamilton. *Irish Rhode Islanders in the American Revolution: with Some Mention of Those Serving in the Regiments of Elliott, Lippitt, Topham, Crary, Angell, Olney, Greene, and other Noted Commanders*. Providence, Rhode Island: American Irish Historical Society, 1903.

Smith, Joseph Jencks. *Civil and Military List of Rhode Island*, 2 vols. Providence, Rhode Island: Preston and Rounds, 1900-1901. (Volume 2 includes Revolutionary War.)

South Carolina
Burns, Annie Walker. *Abstracts of Pensions of South Carolina Soldiers of the Revolutionary War, War of 1812 and Indian Wars*. 12 vols. Washington, D.C.: A.W. Burns, [1960].

Jackson, Ronald Vern. *South Carolina Military Pay Rolls, 1775-1780*. Salt Lake City, Utah: Accelerated Indexing Systems, 1989.

Moss, Bobby Gilmer. *Roster of South Carolina Patriots in the American Revolution*. Baltimore, Maryland: Genealogical Publishing Co., 1983.

Pierce, Alycon Trubey. *South Carolina Revolutionary Records, Selected Final Pension Payment Vouchers, 1818-1864: South Carolina, Charleston*. Athens, Georgia: Iberian Publishing Co., 1996.

Salley, Alexander Samuel. *Accounts Audited of Revolutionary Claims Against South Carolina*. 3 vols. Columbia, South Carolina: Historical Commission of South Carolina, 1935, 1938, 1943.

Salley, Alexander Samuel. *Journal of the Commissioners of the Navy of South Carolina, October 19, 1776-March 1, 1779; July 22, 1779-March 23, 1780*. 2 vols. Columbia, South Carolina: Historical Commission of South Carolina, 1912-1913.

Salley, Alexander Samuel, Wylma Anne Wates. *Stub Entries to Indents Issued in Payment of Claims Against South Carolina Growing out of the Revolution*. 12 vols. Columbia, South Carolina: Historical Commission of South Carolina, 1910-1957.

Tennessee

Allen, Penelope Johnson. *Tennessee Soldiers in the Revolution*. Baltimore, Maryland: Genealogical Publishing Co., 1982.

Armstrong, Zella. *Twenty-four Hundred Tennessee Pensioners: Revolution – War of 1812*. Chattanooga, Tennessee: Lookout Publishing Co., [1937].

Bates, Luck Womack. Roster of Solders and Patriots of the American Revolution Buried in Tennessee. Johnson City, Tennessee: State Regent's Bicentennial Project Tennessee Society NSDAR, 1974.

Hudson, Mary Kay Parrish and Nelly Galloway Shearer. *Register of Qualified Soldiers and Patriots of the American Revolution Buried in Tennessee*. Memphis, Tennessee: NSDAR, Tennessee Society, 2000.

Some Tennessee Heroes of the Revolution: Compiled from Pension Statements. Chattanooga, Tennessee: Lookout Publishing, 1933.

Whitley, Edythe Johns Ricker and Carolyn West Stricklin. *Membership Roster and Soldiers: Tennessee State Society of the National Society Daughters of the American Revolution*. 3 vols. [S.l.]: Daughters of the American Revolution. Tennessee Society, 1961-.

Vermont

Fisher, Carleton Edward and Sue Gray Fisher. *Soldiers, Sailors, and Patriots of the Revolutionary War, Vermont*. Camden, Maine: Picton Press, 1992.

Goodrich, John E. *Rolls of the Soldiers in the Revolutionary War, 1775 to 1783: the State of Vermont*. Rutland, Vermont: Tuttle, 1904.

Virginia

Brown, Margie G. *Genealogical Abstracts, Revolutionary War Veterans, Scrip Act, 1852*. Oakton, Virginia: M. Brown, 1990.

Burgess, Louis A. *Virginia Soldiers of 1776: Compiled from Documents on File in the Virginia Land Office, Together with Material Found in the Archives Department of the Virginia State Library, and Other Reliable Sources*. Baltimore, Maryland: Genealogical Publishing Co., 1973.

Dorman, John Frederick. *Virginia Revolutionary Pension Applications*. Washington, D.C.: J. F. Dorman, 1958-.

Gwathmey, John Hastings. *Historical Register of Virginians in the Revolution, Soldiers, Sailors, Marine, 1775-1783*. Baltimore, Maryland: Genealogical Publishing Co., 1973.

Kegley, Mary B. *Revolutionary War Pension Applications of Southwest Virginia Soldiers*. [Virginia?]: M. B. Kegley, 1997.

McAllister, Joseph Thompson. *Virginia Militia in the Revolutionary War: McAllister's Data*. Bowie, Maryland: Heritage Books Inc., 1989.

McGhee, Lucy Kate. *Virginia Pension Abstracts of the Revolutionary War, War of 1812 and Indian Wars*. Washington, D.C.: [s.n.], 1960, 1965, 1966.

Virginia Genealogical Society. *Virginia Revolutionary War State Pensions*. Easley, South Carolina: Southern Historical Press, 1982.

Wardell, Patrick G. *Virginia/West Virginia Genealogical Data from Revolutionary War Pension and Bounty Land Warrant Records*. 6 vols. Bowie, Maryland: Heritage Books, Inc., 1988-1998.

West Virginia

Johnston, Ross B. *West Virginians in the American Revolution*. Baltimore, Maryland: Genealogical Publishing Co., 1977.

Lewis, Virgil A. *The Soldiery of West Virginia*. Baltimore, Maryland: Clearfield Press, 1991, 1996, 1998. (This is an Ancestry.com database.)

Reddy, Anne Waller. *West Virginia Revolutionary Ancestors: Whose Service were Non-Military and Whose Names, Therefore, do not appear in Revolutionary Indexes of Soldiers and Sailors: An Index from Manuscript Public Claims of the Revolutionary War in the Virginia State Library*. Kokomo, Indiana: Selby Publishing & Printing, 1988. (This is an Ancestry.com database.)

Wardell, Patrick G. *Virginia/West Virginia Genealogical Data from Revolutionary War Pension and Bounty Land Warrant Records*. 6 vols. Bowie, Maryland: Heritage Books, Inc., 1988-1998.

War of 1812

What is called the War of 1812 was part of the larger Napoleonic Wars. Its legacy is seen from two different perspectives, depending on a history lesson in the United States as opposed to a history lesson in Canada. Britain had imposed a naval blockade against France, not allowing neutral trade to reach France. The United States contested the action, and the British pressed American merchant sailors into the Royal Navy against their wills. The British had also been arming the native tribes who fought against the American expansion on the western frontiers in what is today Illinois, Indiana, Michigan, and Wisconsin. A matter of historical debate is how eagerly the Americans wanted to also expand into what is today Canada. The American troops did invade what is now Quebec and Ontario but were defeated. The British attacked Washington, D.C., and burned the White House, but they were repelled in their march into Maryland and New York.

When Britain ended the war with France, the impressments of American sailor merchants were no longer needed. Trade reopened, and both Britain and the United States signed a peace treaty. In addition, no boundaries changed between British North America (Canada) and the United States.

The War of 1812 is often termed the "forgotten war" because most Americans have a vague knowledge of what it was and why it happened. However, for the family historian, it is a boon to records because it was fought almost entirely by the local militias. For example, at the end of the war, the U.S. Army had 35,800 enlisted men, whereas the militia units comprised around 458,463 soldiers. The United Kingdom had its First Nation allies, and the United States had Native American allies in the Cherokee, Choctaw, Muscogee (Creek), and Seneca tribes.

After the war, many young men headed westward to begin new lives, especially in the Midwest. Whether the soldier in the conflict was the Ulster immigrant or his second or third generation, the War of 1812 records can help push the family records back in time. If the search is for the immigrant, the goal is finding a record that states the birthplace in Ulster. If seeking the second or third generation American, the objective is to document the lineage properly so that the immigrant can at some point be identified. The link between the War of 1812 and the immigrant ancestor is of great magnitude, especially as families moved westward onto the frontiers.

A composite service records index is available on Ancestry.com, Fold3.com, and FamilySearch.org, among other websites. While the index is basic, the records themselves were questionnaires for the soldiers that can provide birthplaces. They are only the countries of birth, yet they will help identify the immigrants if they were not known beforehand. The massive index includes around 600,000 men, and listed with some amount of data are those mustered between 1812 and 1815. If a regiment is unknown or a deeper study of the other men in the regiment is needed, the search feature of the databases can be helpful.

For example, if an ancestor was in Ohio, and it was determined he had been from Virginia, first find the ancestor, or who is thought to be the ancestor, serving in a Virginia unit. At that point, begin exploring the ancestor's neighbors in Ohio who had also served in the War of 1812, and

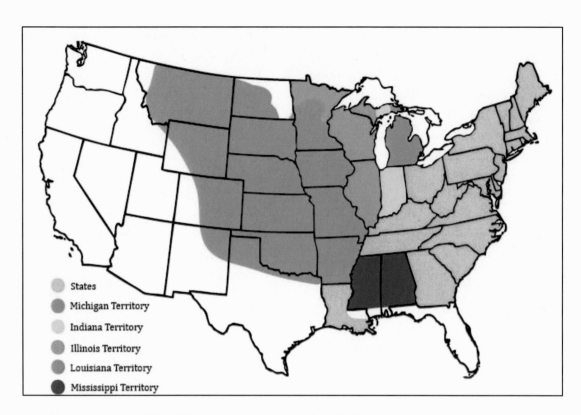

Figure 33: American possessions at launch of the War of 1812.

if they are in a regiment with the ancestor, it could be the necessary clue. It links the veteran in Ohio to the soldier in Virginia and demonstrates that a group of these men after the war traveled together and settled together in Ohio. Most important is whether some in the group were from Ulster, and if they were, their association might have extended past Virginia, possibly into another state or into Ireland itself. If the soldier was not from Ireland but was the second generation, such a fact is still the next step in a holistic approach to the family history. In short, once the county in Virginia is identified, the search for the next generation back can be undertaken. That may be the immigrant. It also may be that the second generation included the children of those who came over from Ulster as a group and settled in one area.

Pensions are a good resource for places of birth in Ulster, if not for the immigrants, for the counties and states where the veterans were born. The Act of 14 February 1871 granted pensions to surviving soldiers and sailors who had served at least 60 days in the War of 1812 and who were honorably discharged. Any widow was eligible for a pension if the marriage took place before 17 February 1815. Because so many of the veterans were already deceased by 1871, the widows' pensions can act as substitutes. Through the Act of March 1878, pensions were granted to surviving soldiers and sailors who had served for 14 days and were honorably discharged. Any widow was included with no restriction on her date of marriage. The index to the pensions is on Ancestry.com, Fold3.com, and FamilySearch.org, along with other websites. The digital versions of the 180,000 pension applications are on Fold3. While most online indexes, including the one from the National Archives, do not provide the birthplaces of the veterans, there is one that does.

A recognized and standard published index to the pension files is Virgil D. White's *Index to War of 1812 Pension Files*, 2 vols. (Waynesboro, Tennessee: National Historical Publishing Co., 1992). If the online indexes are difficult to use or if distinguishing people with the same name is troublesome, a work analogous to White's can provide a new way of looking at information. It gives a short synopsis of what is in the files, such as ages and family members.

An odd source, but one well worth considering for immigrants, is for British citizens living in the United States at the time the war broke out. Many had been in the U.S. for some time, but they were required to register with the U.S. Marshalls of their states of residences. The records produced do not have places of birth other than Ireland, but Ireland can be enough to continue the search in other directions. They at least document who the immigrants were. The index is in Kenneth Scott's *British Aliens in the United States During the War of 1812* (Baltimore, Maryland: Genealogical Publishing Co., 1979), but the originals are part of a larger collection that is on Ancestry.com in the database "War of 1812 Papers, 1789-1815."

Numerous key compilations and databases were constructed for the War of 1812 soldiers and their pensions and burials. Some have been made into

databases on Ancestry.com, and many books have been digitized on both Ancestry.com and FamilySearch.org. The list below is a selection of the published and digitized works that can be helpful in beginning the search within a state:

Alabama

Gandrud, Pauline Myra Jones and Desmond Walls Allen. *Alabama Soldiers: Revolution, War of 1812, and Indian Wars*. Hot Springs, Arkansas: B. J. 1975-2006.

War of 1812 Pensioners Living in Alabama During the 1880s. Cullman, Alabama: Gregath, 1982.

Arkansas

Payne, Dorothy E. *Arkansas Pensioners, 1818-1900: Records of Some Arkansas Residents who Applied to the Federal Government for Benefits Arising from Service in Federal Military Organizations (Revolutionary War, War of 1812, Indian and Mexican Wars)*. Easley, South Carolina: Southern Historical Press, 1985.

War of 1812 Pensioners Living in Arkansas During the 1880's: Abstracted rom the Executive Documents. Cullman, Alabama: Gregath, 198?.

Connecticut

Adjutants-General Office. *Record of Service of Connecticut Men in the I. War of the Revolution, II. War of 1812, III. Mexican War*. Hartford, Connecticut: Case, Lockwood & Brainard, 1889.

Delaware

Penden, Jr., Henry C. *The Delaware Militia in the War of 1812*. Lewes, Delaware: Colonial Roots, 2003.

Georgia

Kratovil, Judy Swaim and R. J. Taylor, Jr. Foundation. *Index to War of 1812 Service Records for Volunteer Soldiers from Georgia*. Atlanta, Georgia: J. S. Kratovil, 1986.

Payne, Dorothy E. *Georgia Pensioners*. McLean, Virginia: Sunbelt Pub. Co., 1985-.

War of 1812 Pensioners Living in Georgia During the 1880s. Cullman, Alabama: Gregath, 1982.

Illinois

Ancestry.com. *Web: Illinois, Databases of Illinois Veterans Index, 1775-1995* [database on-line]. Provo, Utah: Ancestry.com Operations, Inc., 2015.

Illinois Soldier Burial Places, 1774-1974." Database. FamilySearch. http://FamilySearch.org : 14 June 2016. Illinois State Archives, Springfield.

Walker, Homer A. *Illinois Pensioners List of the Revolution; 1812 & Indian Wars*. Washington, D.C.: s.n., 1955.

Indiana

Franklin, Charles M. *Indiana Territorial Pioneer Records*. [S.l.]: Heritage House, 1983. (Volume 3 in this series includes militia rolls.)

Mikesell, Shirley Keller. *Early Settlers of Indiana's "Gore," 1803-1820*. Bowie, Maryland: Heritage Books Inc, 1995.

Kentucky

Burns, Annie Walker and Lucy Gates McGhee. *Record of Abstracts, Pension Papers, Pertaining to Soldiers of the Revolutionary War, War of 1812, and Indian Wars, Who Settled in Kentucky*, 7 vols. Washington, D.C.: A.W. Burns and L.G. McGee, [n.d.].

Broglin, Jana Sloan, ed. *Kentucky Abstracts of Pensions: Revolutionary War, War of 1812 and Indian Wars*. Indianapolis, Indiana: Heritage House, 1999.

Wilder, Minnie S. *Kentucky Soldiers of the War of 1812*. Baltimore, Maryland: Genealogical Publishing Co., 1969. (This is an Ancestry.com database.)

Louisiana

Ancestry.com. *Louisiana, Soldiers in the War of 1812* [database on-line]. Provo, Utah: Ancestry.com Operations, Inc., 1998.

Ancestry.com. *Louisiana, War of 1812 Pension Lists* [database on-line]. Provo, Utah: Ancestry.com Operations, Inc., 2014.

Maine

Ancestry.com. *Maine, Compiled Military Records, 1812-1865* [database on-line]. Provo, Utah: Ancestry.com Operations, Inc., 2011.

"Maine, State Archive Collections, 1718-1957." Database with images. FamilySearch. http://FamilySearch.org : State Archives, Augusta, 14 June 2016. (Includes the collection "Maine Militia Records, 1812-1814, 1820-1850.")

"Maine, Veterans Cemetery Records, 1676-1918." Database with images. FamilySearch. http://FamilySearch.org : State Archives, Augusta, Maine, 14 June 2016.

Maryland

Blizzar, Dennis F. and Thomas L. Hollowak. *A Chronicle of War of 1812 Soldiers, Seamen and Marines*. Baltimore, Maryland: Society of the War of 1812 in Maryland, c1993.

Huntsberry, Thomas V. and Joanne M. Huntsberry. *Maryland Privateers, War of 1812*. Baltimore, Maryland: J. Mart, 1983.

Johnson, Eric Eugene. *Maryland Regulars in the War of 1812*. Berwyn Heights, Maryland: Heritage Books, Inc., 2018.

Marine, William M. and Louis Henry Dielman. *The British Invasion of Maryland: 1812-1815*. Baltimore, Maryland: Genealogical Publishing Co., 1977. (This is an Ancestry.com database.)

McGhee, Mrs. Carl W. *Maryland Revolutionary War Pensioners, War of 1812 and Indian Wars*. Washington, D.C., C. W. McGhee, 1952.

Wright, F. Edward. *Maryland Militia, War of 1812*. Silver Spring, Maryland: Family Line Publications, 1979-.

Massachusetts

Records of the Massachusetts Volunteer Militia: Called Out by the Governor of Massachusetts to Suppress a Threatened Invasion During the War of 1812-14. Boston, Massachusetts: Gardner W. Pearson, 1913. (This is an Ancestry.com database.)

Michigan

Miller, Alice Turner. *Soldiers of the War of 1812, Who Died in Michigan*. Ithaca, Michigan: A. T. Miller, 1962.

Minnesota

Finnell, Arthur Louis. *Known War of 1812 Veterans Buried in Minnesota*. Roseville, Minnesota: Park Genealogical Books, 1997.

Mississippi

Ancestry.com. *Mississippi, Compiled Service Records of Volunteer Soldiers, 1812-1815* [database on-line]. Provo, Utah: Ancestry.com Operations, Inc., 2012.

Rowland, Mrs. Dunbar. *Mississippi Territory in the War of 1812*. Baltimore, Maryland: Genealogical Publishing Co., 1968. (This is an Ancestry.com database.)

Missouri

McGhee, Lucy Kate. *Missouri Revolutionary Soldiers, War of 1812, and Indian Wars: Pension List*. Washington, D.C.: [s.n., 1957?].

War of 1812 Pensioners, Missouri: Transcribed from Government Printing Office Material, 1883. Wyandotte, Oklahoma: Gregath, 1983.

Nebraska

Allen, John C., Secretary of State. *Roster of Soldiers, Sailors and Marines of the War of 1812, the Mexican War, and the War of the Rebellion...: Residing in Nebraska, June 1, 1891*. Lincoln, Nebraska: State Journal, 1892.

New Jersey

Jackson, Ronald Vern. *Index to Military Men of New Jersey, 1775-1815*. Bountiful, Utah: Accelerated Indexing Systems, 1977.

Office of the Adjutant General. *Records of Officers and Men of New Jersey in Wars 1791-1815.* Trenton, New Jersey: State Gazette Pub. Co., 1909. (This is an Ancestry.com database.)

New York
Ancestry.com. *New York City and vicinity during the war of 1812-1815* [database on-line]. Provo, Utah, Ancestry.com Operations Inc, 2005.

Ancestry.com. *New York, War of 1812 Payroll Abstracts for New York State Militia, 1812-1815* [database on-line]. Provo, Utah: 2013.

New York Adjutant General's Office. *Index of Awards on Claims of the Soldiers of the War of 1812.* 1860. Baltimore, Maryland: Clearfield Co., 1994, 1969. (This is an Ancestry.com database.)

North Carolina
Burns, Annie Walker. *Abstract of Pensions of North Carolina Soldiers of the Revolution, War of 1812 & Indian Wars,* 15 vols. Washington, D.C.: A. W. Burns, 1960. (This is an Ancestry.com database.)

Jackson, Ronald Vern. *North Carolina Military Muster Rolls, 1812 & 1814.* Salt Lake City, Utah: Accelerated Indexing Systems, 1989.

North Carolina War of 1812 Pensioners and Others on the Pension Rolls as of January 1, 1883. Cullman, Alabama: Gregath, 1983.

Toler, Maurice S. *Muster Rolls of the Soldiers of the War of 1812 Detached from the Militia of North Carolina in 1812 and 1814.* 1851. Baltimore, Maryland: Genealogical Publishing Co., 1976. (This is an Ancestry.com database.)

Ohio
Ancestry.com. *Index to the grave records of soldiers of the War of 1812 buried in Ohio* [database on-line]. Provo, Utah: Ancestry.com Operations Inc, 2004.

Ancestry.com. *Roster of Ohio soldiers in the War of 1812* [database on-line]. Provo, Utah: Ancestry.com Operations Inc, 2004.

Adjutant General's Department. *Roster of Ohio Soldiers in the War of 1812.* Bowie, Maryland: Heritage Books Inc., 1995.

Index to the Grave Records of Servicemen of the War of 1812, State of Ohio. Lancaster, Ohio: National Society of United States Daughters of 1812, 1969.

Johnson, Eric Eugene. *Ohio's Regulars in the War of 1812.* Berwyn Heights, Maryland: Heritage Books Inc, 2014.

Linscott, Jeff A. *An Organized Listing of the Soldiers of Ohio Who Served in the War of 1812.* Colorado Springs, Colorado: J. A. Linscott, 1993.

Miller, Phyllis Brown, ed. *Index to the Grave Records of Servicemen of the War of 1812, State of Ohio.* Brookville, Ohio: Dillon's Printery, 1988.

Oliver, Bill. *Index to Roster of Ohio Soldiers in the War of 1812: Published Under Authority of Law by the Adjutant*

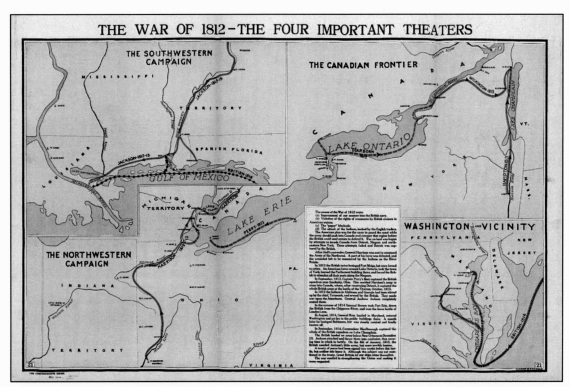

Figure 34: Four important regions of battle during the War of 1812. E.W.A. Rowles, Modern School Supply, 1919. Image from Library of Congress, Geography and Map Division. (Public Domain, published before 1922.)

General of Ohio 1916. Bowling Green, Ohio: Ohio Genealogical Society. Wood County Chapter, 1997.

Phillips, W. Louis. *Index to Ohio Pensioners of 1883*. Bowie, Maryland: Heritage Books Inc., 1987.

Pennsylvania
Ancestry.com. *Pennsylvania, Veterans Burial Cards, 1777-2012* [database on-line]. Provo, Utah: Ancestry.com Operations, Inc., 2010.

Ancestry.com. *Pennsylvania, Volunteers in the War of 1812* [database on-line]. Provo, Utah: Ancestry.com Operations, Inc., 1998.

Ancestry.com. *Pennsylvania, War of 1812 Pensions, 1866-1879* [database on-line]. Provo, Utah: Ancestry.com Operations, Inc., 2012.

McGhee, Lucy Kate. *Pennsylvania Pension Abstracts of Soldiers of the Revolutionary War, War of 1812, and Indian Wars*. Washington, D.C.: L. K. McGhee, 1964.

Muster Rolls of the Pennsylvania Volunteers in the War of 1812-1814. Baltimore, Maryland: Genealogical Publishing Co., 1967.

Rhode Island
Smith, Joseph Jencks. *Civil and Military List of Rhode Island*, 2 vols. Providence, Rhode Island: Preston and Rounds, 1900-1901. (Volume 2 includes a list of officers in the War of 1812.)

South Carolina

Burns, Annie Walker. *Abstracts of Pensions of South Carolina Soldiers of the Revolutionary War, War of 1812 and Indian Wars.* 12 vols. Washington, D.C.: A.W. Burns, 1960.

Tennessee

Armstrong, Zella. *Twenty-four Hundred Tennessee Pensioners: Revolution – War of 1812.* Chattanooga, Tennessee: Lookout Pub. Co., 1937.

Douthat, James L. 1814 *Court Martial of Tennessee Militiamen.* Signal Mountain, Tennessee: Institute of Historic Research, 1993

Fox, George and Juanita Fox. *East Tennesseans in the War of 1812: 150 Muster Rolls – 8,500 Men.* [S.l.]: G. & J. Fox, 2011.

McCown, Mary Hardin, comp. *Soldiers of the War of 1812 Buried in Tennessee: Names Abstracted from Colonel David Henley's "Wastebook" Regular and Militia Personnel for Period 1793-1798 in Southwest Territory (Tennessee).* Johnson City, Tennessee: Tennessee Society, United States Daughters of 1812, 1959.

Moore, Mrs. John Trotwood. *Record of Commissions of Officers in the Tennessee Militia, 1796-1815.* Baltimore, Maryland: Genealogical Publishing Co., 1977. (This is an Ancestry.com database.)

Sistler, Byron and Samuel D. Sistler. *Tennesseans in the War of 1812.* Nashville, Tennessee: Byron Sistler & Associates, 1992.

War of 1812 Pensioners Living in Tennessee During the 1880's. Cullman, Alabama: Gregath, 1983.

Texas

Fay, Mary Smith. *War of 1812 Veterans in Texas.* Greenville, South Carolina: Southern Historical Press, 1979, 1994.

War of 1812 Pensioners and Others on the Pension Rolls as of January 1, 1883, Texas. Cullman, Alabama: Gregath, 199?.

Vermont

Clark, Byron N. *A List of Pensioners of the War of 1812.* Baltimore, Maryland: Genealogical Publishing Co., 1969. (This is an Ancestry.com database.)

Johnson, Herbert T. *State of Vermont: Roster of Soldiers in the War of 1812-14.* Baltimore, Maryland: Clearfield Co. 1995.

Virginia

Butler, Stuart Lee. *Virginia Soldiers in the United States Army, 1800-1815.* Athens, Georgia: Iberian Pub. Co., 1986.

Douthat, James L. *Roster of the War of 1812: Southside Virginia, Shenandoah Valley.* Signal Mountain Press, 2013. (This work is also known as *1812 Militia of Virginia for the Shenandoah Valley.*)

Lyman, Myron E. and Craig M. Kilby. *Burials of the War of 1812 Veterans in the Commonwealth of Virginia.* Berwyn Heights, Maryland: Heritage Books Inc., 2012-2018.

McGhee, Lucy Kate. *Virginia Pension Abstracts of the Revolutionary War, War of 1812 and Indian Wars*. Washington, D.C.: [s.n.], 1960, 1965, 1966.

Virginia Militia in the War of 1812: From Rolls in the Auditor's Office at Richmond. Baltimore, Maryland: Genealogical Publishing Co., 2001. (This is an Ancestry.com database.)

Wardell, Patrick G. *War of 1812: Virginia Bounty Land & Pension Applicants: A Quick Reference Guide to Ancestors Having War of 1812 Service Who Served, Lived, Died, or Married in Virginia or West Virginia*. Bowie, Maryland: Heritage Books Inc., 1987.

West Virginia

Lewis, Virgil A. *The Soldiery of West Virginia*. Baltimore, Maryland: Clearfield Press, 1991, 1996, 1998. (This is an Ancestry.com database.)

Wardell, Patrick G. *War of 1812: Virginia Bounty Land & Pension Applicants: A Quick Reference Guide to Ancestors Having War of 1812 Service Who Served, Lived, Died, or Married in Virginia or West Virginia*. Bowie, Maryland: Heritage Books Inc., 1987.

Bounty Land Warrants

The bounty lands were tracts of territories on the frontiers set aside for veterans of the Revolutionary War and War of 1812. A bounty land warrant can explain the westward migration of a family. Free land was an incentive for military service, and so the warrant is both a land record and a military record.

Obtaining lands from the government was based on claims of wartime service between 1775 and 3 March 1855. The applications are similar to pension files and are often combined with pension applications. Bounty Land Warrant Applications can be found on Fold3.com and on the Ancestry.com database "U.S. Bounty Land Warrants, 1789-1858." The collection includes warrants issued to veterans of the Revolutionary War between 1789 and 1833 and of the War of 1812 between 1815 and 1858. The warrants were essentially certificates given to veterans or their heirs for the rights to free lands on the public domains. They do not carry birthplaces, but they can help establish residences, regiments, and family members.

Revolutionary War warrants could be transferred to other people or sold on open markets, which should be noted on the certificates. The War of 1812 warrants could not be sold but could be transferred through inheritances. The federal government no longer gave bounty lands after 1855.

The states, too, granted bounty lands, and Lloyd D. Bockstruck's *Revolutionary War Bounty Land Grants Awarded by State Governments*, (Baltimore, Maryland: Genealogical Publishing Co., 1996) is an index to them, which is also an Ancestry.com database, "Revolutionary War Bounty Land Grants." Some states did not have enough vacant territories to support bounty warrants. Those states included Delaware, New Hampshire, New Jersey, and Vermont. Connecticut, Maryland, Massachusetts, New York,

Year	Military Reserves	Modern Location
1778	South Carolina Military Reserve	Western South Carolina
1778	Virginia Military Reserve	South and West Kentucky
1780	North Carolina Military Reserve	Upper East Tennessee
1781	Maryland Military Reserve	Western Maryland
1781	Virginia Military Reserve	South and West Kentucky
1782	New York Military Tract	Western New York
1783	Pennsylvania Donation Lands	Western Pennsylvania
1783	Pennsylvania Depreciated Lands	Western Pennsylvania
1783	North Carolina Military Reserve	Upper Middle Tennessee
1784	Georgia Military Reserve	Northern Georgia
1784	Virginia Military Reserve	South Central Ohio
1787	U.S. Military District	Central Ohio
1796	U.S. Military District	Central Ohio
1812	U.S. Bounty Lands	Eastern Arkansas
1812	U.S. Bounty Lands	North Central Missouri
1812	U.S. Bounty Lands	Western Illinois
1816	U.S. Bounty Lands	North Central Missouri
1816	U.S. Bounty Lands	Western Illinois

North Carolina, Pennsylvania, South Carolina, and Virginia did have lands, but they were in their western reserves. For example, North Carolina granted bounty lands in what is today Tennessee, and Massachusetts granted lands in what is today Maine. Soldiers in the Continental Line could take both federal and state grants, providing bounty lands outside the original eastern states. The states had a formula for who received how much land. Bockstruck's work has an excellent introduction about how each state handled its bounty land grants.

A list of some informative compilations of bounty lands indexes, both state and federal are:

Arkansas
Christensen, Katheren. *Arkansas Military Bounty Grants (War of 1812)*. Hot Springs, Arkansas: Arkansas Ancestors, 1971.

Georgia
Ancestry.com. *Land Grants to Georgia Revolutionary War Veterans* [database on-line]. Provo, Utah: Ancestry.com Operations Inc, 2003.

O'Kelley, Nicole M. and Mary Bondurant Warren. *Georgia Revolutionary Bounty Land Records, 1783-1785*. Athens, Georgia: Heritage Papers, 1992.

Illinois
Walker, James D. and Lowell M. Volkel. *War of 1812 Bounty Lands in Illinois*. Thomson, Illinois: Heritage House, 1977.

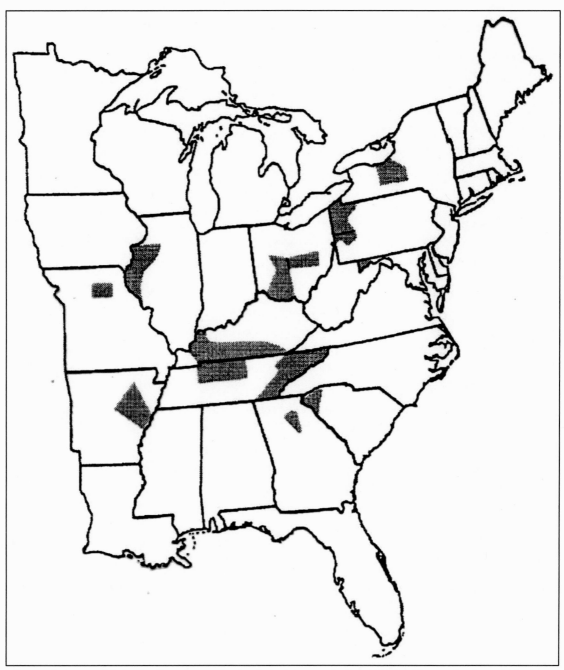

Figure 35: State and federal military bounty land redemption areas for Revolutionary War service through Mexican War, the last congressional act dating 1855.

Kentucky

Brookes-Smith. *Master Index, Virginia Surveys and Grants 1774-1791*. Frankfort, Kentucky: Kentucky Historical Society, 1976.

Jillson, Willard Rouse. *Old Kentucky Entries and Deeds: A Complete Index to all the Earliest Land Entries, Military Warrants, Deeds and Wills of the Commonwealth of Kentucky*. Baltimore, Maryland: Genealogical Publishing Co., 1978, 1969.

Key Timelines for Federal Bounty Land Distribution

Act of 16 September 1776
Offered 100-500 acres for enlistment because there was no money to offer.

Northwest Ordinance of 1787
Allotted lands to Ohio Land Company and select others. They could use redeemed bounty warrants as payment to government. This led to buying up of warrants by speculators. Warrants distributed at this time for 160 acres.

Act of 1 June 1796
Established Congressional Military Tract.
Minimum purchase was 4000 acres, reduced to 100 acres in 1800. Only speculators who paid to have warrants assigned to them could afford this.

Acts of 1803
First to include description of land directly on the warrant.

Acts During the War of 1812
3 new districts were created for new enlistees: Michigan Territory, Illinois, and Louisiana (present-day Arkansas).
Lands were in lottery format for lands within each district, and they could not be assigned or mortgaged until patent issued. This was to prevent abuse by speculators. Michigan tract was abandoned, labeled as undesirable, and lands were reallotted in Missouri Territory, with additional acreage in Illinois and Arkansas.
160 acres granted in 1812, 320 granted in 1814.

Act of 30 May 1830
Acknowledged shortage in Virginia Military Tract, and thus provided for Revolutionary War Scrip, which could be redeemed in Ohio, Illinois, and Indiana.

Act of 2 Mar 1833
Removed all restrictions of location from all Revolutionary War bounty warrants.
They could be redeemed in any federal land office for public lands.
Redemption only after initial auction for areas and could not be redeemed for Indian Trust Lands.

Acts of 1835, 1842, 1854
Extended length of time in which to apply for Revolutionary War and 1812.
Could also be redeemed at that value for taxes or other government payments/purchases.

Keep in mind, descendants of the original qualifier for bounty lands could file for their deceased ancestral soldier.

Key Timelines for Federal Bounty Land Distribution

Acts during the Mexican War (1847)

160 acres for one year of service/or 100 dollars.

40 acres for less/ or 25 dollars.

Could also be redeemed at that value for taxes or other government payments/purchases.

Nearly 81,000 warrants were issued for 160-acre tracts.

Nearly 8,000 warrants for 40-acre tracts.

This was the last conflict for which bounty lands were given.

Act of 1850

Catch-all for any previous wars or conflicts prior to 1790, including various Indian conflicts, and it reduced the service requirements.

9 months of service = 160 acres.

4-9 months = 80 acres.

1-4 months = 40 acres.

This opened lands to many that were previously ineligible!

Act of 31 Aug 1852

Any outstanding Virginia warrants MUST be exchanged for scrip.

Virginia ceded any remaining lands in Ohio to government.

Another act in 1852 lifted ban on assignment clauses, and extended privileges to militiamen who were called into service after 1812.

Act of 1855

Length of service reduced to as little as 14 days or at least have traveled 1200 miles.

Included Native Americans into all acts.

Any who had received less than 160 acres were qualified for the difference.

From 1847-1855 there were 552,494 warrants issued, totaling more than 34 million acres.

What does this mean? By 1855, most Revolutionary War soldiers were dead, as were many from other conflicts. Their heirs were qualifying on the soldiers' behalf, having to prove their lineage to the soldier and account for all other heirs! Ancestors who previously did not qualify almost always qualified under the later acts that reduced service requirements.

Act of 1858

Issue of bounty warrants ceased. No bounty lands were given after 1858, and none could be redeemed after 1863.

Act of 1872

Congress ceded remainder of U.S. Military Tract to the state of Ohio.

Quisenberry, Anderson Chenault. *Revolutionary Soldiers in Kentucky*. Baltimore, Maryland: Genealogical Publishing Co., 1968.

Taylor, Philip Fall. *A Calendar of the Warrants for Land in Kentucky, Granted for Service in the French and Indian War*. Baltimore, Maryland: Genealogical Publishing Co., 1967, 1975, 2001.

Wilson, Samuel M. *Catalogue of Revolutionary Soldiers and Sailors of the Commonwealth of Virginia: to Whom Land Bounty Warrants were Granted by Virginia for Military Service*. Greenville, South Carolina: Southern Historical Press, 1994. (This work is also known as *Kentucky Land Warrants for the French, Indian & Revolutionary Wars.*)

Maine

Ancestry.com. *Maine, Revolutionary War Land Grants, 1776-1780* [database online]. Provo, Utah: Ancestry.com Operations, Inc., 2011.

House, Charles J. *Names of Soldiers of the American Revolution: Who Applied for State Bounty Under Resolves of March 17, 1835, March 24, 1836 and March 20, 1836 as Appears of Record in Land Office*. Baltimore, Maryland: Genealogical Publishing Co., 1967.

"Maine Revolutionary War Bounty Land Applications, 1835-1838." Database with images. FamilySearch. http://FamilySearch.org : 7 October 2016. Citing Maine State Archives, Augusta.

"Massachusetts Revolutionary War Bounty Land Applications, 1805-1845." Database with images. FamilySearch. http://FamilySearch.org : 7 October 2016. Citing Maine State Archives, Augusta.

Maryland

Carothers, Bettie Stirling. *Maryland Soldiers Entitled to Lands West of Fort Cumberland*. [S.l.: s.n.], 1973.

Meyer, Mary K. *Westward of Fort Cumberland; Military Lots Set off for Maryland's Revolutionary Soldiers: with an Appended List of Revolutionary Soldiers Granted Pensions by the State of Maryland*. Finksburg, Maryland: Pipe Creek, 1993.

Newman, Harry Wright. *Maryland Revolutionary Records*. Baltimore, Maryland: Genealogical Publishing Co., 1967, 1980, 2002.

Massachusetts

House, Charles J. *Names of Soldiers of the American Revolution: Who Applied for State Bounty Under Resolves of March 17, 1835, March 24, 1836 and March 20, 1836 as Appears of Record in Land Office*. Baltimore, Maryland: Genealogical Publishing Co., 1967.

"Massachusetts Revolutionary War Bounty Land Applications, 1805-1845." Database with images. FamilySearch. http://FamilySearch.org : 7 October 2016. Citing Maine State Archives, Augusta.

Missouri

Till, Louise Gay Rogers. *Military Land Warrants in Missouri, 1819: Alphabetical Index of Missouri Patentees*. [S.l.: s.n.], 1988.

New York

Ancestry.com. *New York, Pension Claims by Disabled Revolutionary War Veterans, 1779-1789* [database on-line]. Provo, Utah: Ancestry.com Operations, Inc., 2014.

Cook, Joyce H. *The allotting Book and Other Documents Relating to Military Bounty Lands in the State of New York.* Syracuse, New York: New York State Council of Genealogical Organizations, 2011.

North Carolina

Ancestry.com. *North Carolina and Tennessee, Revolutionary War Land Warrants, 1783-1843* [database on-line]. Provo, Utah: Ancestry.com Operations, Inc., 2013.

Ohio

Brumbaugh, Gaius Marcus. *Revolutionary War Records: Virginia Army and Navy Forces with Bounty Warrants for Virginia Military District of Ohio and Virginia Military Script, from Federal and State Archives.* Baltimore, Maryland: Genealogical Publishing Co., 1995.

Jackson, Ronald Vern. *Ohio Military Land Warrants, 1789-1801.* North Salt Lake, Utah: Accelerated Indexing Systems, 1988.

Maxwell, Fay. *Ohio's Virginia Military Tract: Index of 1801 Tax List.* Worthington, Ohio: Ohio Genealogy Center, 1991.

Pennsylvania

Busch, C. M. *Donation or Military Tracts of Land Granted the Soldiers of the Pennsylvania Line.* Harrisburg, Pennsylvania: C. M. Busch, state printer, 1896.

Egle, William Henry and Robert H. Foster. *Old Rights, Proprietary Rights, Virginia Entries and Soldiers Entitled to Donation Lands with an Explanation of Reed's Map of Philadelphia.* Harrisburg, Pennsylvania: C. M. Busch, state printer, 1896.

South Carolina

Draine, Tony. *Revolutionary War Bounty Land Grants in South Carolina.* Columbia, South Carolina: Congaree Publications, 1986.

Tennessee

Ancestry.com. *North Carolina and Tennessee, Revolutionary War Land Warrants, 1783-1843* [database on-line]. Provo, Utah: Ancestry.com Operations, Inc., 2013.

Burgner, Goldene Fillers. *North Carolina Land Grants in Tennessee, 1778-1791.* Greenville, South Carolina: Southern Historical Press, 1981.

Rice, Shirley Hollis. *The Hidden Revolutionary War Land Grants in the Tennessee Military Reservation.* Lawrenceburg, Tennessee: Family Tree Press, 1992.

Virginia

Brumbaugh, Gaius Marcus. *Revolutionary War Records: Virginia Army and Navy Forces with Bounty Warrants for Virginia Military District of Ohio and Virginia Military Script, from Federal and State Archives.* Baltimore, Maryland: Genealogical Publishing Co., 1995. (This is an Ancestry.com database.)

Burgess, Louis A. *Virginia Soldiers of 1776: Compiled from Documents on File in the Virginia Land Office, Together with Material Found in the Archives Department of the Virginia State Library, and Other Reliable Sources*. Baltimore, Maryland: Genealogical Publishing Co., 1973.

Wilson, Samuel M. *Catalogue of Revolutionary Soldiers and Sailors of the Commonwealth of Virginia: to Whom Land Bounty Warrants were Granted by Virginia for Military Service*. Greenville, South Carolina: Southern Historical Press, 1994. (This work is also known as *Kentucky Land Warrants for the French, Indian & Revolutionary Wars*. It is an Ancestry.com database.)

Figure 36: "Drawing shows the ruins of the U.S. Capitol following British attempts to burn the building; includes fire damage to the Senate and House wings, damaged colonnade in the House of Representatives shored up with firewood to prevent its collapse, and the shell of the rotunda with the facade and roof missing." "1 drawing on paper: ink and watercolor" "Historical context: George Munger's drawing, one of the most significant and compelling images of the early republic, reminds us how short-lived the history of the United States might have been. In the evening hours of August 24, 1814, during the second year of the War of 1812, British expeditionary forces under the command of Vice Admiral Sir Alexander Cockburn and Major General Robert Ross set fire to the unfinished Capitol Building in Washington, D.C. All the public buildings in the developing city, except the Patent Office Building, were put to the torch in retaliation for what the British perceived as excessive destruction by American forces the year before in York, capital of upper Canada. At the time of the British invasion, the unfinished Capitol building comprised two wings connected by a wooden causeway. This exceptional drawing, having descended in the Munger family, was purchased by the Library of Congress at the same time the White House purchased the companion view of 'The President's House." (This work is in the public domain in its country of origin and other countries and areas where the copyright term is the author's life plus 100 years or fewer.)

Chapter Nine

Naturalization Records

The procedure by which someone became a citizen of the United States generated papers at every step. For Scots-Irish research, the goal of examining naturalization and citizenship records is to determine whether they convey, in response to the question about birthplace, where in Ulster a person was born. Whether they do or do not is unpredictable. When a location is present, it can range from Ireland to the county in Ireland to the city in Ireland. Oddly enough, within one manuscript book that contains a particular piece of the citizenship process, the entries can vary from all to one to none of the aforementioned birthplaces. As with so many United States records, what will be found is inconsistent, and so searching all documents is part of a holistic strategy.

The English colonies did not have citizenship requirements because Ireland was a country in its empire. However, when the United States was being created in 1776, former British citizens were residents. They were a "collective citizenship," groups of people who became citizens without any certification. At that time, all people living in the new United States were citizens with the exception of Native Americans and African Americans.

The first naturalization law was in 1790. Although requirements in the laws changed throughout the years, some did not. Unaltered was the filing of a declaration of intention and petition to become a citizen, after which the certificate of naturalization was granted. The person applying had to be a resident of the United States for a fixed number of years, such as 5 in the United States and one in his state of residence, but the lengths of time, too, changed. Naturalization was the final stage and was a court procedure. The entire process produced sets of records for immigrants throughout the United States that are diverse in content and between courts.

An alien could undertake any part of the course for citizenship in a choice of courts that included chancery, criminal, marine, municipal, police, probate, and surrogate. Sometimes, checking all available courts in an area, which can encompass a geographical region or just a county, is prudent.

Citizenship papers are so relevant to the family historian that the subject in instruction books, if not entire stand-alone volumes, always requires at least a chapter. Many of the standard works are dated because they address records that are now online at Ancestry.com or

FamilySearch.org. In other words, the discussion of the records themselves is current and a substantial research tool, but the directions for accessing the records is outmoded. Some of the recommended standards in the genealogy field are:

Greenwood, Val D. "Court Records and Family History" in *The Researcher's Guide to American Genealogy*, 4th ed. Baltimore, Maryland: Genealogical Publishing Co., 2017, pp. 560-567.

Luebking, Sandra Hargreaves. "Immigration Records" in *The Source: A Guidebook of American Genealogy*, 3rd ed., edited by Loretto Dennis Szucs and Sandra Hargreaves Luebking. Provo,

Utah: Ancestry Publishing, 2006, pp. 399-408.

Newman, John J. *American Naturalization Records 1790-1990*. Bountiful, UT: Heritage Quest, 1998.

Schaefer, Christina K. *Guide to Naturalization Records of the United States*. Baltimore, MD: Genealogical Publishing Co., Christina K. Schaefer, 1997.

Szucs, Loretto Dennis. *They Became Americans: Finding Naturalization Records and Ethnic Origins*. Salt Lake City, Utah: Ancestry Publishing, 1998.

Many laws continue to regulate who can become a citizen and who cannot. The

Date	Provision
26 Mar 1790	One visit to court; two-year residency; free white alien; children of naturalized citizen are to be considered citizens.
29 Jan 1795	Free white aliens of good moral character; five-year residency with one year in state; declaration of intention filed after two years; petition filed three years after declaration.
18 Jun 1798	14-year residency; declaration of intention filed 5 years before granting of citizenship.
14 Apr 1802	Reasserted residence requirements of 1795 act; children of naturalized citizens considered to be citizens.
26 May 1824	Alien minors naturalized upon reaching 21 years of age if alien had lived in United States for five years.
10 Feb 1855	Alien women married to United States citizens considered to be citizens.
17 Jul 1862	Aliens who received honorable discharges from U.S. Army were not required to file declarations.

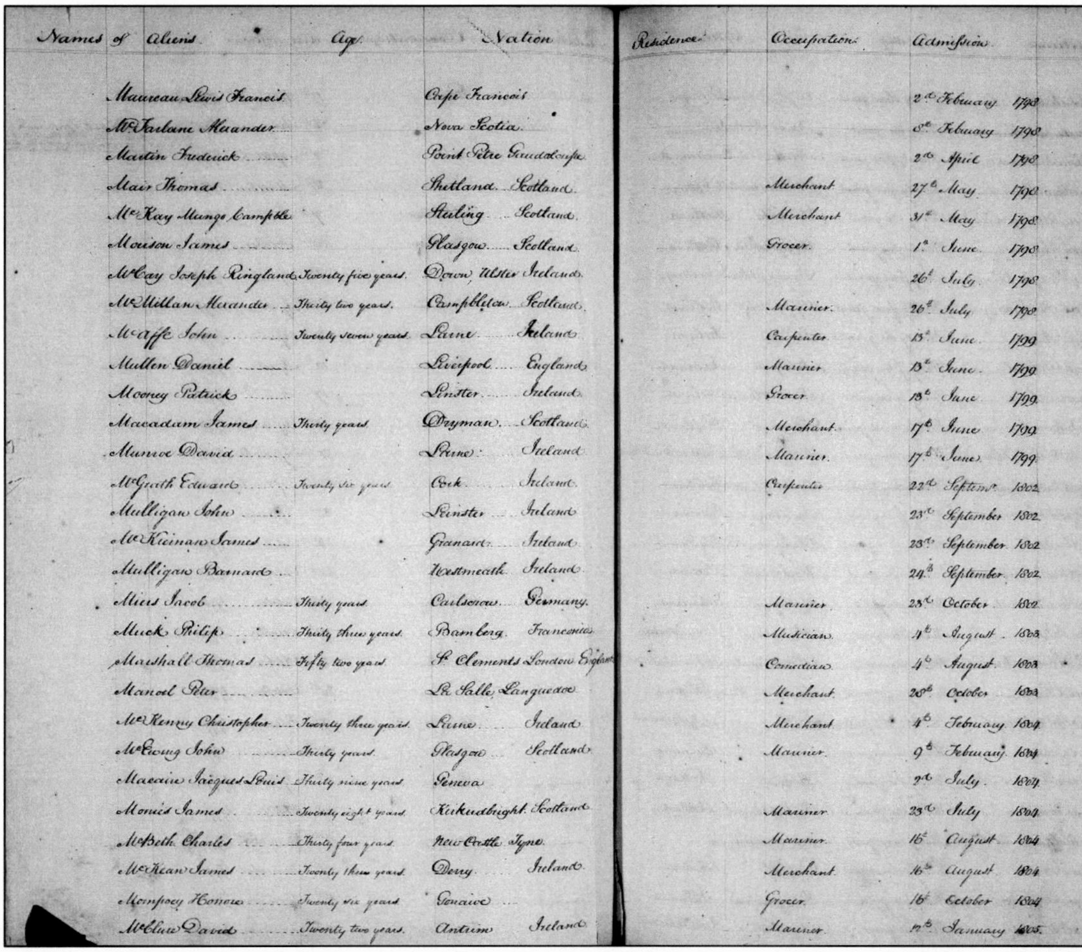

Names of Aliens	Age	Nation	Residence	Occupation	Admission
Maureau Louis Francois		Cape Francois			2d February 1798
McFarlane Alexander		Nova Scotia			8th February 1798
Martin Frederick		Point Petre Guadaloupe			2d April 1798
Mair Thomas		Shetland Scotland		Merchant	27th May 1798
McKay Mungo Campble		Sterling Scotland		Merchant	31st May 1798
Morison James		Glasgow Scotland		Grocer	1st June 1798
McCay Joseph Ringland	Twenty five years	Down, Ulster Ireland			26th July 1798
McMillan Alexander	Thirty two years	Campbleton Scotland		Mariner	26th July 1798
McAffe John	Twenty seven years	Laine Ireland		Carpenter	13th June 1799
Mullen Daniel		Liverpool England		Mariner	13th June 1799
Mooney Patrick		Linster Ireland		Grocer	13th June 1799
Macadam James	Thirty years	Dryman Scotland		Merchant	17th June 1799
Munroe David		Laine Ireland		Mariner	17th June 1799
McGrath Edward	Twenty six years	Cork Ireland		Carpenter	22d Septemr 1802
Mulligan John		Leinster Ireland			23d September 1802
McKiernan James		Granard Ireland			23d September 1802
Mulligan Barnard		Westmeath Ireland			24th September 1802
Miers Jacob	Thirty years	Carlsonow Germany		Mariner	28th October 1802
Muck Philip	Thirty three years	Bamberg Franconia		Musician	4th August 1803
Marshall Thomas	Fifty two years	St Clements London England		Comedian	4th August 1803
Manoel Peter		La Salle Languedoc		Merchant	28th October 1803
McKenny Christopher	Twenty three years	Laine Ireland		Merchant	4th February 1804
McEwing John	Thirty years	Glasgow Scotland		Mariner	9th February 1804
Macaire Jacques Louis	Thirty nine years	Geneva			2d July 1804
Morris James	Twenty eight years	Kirkudbright Scotland		Mariner	23d July 1804
McBeth Charles	Thirty four years	New Castle Tyne		Mariner	16th August 1804
McKean James	Twenty three years	Derry Ireland		Merchant	16th August 1804
Mompoey Honore	Twenty six years	Gonaive		Grocer	16th October 1804
McClure David	Twenty two years	Antrim Ireland		Mariner	17th January 1805

Figure 37: U.S. District Court of South Carolina, naturalization documents from their collection dating 1790-1906, currently housed at the National Archives in East Point, Georgia. Note that the list of names often provides the county in Ireland where the immigrant derived. (This work is in the public domain in the United States because it is a work prepared by an officer or employee of the United States Government as part of that person's official duties under the terms of Title 17, Chapter 1, Section 105 of the U.S. Code.)

laws and the documents constructed by courts are discussed in the books listed above. Citizenship laws began in 1790, and for the purpose of Scots-Irish research, the main ones are listed below through the 1862 law in place during the American Civil War. The chart on the opposite page is adapted from the online National Archives' "Major United States Laws Relating to Immigration and Naturalization: 1790-2005:"

Knowing some facts about citizenship will simplify genealogical pursuits. First, in the early years, only men were naturalized. Women did not have the right to vote until 1920, and, therefore, women did not need to submit declarations because they received citizenship through their husbands. Second, not all who started the procedures finished them, explaining why declarations of intention were filed but naturalization certificates cannot be found. Third, the steps in the system can take place in different courts within each state, or people can move to other states to complete their naturalizations. A fourth consideration is that no laws require immigrants to become citizens. In conclusion, the naturalization records of the United States may or may not lead to Ulster origins, but despite the results, they still have to be studied.

The Naturalization Process

Before 1906, citizenship records were not standardized. Each court kept its own documents whose details could contrast from basic to extensive, thus offering a set of difficulties when studying them. However, some essential data is always given:

- Name of immigrant
- Residence of immigrant
- Country of origin or allegiance

Researchers seek additional information, which may or may not be common. Depending on the court, some of the following can be contained:

- Port of arrival
- Date of arrival
- Age of immigrant
- Residence of immigrant
- Birthplace of immigrant

The papers do not provide parents' names, and so sorting through people with the same name is obligatory. In the case of the Scots-Irish, Scots or Irish Catholics may have had the same name, and connecting with the wrong person can be easy. When additional knowledge beyond the basics is found in the records, the categorizing can begin in earnest. One way certainly would be by

locality. If an address is given for the person, determining where an ancestor lived becomes the objective. If, for some reason, the port from which he sailed is noted, knowing that most Protestant Scots-Irish left through Londonderry (Derry) or Belfast in the north can be helpful, separating the ancestor further from potential Irish Catholics from outside Ulster, who left from the ports of Cork or Dublin. Citizenship papers cannot be used as guides to religious affiliations because religions are not listed.

The character witnesses can be important, and they were named on the documents. Who were they, and what was their relationship to the person being naturalized? Possibly, they were relatives or friends from Ireland, and so they are another significant subject to explore.

Requesting citizenship typically involved a Declaration of Intention, called a "first paper," the pronouncement to become a citizen. Questions were asked for it, and the birthplace was frequently recorded. Two or three years after the declaration was filed, the Petition, called the "second or final paper" on which the man signed an Oath of Allegiance to the United States, was submitted. The last paper was the Naturalization Certificate from the court maintaining the Petition. The immigrant was then sworn in as a citizen, and his citizenship certificate was issued.

The easiest way to look at all documentation is through Ancestry.com, FamilySearch.org, and the National Archives. All federal records are in the National Archives. FamilySearch collections are in the FamilySearch Catalog under the state levels, such as "New York/Naturalization and Citizenship" or under the county levels, such as "New York/Ontario/Naturalization and Citizenship." The massive microfilm collections at the Family History Library are digitized, where contracts allow, on the FamilySearch.org website, and they can be viewed at home or at a FamilySearch Center.

Report and Registry of Aliens

From 1798 to 1828, new immigrants were required to appear before a local court and register their arrivals in the United States. Their information was kept in the court minutes, although some counties had separate registries. At that point, an immigrant could obtain a certificate from the court that could be used in a later citizenship process. The paper was the proof of the length of residence in the country when applying for citizenship. The registration did not have to occur in the court where the declaration of intention was filed.

The questions asked and recorded by the courts were not uniform in states and courts. Generally, they were:

- Name of immigrant
- Birthplace
- Age
- Nation of allegiance
- County of migration
- Place of intended settlement
- Occupation

The information in the contents was from basic to exhaustive. An example of some maximal facts in Ulster alien registrations comes from the Orange County, New

York, Court of Common Pleas (1817-1828). It is an Orange County record digitized through FamilySearch:

> To James W. Wilkin Esq. Clerk of the Court of Common Pleas in & for the County of Orange in the State of New York
>
> I Michael Mount of the Town of Wallkill in the County of Orange and State of New York do report my name to be Michael Mount that I was born in the County of Tyrone (Ireland) that I am forty three years ten months two weeks & six days of age that I am of the English Nation and my allegiance is to George the Fourth King of Great Britain that I emigrated from Ireland the port of Londonderry (Ireland) for the City of New York & that I intend to settle myself in the Town of Wallkill in the County of Orange aforesaid all which I do hereby report to you in pursuance of the laws of the United States Dated June 1, 1820. Michael Mount (Image 130/728).

Some are more specific, proving the places within the counties, while others, even from the same register, are in fill-in-the-box formats, with no elaborations whatsoever. The same Orange County, New York, Court of Common Pleas, as above, recorded the following:

Report of Thomas Bell an Alien in order that he may be naturalized (Image 131/728):

Name, Thomas Bell
Birthplace, County Down
Age, 21
Nation, Ireland
Allegiance, King of Great Britain & Ireland
Country Whence Migrated, Ireland
Place of Intended Settlement, Orange Co., N. York

Newburgh Orange County State of New York May 27, 1820

Above record entered 2nd day of June 1820

Still more are extensive, such as the collection of "Landing Reports of Aliens, 1798-1828" that covers the United States District Court for the Eastern District of Pennsylvania. They are National Archives documents, digitized through FamilySearch. Ulster immigrant Archibald Armstrong, as an illustration, appeared before the court on 27 July 1810. He was listed on the fill-in-the-blank form as being born in County Cavan, Ireland, on or about 18 July 1778 and was 32 years old. He migrated from Dublin to New York on or about 28 October 1804, and he intended to settle in Pennsylvania (Image 122/636). In another example, on 17 September 1814, Samuel McCaman appeared before the United States District Court, stating that he was born in County Armagh, Ireland, on or about 12 February 1768 and was 46 years old. He had migrated from Belfast on or about 11 June 1811, and it was his intention to settle in Pennsylvania (Image 217/636).

Indexes to Records

Indexes can be troublesome to use if their information is basic. Chances are researchers do not know an ancestor's year of naturalization or the court where it took place. For this reason, with common names, it is problematic to know who, if anyone, the ancestor was unless an index is precise enough so that a county of residence or a span of years can be used as a guide. The problem is sizeable with state courts or in larger collections in which copious records have been indexed from numerous courts covering several counties.

One place to start is in the county where an ancestor is known to have lived. Search the FamilySearch Catalog to see what it covers. If the collection includes the years needed, look at the digital images for indexes to the appropriate volume. Keep in mind that neither FamilySearch.org nor Ancestry.com has images and indexes to all citizenship papers, and thus it may be necessary to contact a county courthouse or state archives. However, for most family historians, the two websites are a solid beginning.

When examining an index, note the court, volume, page, or number assigned to the particular declaration, petition, or certificate. Find that volume to read the entry, and if an image is attached to the online index, the answer is a click away. If only the index has been digitized or microfilmed, determining the repository retaining the original papers is required. Is

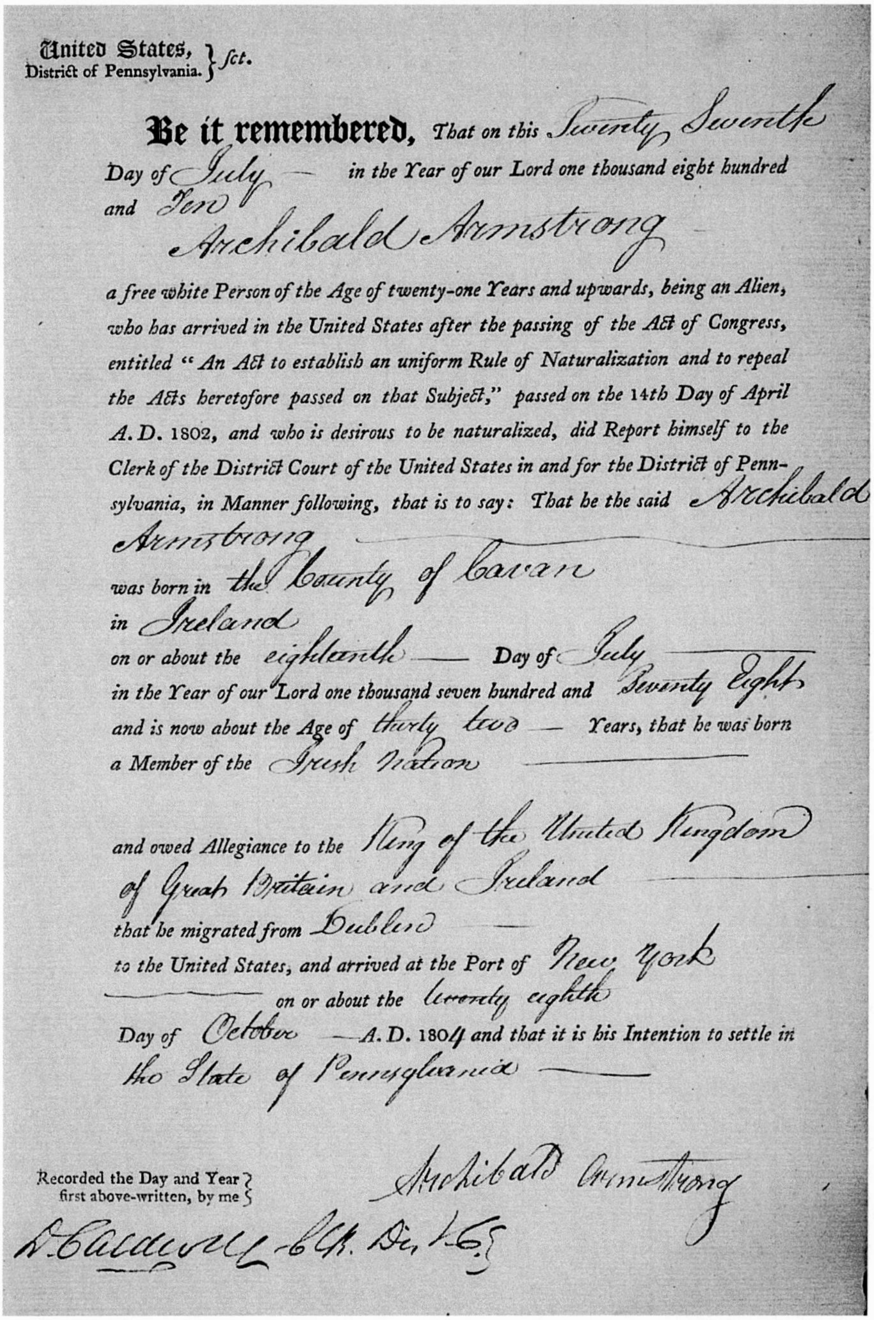

United States, } sct.
District of Pennsylvania. }

Be it remembered, *That on this* Twenty Seventh *Day of* July *in the Year of our Lord one thousand eight hundred and* Ten Archibald Armstrong *a free white Person of the Age of twenty-one Years and upwards, being an Alien, who has arrived in the United States after the passing of the Act of Congress, entitled "An Act to establish an uniform Rule of Naturalization and to repeal the Acts heretofore passed on that Subject," passed on the 14th Day of April A. D. 1802, and who is desirous to be naturalized, did Report himself to the Clerk of the District Court of the United States in and for the District of Pennsylvania, in Manner following, that is to say: That he the said* Archibald Armstrong *was born in* the County of Cavan *in* Ireland *on or about the* eighteenth *Day of* July *in the Year of our Lord one thousand seven hundred and* Seventy Eight *and is now about the Age of* thirty two *Years, that he was born a Member of the* Irish Nation *and owed Allegiance to the* King of the United Kingdom of Great Britain and Ireland *that he migrated from* Dublin *to the United States, and arrived at the Port of* New York *on or about the* twenty eighth *Day of* October *A. D. 1804 and that it is his Intention to settle in* the State of Pennsylvania

Archibald Armstrong

Recorded the Day and Year first above-written, by me

D. Caldwell Clk. Dis. C.

Figure 38: Landing Reports of Aliens, 1798-1828 from the U.S. District Court for Eastern Pennsylvania. (This work is in the public domain in the United States because it is a work prepared by an officer or employee of the United States Government as part of that person's official duties under the terms of Title 17, Chapter 1, Section 105 of the U.S. Code.)

it a county courthouse, a state archive, or perhaps the National Archives?

In some circumstances, targeting and studying the books covering the period in question may be more sensible. Search page by page even though it appears indisputable that the person in the index is the one being sought. In doing so, it will be assured that nothing has been missed!

Strategies for Using Citizenship Records

When additional information is in the records, it still may not be specific enough to further the research goals. Therefore, the search should expand past the ancestor's declaration or naturalization. For example, because the pre-1906 records were not standardized, the one for an ancestor may note the birthplace as simply Ireland, whereas the citizenship papers for someone else, such as a brother or a cousin of the ancestor, may state County Donegal. Consequently, keeping track of people with the same surname as an ancestor in the records during the same time is wise.

Even if none of the people with the same last name is registered with anything other than Ireland as a birthplace, the citizenship papers have provided a means to extend the search. Often, a brother or cousin was naturalized in the same county and court as an ancestor was, yet the ancestor moved away soon afterward and did not appear in any other record for that county. The possible relative can be researched in other records in another place. If he is related, likely he was from the same place in Ulster as the ancestor was.

If it is already known, for instance, that an ancestor was from County Fermanagh but no Irish records indicate precisely where in the county, studying who was born in County Fermanagh was being naturalized during the same period is important. The surname does not matter. All the men might have known one another in Fermanagh or have been from the same parish. Also remember that in Ulster, the Ulster-Scots married the English and Welsh, and so a Scot-Irish immigrant may not have had a name that appears to be Scottish. A Jones and Williams (Welsh names) from County Fermanagh are as worth noting as a McDougal or a Campbell. Conversely, if the person was a friend, that other person from Fermanagh may not have been Scot-Irish. Perhaps a Presbyterian ancestor and his Quaker friend, who was from an English background, immigrated together!

The principle can be applied as well to Irish Catholics from County Fermanagh who were naturalized during the same period. Catholics and Protestants could have been friends in Ulster, or even relatives. Follow the other Irish for their identities and from where they came in County Fermanagh. Continuing with the example of County Fermanagh, the probability is that all men from Fermanagh might have been from one area of the county regardless of surname and religion because Fermanagh certainly never was as heavily populated as Belfast. Fermanagh is a rural county, and as word was received that a county in the United States had good land, a chain migration might have ensued from a few parishes.

In records such as citizenship, be aware of the discrepancies. Start the inquiry with what is known, Scots-Irish and Protestant, and enlarge it to other Scots-Irish, related or not, and then to those who were not Scots-Irish (the Welsh and English surnames). If the search needs to reach to Catholics during the same years, do not hesitate to do so. Remember,

chain migrations, in which one after another after another over decades joined
people in a foreign place, could mean,
apart from the surnames or religions,
that all people being naturalized in a
given time in a given county may have
been from a cluster of parishes in an Ulster county.

Figure 39: Naturalization of Foreigners, Scene in Tammany Hall, New York City. "Drawn from life." From Frank Leslie's Illustrated Newspaper, vol. 2, no. 48, 8 November 1856, p. 352. (Image from Library of Congress, Prints and Photographs Division. Public Domain, published before 1922.)

Figure 40: A cropped view of "Two Ships" by an unknown artist dating in the 1700s. (Image from Library of Congress, Prints and Photographs Division. This work is in the public domain in its country of origin and other countries and areas where the copyright term is the author's life plus 100 years or fewer.)

Ulster

Chapter Ten

Passenger Lists (Pre-1820)

Scots-Irish immigrants came to America through all ports. In the colonial days, Philadelphia was the favored entry, although certainly not the only one. By 1820, when records officially began, Scots-Irish were arriving at the major harbors of Baltimore, Boston, Charleston, Mobile, New Orleans, and New York as well as Philadelphia.

The United States government arrival lists are indexed and scanned on Ancestry.com and on other websites, such as FamilySearch.org. To fill in the gaps in government registers before 1820, diverse sources are used, but they are appreciably incomplete for incoming passengers. Because the problem for Scots-Irish research is pre-1820 immigration, it is the focus of the present study. The post-1820 passengers' lists are readily available, digitized, and indexed, and

they have been analyzed extensively. Two helpful works on post-1820 passenger arrival records have to include:

Colletta, John Phillip, *They Came in Ships: Finding Your Immigrant Ancestor's Arrival Record*, 3rd ed., Orem, Utah: Ancestry.com, 2002).

Tepper, Michael, *American Passenger Arrival Records: A Guide to the Records of Immigrants Arriving at American Ports by Sail and Steam*, revised and enlarged edition (Baltimore, Maryland: Genealogical Publishing Co., 1999).

Many compilations and databases are for passenger arrivals before 1820. They were obtained from a number of sources and can include court records, newspapers, published books and journal articles, and town records, to mention a few. Even though the collections are sizeable, it is possible to go through them and still not find an ancestor's name. Therefore, the pre-1820 passengers' lists may not be the first source to be explored, but they are worth examining for the prospect that an ancestor might have been documented.

An example of a pre-1820 published compilation demonstrates how localized and sketchy the lists are. Extracts from the Council Journals are in Janie Revill's *A Compilation of the Original Lists of Protestant Immigrants to South Carolina, 1763-1773* (Baltimore, Maryland: Genealogical Publishing Co., 1981). Another odd source, which documents both Catholics and Protestants, is the extracts from the town records in New England in the colonial period. One is George F.

Donovan's *The Pre-Revolutionary Irish in Massachusetts, 1620-1775* (Washington, D.C.: L. C. Photoduplication Service, 1986). The two illustrate how essential recognizing an exact compilation is so that it can be used properly and in context. Such evidence is limited in its coverage to a geographical area and to its availability.

In regard to South Carolina and its compilations, it is important to understand the state was a Protestant colony set up as a buffer between Spanish Florida and the English colonies. Thus, those listed in the Council Journals were loyal Protestants by default, despite the country from which they came. On the other hand, while New England was also predominantly Protestant, with the Congregational Church as the majority faith, Irish Catholics did immigrate during the colonial period. In the New England compilation, it cannot be assumed that all the Irish listed were Protestant, and so the source is more difficult to use because of the crossover between Irish Catholic surnames and Ulster-Scots surnames. Even if the town records were, in essence, the Congregational records, Catholics will be found in them. In the South Carolina Council Journals, it is safe to assume those named as arriving were Protestants. The guideline in undertaking colonial immigrant research is forethought about the history of the colony and who the people were who settled in it.

Passenger and Immigration Lists Index

The series *Passenger and Immigration Lists Index*, edited by P. William Filby and Mary K. Meyer, is an enormous index to already published passenger and immigration lists, probably the most extensive one of pre-1820 arrivals. Popular for decades in its printed form, it has been made into a comprehensible database on Ancestry.com as "U.S. and Canada, Passenger and Immigration Lists Index, 1500s-1900s." The Ancestry.com edition allows the information to be manipulated in a number of ways not possible with the books. The work is so well known and utilized that in genealogical circles, it is simply nicknamed *Filby's* and is widely understood by that reference. The compass of the work is astounding because a quantity of varied and totally unrelated sources was gathered for it. Once an entry is found, the Ancestry.com version will display the published work that contains the entry with its page number. Whether using the published *Filby's* or the Ancestry.com database, remember that *Filby's* is just an index to the wider collections and is by no means the end of the search. The published book in which a record was originally printed still needs to be consulted and should be studied for further information, background, and names of people who might have been listed alongside the ancestor.

Filby's can be valuable in tracing colonial ancestors and covers all periods. For each individual, at least some of the following information can be found:

- Name and age
- Year and place of arrival
- Naturalization
- The source of the information
- Accompanying family members.

Known Ports with Records Prior to 1850

Alabama
Mobile (1832, 1849-1852, 1890-1924)

Connecticut
Fairfield (1820-1821)
Hartford (1837)
New Haven (1820-1873)
New London (1820-1847)
Saybrook (1820)

Delaware
Havre de Grace (1820)
Wilmington (1820, 1830-1831, 1833, 1840-1849)

Florida
Key West (1837-1852, 1857-1868, 1898-1945)
Port St. Joe (1823, 1839)
St. Augustine (1821-1824, 1827, 1870)

Georgia
Darien (1823, 1825)
Savannah (1820-1826, 1831, 1847-1851, 1865-1868, 1906-1945)

Louisiana
New Orleans (1820-1952)

Maine
Bangor (1848)
Bath (1825, 1827, 1832, 1867)
Belfast (1820-31, 1851)
Frenchman's Bay (1821-1822, 1825-1827)
Kennebunk (1820-1842)
Passamaquoddy (1820-1859)
Portland (1820-1853, 1856-1868, 1893-1943)
Waldeboro (1820-1821, 1833)
Yarmouth (1820)

Maryland
Annapolis (1849)
Baltimore (1820-1952)

Massachusetts
Barnstable (1820-1826)
Boston (1820-1943)
Dighton (1820-1836)
Egartown (1820-1870)
Fall River (1837-1865)
Gloucester (1820, 1832-1839, 1867-1868,1870, 1906-1942)
Marblehead (1820-1836, 1849)
Nantucket (1820-1851, 1857-1862)
New Bedford (1826-1852, 1902-1942)
Newburyport (1821-1839)
Plymouth (1821-1836, 1843)
Salem (1823, 1865-1866)

New Hampshire
Portsmouth (1820-1861, fragmented)

New Jersey
Bridgeton (1828)
Cape May (1828)
Little Egg Harbor (1831)
Newark (1836)
Perth Amboy (1820, 1829-1832)

New York
New York (1820-1954)
Oswegatchie (1821-1823)
Sag Harbor (1829, 1832, 1834)

North Carolina
Edenton (1820)
New Bern (1820-1845, 1865)
Plymouth (1820, 1823, 1825, 1840)
Washington (1828-1831, 1836-1837, 1848)

Known Ports with Records Prior to 1850, cont.

Pennsylvania Philadelphia (1820-1952) **Rhode Island** Bristol (1820-1828, 1843-1871) Newport (1820-1852, 1857) Providence (1820-1867, 1911-1943) **South Carolina** Charleston (1820-1829, 1890-1924)	**Texas** Galveston (1846-1871, 1896-1951) **Virginia** Alexandria (1820-1865) East River (1830) Hampton (1820-1821) Norfolk (1820-1857) Portsmouth (1820-1857) Petersburg (1819-1822) Richmond (1820-1824, 1826-1830, 1832, 1836-1837, 1844)

Even as massive as *Filby's* is, with its millions of entries, not finding an ancestor's arrival information still is not unusual. It is common to find several individuals by the same name in different lists, and whether any one of them is the ancestor can be uncertain.

As *Filby's* and its over five million entries are from published sources, it acts as the "go to" beginning for Scots-Irish research. Many Irish and Scots-Irish-related databases were on CD-ROMs when they were on the market, but they were from the same printed material as *Filby's*. It is easier to use the Ancestry.com version of *Filby's* than to sort through the myriads of old CD-ROM databases or current websites. Once an entry is found, it might be necessary to consult websites and other databases for more current content about that person and the passengers on his or her ship. Websites such as Joe Beine's "Irish Passenger Lists Research Guide: Finding Ship Passenger Lists and Immigration Records – Ireland to America" can certainly supplement *Filby's*, although one of the sources listed on his website is, to no surprise, *Filby's!*

Records Leaving Ireland

One frequent question that researchers ask is related to the one about ships' lists themselves: the location of passengers' lists leaving Ireland. For the pre-1820 period, they are scarcer than those in the United States. However, two main collections should not be ignored in trying to provide a substitute for missing incoming records on the American side.

One source specific to Ulster is what has been termed the "letter of thanks." During the 1700s, the passengers on ships from Ulster customarily signed "letters of thanks" to their captains for good voyages. The letters with the names of the passengers were published in Ulster newspapers to encourage others to sign up for passages with the captains—in other words, free advertising—although not every ship did so.

Between 1737 and 1772, the major newspaper in Ulster was the *Belfast Newsletter,* which printed notices regarding ships (including the "letters of thanks") from ports throughout Ulster. *Belfast Newsletter Index, 1737-1800* (Ann Arbor, Michigan: UMI, 1993), compiled by John C. Greene, is a detailed index to the paper in five parts on microfiche and has surnames, places, ships, general topics, and advertisements. It also is online at the University of Louisiana Lafayette website. In the online edition, every significant word and date in the 20,000 surviving pages is indexed. The website does highlight some limitations. For example, only one-quarter of the newspapers survived from 1737 to 1750, yet they are nearly complete from 1750 to 1800. The database contains 300,000 items of news and advertisements.

The same kind of emigration information may be in the *Londonderry Journal*, which began publication in 1772. Along with other items, it has been abstracted in Donald M. Schlegel's *Irish Genealogical Abstracts from the Londonderry Journal, 1772-1784* (Baltimore, Maryland: Clearfield Co., 1990). The book has been scanned and converted into an Ancestry.com database.

The second source, which covers all of Ireland, is narrow in its time frame, but if an ancestor is named in it, it could hold the only facts about people leaving Ireland. Between March 1803 and March 1806, masters of ships were required by law to provide registers of their passengers as they left Irish ports. The lists are called the Hardwicke Papers. They give each passenger's name, age, occupation, and residence. The law was intended to keep skilled laborers from leaving the country, and so the occupations recorded may be questionable as people tried to avoid the law. Brian Mitchell extracted and indexed the records in *Irish Passenger Lists, 1803-1806: Lists of Passengers Sailing from Ireland to America Extracted from the Hardwicke Papers* (Baltimore, Maryland: Genealogical Publishing Co., 1995). The book has been scanned and converted into an Ancestry.com database.

Otherwise, not much in the pre-1820 period can be obtained from the collections of Ireland's data to link to ones in America. Accordingly, passengers' lists, whether in Ireland or in America, are not among the first sources to explore.

Figure 41: Etching of passengers preparing to board. (Image from Our First Century...published by C.A. Nichols and Co., 1877. Public Domain, published before 1922.)

1883, he was married to Belle, daughter of William Dunbar, of Cross Creek township, and one child, Edna Belle, was born to them; John R. is a Republican in politics, and holds the office of road commissioner); James P., a Presbyterian minister of Eagle Pass, Tex.; Eliza C. (wife of Alexander Irwin, of Washington county, Ohio); William Henry (deceased in youth); Rucina E. (a school teacher, living at home); Ulysses L. (a Presbyterian minister of Venango county, Penn.), and Brainard C. (residing at home). James and Rebecca Lyle lived on the home farm some time after their marriage, then purchased and moved upon the well-improved farm where they are now residing. When they came to their present farm it was wild and uncultivated, and they have made all improvements.

A worthy representative of a noble ancestry, James J. Lyle is among the foremost of the highly esteemed farmers, not only of his township, but of Washington county. He has never cared to enter the turmoil of active political life in which his ancestors have made such brilliant record, choosing rather "the low of cattle and song of birds, and health with quiet and loving words." However, he voices his political opinions by his vote, having formerly been a Whig, now a Republican. He and his wife are members of and liberal contributors to the Presbyterian Church at Cross Creek village.

WILLIAM MALCOLM DINSMORE. The family of which this gentleman is a worthy representative is one of the oldest in Canton township, and comes of pure Scotch-Irish stock. The remote ancestor was the Laird Achenmede, on the river Tweed, in Scotland, one of whose sons emigrated to Ireland about 1690, and settled at Ballywattick, near Ballymoney, County Antrim. The first in America came from there in 1719, and settled near Londonderry, N. H. His name was John Dinsmore, and he became the ancestor of a numerous and respectably posterity, several of whom attained eminence in public and business life. Two of his descendants have been governors of New Hampshire; W. B. Dinsmore (lately deceased), president of Adams Express, and a great railroad magnate; Col. Silas Dinsmore, of whom so much is said in Parton's "Life of Jackson," and who beat him at his own game, and others, were members of this family.

The direct ancestor of the Washington county branch was James Dinsmore, who was born at Ballywattick, Ireland, April 24, 1742. He emigrated to America in 1761, and settled in York county, Penn. There he married, had three daughters, and buried his wife. In 1774–75 he re-moved to Miller's Run, in what is now the edge of Allegheny county. There he married again, and had two sons and two daughters. At that time Pittsburgh was but a straggling hamlet, the country was a wilderness, swarming with savage beasts and wild men. That land is still owned by his descendants in the direct line, and it is situated not far from Venice. In 1794 he bought, and in 1796 removed to a large tract of land in what is now Canton township, Washington county, and on that estate the fifth generation of his name and blood are living to-day; this land is situated six miles a little north of west from Washington. This James Dinsmore was a very bulky man, weighing above three hundred pounds; he died in 1817. He was eminent for saintliness, and was an elder in the Presbyterian Church for a great many years. He had two sons, John and James, between whom his landed estate was divided.

John Dinsmore, the grandfather of subject, was born at Miller's Run, in Pennsylvania, July 14, 1779. When a boy he removed with his father to Washington county, as above stated, and there spent his life, dying July 12, 1858. He was a man of great force of character, an elder in the Upper Buffalo Presbyterian congregation for nearly fifty years, distinguished for piety and greatly respected. He was a thrifty man, and became a large land-holder. In 1808-10 he built the large, solid, old-fashioned house which has been the nest of the family for more than eighty years, and the children of its present owner are the fifth generation to live in it. John Dinsmore had four sons—William, James, John and Robert—and one daughter —Mary. They all settled at their birthplace (William inheriting the old homestead), and are all gone out of this world.

William Dinsmore, father of subject, was born October 14, 1801, and died March 31, 1883, on the spot on which he was born. He was an intelligent, upright, God-fearing man, very industrious, affectionate and greatly beloved by his neighbors, and especially by his family. He was the liberal friend of every good cause. He was married March 12, 1838, to Rebecca Anderson, daughter of Capt. James Anderson, of the army of the Revolution. Capt. Anderson was also an early settler in the same neighborhood, and the farm on which he lived and died afterward became part of the Dinsmore estate. William and Rebecca (Anderson) Dinsmore had four children who lived to maturity, and one, James Anderson, who died when quite young; John Walker, the eldest in the family, was born March 13, 1839, and will have special mention further on in this sketch; Jane Melissa and Mary Virginia (twins), born May 1, 1841 (Jane Melissa married M. Wilson McClane, and lives near Washington; she has seven children. Mary Virginia married J. Hamilton M'Carrell, and

Figure 42: Published biography of William Malcolm Dinsmore, recounting a great many details for research consideration, including prior origins of "Ballywattick." Books such as this offer an excellent starting point for Scots-Irish research but must be audited for accuracy with additional research. (Commemorative Biographical Record of Washington County, Pennsylvania by J.H. Beers, 1893. Public Domain, published before 1922)

Ulster

Chapter Eleven

Published and Internet Family Histories

When approaching a Scots-Irish research problem in America, especially for early immigrants, begin by determining what has been compiled about the family. So many Scots-Irish came to America in the 1700s that immigrants logically will have hundreds of thousands of descendants today. Consequently, the probability is that a reference to an early Scot-Irish ancestor is in one or more branches of the family regardless of color lines. The research may not be correct, but some type of family history likely is in a published book, a journal article, or an Internet site.

Remember that the Scots-Irish were among the founders of communities, states, and religious organizations. Also, as plantation holders and traders with the native tribes, they had children with African Americans and Native Americans,

casting the net even wider for family histories and improving the prospect of biographies about them being preserved. Moreover, the immigrants or their children were at the forefront of conflicts, such as the Revolutionary War and the War of 1812, and so the chance of something being written about them is further increased.

Getting the Most out of Old County Histories

It is not unusual to find a biographical or genealogical sketch of a branch of the family in an old county history book written in the late nineteenth or early twentieth century. Such family summaries may be inexact, depending sometimes on what descendants remember hearing from their ancestors and relatives, but the books are a place to start.

By returning to the idea that early Scots-Irish recurrently traveled in groups from Ulster directly to America, some new research possibilities are opened. People who have studied the old county histories know about the treasure of information contained within the volumes. The books were commonly printed from the 1870s through the early 1900s in the Midwest, Middle Atlantic, New England, and West. Fewer were published in the southeastern part of the country. They generally were offered as general histories of counties and of each township within them. The township sections typically presented histories of the churches, lodges, early settlers, villages, and anything else considered interesting, a ready reference for identifying area churches and lodges with which an ancestor might have been associated. From the information, records can be sought with a degree of accuracy.

Sometimes, biographical and genealogical sketches are in the township or town sections, at the ends of the books, or in biographical volumes following the historical sections. Basic indexes to the biographies are ordinarily printed with the books; however, do not rely on them to include every name mentioned. Because the books are so historically valuable, it is customary for genealogy societies or individuals to index all the names included within the volumes, although place names often are not indexed.

Technology, though, has overcome the limitation and can be an amazing tool in developing new research strategies that were closed before. For example, if an old history book, which is out of copyright as a rule, has been digitized, word searches (ctl + f on a PC) can be undertaken. The book may merely need to be downloaded so that searches can be performed.

Some helpful strategies can be utilized for place names. Type in the name of the county or state from where an ancestor emigrated to learn who else came from the same area. For example, if seeking information on a family who settled in a specific county in Illinois in 1830 from New York, use the word search to find others from New York. If the county in New York is already known, conduct a word search for the name of the county to allow a study of migration patterns into the Illinois county from the New York county. If a pattern emerges, especially from the targeted county in New

York, the group could qualify as the one with which the ancestor traveled to Illinois. From an identified pattern, research can proceed with the names in the county in New York to establish whether the next generation back was from Ulster. The old family profiles often mention when the family came to the county, and so it is possible to isolate those who arrived about the same time that the ancestors did. Do not be too literal because the histories may be mistaken about locations, but within reason, patterns can be revealed.

If a county in Ulster is unknown, do the word searches for persons coming from Ulster or Ireland and settling in that county—which can be a little complicated. For example, when the histories were written, Irish Catholics migrating into the same areas were abundant, and they lived next to the Scots-Irish, whose descendants might have arrived generations before. To sort through them, the biographies will normally provide churches to which the subjects or families belonged. Discard the Catholic ones and keep studying the Protestant ones. Do not limit the search to only Presbyterians but include all Protestants. The goal is to ascertain whether a pattern among the Scots-Irish begins to emerge. Are all the Irish-born people coming from one county in Ulster? That could be a principal clue.

If the county in Ulster is already known, do the word search in reverse by county, such as Armagh, for immigrant Protestant families. Ignore the Catholic families from County Armagh.

All the same strategies can be applied to the town histories of New England. Most towns have some form of older ones. If an ancestor moved to the frontier of western Massachusetts, download the old town history and do the word searches for a pattern of Ulster homes of the Ulster immigrants in that town. It is easy to forget that the frontiers once were western Massachusetts, Upstate New York, and Vermont.

Tracking the ancestors back eastward from an area will situate them closer to where the original group settled. Bear in mind that as good as New England vital records are for research, they can be incomplete. For example, if a family suddenly disappears from the New England town vital records or published versions of them, it may be because of its conversion to the Baptist faith. Baptists held to believers' baptisms, and so the christenings of children were not part of the Congregational Church registers, which in the colonial period, could be the same as the town records. Migration patterns have to substitute for the town records. As an illustration, eventually tracing a family from an area back, to say, Londonderry, New Hampshire, has its own significance. In this instance, the original Scots-Irish settlers arrived in 1718 and were part of a congregational migration from Aghadowey Parish, County Londonderry. Once followed eastward to a town, that town history can be studied for a group migration from a particular part of Ulster. If it traces back to Londonderry, New Hampshire, around 1718, the case is solved!

Getting the Most out of Family Histories

The Library of Congress and the Family History Library have the largest collections of published family histories in the United States, but globally, the Family History Library has the distinction. Intercontinental thinking is essential because a branch of the family might have gone to Australia (as convicts or free settlers) when the ancestral family went to the United States. It is not exceptional for genealogists in Australia, Canada, New Zealand, South Africa, and the United Kingdom to be researching and writing family histories. Their published works may be at the Family History Library, which acquires from throughout the world.

Many published family histories, whether in books or on the Internet, claim to know families' exact origins in Ulster. If properly sourced, where that information was obtained is evident. If it is only raw information with no sources, it does not have much substance, and original research will still need to be undertaken. The unsourced family history, however, is not worthless. Quite the contrary, it might have rare clues not preserved and found elsewhere, allowing research to try to prove or disprove undocumented claims. Even if unsourced but definite dates are given, the author possibly had access to tombstones, a family Bible, or church registers. Where else would precise birth and death dates be discovered if no civil records are in that area?

Frequently, online or published books will give a specific parish within the Ulster county from where the family came. If sourced, evaluating the information for accuracy will be important. Oftentimes, it comes from an old county history or someone else's research. If not sourced, the Irish tax lists can be quickly checked. Certainly, tax lists such as the Tithe Applotment Books (1823-1837) or Griffith's Primary Valuation (1847-1864) can provide conclusive evidence. Even if ancestors were gone for a lengthy period before the valuations were generated, the lists can be used to locate relatives who did not leave Ireland. Thus, if the surname remained in the claimed area, even a century after the ancestors left, the unsourced family history may be correct!

If a family history states a couple was married in Ireland, the marriage, too, can be verified by determining whether both surnames are in the same or neighboring parishes in the Irish tax lists. Sometimes, it is just a matter of logic. The family history may assert that the couple married in Ulster and all their children were born in the United States, and so the couple was likely married in the United States. The observation may be obvious, but many novices fail to notice it. Its alternative would have been the honeymooners boarding a ship and immediately sailing to America. Again, inspecting the Irish tax lists is simple if a woman's birth surname is known.

Using Genealogy Periodicals as a Source

One overlooked resource in the search for family histories is the thousands of genealogy periodicals published worldwide. They are neglected because access to needed articles requires an index or inventory. Fortunately, the articles have a register by title and subject, known as

Periodical Source Index (PerSI). Without it, the vast library of knowledge is locked. Periodicals are a library within a library for articles not found in a typical library catalog, an absence that thus obscures their presence and value.

Periodical Source Index, known in genealogy circles as PerSI, is the product of the Allen County Public Library in Fort Wayne, Indiana, a major genealogical library in the United States. One of its main holdings is genealogy periodicals from around the world. It houses the largest international collection of them, with the Family History Library in Salt Lake City maintaining the second largest collection.

The purpose of PerSI is simple. Articles are published worldwide, but what has been published is unknown. An example is a family historian from California vacationing in Virginia and spending time extracting inscriptions from every tombstone in the rural cemetery where ancestors are interred. Upon returning home, the hometown California genealogy society periodical publishes the extractions. How would anyone find the item? No one could without PerSI, which allows a search of all articles using the name of that one Virginia county. The search even can be limited to the topic of cemeteries and found, no matter where the article was eventually printed.

PerSI has been available in books, with updates, for years, although it is cumbersome to use. An electronic version is on Findmypast.com and can be manipulated any number of ways. It is also continually revised. To begin, use the Findmypast.com catalog and narrow its entire database to "Periodical Source Index." Only that database will be searched, and all of the millions of articles are restricted to the county where the ancestors are known to have lived. Hundreds of articles may pertain to that one county, and so to reduce them further, "optional keyword" searches within the "Periodical Source Index" database can be explored with various words, such as deed, church, Presbyterian, Scots, Scotch, Irish, or a surname. Using the "optional keyword" to access a specific topic urges thinking creatively.

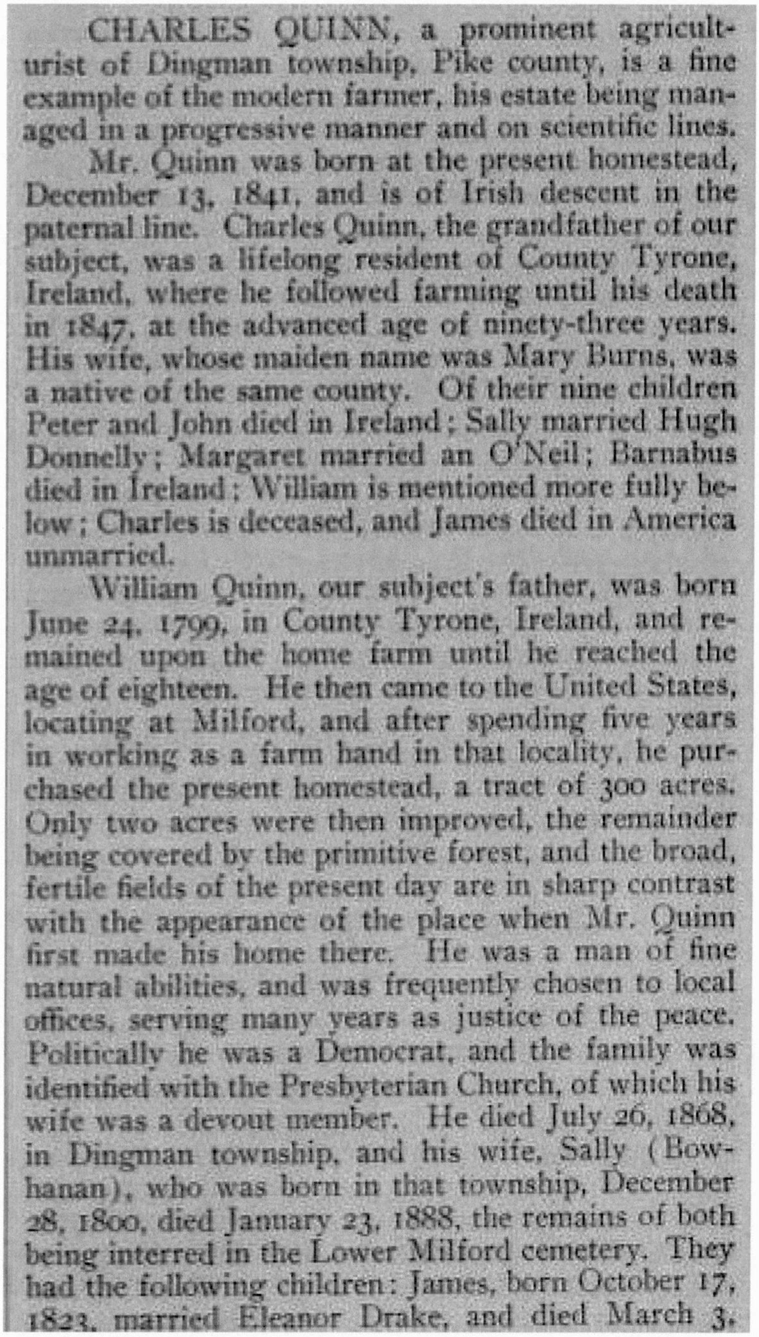

The "Periodical Source Index" database also works for international periodicals, but it is not as easy. If an international subject is desired, the United States information, such as state and county, needs to be left blank and the "optional keyword" search utilized instead with, for instance, Tyrone or Tyrone church as the search parameters.

Once articles of interest are found, the names of periodicals and their years, issues, and numbers will appear. The

CHARLES QUINN, a prominent agriculturist of Dingman township, Pike county, is a fine example of the modern farmer, his estate being managed in a progressive manner and on scientific lines. Mr. Quinn was born at the present homestead, December 13, 1841, and is of Irish descent in the paternal line. Charles Quinn, the grandfather of our subject, was a lifelong resident of County Tyrone, Ireland, where he followed farming until his death in 1847, at the advanced age of ninety-three years. His wife, whose maiden name was Mary Burns, was a native of the same county. Of their nine children Peter and John died in Ireland; Sally married Hugh Donnelly; Margaret married an O'Neil; Barnabus died in Ireland; William is mentioned more fully below; Charles is deceased, and James died in America unmarried.

William Quinn, our subject's father, was born June 24, 1799, in County Tyrone, Ireland, and remained upon the home farm until he reached the age of eighteen. He then came to the United States, locating at Milford, and after spending five years in working as a farm hand in that locality, he purchased the present homestead, a tract of 300 acres. Only two acres were then improved, the remainder being covered by the primitive forest, and the broad, fertile fields of the present day are in sharp contrast with the appearance of the place when Mr. Quinn first made his home there. He was a man of fine natural abilities, and was frequently chosen to local offices, serving many years as justice of the peace. Politically he was a Democrat, and the family was identified with the Presbyterian Church, of which his wife was a devout member. He died July 26, 1868, in Dingman township, and his wife, Sally (Bowhanan), who was born in that township, December 28, 1800, died January 23, 1888, the remains of both being interred in the Lower Milford cemetery. They had the following children: James, born October 17, 1823, married Eleanor Drake, and died March 3,

Figure 43: From Commemorative Biographical Record of Northeastern Pennsylvania, J.H. Beers & Co., 1900, this not only proposes the county of origin in Ireland, but various marriages and deaths that occurred there. As mentioned, the information must be corroborated. (Public Domain, published before 1922.)

"Periodical Source Index" often displays the major libraries, even though the list is not current, where the periodicals can be found. However, copies are always at the Allen County Public Library, where they can be ordered. Most, but not all, also will be at the Family History Library. The database does not index what is in the articles but furnishes the subjects and titles only. The original articles need to be obtained. Currently, many of the journals are being scanned on the PerSI database on Findmypast.com, a continuing project because the periodicals themselves are still under copyright. As with any other source, some of the articles will be comprehensive, and others will not be as detailed.

Irish Local Histories

Over the past few decades, historians and genealogy societies have had an interest in publishing books about their local parishes or counties in Ireland. Some online sources can be thorough. The best way to find them is to type in a name in a search engine for, as an example, "Down Genealogy," or consult a website of links, such as Genealogy United Kingdom and Ireland (GENUKI). Sites similar to GENUKI are constantly being updated.

Locally published civil or religious parish histories usually have family sections that can be helpful, especially if emigrations are addressed. Probably the largest collection of these outside of Ireland and Northern Ireland is at the Family History Library and will be in its catalog under the names of counties and civil parishes. In Ireland and Northern Ireland, the histories will be at the National Library of Ireland in Dublin or the Public Record Office of Northern Ireland (PRONI) in Belfast. Each has online catalogs that can be searched by the name of the parish.

Generation-Linked Databases

Likely, the two largest generation-linked online databases are on Ancestry.com and FamilySearch.org, although they are by no means the only ones. Many researchers have Trees on both because the two sites are not connected. Many people also use MyHeritage.com. One major difference between them all is that the FamilySearch.org version, known as "Family Tree," is a community tree, and once a Tree is started, anyone can alter it or insert information into it. While perhaps most additions are positive, those that are erroneous are frustrating. As various researchers hash over why one version is correct and the other should be deleted, the battle of the egos can almost escalate into the opponents wishing it were a contact sport. Regardless, a lot of Ulster origins are listed—and debated—through the Trees.

The pedigrees are no different than the published and online family histories. Is the source valid or hearsay? Did someone along the way find a "Helpful Hint" or "Suggested Record" that seemed reasonable and simply clicked it and added it to the Tree? Such factors are important in considering any generation-linked program. Sometimes, the information does not make sense, but whoever added it never questioned it. Therefore, it is necessary to examine everything and attach documentation to alleviate the many problems, especially for a community tree. The difficulty is that a community tree places the person who has been researching for 3 hours on equal footing with the person who has been doing so for 30 years. Nonetheless, as with other programs, the various people using "Family Tree" can communicate.

Ancestry.com "Public Member Trees" (which can be made private) share some of the same issues, but an Ancestry Tree belongs to one person. The difficulty with "Public Member Trees" is people attaching flawed Trees to their own Trees, thus spreading the errors at record speed and ingraining that information further into the various branches of the families. Again, some of the work is illogical, and so scrutinize the cited sources for whether the migration patterns fit or the dates are right. Happily, the various users of the "Public Member Trees" can contact one another. Even though most Trees tend to be raw data only, with no proof, some are well documented. The profiles do list how many sources are attached, which can be a good indication of good or poorly executed research.

Inexperienced researchers on Ancestry.com or FamilySearch.org are prone to attach "Helpful Hints" or "Suggested Records" that the computer provides for their lineages. They often have nothing to do with the ancestor and are major and frustrating distractions. Consequently, even when sources are attached to an individual in a pedigree, they must be assessed carefully.

The Rule of Thumb

The rule of thumb when utilizing online material or published books is that at times, almost too much is available whereas only a few years ago, there was not enough. The material can be overwhelming until it is understood that a good share of what is seen in print or online is not documented and needs to be evaluated. After analyzing a lineage for clues, it must be confirmed through

documentation or discarded if evidence cannot support it. Do not automatically accept everything. Because it is in print or on the Internet does not make it true!

"The difficulty with "Public Member Trees" is people attaching flawed Trees to their own Trees, thus spreading the errors at record speed and ingraining that information further into the various branches of the families."

"Inexperienced researchers on Ancestry.com or FamilySearch.org are prone to attach "Helpful Hints" or "Suggested Records" that the computer provides for their lineages. They often have nothing to do with the ancestor and are major and frustrating distractions. Consequently, even when sources are attached to an individual in a pedigree, they must be assessed carefully."

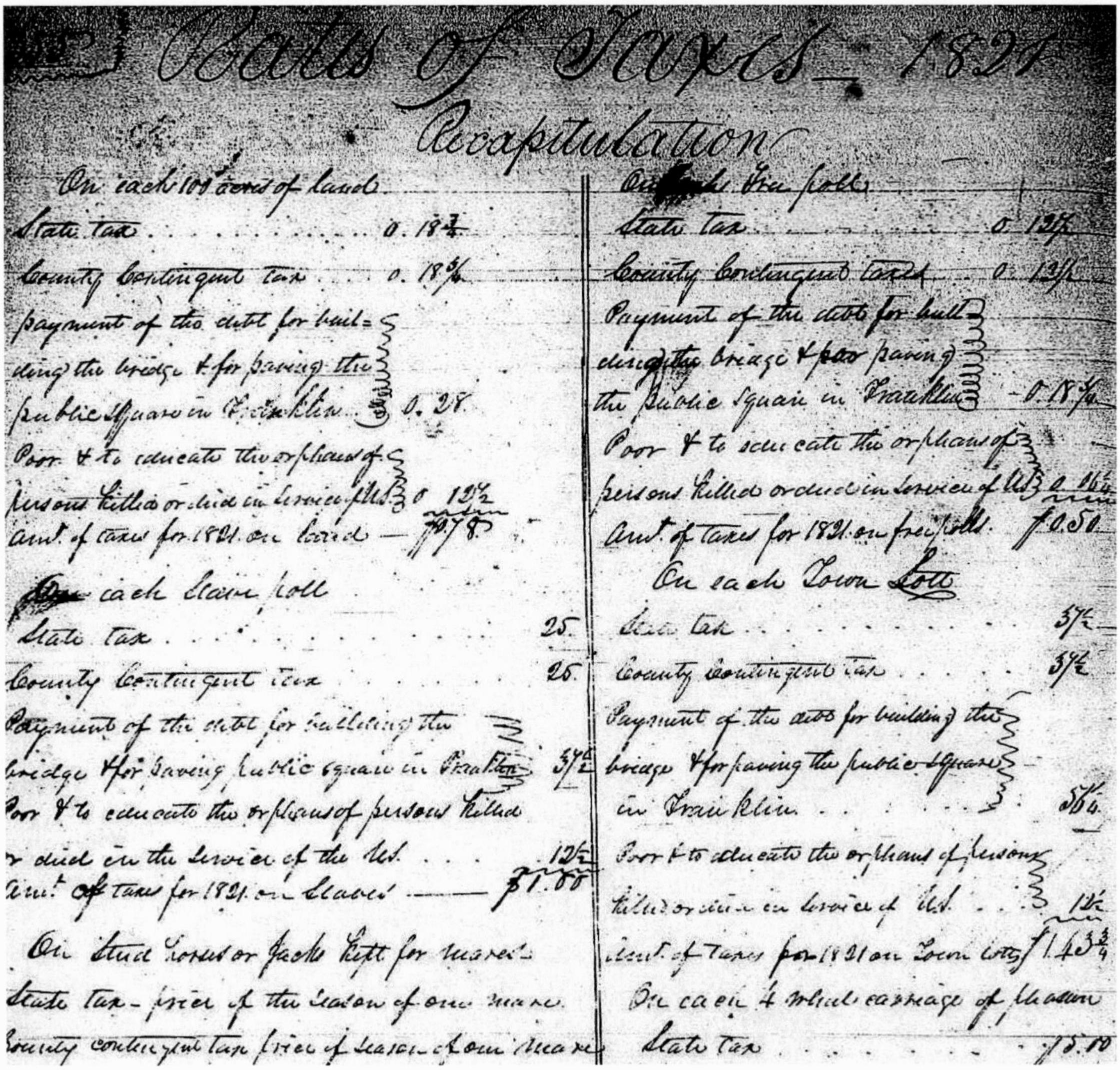

Rates of Taxes – 1821

Recapitulation

On each 100 acres of land
State tax 0. 18¾
County Contingent tax 0. 18¾
Payment of the debt for building the bridge & for paving the public Square in Franklin ... 0. 28
Poor & to educate the orphans of persons killed or died in service of U.S. 0 12½
Amt. of taxes for 1821 on land — $0.78

On each slave poll
State tax 25
County Contingent tax 25
Payment of the debt for building the bridge & for paving public square in Franklin 37½
Poor & to educate the orphans of persons killed or died in the service of the U.S. ... 12½
Amt. of taxes for 1821 on slaves —— $1.00

On stud horses or jacks kept for mares
State tax - price of the season of one mare.
County contingent tax price of season of one mare

On each free poll
State tax 0 12½
County Contingent tax 0 12½
Payment of the debt for building the bridge & for paving the public Square in Franklin - 0.18¾
Poor & to educate the orphans of persons killed or died in service of U.S. 0 6¼
Amt. of taxes for 1821 on free polls $0.50

On each Town Lott
State tax 37½
County contingent tax 37½
Payment of the debt for building the bridge & for paving the public square in Franklin 56¼
Poor & to educate the orphans of persons killed or died in service of U.S. ... 12½
Amt. of taxes for 1821 on Town Lotts $1.43¾
On each 4 wheel carriage of pleasure
State tax $5.10

Figure 44: Instructions to a Tennessee County Tax Assessor describing tax amounts to help fund a public square in Franklin. It listed state tax amounts, as well as local and county taxes to be gathered. Four-wheeled carriages were even to be taxed. Image from Williamson County, Tennessee, Trustee Office, courtesy of the Tennessee State Library and Archives.

Ulster

Chapter Twelve

Tax Records

Among the last sources researchers consult are tax lists but, along with land deeds and censuses, they should be the first. One reason for the aversion to them is that they are tedious, and at first glance, most people dismiss them as bearing little information. Moreover, the rolls can be a confusing encounter because tax laws differ from state to state and all are subject to change over the years. Knowledge of what is contained in a typical tax record, however, and what pieces of that information are of genealogical significance can transform this otherwise dull source into one of the most informative.

Although not much reference material is dedicated to American tax records in a stand-alone book, some good guides should be consulted. Among them are:

Carroll, Cornelius. *The Beginner's Guide to Tax Records*. Baltimore, MD: Clearfield Co., 1996. (Focused on the tax lists of Virginia, North Carolina, Kentucky and Tennessee).

Darrow, Carol Cooke and Susan Winchester. *The Genealogist's Guide to Researching Tax Records*. Westminster, Maryland: Heritage Books, 2007.

Hansen, Holly T., James L. Tanner, and Arlene H. Eakle. *U.S. Land and Tax Records*. Morgan, Utah: Family History Expos, Inc., 2016.

Greenwood, Val D. "Local Land Records" in *The Researcher's Guide to American Genealogy*, 4th ed. Baltimore, Maryland: Genealogical Publishing Co., 2017, pp. 505-506, 512-518.

Luebking, Sandra Hargreaves. "Land Records" in *The Source: A Guidebook of American Genealogy*, 3rd ed., edited by Loretto Dennis Szucs and Sandra Hargreaves Luebking. Provo, Utah: Ancestry Publishing, 2006, pp. 458-460.

The present chapter focuses on some basic concepts that will allow researchers to look at tax lists from a new perspective to seek correct explanations to inquiries. Throughout this chapter, the Kentucky tax records are referenced because they demonstrate how much can be extracted from the lists. In states with few vital records, tax records can be replacements for birth and death records.

Tax Lists as a Substitute Census
Experts habitually talk about tax lists in Ireland as "census substitutes." Although

the exchange of a record for another is not accurate, it does convey the meaning of a "census alternative." Ireland, though, is not the only place where the strategy works because tax lists can fill in for sketchy or non-extant documents. Two are John and E. Diane Stemmon's *Pennsylvania in 1780: A Statewide Index of Circa 1780 Pennsylvania Taxlists* (Laughlintown, Pennsylvania: Southwest Pennsylvania Genealogical Services, 1978) and Charles A. Sherril's *The Reconstructed 1810 Census of Tennessee: 33,000 Long-Lost Records from Tax Lists, Court Minutes, Church records, Wills Deeds and Other sources* (Mount Juliet, Tennessee: C. A. Sherrill, 2001).

The 1780 Pennsylvania compilation comprises tax lists for Bedford, Berks, Bucks, Chester, Cumberland, Lancaster, Northampton, Northumberland, Philadelphia, Westmoreland, and York Counties. It is a remarkable source for tracking people who first appear in the census in 1790 but whose origins before then are unknown. When studying a source, such as this index, consider whether the author used only the personal property books or real estate books or both in the compilation. The content makes a difference in what can be determined from an index. Since not everyone owned land, a tax list that included personal property is the most helpful especially if a "head tax" was placed on young men when they reached a certain age. Always consult the introductions to published extractions for exactly what was indexed.

The 1810 Tennessee compilation is more problematic. The tax lists are only part of the compilation because a variety of sources were used for the index, which is the nature of frontier Tennessee research. Although Tennessee became a state in 1796, its first complete census was in 1830. Tax lists before 1830 are thus valuable, but not all tax lists have survived for the pre-1830 period. Hence, the 1810 compilation consists of almost any other record that its author could find for either side of 1810. In Tennessee, it is not only necessary to understand whether the tax lists contain both real and personal property but also whether lists survived at all.

What Information is Important?

Not all information from tax lists is needed, but some data should never be neglected. The first observations when viewing tax rolls should be what was being taxed. For genealogical purposes, a carriage or a clock, albeit interesting, is not that useful. Those taxable items do not tie the research back into records such as deeds, church records, or probates, let alone other family members. Neither do cattle. Although perhaps purchase agreements for cattle might or might not have been registered, remember that cattle are foodstuffs, and so their use in joining families together, when no other record will, is certainly questionable. For example, John Brown being taxed for 3 cows in 1801, and 2 in 1802, and James Brown picking up an extra cow in 1802 does not mean John sold James that cow. John could have eaten his one missing cow! Also, a family relationship between John and James is not indicated. Horses and slaves are a different matter.

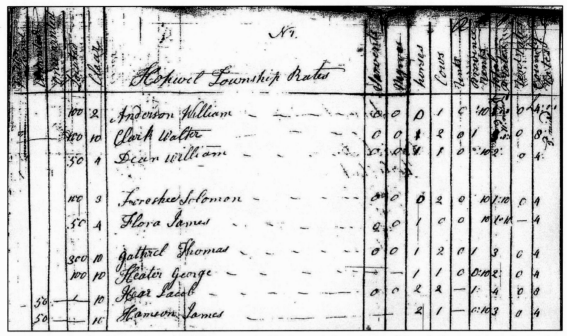

Figure 45: Sample of Pennsylvania's 1780 tax records. This image is from Hopewell Twp. in Beaver County, Pennsylvania, courtesy of Pennsylvania State Archives in Harrisburg, Pennsylvania.

The number of horses and slaves is essential information. Neither horses nor slaves were food, and so the number remains a taxable constant in a household until they were sold or they died. If John Brown had 3 taxable slaves or horses in 1801 and lost one in the 1802 tax lists but a James Brown gained one, it is noteworthy. In frontier research, it may be the sole record that suggests they were father and son when no probate or deed stating such was left. The proof is not the best but may be the only evidence on the frontiers or in counties where records were burned! Horses and slaves were considered personal property, and occasionally they were combined in taxes with real estate or were divided into separate books. Be careful in noting how the tax registers were arranged.

Land transactions are as significant as the sales of horses and slaves, resulting in real estate taxes. Not only do they sometimes provide the first clue that an ancestor owned land but also the tax lists are the only proof in many cases. Again, depending on the state laws, not all deeds were registered. Land often was passed through many family members, only to be officially registered when the need occurred, which could have been decades later. Nonetheless, a party was always taxed for the land each year.

The land taxes of Kentucky provide insight into where the families and their neighbors were living. Material for the real estate taxes could be plentiful. In some tax years, listed are sorts of land genealogies dating back to the original persons who obtained the properties. When those questions stopped, the fill-in-the-blank forms changed, and property histories were no longer requested. Was an earliest owner a family member or someone not related?

Geographically, the acres and "watercourse" information are most important. Watercourse is the term used in the Kentucky tax books, and it could be a river, branch, lick, or stream, all having to do with water running through an area. If the common name of Smith is being researched, or better yet, John Smith, do not panic. The watercourse will assist in distinguishing him. The first clue the John Smith on Possum Lick is not ancestral is the ancestral John Smith who had land on Buzzard Creek.

The same principle is true with other Smith families. If other Smiths were on Buzzard Creek along with the ancestral John, the supposition is they were relatives. A map showing the watercourses will establish the length of Buzzard Creek in the county. If it runs from one end of the county to the next, perhaps the assumption cannot be made quickly about whether the other Smiths were related to the ancestral John. If it runs for only a short distance, the assumption is much safer, if not a certainty. In addition, the strategy of using the watercourse as a guide can be utilized to sort through the five John Smiths in the county. Take into account that states such as Kentucky do not have townships, and so the watercourses, in essence, become the theoretical townships, which also can be helpful when sorting through county deeds. The watercourses, or at least the neighbors on them, are on the lists. When the watercourses have other names, they, too, are reflected in the books, sometimes alternating over the years.

Divisions Used in the Tax Lists

The tax lists, too, can be used to determine in which civil division within a county a person lived. In states such as Kentucky, the tax lists may be divided by companies or districts. In the early days, the districts were basically militia ones, and a question asked might have been the number of free white males in an age group, perhaps below 21 years of age. If so, a geographical part of the county may be in the tax lists as Captain Stone's Company or simply as District 1. If a district name or number was not specified and more than one is in the county, the researcher should assign a letter or number to it to organize who is where. While the company and district numbers do change over the years, the same populations should remain somewhat constant within parts of the counties, again aiding in separating families with common surnames to particular sections of a county.

The compositions of the residences also changed when new districts or companies were created. In states such as Kentucky, new counties were being established quickly as the population swelled and moved westward. An entire district might have disappeared from a county tax list, only to be found as part of the newly formed county. A family might not have moved, but, instead, boundaries moved around it. Having never relocated, a family can possibly be documented as part of three or more counties in the tax lists.

The Finer Details

Once in a while, the finer details need to be studied closely. In the records, as an example, are John Smith, Jr., and John Smith, Sr. Did the John Smith, Jr., become the John Smith, Sr., when the latter died or was Sr. exempt from the taxes? They were not necessarily a father and son, but the entries could have been designations for older and younger. The point requires thought, and in Kentucky, if both Sr. and Jr. are found on the same or neighboring watercourses or in the same district, they might have been father and son. While probates and land deeds certainly can resolve the relationship, not everyone left a will or owned land.

Depending on the state laws and periods, when a man dies, his widow may be in the tax list for a year or two, maybe even listed as a widow. Typically, when the male taxable is no longer in the books and a female appears in that man's place, a death has occurred. In the absence of a will or probate, the man's disappearance from the tax lists may be the only proof of the year of death, place of death, and the widow's name.

Aside from determining a death date, states such as Kentucky provide an excellent method of discovering birth dates. In Kentucky, it is the head tax: When a young man became 21 years old, he was placed on the tax rolls, and so the approximate birth year is 21 years before the first year the young man appears. Placing taxables into generations is thereby facilitated. Another clue that a person was young, perhaps single and 21, is that he or she was not taxed for anything other than the head. A person listed for the first time with land, horses, and slaves was well established and not just turning 21 years old.

Understanding ages for people in the tax laws of states is important. Were there head taxes or were persons considered taxable only if they were over 21 years of age and owned real or personal property? The answers are a matter of studying the tax laws or consulting a genealogy reference book for the state in question. For example, Kentucky was originally Kentucky County, Virginia, and so its tax laws resembled those of Virginia. Tennessee, on the other hand, was originally part of North Carolina, and its tax laws corresponded to the ones of its parent state. Because Virginia and North Carolina had dissimilar laws for who and what were taxable, their tax rolls do not look alike, and they were passed down to Kentucky and Tennessee.

An indication of a person's move out of the county is the disappearance of the name from the tax rolls, which is an excellent method of tracing the migration of a family. The rolls can act as substitutes on the frontiers for the lack of birth records or church records. If a family was documented in the tax lists in a county between 1825 and 1835, any children born between those years were born in that county. Where else could they have been born? If the father owned land on Raccoon Run, he and his wife were certainly on the farm on that watercourse. The tax list is the indirect proof of birthplace and may be the only record denoting the information even if the conclusion is through the preponderance of evidence.

Other minute details include race. Some parts of the country were riddled with mixed-race families, either bi-racial or tri-racial. The censuses before 1850 can reveal them, and so may the tax lists, depending on the state laws. Free color typically means a family was of European-African ancestry or European-Native ancestry or European-African-Native ancestry. Academics know the last as tri-racial isolates, and in places such as the Carolinas, eastern Tennessee, eastern Kentucky, Virginia, and West Virginia, they were quite numerous. In addition, free color can be found in Delaware, Maryland, and New York. The use of race in the records was one way the majority white population restricted the civil rights of all others, maybe as simple as with state laws not allowing free color to own guns during a specific period.

Sometimes, persons of free color owned slaves, as did a class in South Carolina and Louisiana, and needs to be considered; it is reflected in both the censuses

and the tax lists. More likely, the situations were family members purchasing other family members and calling them slaves for the records. Here, reading between the lines is beneficial.

Another subtle detail is the location of persons' names on the tax pages. Most tax lists are not alphabetical by surnames, but, rather, by the first letters of the surnames. All the C's are together, for instance. If one is researching Campbell, and the ancestral Alexander Campbell was taxed and several other Campbells also were listed right before or after Alexander on the page, the assumption can be made with some assurance that they were connected. The conjecture is logical. Because people were busy on the farms, several family members might have climbed onto the back of a wagon to ride to the courthouse to pay their taxes on the same day. Thus, their names

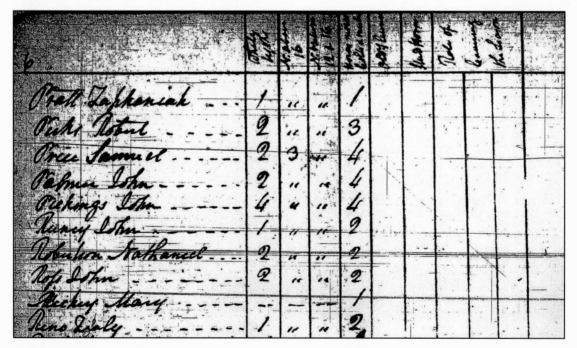

Figure 46: Portion of a poll-tax (or head-tax) page from Kentucky. In Kentucky and Virginia as well as some other southern states, there were often two lists. One for general taxables—the poll-tax—and one for land taxes. It is important to check both. Courtesy of Kentucky Historical Society in Frankfort, Kentucky.

Year 1800	Place: *Christian County, Kentucky* Extracted by: *John P. Doe*					
District	Name	Watercourse	Acres	#Horses	#Slaves	Page
2nd	*Hugh McMurray*	*Little River*	*63.5*	*2*	*None*	*8*

were recorded together on a page of the tax rolls. The strategy does not always work but buttresses the theory when the tax books have the days the people paid the taxes. On the frontiers, the cluster of names may be the only proof of a family relationship, especially if researching a family who never owned land, belonged to a church, or left a will.

Tallying the Findings

To simplify the analysis of the data from tax lists, findings can be plotted on an Excel or Word sheet or a word processing program. Starting with a ten-year period and noting everyone with the surname of interest is wise, and at the end, who is who and where they were living becomes apparent. A simple chart for Kentucky might look something like the image above.

Next, list everyone by the surname. The process works well with common names, such as Smith, McDonald, and Brown, by allowing the researcher to sort through everyone by districts and watercourses. It is a simple form, but it will need to be modified as the tax laws changed and different questions were asked, for instance, the number of white males between such and such an age.

Becoming apparent after about 10 years is that District 1 has a group with familiar names and watercourses. Remember that the watercourses were the substitutes for townships in other parts of the country and must be thought of as the "neighborhoods." From a chart, it is possible to determine who might have moved in and out of the county and who stayed, died, or perhaps applied for some exemption based upon age or occupation.

Using Tax Lists in Eastern States

The examples above, centering on Kentucky, are suggestions for how to successfully trace family associations, identify potential relatives, and track movements through tax lists. They are of great worth on the frontiers since people traveled together for security. An individual was not safe moving westward alone, and so people went in groups that were often composed of relatives and friends from their original places in the eastern parts of the country. The goal of studying tax lists for frontier research is much different than that for eastern states. The objective in frontier research is to move the families back to the East and not necessarily to identify immigrants' origins.

The eastern states were more populated and had no safety worries. The concern was making a living and if doing so by farming, to ensure that enough land was available for crops and livestock. When land was no longer accessible or the soil gave out from erosion or was depleted of nutrients, people went to the frontiers where land was plentiful. In the more settled areas of the East, the research aim is to track movements and family associations and work back to the immigrant ancestors. Occasionally, people were noted in tax lists as being from Ireland. Furthermore, in places such as Virginia, servants were named for a time, and many of them were from Ireland.

The compilation of the New Jersey tax lists is one illustration of how to use eastern states' tax lists. The first complete United States census for New Jersey was 1830, leaving a gap in locating families from 1790 to 1820. The tax lists when compiled for the entire state, as in Ron Vern Jackson's *New Jersey Tax Lists, 1772-1822* (Salt Lake City, Utah: Accelerated Indexing Systems, 1981), solves the issue. It also begins the process of linking people who moved to the frontiers from places such as New Jersey. If a man disappeared from the New Jersey tax lists and reappeared soon after on a frontier in the tax lists of Ohio, some important conclusions can be drawn. The lists also can follow the ancestor's neighbors in Ohio back to the same county or town in New Jersey.

To continue with New Jersey as a model, once it is certain that the correct person has been identified, a research gateway is opened to an assortment of other records for that town and county. The documents can consist of those for churches, lands, and probates.

Below is a short list of some tax compilations from each of the Eastern Seaboard states reflecting the period from the 1780s forward, when people were beginning to move westward onto the frontiers. The collections can provide the links between the frontier areas and the settled eastern states. New England is not among them because it has town vital records to form the connections, and Spanish and French America are not included either:

Delaware
Ralph D. Nelson and Delaware Genealogical Society, *Delaware 1782 Tax Assessment and Census*. Wilmington, Delaware: Delaware Genealogical Society, 1994.

Georgia
Alice Jeffery. *Georgia Tax Index, 1789-1799* [database online]. Provo, Utah: Ancestry.com Operations Inc, 1998.

Ancestry.com. *Georgia, Property Tax Digests, 1793-1892* [database online]. Provo, Utah: Ancestry.com Operations, Inc., 2011.

R. J. Taylor, Jr., Foundation, *An Index to Georgia Tax Digests, 1789-1817*, 5 vols. Spartanburg, South Carolina: Reprint Co. Publishers, 1986.

Maryland
Bettie Carothers, *1783 Tax List of Maryland*. Lutherville, Maryland: [B. Carothers], 1977.

New Jersey
Ron Vern Jackson, *New Jersey Tax Lists, 1772-1822* (Salt Lake City, Utah: Accelerated Indexing Systems, 1981).

Kenn Stryker-Rodda, *Revolutionary Census of New Jersey: an Index, Based on Ratables, of the Inhabitants of New Jersey during the period of the American Revolution*. Cottonport, Louisiana: Polyanthos, 1972.

New York

Ancestry.com. *New York, Tax Assessment Rolls of Real and Personal Estates, 1799-1804* [database online]. Provo, Utah: Ancestry.com Operations, Inc., 2014.

North Carolina

Dorothy Williams Potter, *1820 North Carolina Census: Supplemented with Tax Lists*. Nashville, Tennessee: D. W. Potter, 1974.

Clarence Earl Ratcliff, *North Carolina Taxpayers*, 2 vols. Baltimore, Maryland: Genealogical Publishing Co., 2002. (Note: vol. 1: 1701-1786; vol. 2: 1679-1790.)

Pennsylvania

Ancestry.com. *Pennsylvania, Tax and Exoneration, 1768-1801* [database online]. Provo, Utah: Ancestry.com Operations, Inc., 2011.

Ancestry.com. *Pennsylvania, U.S. Direct Tax Lists, 1798* [database online]. Provo, Utah, Ancestry.com Operations, Inc., 2012.

John and E. Diane Stemmon, *Pennsylvania in 1780: A Statewide Index of Circa 1780 Pennsylvania Taxlists* (Laughlintown, Pennsylvania: Southwest Pennsylvania Genealogical Services, 1978).

South Carolina

Ancestry.com. *South Carolina, Compiled Census and Census Substitutes Index, 1790-1890* [database online]. Provo, Utah: Ancestry.com Operations Inc, 1999.

Daughters of the American Revolution (South Carolina), *South Carolina Name Index to Genealogical Records Collected by South Carolina Daughters of the American Revolution (DAR)*. Salt Lake City, Utah: Filmed by the Genealogical Society of Utah, 1988 (102 microfiche).

Virginia

Augusta B. Fothergill and John Mark Naugle, *Virginia Tax Payers, 1782-87, Other Than Those Published by the United States Census Bureau*. Baltimore, Maryland: Genealogical Publishing Co., 1966, 1971, 1974, 1978.

Netti Schreiner-Yantis and Florene Speakman Love, *The 1787 Census of Virginia*, 3 vols. Springfield, Virginia: Genealogical Books in Print, 1987.

Netti Schreiner-Yantis, *A Supplement to the 1810 Census of Virginia: Tax Lists of the Counties for Which the Census is Missing*. Springfield, Virginia: Genealogical Books in Print, 1971.

Robert F. Woodson and Isobel B. Woodson, *Virginia Tithables from Burned Record Counties: Buckingham, 1772-1774; Gloucester, 170-1771, 1774-1775; Hanover, 1763 and 1770; James City, 1768-1769; Stafford, 1768 and 1773*. Richmond, Virginia: R. F. Woodson, 1970.

BOLTON MARRIAGES. 149

LONGLEY, Robert and Anna Whetcomb, March 17, 1756.*
Robert and Elizabeth Whitman of Stow, May 21, 1797. At Stow.
Sarah and Ephraim Whitcomb, Jan. 14, 1777.*

LORING, Mary of Marlborough and Calvin Nurse, int. Oct. 9,
1808.

LOVEGROVE, James of Batimore [?] and Lydia Pope of Marlborough, Aug. 14, 1812. C.R.2.*

LOW, Jabez B. and Sophia Sawyer, Oct. 6, 1805.

LUN, Jesse and Caty Parker, July 25, 1803.

LYMAN, Charles A. of Lancaster and Sarah Townsend, March 28,
1833.

LYNN, Nancy and Lowell Chatman, both of Sterling, April 27,
1831.*

McBRIDE, Amos and Lucy Burnam, Feb. 21, 1797.
Gardner and Abigail Hastings, Jan. 18, 1796.
Jeames and Lydia Wilson, Dec. 8, 1763.*
John and Phebe Wheelar, Sept. 17, 1776.*
John Jr. and Mrs. Rachel Barrett of Carlisle, int. July 29, 1813.
John and Sally Russell, Dec. 26, 1822.
Nancy and Benjamin Bruce, Dec. —, 1768.*
Obediah McBride to marry Amity Aldrich, Aug. 26, 1812. Cert.
to Uxbridge given.*
Thomas and Sarah Snow, April 19, 1769.*
William and Susanna Bailey, July 20, [1781 ?].*

McELWAIN (see McIlwain), James and Rebekah Whetcomb,
Oct. 10, 1769.*
John and Joanna Burge, Nov. 2, 1769.*
Lydia and Elijah Whetney, Jr., Jan. 25, 1773.*
William and Anna Stone, Nov. 3, 1772.*

McFADDEN, Sarah and George Pines, Feb. 14, 1755.*

McKENNIE [Kenne in int.], James and Sarah Wheeler, Jan. 7,
1822.

McKEVER [McKeever, C.R.1], Mary and Franklin Atherton, int.
May 11, 1845. [Married May 15, C.R.]

McLWAIN (see McElwain), Hezediah and Andrew Haskell
April 18, 1764.*

* Intention not recorded.

Figure 47: Vital Records of Bolton, Massachusetts, to the End of the Year 1849, by Franklin P. Rice, 1910. Town records are an excellent source of vital records for the New England region, and many have been published for Massachusetts. (Public Domain, published before 1922.)

Chapter Thirteen

Vital Records

Vital records are usually considered to be births, marriages, and deaths/burials and are typically categorized as civil ones that are contained in records such as county marriage registers and town or city birth ledgers. Over the years, to reconstruct births, marriages, and deaths, many towns, especially in New England, have merged various types of records into collections, which have been published as vital records to 1850. Since most of the books of compilations are in the public domain of copyright, they are readily available on major websites such as AmericanAncestors.org, Ancestry.com, FamilySearch.org, and others. Codes in the fronts of the volumes identify the sources for the entries. For example, for the town of Bolton, Worcester County, Massachusetts, sources for the book *Vital Records of Bolton, Massachusetts to the End of the Year 1849* (Worcester, Massachusetts: Franklin P. Rice, 1910) are:

C.R.1. - Congregational Church Record
C.R.2. - Quaker Church Record
C.R.3 - Wilder Church Record
G.S.1. - Gravestone, Old Cemetery on Berlin Line
G.S.2. - Gravestone, Quaker Cemetery near Fryville
G.S.3. – Gravestone, Old Cemetery
G.S.4. - Gravestone, Cemetery, Bolton Pan
G.S.5. - Gravestone, Cemetery, east part of Bolton
G.S.6. - Gravestone, West Cemetery
G.S.7. - Gravestone, Eastwood Cemetery
H.P.B. - Houghton Pocket Book, Lancaster Library
Int. - Publishment of Intention of Marriage
P.R. - Private Record

For those not familiar with how New England is governed, many towns are within a county but are not townships or towns as defined in other states. Each town is a geographically surveyed piece of ground that may have one or more villages, communities, or cities within its boundaries. The towns historically kept the records of births, marriages, and deaths, among other types, and the counties maintained books documenting their populations. Therefore, both levels of governance need to be consulted in general research. The towns' compilations are the most essential because the vital records are drawn from throughout their communities.

Newer published vital record compilations, still within copyright, can usually be found in libraries that emphasize New England genealogy, such as the New England Historic Genealogical Society and the Family History Library. The collections may or may not be online as regulated by the copyrights.

Sources for such vital record compilations are from church registers, tombstone transcripts, town vital records, and any number of others, and for generations, the collections have been the core of New England genealogy. In the early days, the government and the Congregational parish of every town were one and the same, and so registers were important.

The Congregational Church was the historic main church in New England, and finding early Catholics in its registers is not rare. Because the surname of interest is in the vital records or Congregational registers does not mean the person was Protestant. Regardless of the denomination, remember that during the period, Catholic priests were scarce in some areas of the country.

Scottish immigrants to New England were in the identical situation as the Catholics. They were attending the Congregational churches with the Scots-Irish. Even when a Presbyterian minister arrived and a separate congregation was formed, both Scots and Ulster-Scots were worshiping together. Verify that the family being researched is Scot-Irish and not Scot. Even if it has the same surname in the same congregation, be mindful about the country of origin when studying the vital record compilations.

The vital records are not as plentiful in other parts of the country. In the American South, a good segment of the

population belonged to churches that did not baptize infants, but, rather, practiced believers' baptisms, and so creating birth or christening records for the memberships was not needed. Literacy and poverty were issues, not to mention the enslavement of a percentage of the population that had Scots-Irish ancestry. The early marriage records for the counties in the South may be sketchy, too, because state laws might not have mandated registrations until specific years. In localities like the Midwest, each frontier area would be visited by a Methodist circuit-riding minister once every few years, and marriages and christenings could have been performed at those times. All the same, everyone in the communities looked upon common-law marriages as legitimate with the ministers only acknowledging them.

Vital records in Scots-Irish research may identify family members, push lineages back in time, separate unrelated families with the same surname, or locate birthplaces in Ulster. The goal is not finding just one of the records, and one general rule cannot apply to their uses.

Using Vital Records to Identify Ulster Origins

The earlier the record, the less likely personal details, such as a birthplace or parents' names, will be on it. One notable exception is a Quaker record substituting as a vital record. Outside of New England, most of what became the United States did not document births and deaths, some states not doing so until the beginning of the twentieth century. Depending on the area, marriage records may or may not be complete, but they can provide good clues and many helpful research strategies. If a county-registered marriage has the name of the minister performing the ceremony, the next task is to find where the minister pastored. Sometimes, this is as easy as an Internet search or looking through an old history book. The "Global Christian Leaders Index" on Findmypast.com may be of assistance. The record from the church may disclose a different version of the marriage than the one the county produced, perhaps listing parents' names and even birthplaces. What it will offer is unpredictable.

The names of the witnesses to a marriage can be informative. They could have been parents, other family members, or friends from Ulster, although entirely unrelated people, on call, sometimes witnessed multiple marriages on a given day. Determining whether they did so is as simple as scanning a few pages of the church marriages for their names appearing continually.

Death records, whether church or civil, can be among some of the most valuable. They may impart personal information, such as birthplaces or parents' names, but carefully evaluate death certificates for the persons who supplied the information. The details were not from the deceased, and the informants were often under the stress of grieving.

When using early compilations, such as the New England town sources cited on the previous page, the entries typically do not have birthplaces in Ireland. Their value is not measured by the places of birth though. If an ancestor's vital record is in a published compilation of registers of a county or town, others with his or her surname listed during the same period are of interest in a generational approach. Everyone with the same surname who was married in that town within, for instance, ten years on either side of when an ancestor married, could have been a sibling or cousin of the ancestor, which is an excellent starting point. The others of the same generation can be researched, and if they are also immigrants, birthplaces in Ulster may be in other registers documenting their lives. Part of the generational approach is to keep in mind that in the same town might have been Scottish immigrants as well as Scots-Irish with the same surname. Make sure to consider the possibility, not just in New England town records but in county marriage registers nationwide, too.

Many databases for vital records are on AmericanAncestors.org, Ancestry.com, FamilySearch.org, Findmypast.com, MyHeritage.com, state archives, and local websites. One of the largest for marriages is "United States Marriages," which currently has over 200 million entries on Findmypast.com. One site to seek information by state and county is USGenWeb.org.

Church Records as Vital Record Compilations

In areas of the country where county vital records, including marriages, are almost non-existent, the church compilations of registers from various denominations, such as those in Pennsylvania, become the main resource for vital records. Quaker records are unrivaled because they contain birthplaces in Ulster or parents' names, as do Moravian records; however, not everyone was Quaker or Moravian. Sometimes, the church records for several denominations are combined into one book. For example, a single published work documenting the population in any given county in Pennsylvania or New Jersey may include a combination of Brethren, Episcopal, Lutheran, Methodists, Presbyterian, Quaker, and Reformed, among others.

Often, German churches are ignored in Scots-Irish research because the family roots were Ulster Presbyterian and not German Reformed or Lutheran. Nevertheless, perhaps reassess where an ancestor went to church or, at the least, was married and had children christened. In some regions of Pennsylvania, the dominant church was the German Reformed, and in parts of New Jersey and New York, it was the Dutch Reformed. The Reformed Church is part of the Calvinist family tree of denominations, and like the Presbyterian, they shared roots, although the language and culture were unfamiliar to the Scots-Irish. The Reformed is a primary church in Pennsylvania, New Jersey, and New York to continue the search for a Scot-Irish family— but still not the only one.

The ethnic composition of a county that was preponderantly German is not an historical fact to be overlooked. The incoming Scots-Irish in Pennsylvania commonly settled, associated, and intermarried with the German families, and thus a Scot-Irish family may be in a Lutheran family. Do not discount church record compilations just because they are German.

Some compilations can offer new idiosyncrasies to the search. For example, in New York City, the Methodist marriages have been indexed in William Scott Fisher's *New York City Methodist Marriages, 1785-1893* (Camden, Maine: Picton Press, 1994). Across the United States, the communities' churches were Methodist. People of all faiths were married in them or had children baptized by Methodist ministers, yet they did not attend the Methodist Churches, which were neutral in the religious turf wars of the time. In New York City, it is not unusual for the records to have Irish Catholics. They were Catholics who, for whatever reason, were not associated with or at least were not married by Catholic priests, perhaps because of marriages to Protestants. As some Gaelic Irish surnames and Scottish surnames can be the same, researching the wrong family would be easy. Make sure the family being researched does not appear again in a Roman Catholic record. The records of the Archdiocese of New York are online at Findmypast.com, completely indexed and with images, and a conclusion can be reached quickly.

In areas of the country, such as the South, compilations of church records may be rare. Congregations, especially rural ones, might not have had records. If they did, sometimes they are partial or have not withstood the damages of time. The literacy of a percentage of the population was an issue as well.

When churches kept only church minutes or practiced believers' baptisms, the membership records can be the vital records because membership registers documented people and their activities. Even if the information is basic, at least membership records verify a person's presence at a specific period. The next question is who the others were on that membership record. Were the like-minded persons with whom the ancestors associated the in-laws, relatives, or close friends? The answer may be the first step toward pushing the lineage back in time because a group of congregants might have come together from Ulster and settled together, founding the congregation. Discovering their emigration moves research one step closer to addressing Ulster origins.

Using a membership record as a substitute for a vital record is easier than it seems it could be at first glance because the congregations were not megachurches, as found today with thousands upon thousands of members. Small one-

room buildings had approximately 100 to 150 people in each, which was the average size of most countryside congregations. Such congregations still dot the landscapes across rural America.

422	NEW YORK CITY METHODIST MARRIAGES 1785-1893		
McFarland, Daniel	Fitzgerald, Mary Ann	15 Nov 1840	41/385
McFarland, Ephraim W.	Smith, Emma S.	16 June 1845	41/395
McFarland, John	Wallace, Agnes	9 Oct 1837	41/377
McFarland, Joseph	Garrettson, Elizabeth	1 Nov 1810	6/352
McFarland, Robert	Colvill, Jennett	11 Oct 1838	41/380
McFarland, Robᵗ Russell	McKelvey, Elizabeth Jane	19 Oct 1888	26/140
McFarland, Robt. A.	Stewart, Mary E.	21 Aug 1865	11/031
McFarlane, ----	Randle, Frances	15 June 1828	9/500
McFarlane, Fredrick B.	Lynch, Jenny	13 July 1862	29/076
McFarlane, James S. (M.D.)	Norman, Eliza	5 Apr 1821	9/494
McFarlin, Frederic	Cricy, Ann	2 June 1825	9/495
McFarlin, Frederick	Cricy, Ann	2 June 1825	41/359
McFarling, Wright	Drake, Mary	20 Jan 1805	6/335
McFarquhar, John	Rush, Harriet	8 May 1856	40/254
McFarran, John	Troughton, Rebecca	25 Oct 1843	36/135
McFarren, James	Elsworth, Mary	27 Feb 1848	2/159
McFaul, James Blair	Webbers, Mary	10 Dec 1808	6/344
McFee, Daniel	Duyer, Mary C.	5 May 1825	1/011
McFee, William	Holt, Eleanor	27 Apr 1836	2/085
McFerran, Robert	Murphy, Jane	9 Aug 1862	39/105
McGarah, Jacob M.	Rhoades, Mary A.	25 Sep 1862	12/108
McGarr, Andrew	McClellen, Elizabeth	17 March 1853	41/421
McGarrigheal, Archibald	Cochran, Mary Ann	6 Jan 1834	41/367
McGarry, James	Dickinson, Elizabeth	12 March 1837	41/375
McGarvey, Danˡ	De Starr, Elizabeth Ann	10 Oct 1852	23/330
McGary, James	Hayes, Ann	23 Nov 1852	39/100
McGary, Robert	Thompson, Mary Ann	15 Jan 1846	18/156
McGav, Henry H.	Laurence, Ella	20 July 1865	39/108
McGee, Abraham	Gilbert, Mary Ann	4 Oct 1852	41/419
McGee, Ephraim	Delany, Esther	5 Oct 1828	9/499
McGee, James	Merklee, Elizabeth A.	31 Jan 1850	18/165
McGee, James	Finnegan, Ann	10 Jan 1853	41/420
McGee, John	Woodrow, Rebecca	?5 Jan 1795	6/324
McGee, John	Jones, Lidia	18 Apr 1829	9/500
McGee, Robert	Colburn, Hannah	23 Nov 1836	40/247
McGee, Robert	Way, Mary F.	1 Jan 1866	30/140
McGee, Temonie	Servis, Anna	2 Feb 1856	31/229
McGerald, James	Dakin, Harriet	16 Nov 1870	15/330
McGerald, John	Gildersleeve, Kate	24 March 1862	39/105
McGheen, James	Hazleton, Alice	14 Sep 1859	39/104
McGiff, John	Kelly, Bridget	9 June 1845	2/142
McGill, Daniel	Somers, Elizabeth B.	22 May 1865	38/289
McGill, Edward	Kennedy, Mary	1 March 1863	40/256
McGill, Jno.	Snodgrass, Agnes	1 March 1863	40/256
McGill, John	Etzberger (or Ertzberger), Rachel	13 March 1826	9/496
McGill, John	Etzberger, Rachel	13 March 1826	41/360
McGill, John W.	Holston, Elisabeth	16 May 1838	10/628
McGill, Richard	Hughes, Harriet	19 July 1852	21/246
McGill, Wm.	McKann, Elizᵗʰ	28 Apr 1848	31/224
McGinnis, Edwᵈ	Sink, Mary Ann	10 June 1847	27/171
McGinnis, George	Lisbon, Sophia	24 Apr 1861	3/170
McGiven, James	Allen, Hannah	14 Oct 1850	40/253
McGiven, Patrick	Hannas, Louisa	13 June 1839	10/628
McGivney, John	Hoyt, Julia	5 July 1825	9/495
McGivney, John	Hoyt, Julia	5 July 1825	41/359
McGlaughan, William	Williams, Jane	26 Nov 1851	23/329

Figure 48: Page from William Scott Fisher's New York City Methodist Marriages. (Used with written permission from author.)

The Cemetery as a Vital Record

Ordinarily, Scots-Irish immigrant tombstones do not bear inscriptions of birthplaces. The custom of doing so tended to be more Irish Catholic. Research should not be narrowed because of their absences. For example, a person who was buried in an Episcopal churchyard and who might have attended that denomination could have been Scot-Irish or from Ulster. The person may not have had a Scottish surname but nevertheless descended from Ulster-Scots. In places, such as Virginia, where the Episcopal Church was the historic colonial faith, the church cemeteries might have been the communities' cemeteries. Scots-Irish may be found in the church registers or interred in the cemeteries. In Ulster were intermarriages between Anglicans and Presbyterians, and so an immigrant might have arrived as either. Staunton Moore's *The Annals and History of Henrico Parish, Diocese of Virginia, and St. John's P.E. Church* (Richmond, Virginia: Williams Print. Co., 1904), pp. 413-529 shows the following tombstones:

In Memory of John Ballentine, a native of Antrim, Ireland who died Aug. 1st, 1838 aged 28 years

Mary, relict of Florence Downey, born at Moville, County Donegal, Ireland, Aug. -----

In Memory of Mr. Samuel Henry, of Ura County, Antrim, Ireland who died the 6th April 1819, aged 48 years.

In Memory of John Henderson, who was born near Money More County, Derry, Ireland. Aged 36 years. Departed this life 5th April 1817.

In Memory of James Kennedy, a native of the county of Downs, Ireland, who departed this life August 11th, 1823, aged 37 years.

In memory of Daniel McDermott, who died Oct. 6, 1814, a native of Ireland, County of Dusmegal, and parish of Fahan. (Note: The county is Donegal.)

In Memory of Daniel McFall, who died Nov. 5th, 1837, in the 56th year of his age, a native of Londonderry, Ireland, and for 24 years a resident of Richmond, Va.

Sacred to the memory of Isabella Neilson a native of the county of Donegal, Ireland who died January 29th, 1825, aged 39 years.

In memory of John Purse, a native of County Down, Ireland, who departed this life the 1st Jany, 1814, aged 42 years.

Here repose the mortal remains of Robert Sloan, a native of the Parish of Connor in the county of Antrim and a member of the Connor Lodge No. 832. He departed this life Dec. 10th, 1816, aged 35 years.

Sacred to the memory of Isabella Tuson, a native of the county of Donegal, Ireland, who died Jan. 29, 1825, age 39 years.

In studying the above cemetery inscriptions as a whole, some patterns can be discerned. For example, not all tombstones are marked with birthplaces, and on the ones that are, not all are Ulster counties. They are for a wider diversity of people from Ireland than only Scots-Irish, which is unsurprising in a major hub of commerce like Richmond. Not every tombstone has a county in Ireland, listing just Ireland. For the people who had enough money for substantial, engraved tombstones, the inscriptions may be the only records for documenting their birthplaces. Again, in a city such as Richmond, the class of people who had them is expected. A couple of features are noteworthy. Of the tombstones listing Ulster locales, all were between 1814 and 1838, which may reflect an emphasis of the period or perhaps the engraving design of the tombstone company. The explanation may never be known. Perhaps most interesting is that the concentration of this selection of tombstones is:

- 3 from Antrim
- 4 from Donegal
- 2 from Down
- 2 from Londonderry

If the subject of the search is Daniel McFall from Londonderry (Derry), of interest is John Henderson of Moneymore, County Londonderry. A valid question is whether the McFall family was also from Moneymore, or whether two families from the county happened to immigrate to Richmond? More Henrico County and Richmond investigations are in order. Additionally, a surname distribution search of the indexes of Irish records, such as the tax lists, for the surnames of McFall and Henderson in the Moneymore area is encouraged.

If the subject of the pursuit is Daniel McDermott from Fahan, County Donegal, who died on 6 October 1814, a research strategy has to be taken a step further. The other three Donegal tombstones were for married women, and unless research indicates otherwise, their husbands might not have been from County Donegal or even Irish-born. The maiden names have to be found so that research could proceed to determine whether they were from Fahan, County Donegal, or a neighboring parish. If any of their birth names were McDermott, the first assumption is that they were related to the Daniel McDermott in question.

In both cases, although the places of origin in Ireland have been identified from the tombstones, researching the others from that county is still reasonable. Foremost, discovering the locations in Ireland may not be enough to document the families in those parishes. Church registers tend to have begun late in Ireland or they have been destroyed. The main collections of wills were destroyed, too. Although some abstracts or second copies survive, they may not be for the upper-class people in Ireland whose pedigrees were registered at the Genealogical Office in Dublin. Neither may they be for the lease-holding class in Ireland that did not have documents in the Registry of Deeds in Dublin. Therefore, knowing the place within the county may not be adequate, but it is an excellent start to Irish research. By finishing reconstructing the family in Richmond, the answers being sought in Ulster may be found in Richmond. At that stage, the status of records and records' survival in Ireland becomes less crucial.

ST. JOHN'S CHURCH.   511

Here
repose the mortal remains of
ROBERT SLOAN,
a native of the Parrish of Connor
in the county of Antrim,
and a member of the Connor Lodge No. 832,
Ireland.*
He departed this life Dec. 10th, 1816,
aged 35 years.
Erected by M. Crawford.

Sacred
to the memory of
MARTHA STREET,
of the Borough of Norfolk,
who died the 7th day of August, 1813,
on her passage to Richmond,
aged 56 years.

SARAH TAYLOR,
February 14th, 1791.

In memory of
ELIZABETH TAYLOR,
daughter of Jno. and
Sarah Taylor, born
4th May, 1794, died 13th
Aug., 1796, aged 2 years
and 3 months.

MARY FRANCES TAYLOR,
born Oct. 10, 1845,
died June 27, 1847.
Buried in the same grave.
GEORGE EDWARD TAYLOR,
born Dec. 3, 1849,
died Jan. 29, 1855.

*It will be observed that "Scotia" and "Erin" furnished many
citizens of early Richmond—the Scotch being especially prominent
and enterprising as merchants, and later as millers, the hardy
representative of whom it has been urged that he might find existence and thrive on a "bare rock," was ubiquitous in Virginia from
early Colonial days.

Figure 49: From The Annals and History of Henrico Parish, Diocese of Virginia, and St.
John's P.E. Church, conveying the depth of vital record information that can be found
on tombstones. (Public Domain, published before 1922.)

It must be stated that because someone was buried at St. John's Episcopal Cemetery, the person might or might not have been a member of St. John's Episcopal Church. Exploring the Ulster immigrants interred in the cemetery is a beginning.

An assumption is upper-class Protestants in Richmond would have been associated with other upper-class Protestants in St. John's Parish. In the rural regions of the country, farmers would have been involved with farmers, and the church buildings themselves possibly were close to the farms. Upper-class plantation owners in rural areas, though, might have been part of prominent Episcopal, Methodist, or Baptist congregations, usually located within towns. Besides the miscellaneous details for merchants and business classes, apply the same research strategies as those employed for St. John's Episcopal in Richmond.

When evaluating tombstones and cemetery transcripts, some important clues may be:

- Because a family was buried in a graveyard attached to a Methodist church does not mean the family was Methodist. A graveyard might have been for the community. On the other hand, the family could have been in the congregation. In many parts of the United States, the Methodist was the "community church." Whether a person physically attended is another issue.

- The information on the tombstones may be the vital records in parts of the country where few sources exist. It is safe to say, as an example, that especially before embalming was routine, a person died within a short geographical distance of the cemetery in which he or she was buried. In essence, the marker is a death certificate and proof of where someone died. Everyone, to some degree, buried in that cemetery was part of that geographical community.

- Who are the others with the surname in question interred in the cemetery? They may have been relatives and are worth investigating. The same could be said for those whose graves lie physically close to the ancestor's regardless of the surname. Were they in-laws, cousins, or friends from Ulster? The questions definitely are worth further research.

- Are burial records kept by the cemetery? In rural areas, they likely were not until the late nineteenth or early twentieth century. In urban areas, the records may be old. Do the cemetery books provide additional information? If the people were buried beside a church, were the church burial registers the cemetery records? Do they have more information? Are early urban city death records also the burial records for the cemetery? All are logical deliberations and need to be pursued.

- An excellent clue is a large number of Scots-Irish burials in a cemetery. If the area was predominantly Scots-Irish in origin, did the interconnecting families know one another either in Ulster or before moving to the area where the cemetery is?

It is not uncommon that all the tombstones within a county have been transcribed and indexed, which is a research tool for discovering other people in the county. In some parts of the country, though, most people historically did not have tombstones. It is not exceptional in regions such as the South for tombstones to be no more than simple limestone or sandstone rocks without inscriptions. Work with what is available, especially in a county with little or no church or vital records. With access to all cemeteries in a county, the research strategies for one cemetery can be adapted for others in the entire county.

Be aware that although tombstone and cemetery indexes on websites, such as Findagrave.com, Billiongraves.com, and others, are amazing research tools, they do not always convey the whole report. They are on the databases only if someone adds them. Consequently, the issue is always whether the listings for cemeteries are complete. Some have all-inclusive listings while others do not. Unless it can be confirmed, do not assume the register for a cemetery is comprehensive. In addition, on websites such as Findagrave.com, submitters add genealogical information, which can be accurate or totally erroneous.

Obituaries as a Vital Record

Although an obituary is a newspaper related article, it can divulge needed information in the same way a birth, marriage, and death certificate will—and it may supply more. Obituaries are especially helpful for pioneers or their children. They often preserve birthplaces of the Irish immigrants, even if the obituary is for a child of an immigrant. The purpose of obituaries for pioneers or prominent citizens of communities is to describe the persons and their struggles to obtain their positions in their areas.

As the founders of communities, organizations, and churches, the Scots-Irish left behind a proud legacy that cannot be refuted. Their celebrity extended into the political and religious realms. In decades past, a mythos in the United States developed about them that at times reached epic proportions. Images ranged from the noble, Indian-fighter trailblazer wearing a coonskin hat to the musket-toting defender of liberty, justice, and all things God-given. According to the legends, whether stated or insinuated, all that is good in America is because of the Scots-Irish, all that is admirable in American values is because of the Scots-Irish, and all that is divinely ordained in America is because of the Scots-Irish.

The notions are not heard as much at present as they were in the past. By today's standards, such opinions seem overly simplistic and naïve. However, they can be assets to the family historian because they created paper trails safeguarding relevant memories, as represented by obituaries. For many communities, the Scots-Irish were deemed the movers and shakers even though the viewpoint might not have been any more realistic than it could have been for any other ethnic group. Nonetheless, perhaps the period mind-set does not matter if it provided birthplaces in Ulster. Like all family lore, it protected some significant truths.

Ulster

Chapter Fourteen

Special Strategy: Using Ulster Records

Researchers customarily begin their quests for the birthplaces of their immigrant ancestors in the Ulster records, and under certain circumstances, they have positive results. However, the reality is that the records become scarcer in Ireland as the search progresses further back in time. One, but not the only, reason for their absence is that in 1922, during the Irish Civil War, the Public Record Office in Dublin was burned. Many primary records such as marriage bonds, pre-1858 wills (some second copies and some abstracts survived), the 1841 and 1851 Irish censuses (a few abstracts survived), and half the Church of Ireland registers were turned into ashes. Because most immigrant Scots-Irish in the pre-1858 period did not come from families of means, the loss of the wills was not

devastating for them. The destruction of half the Church of Ireland registers did affect Scots-Irish because so many were either intermarried with Anglicans or their baptisms, marriages, and burials were documented in the registers. As the state religion, the Church of Ireland was a central denomination even for non-conformists such as Presbyterians. The missing censuses affect the search for the Ulster-Scots who stayed. The eradication of records is complicated by the fact that most Presbyterian registers did not begin until the 1820s and 1830s.

Typically, church registers are the first sources people want to pursue, but for the 1600s and 1700s, ones from which to document early ancestors are rare. For the 1800s, locating them is possible, and they are coming online at RootsIreland.ie and on the databases of the Ulster Historical Foundation's website, AncestryIreland.com.

People leaving Ireland did so for reasons. The Scots-Irish migrating in the 1700s were not necessarily the poorest of the poor. They had at least enough money to contract passages on ships and depart in droves. Periodic famine, economic downturns, drops in crop prices, and landlords' rent increases were among the main motivations for emigrating. Immigration to the United States in the 1800s might have been for other purposes because the public institutions for the poor during the Irish Potato Famine (1845-1851) had their share of destitute Protestants, just as they did of Catholics. While the Potato Famine ravaged the west and south of Ireland, it was also felt in Ulster, although not as severely.

The assertion can be made that the average Ulster-Scot immigrant to America, especially from the 1700s, was never named in an Irish record. The statement does not purport that a place in Ulster cannot be identified but simply that the chance of finding a record in the 1700s in Ireland is improbable because of the incomplete collection of records for eighteenth-century Ireland. The research will always remain a United States puzzle, but solving it is not impossible.

The current chapter offers sources that if strategically explored after enough information is gathered in the U.S., increase the likelihood of identifying a place of origin in Ulster. Not all sources are treated, only those that are deemed the most effective in this type of research.

For a more complete initiation to Irish sources, the reference books and websites presented below are excellent, but remember that books written by authors living in Ireland or Northern Ireland are not meant to solve immigration problems. Relocation is outside their scopes. Their intentions are to educate when the efforts have advanced to studying Irish records. Some of the books are dated or out of print, but since the sources and their history are the same, a dated book remains useful. Where records are located and how to access them changes. For example, many sources, such as the Irish Registry of Deeds, have been on microfilm through the Family History Library for decades. They are now digitized and can be viewed from home on the FamilySearch.org website. Also, many Protestant church registers are now indexed on RootsIreland.ie.

The distinguished Irish genealogy reference books and websites are as follows, with two that are noteworthy for Ulster research. The first is William J. Roulston's *Researching Scots-Irish Ancestors: The Essential Genealogical Guide to Early Modern Ulster, 1600-1800,* and the second is AncestryIreland.com, the website of the Ulster Historical Foundation in Belfast. Both are essential tools for maneuvering through Ulster records.

Reference Books

Blatchford, Robert and Elizabeth Blatchford. *The Irish Family and Local History Handbook*. Poppleton, UK: Robert Blatchford Pub., 2012.

Begley, Donald F. *Irish Genealogy: A Record Finder*. Dublin, Ireland: Heraldic Artists, Ltd., 1981.

Daly, Marie E. and Judith Lucey. *Genealogist's Handbook for Irish Research*. Boston, Massachusetts: New England Historic Genealogical Society, 2016.

Falley, Margaret Dickson. *Irish and Scotch-Irish Ancestral Research: A Guide to the Genealogical Records, Methods and Sources in Ireland*. 1962. 2 vols. Baltimore, Maryland: Genealogical Co., 1998, 1988.

Grenham, John. *Tracing Your Irish Ancestors*. Dublin, Ireland: Gill Books, 2019.

Maxwell, Ian. *Tracing Your Ancestors in Northern Ireland: A Guide to Ancestry Research in the Public Record Office of Northern Ireland*. Edinburgh: The Stationery Office, 1997.

Ouimette, David S., *Finding Your Irish Ancestors: A Beginner's Guide*. Provo, Utah: Ancestry, 2005.

Paton, Chris. *Tracing Your Irish Family History on the Internet: A Guide for Family Historians*. Barnsley, South Yorkshire, UK: Pen and Sword Family History, 2013.

Radford, Dwight A. and Kyle J. Betit. *A Genealogist's Guide to Discovering Your Irish Ancestors: How to Find and Record Your Unique Heritage*. Cincinnati, Ohio: Betterway Books, 2001.

Roulston, William J. *Researching Scots-Irish Ancestors: The Essential Genealogical Guide to Early Modern Ulster, 1600-1800*. Belfast, Northern Ireland: Ulster Historical Foundation, 2018.

Websites

Ancestry.com quickly is emerging as a significant holder of databases for Ireland. For Ulster-Irish research, the Tithe Applotment, Griffith's Valuation, Grand Lodge of Ireland membership records, and published books, Ancestry.com is essential.

AncestryIreland.com is the website of the Ulster Historical Foundation, a non-profit organization in Belfast that focuses on the historic province of Ulster. It has many databases, and its church records' indexing is on RootsIreland.ie. Many of its online databases are open to members.

Askaboutireland.ie has scanned images of Griffith's Primary Valuation and the maps that accompany them.

FamilySearch.org is the website of the Family History Library in Salt Lake City and hosts its library catalog. It has numerous and varied Irish databases. Because FamilySearch is currently digitizing its collections of microfilm, searching them from anywhere for free is now possible.

Findmypast.com has many Irish record collections. Major ones for Ulster-Scots research include Landed Estate Court Rentals, 1850-1885; Irish Quaker records; prison records; petty court sessions; migration records; and Griffith's Primary Valuation.

GENUKI.org.uk is UK+Ireland and has regional sections on England, Ireland, Scotland, Wales, Channel Islands, and Isle of Man. Each county in Ireland and Northern Ireland has links associated with it, and the links are updated periodically on the website.

JohnGrenham.com is the website "Irish Ancestors," which is maintained by Irish genealogist John Grenham. He has extensive reference material for Irish genealogy that includes featured periodicals with free articles. The "Browse" section has an overview of some of the records relevant to Irish family history research. It is useful for civil parish maps and for surname distribution studies.

Irishgenealogy.ie is an Irish government website. For later Ulster-Scots research, the civil registration indexes and the digital images of births, marriages, and deaths are online for free.

Logainm.ie is the "Placenames Database of Ireland" hosted by the government of Ireland. It covers the historic province of Ulster. Official place names are in the database as well as minor place names within the official townlands.

NationalArchives.ie (NAI) is the website of the National Archives of Ireland in Dublin. It has the Tithe Applotment index with scanned images and surviving portions of censuses, such as the one for Londonderry (Derry) for 1831.

NLI.ie is the website of the National Library of Ireland in Dublin. The research guides to its collections are excellent for finding sources such as the estate records of the landlords. The NLI catalog allows an expanded search for the inclusion of other repositories.

PRONI – Indirect.gov/uk/proni - (Public Record Office of Northern Ireland) is a free database. The "Name Search" and databases such as the "Freeholders' Records" are excellent research aids for Ulster-Scots. PRONI hosts the digital images for the revision books taken after Griffith's Primary Valuation that documents lands within each townland. The PRONI "Online Guides," such as "Guide to Church Records" and "Introductions to Significant Privately Deposited Archives," are especially beneficial.

Surname Distribution Survey

The surname distribution strategy is effective for researching immigrants from the 1700s and into the 1800s. Given the theory that not all family members emigrated, the assumption is reasonable that some family members remained close to the ancestral property, and if not on the property itself, perhaps in the parish or a neighboring parish. If surnames are uncommon or several people with the surname are known to have been in the same area, the tax lists can determine where surnames are distributed so that they can be documented in Ulster. This can be done even if the ancestors immigrated a century before.

If a couple married in Ulster and the woman's birth surname is known, a surname distribution search can be successful because working with two surnames doubles the possibility of identifying where the couple lived. The theory is that a man and woman meeting and courting before they married placed them in the same geographical area, perhaps if not in the same civil parish, then in neighboring ones. The exception would have been a couple meeting at a market town on market day. If so, some distance could have been between them since the market town drew from a large region. However, the market town is the clue and should not be ignored. From where did the market town bring in buyers and sellers?

The same strategy is productive for a group of names. If United States research has determined a group of people from Ulster settled in the same area in America, look at all the surnames for a pattern of residence emerging in a particular county, part of a county, or a civil parish in Ulster. The idea is that they all knew one another or knew someone who knew the ancestors, which is why they emigrated together and settled in the same locale in the United States.

Although almost any type of record regardless of date can be used for the surname approach, the breadth of the record has to be considered. For example, if using the index to the Grand Lodge of Ireland Masonic records on Ancestry.com, realize who belonged to a Masonic lodge. The members had enough money to pay dues, which automatically discounts a class of people and narrows the search considerably. Also, keep in mind that the men in the Grand Lodge of Ireland were Protestant and Catholic until at least the 1830s, when a Papal Bull was issued prohibiting lodge membership. Afterward, the organization became mostly Protestant, and so make sure a name found in the index is Protestant in Ulster and not Catholic.

Protestant church record indexes can also reveal in what geographical areas surnames are found. The average Methodist and Presbyterian registers in Ulster began in the 1820s and 1830s. The half of the Church of Ireland parish registers that survived typically began in the late 1700s or early 1800s. Indexes to a wide variety of Protestant church registers can be found on RootsIreland.ie. Although the RootsIreland.ie indexes do not currently encompass all congregations in every denomination, they have ranges broad enough to facilitate a surname distribution search.

Although starting later, the Civil Registration of births and marriages can also assist in determining where surnames are found geographically. The Civil Registration of Protestant marriages began in 1845, and in theory, of all births and deaths in 1864. Registrations of marriages are typically good in Ireland, but many people tended not to comply with registering births and deaths for several decades after 1864. While problematic, enough were registered so that a surname survey can be done with the indexes to these valuable records. Complete or partial collections of them can be found on several websites, such as FamilySearch.org and RootsIreland.ie. The most complete one is on IrishGenealogy.ie, which has the digital images as well. The FamilySearch index is easier to use, but it covers only what is in its collections.

Probably the best sources for a surname distribution in Irish research are the two tax lists that function as census substitutes or no less than census alternatives: the Tithe Applotment (1823-1837) and Griffith's Primary Valuation (1847-1864). That the ancestors had been gone for over one hundred years does not matter. If families stayed, the tax lists can provide the first clues to origins. The strategy works especially well if the concentrations of the surname or surnames being sought are found in a few parishes or in one county.

Within the civil parishes are townlands, surveyed parcels of land from the 1830s that historically were the addresses of most rural residents. Today, in Northern Ireland, they are historical only as street addresses replace them. In rural Republic of Ireland, they can still be people's addresses. Townlands can range from under one hundred acres to several thousand, and historically, 64,000 of them were surveyed and named throughout Ireland. In sources such as the tax records, not only are the civil parishes designated but also the townlands of residences. Both will assist in restricting where surnames are found.

When using any source in a surname distribution search, it is helpful to have a civil parish map at hand. A civil parish is a government parish and in theory, is the same as the local parish of the Church of Ireland, the established Protestant church until 1871. However, as with most Irish matters, it is more complex. Large numbers of Church of Ireland parishes are in Ulster, and a civil parish may have more than one within its boundaries. The two do not correlate, and a civil parish is a government parish. There are no Presbyterian parishes, as in Scotland, but like all other denominations, only congregations within the civil parish.

Civil parish maps can be found online in several places. One website is JohnGrenham.com. They are also published in the standard genealogy reference work by Brian Mitchell, *A New Genealogical Atlas of Ireland*, 2nd ed. (Baltimore, Maryland: Genealogical Publishing Co., 2002). With a civil parish map, sources, such as the Tithe Applotment and Griffith's Primary Valuation, for where surnames were distributed can be tallied in a simple form or spreadsheet as shown below.

If several sources are being used, codes can be assigned to them, for example:

Tithe Applotment (TA), Griffith's Primary Valuation (GPV), Grand Lodge of Ireland (GLI), or Freeholders Lists (FH); however, restrict the list to documented sources and not to compiled family histories or online pedigrees, which are habitually not proven.

In the surname distribution search, realize that the Tithe Applotment was a rural taxation and named only those who paid the taxes. Therefore, if one person collected money from the neighbors, only the person paying was listed. Griffith's is a more complete list of heads of households with owners, lessors, sub-lessors, renters, sub-renters, and even squatters. It did not include people in company housing, such as miners or workers for landlords at the estate houses. Therefore, Griffith's Valuation is favored in a surname distribution search.

Once the statistics are gathered from the study, some conclusions can be drawn. The more surnames one has to work with, the better. Even more advantageous is an uncommon surname or given name. If a rather odd given name is passed down in the family in the United States, look for a distant cousin with that same one in Ulster. This is beneficial, especially if the given name matches the same general area as the surnames being tallied.

Year	Extracted by:				
Surname A	Surname B	County	Civil Parish	Townland	Source

The Census Alternative

A "census substitute," also called "census alternative," is a recreated enumeration that documents a segment of the population. The first complete census for Ireland was in 1901. As the result of the destruction of records or the general lack of registers, almost any source can fill in gaps, for instance, those for religion, education, voting, occupation, military, and membership to organizations. Some of the compilations are well known in Irish research, but others have yet to be created. For the 1700s, they are essential for the Ulster-Scots. Most of the Irish genealogical reference books have a general list of what the authors consider viable census substitutes. The lists do differ among books and also vary in their usefulness depending on the population being included and how, or even if, a particular census alternative applies to the research problem at hand. The website AncestryIreland.com has a diverse collection of all types of census substitutes listed on its website.

One example of a viable census alternative and how to expand upon it is that for the linen trade, which naturally encompassed Ulster. The tougher the research problem, the more creative a strategy needs to be to utilize often random and odd sources, such as the one for the linen trade. Consider, though, whether the ancestors were in the linen industry or whether linen-related sources are for a surname distribution survey purpose only.

To begin with, in 1986, when the "1796 Spinning Wheel Premium Lists" first appeared in a 12-microfiche set as *Surname*

index for the 1796 spinning wheel premium entitlement lists of Ireland (Vienna, Virginia: All-Ireland Heritage, 1986), family historians were exuberant. Yet, even today, it remains a strange source, although it is important enough that it has been made into its own database, "Irish Flax Growers List, 1796" on Ancestry.com. The source was not new. It had been printed originally in a book, but the new index made the 56,018 names readily available and easy to search. A perfect occupational census for 1796, especially in flax growing counties of Ulster, was created, and more in-depth surname distribution searches could be conducted because civil parishes could be attached to particular surnames during a period when few churches had records. The reason the source was generated was because the government was trying to reintroduce the linen industry back into the homes, even furnishing spinning wheels to applicants. The 1796 source can be used and compared to the Tithe Applotment (1823-1837) and Griffith's Primary Valuation (1847-1864) in a surname distribution search. It can be of value even if ancestors were gone from Ulster for over a century.

While the 1796 list is the next logical source before the Tithe Applotment years in Ulster, some sources predate 1796. An early book is Thomas Greer's *Market Book for Crown Linen*. Thomas Greer was a resident of Dungannon, County Tyrone, and in 1758-1759, he kept an account book of the linen he bought at various markets and the people from whom he purchased it. He did not record the residences of the sellers, but their names and the market towns were listed. A reasonable assumption is that the sellers lived in the surrounding areas and brought their linen to the market towns. Thomas Greer made 1,061 purchases and assigned a number to each lot (e.g., 1 through 1,061). When he bought more than one lot of linen from the same seller a "do [ditto]" is placed under the name. About 700 individual names are within the 1,061 entries. His account book was digitized by FamilySearch and is under the title "Transcripts Collection of Genealogies, Leases, Bonds, Etc." The PRONI reference is T1127. Otherwise, the digitized version is almost impossible to find. Greer's book as a census substitute, arranged by market town, civil parish, and Account Book purchase number, is an easier reference to the manuscript book:

- Armagh, Armagh Parish, County Armagh: #88-112, 539-554, 800-811
- Caledon, Aghaloo Parish, County Tyrone: #323-335, 572-598, 716-745, 930-957
- Coagh, Tamlaght Parish, County Tyrone: #381-387
- Dungannon, Drumglass Parish, County Tyrone: #1-87, 113-138, 150-183, 202-234, 240-265, 277-

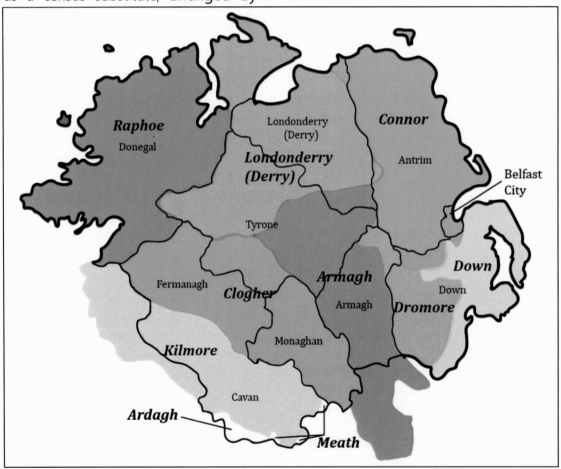

Figure 50: Approximate Church of Ireland Diocese boundaries in Ulster. (Note that most blend across county borders and even the Ulster Province boundaries.)

297, 315-322, 355-361, 375-380, 404-413, 432-443, 458-502, 526-538, 555-574, 599-607, 641-674, 715, 754-770, 822-885, 913-929, 958-979, 1010-1061

- Monaghan, Monaghan Parish, County Monaghan: #771-799, 886-912, 980-1009
- Moneymore, Artrea and Desertlyn parishes, County Londonderry: #139-149, 298-314, 414-431, 608-640, 746-753
- Stewartstown, Donaghenry Parish, County Tyrone: #184-201, 235-239, 266-276, 336-354, 362-374, 388-403, 444-457, 503-525, 675-714, 812-821

What is revealed is that Thomas Greer's main purchases were from County Tyrone markets. The civil parish of the market town provides the center from which to expand further. To extract and index the names with their associated markets creates an unproblematic and workable census alternative for these areas of Ulster, especially for County Tyrone. Other Ulster linen merchants have surviving account books deposited at the Public Record Office of Northern Ireland.

Marriage License Bonds

Before 1845, anyone wishing to obtain a marriage license was required to place a bond with the bishop of the diocese. The original licenses and bonds do not survive, but the indexes for most Diocesan Courts do. The bonds for the Prerogative Court covered all of Ireland.

People listed in the bonds usually had some funds so that they could bypass the banns system, wherein every intended marriage was announced in a couple's church over several weeks. In general, they were moneyed Protestants; however, subject to the cost of the bonds, other classes of Protestants might have been included. Even though the bonds' lists are not complete for all Protestant marriages, they nevertheless are worth studying for clues, even if only for surname distributions.

The Marriage Bonds Indexes are straightforward. They are divided by diocese and have the names of the grooms and the brides along with the years. Church of Ireland dioceses' boundaries frequently crossed counties' boundaries, and so do not confine a search to a county even if it is thought to be known ahead of time.

Diocesan Court Jurisdictions for Accessing Indexes of Marriage Bonds

County	Diocesan Courts
Antrim	Connor, Derry, Down, Dromore
Armagh	Armagh, Dromore
Cavan	Ardagh, Kilmore, Meath
Donegal	Clogher, Derry, Raphoe
Down	Connor, Down, Dromore, (Newry & Mourne as independent jurisdictions)
Fermanagh	Clogher, Kilmore
Londonderry (Derry)	Armagh, Connor, Derry
Monaghan	Clogher
Tyrone	Armagh, Clogher, Derry

To use the indexes, knowing which diocese covered which counties or parts of counties in Ulster is necessary. They are found in the box on the previous page.

Some indexes have missing years, and a few do not survive at all. The indexes are alphabetical with both grooms and brides with the same surnames listed together. Also, the entries have the brides, the grooms, and the dates. Other than a few notations, which may be necessary, they are typically basic. They are indexed on the National Archives of Ireland website as well as on FamilySearch.org and Findmypast.com (see box above).

If an entry or surname of interest is found, the wife's birth name can further narrow a geographical search. The assumption, although not necessarily a rule, is that the bride and groom were from the same county. Tax lists can determine where both names occur. Be careful with this strategy, though, because wealthier families often had multiple houses and land holdings and, therefore, might have changed residences on

a regular basis or met their spouses from families residing away from their traditional homes. In other words, do not expect that both parties were from the same county. If they were not, the Prerogative Court of Armagh might have documented the marriage instead of the diocesan courts.

The Prerogative Court, based in the city of Armagh, issued marriage license bonds. It embraced all of Ireland. Like the diocesan marriage bonds, the license bonds were also destroyed in the 1922 Four Courts Fire. However, the indexes survive as do abstracts made before 1922. The early ones are as follows and were digitized by FamilySearch and Findmypast.com:

Prerogative Court Marriage License Bonds Index (1710-1849)

Betham's Genealogical Abstracts from Prerogative Marriage Licenses (1629-1810) (Note: These were extracted by Sir. William Betham.)

Abstracts of Prerogative Marriage Licenses of Ireland (1629-1858) (Note: These were extracted by Denis O'Callaghan Fisher.)

Having a bond from the court was prestigious because the Prerogative Court issued ones to more well-to-do families.

Church Records Indexed on the National Archives of Ireland, FamilySearch.org, and Findmypast.com Websites

Diocese	Years
Armagh	1727-1845
Clogher	1709-1866
Derry	Destroyed
Down, Connor, Dromore	1721-1845
Kilmore & Ardagh	1697-1844
Meath	1655, 1702-1845
Newry & Mourne	Destroyed
Raphoe	1710-1755, 1817-1830

Genealogical Office, Dublin

The collections at the Genealogical Office in Dublin mainly relate to the gentry and nobility. The office is part of the National Library of Ireland in Dublin and covers all of Ireland. Many of the genealogies extend from Ireland into Scotland and England. Some collections are based on research in records that were destroyed in the 1922 Four Courts Fire, and the compiled pedigrees may be the only remaining proof of lineages. The pedigrees are connected to the upper classes. Nevertheless, most upper-class families had descendants who were not part of a designated social class since fortunes were gained and lost depending on financial, political, and cultural circumstances. The pedigrees of the Genealogical Office, therefore, can be utilized even if gentry connections are not known. As part of a Scots-Irish strategy, the intermarriages between educated Ulster-Scots and the gentry class, commonly of English heritage, are another reason to search the pedigrees of the Genealogical Office.

The Genealogical Office's vast archive of records is available through FamilySearch.org, and it is divided into many different collections and subjects. To the family historian, the records may not make much sense, and approaching them may be daunting. The assorted collections were never meant to be used as they are today. They became essential after the 1922 Four Courts Fire. All researchers have the same problem accessing the archive, but two guides offer directions through the maze:

Virginia Wade McAnlis in *The Consolidated Index to the Records of the Genealogical Office, Dublin, Ireland* 4 vols. (Issaquah and Port Angeles, Washington: by author, 1994-1997) has indexed the Family History Library microfilms alphabetically by surname. The entries include the Genealogical Office collection reference numbers and the Family History Library microfilm numbers. With the microfilm numbers, the current digitized reference is easily found.

Richard Hayes's *Manuscript Sources for the History of Irish Civilisation* (Boston, Massachusetts: G. K. Hall and Co., 1965) has a brief description of the Genealogical Office manuscripts. The guide should be used in conjunction with the NLI catalog online.

The Genealogical Office manuscript numbers are useful for the FamilySearch collection of the Genealogical Office manuscripts. Despite having a manuscript number, finding a particular source cited in a reference book may require reading through the scraps of papers one page at a time even when a reference to a source is found in a "Census Substitute" chapter of an Irish research guide. The Genealogical Office manuscripts consist of handwritten or typescript pages that may not have consistent or consecutive page numbers. Some manuscripts are simply odd pieces of paper with the information written on them. As frustrating as Genealogical Office manuscripts may be, they are perhaps the only copies of such material not destroyed in 1922.

Registry of Deeds

Most of the Ulster-Scots were tenant farmers who leased or rented their lands from landlords. Only one or two percent of the people in Ireland owned their lands outright. Several layers of subleasing or rent arrangements could have been between the landowners and tenant farmers. Land holding arrangements affected peoples' economic prosperities, ways of farming, inheritances, and emigration patterns. The prospect of land ownership was attractive to the Scots-Irish who flooded into Colonial America in the 1700s.

One common type of lease with great potential for genealogical information was the "lease for lives." A "lease for lives" stayed in effect as long as the persons named in the lease were living. As soon as all of the "lives" named in the lease died, the lease ceased to be in effect. A lease agreement for three lives was ordinary. Typically, a lease named the lessee, one of the younger children (who in theory would live the longest), and often the King of England, with no inference that the lessee knew the king. Everyone knew when the king died, and his death would bring the agreement down from three to two or possibly to one "lease for lives."

A lease could be granted for a set number of years, or a tenant could rent from year to year without holding a lease of any kind. A tenant could occupy land completely at the landlord's discretion, called holding land "at will." Many Scots-Irish tenant farmers were in the category of "at will" of their landlords.

Beginning in 1708, land transactions in Ireland were registered with the Registry of Deeds in Dublin. However, because registrations were not mandatory, not all land transactions were registered even though registering them was to the advantage of everyone involved. Within the Registry of Deeds are deeds of sale, lease agreements, marriage settlements, and wills. When a deed was presented in the Registry of Deeds, it was not filed there; rather, it was returned to the party who delivered it for registration. What was filed in the Registry of Deeds was a "memorial," which is a synopsis of the deed. From 1708 to 1832, 588,983 memorials of deeds were registered. A hundred years later were more than 2,500,000 registered deeds.

Even if an ancestor was not rich or prominent, relevant information may be in the Registry of Deeds, such as a deed with a list of the tenants on the land being sold or leased. What is in a deed is not known until a study for a specific locality or seller of land is undertaken.

The reason for registering transactions was for legal purposes, generally between the gentry and nobility, who were more or less equal in wealth. But almost all rules have exceptions. The Tithe Applotment Books and Griffith's Primary Valuation are good starts to addressing social statuses. If a family had one acre, it probably is not in the Registry of Deeds. If it had a large tract or many tracts, a lease might have been registered.

When using the Registry of Deeds, some basics should be considered. They are especially important for Ulster.

- County Tryone has many registered deeds for transactions, and they are a rich archive for the county.

- Compared to County Tyrone, significantly fewer registered deeds are available for County Armagh.

- Small farmers in County Down typically avoided the Registry of Deeds, and thus the number of registered deeds for County Down is appreciably lower than for other counties.

- The Quaker community had few registered deeds because they tended to avoid registration.

- As a whole, the Presbyterians in Ulster had fewer registered deeds than would be expected.

- All parties had to be 21 years old or older to register a deed, and a minor could only execute a deed through a guardian.

- Historically, women did not hold property. Their rights of inheritance came through their husbands or fathers, yet scores of women are listed in the Registry of Deeds. The listings often have the women's maiden names and the names of their fathers. Unmarried women and widows regularly registered deeds along with other relatives.

- If a person abandoned the lease agreement upon immigrating, legal problems could result for the actual owner or lessor of the property. A new lease could be issued only after a release from the older agreement was obtained so that the property would no longer be legally bound. Cases are documented for immigrants having to be located by landlords' agents, and they may be mentioned in U.S newspapers, the Registry of Deeds, and landlords' estate papers. New databases and indexes to both newspapers and the Irish Registry of Deeds open unique aspects of deed research for further exploration.

An excellent guide to the Registry of Deeds is Rosemary ffolliott's chapter "The Registry of Deeds for Genealogical Purposes," in *Irish Genealogy: A Record Finder*, Donald F. Begley, ed. (Dublin: Heraldic Artists, Ltd., 1981): 139-156. Although the book is now out of print, it can be found at most libraries with an emphasis on Irish genealogy.

When studying the Registry of Deeds, remember that a deed might have been registered years after the transaction. Often, a deed cites the earlier buying and selling of the property of the transaction being investigated. Its history can help sort through the layers of owners, lessors, and sub-lessors. Some deeds have only a few townlands involved in a small transaction, whereas others may have hundreds. Remember that spellings of townland names were inconsistent in the deeds. Before the 1830s, sub-denominations (localized names or places) often appear as the townland names, and the sub-denomination names technically were supposed to disappear from the official government records after the 1830s. They often did not, which complicates research because the townlands where the sub-denominations were located have to be determined to fully understand what was being transacted.

The immense archive of deeds and the indexes was digitized by FamilySearch and is in its catalog as "Transcripts of Memorials of Deeds, Conveyances, and Wills, 1708-1929." Access to the archive is through two manuscript indexes:

Surname Index. The "Surname Index," also called the "Grantor Index," is a personal name index to the sellers (grantors) of land. It does not list the buyers (grantees), which is a chief limitation to the index because Irish lands are usually a tangle of owners, lessors, and sub-lessors. Accessing the grantor does not mean transactions cannot be identified but is more difficult if he or she is not known. The grantor may be the main lease holder. It is not unusual for many grantors to be listed in a deed. If so, the second, third, and even fourth parties may also be indexed by name, which may be helpful. The index is arranged alphabetically by first letter of the surname and by periods.

Lands Index. The "Lands Index," also called the "County Index," is organized geographically and is a leading resource for deeds. If a townland name is already

known, all transactions mentioning it can be accessed. In the indexes, often the handwriting is illegible, and reference numbers can be difficult to interpret. In the manuscripts, sometimes the page numbers do not correspond with the volumes they are referencing. Nevertheless, the memorial numbers of the deeds should be correct. While a search of the Lands Index is time consuming, it is currently the only way to retrieve all registered transactions for a specific townland or address at a specific time.

Volunteers are indexing all the names that appear in the memorial books in the Registry of Deeds on the website "Registry of Deeds Index Project Ireland." The indexers are including wills and marriage settlements. They use codes to distinguish the kinds of deeds being indexed and the people involved where titles are concerned. The index can be searched by names, grantors, family names, and memorial numbers, but it is not a place names' index. As it grows, it remains a foremost research tool.

If an ancestor was a landowner or held a registered lease, the Registry of Deeds may supply a wealth of details. It is possible to find information about deaths, inheritances, and the relationships of various family members in the text of the deeds. In addition to deeds, some wills were registered in the Registry of Deeds. They were primarily for prominent families. Wills dating from 1708 to 1832 in the Registry of Deeds have been extracted and published with a place name index as follows:

Beryl P. Eustace. *Registry of Deeds, Dublin, Abstract of Wills*. Volume 1 (1708-45), Volume 2 (1746-88), Dublin, Ireland: Stationery Office for the Irish Manuscript Commission, 1954-56.

Eilish Ellis and P. Beryl Eustace. *Registry of Deeds, Dublin, Abstract of Wills*. Volume 3 (1785-1832), Dublin, Ireland: Stationery Office for the Irish Manuscript Commission, 1984.

The Registry of Deeds has potential for documenting the upper class and lease-holding class of Scots-Irish. If the social class to which the immigrant belonged is unknown, look closely for how much land that person bought upon arrival. If many acres in Virginia were purchased with money in hand upon coming to America, the Irish Registry of Deeds may be the next step in identifying the family's origin in Ulster.

Freeholders and Voters

An important group of records, often ignored in Irish research, is the voter registers. Voters', polls', freemens', and freeholders' records are lists of people entitled to vote or in fact are voting at elections and are normally arranged by counties, cities, or boroughs. Freeholders were property holders who had the right to vote, although freemen or free citizens of cities and boroughs also had votes. In cities, freeholders who qualified through their lands as well as freemen who qualified through their trades voted in elections, but usually borough elections involved only freemen. A borough is a town possessing a municipal corporation (government) and privileges granted by a royal charter.

The voters' sources can also be useful in immigrant research. Even if the immigrants were not of the voting class because their holdings were not valuable enough, the lists of Protestant voters can still be significant from the perspective of a surname distribution search. Indexes to them may have one of the only clues that a surname is found in a particular area during the period. They can also be part of a holistic approach, that is, as one of many records limiting origins to specific parishes or counties. Voters' lists often predate church registers.

A right to vote based upon the value of land owned or leased is complex and provides insights into the class and religious divisions in Ireland. From 1727 to 1793, only Protestants with forty-shilling freeholds or more could vote. In 1793, every Catholic with at least a forty-shilling freehold or over could also vote. However, in 1829, with Catholic Emancipation, all forty-shilling freeholders lost their votes. From that date, a £10 freehold was required to qualify as a voter. In effect, it eliminated an entire class of voters, both Catholic and Protestant.

The poll books registered voters at parliamentary elections, and they contain the names and addresses of the voters and often the addresses of their freeholds. Freeholders' registers have similar information but do not record how people voted at the elections.

The website of the PRONI is the best place to begin the search for the records. It has been indexing and digitizing its pre-1840 records in its online database "Freeholders' Records," a renowned resource for the family historian. If a voter of interest is identified from the database, consulting the Registry of Deeds for the date the person obtained the right to the land and under what circumstances is wise.

Wills and Probates (pre-1858)

Irish wills and administrations can be invaluable for tracing a Scot-Irish family. The key is to know the social class of the immigrant ancestors to determine whether they would have had wills. The majority of Scots-Irish who were tenant farmers emigrated from Ulster because the rents were being raised, and so they were not of the class of families who would have left generations of wills, especially in the eighteenth century. Conversely, a conclusion cannot be reached that ancestors were of this class, for they might have had some means or leases, or they were landlords themselves. A class of Scots-Irish families was well-educated with means and professional members and frequently intermarried with prominent Church of Ireland families. Unless the social statuses of families are already known, do not assume they were always tenant farmers.

By the nineteenth century, the role of wills had expanded in Ireland. Common families might have had estates or been involved in estate matters. A reliable method for researching in the 1600s and 1700s is to ask serious questions about a family's social and economic class. For research in the 1800s, look for a will or administration regardless of social class.

An indication about whether an immigrant's family might have left a will in Ulster is his or her financial status upon arriving in America. If an immigrant purchased a large tract of land in America or had many slaves, he or she might have had a sibling or parent who left a will in Ireland. Another clue is the immigrant's membership in the Freemasons in America. The moneyed class in Ireland was drawn to the Grand Lodge of Ireland. Everyone did not emigrate because of poverty, which is easy to forget. People left for all kinds of reasons that on occasion had nothing to do with need. The upper class registered wills in the Registry of Deeds, and so land records are a source for finding surviving wills.

Wills and administrations are best divided into two categories: pre-1858 and post-1858. Before 1858, wills and administrations were under the jurisdiction of the Church of Ireland. The current chapter focuses on the pre-1858 collections and indexes. The two courts under the Church of Ireland jurisdiction were the Consistorial Court, handling local estates in the diocese, and the Prerogative Court, which covered all of Ireland and handled estates for holdings in more than one diocese.

After the death of a person who had left a written last will and testament, the will was probated by the executors. For a person who didn't leave a written will, the record about his or her estate was the administration of an estate.

An 1857 law required that all wills and administrations older than twenty years be sent to the Public Record Office in

Dublin. Most of the Irish wills and administrations were destroyed during the 1922 Irish Civil War, when the archive was burned. A number of the original indexes survived, and they alone are incredible research assets. Fortunately, to rebuild the collections after the fire, abstracts of a significant number of wills and administrations that had been constructed by researchers before 1922 were donated to the Public Record Office, now the National Archives of Ireland. The National Archives of Ireland collections can cover all of Ireland. PRONI also has its own collections of wills and probates. Large groups of wills from both archives can be found on the FamilySearch.org website.

The first step to using the pre-1858 will collections is to determine if a will of interest might have been created. If so, the task turns to ensuring that a copy or abstract of it exists. Indexes can be found on Ancestry.com, FamilySearch.org, and Findmypast.com, as well as on the websites of the National Archives of Ireland and the Public Record Office of Northern Ireland.

Two major compilations can be obtained from the FamilySearch.org website. The first is known as the "Parsons-Jensen Index," or *Index to Irish Films at the Family History Library*, compiled by Joyce Parsons and Jeanne Jenson. It is an alphabetized listing by surnames and first names of the records of many wills, courts, and lands. In its 5-volume series, the wills are in volumes one and two. The second is the *Super Index: A Compilation of Available Irish Will Indexes 1270-1860,* compiled by Gloria Bangerter and edited and alphabetized by Joyce Parsons and Jeanne Jensen. The 11-volume work is an index to indexes. Most of the material in it was destroyed in 1922; however, it references material from other collections that did survive. The Super Index is one of the best indexes for determining if a will was ever written. If it was, the search for a surviving copy can be undertaken with the name and place. Even if an abstract or second copy of a will has not survived, the index is an exceptional search aid for a surname distribution survey because it still has the residences of the deceased.

The Prerogative Court had jurisdiction over estates of persons who had property worth over £5 in more than one diocese. The Prerogative Court was the responsibility of the Archbishop of Armagh of the Church of Ireland. The indexes to administrations through the Prerogative Court have survived for the years from 1595 to 1858 and are available on Ancestry.com, FamilySearch.org, and Findmypast.com. Even though the original wills were destroyed in 1922, abstracts of the Prerogative wills were made before 1922 and are part of Betham's Genealogical Abstracts. The important collection of abstracts was digitized by FamilySearch. Another collection of the Prerogative wills, compiled from Betham's will abstracts, before 1922, is known as "Burke's collection of [Prerogative] wills for forming Irish pedigrees." The index to its massive collection and the abstracts was digitized by FamilySearch.

To explain the indexes, wills probated through Consistorial Courts means that they were the diocesan courts. Each

Church of Ireland diocese before 1858 proved its estates in its local Consistorial Court for testators and their properties in the diocese. As follows were the courts for Ulster, which make up the bulk of the many online indexes (see chart below). For the most part, the Consistorial Court indexes survived the fire of 1922 even if the records themselves did not.

Whether or not an immigrant's family was of the class that left wills, the indexes can be valuable for research, along with tax, church, and land records, to pinpoint where surnames were located when places in Ulster are not known. The indexes, too, can document where people, likely Protestant, who had something to leave behind lived. They often provide the townlands within the civil parishes and dioceses where people resided.

Getting the Ancestors Back to Scotland

While the emphasis of this book is moving an ancestral family back from the United States to Ulster, a short discussion needs to be presented about a familiar area of concern among researchers: moving the family back to Scotland. Ulster records are difficult, at best, for assisting in forming the link because, with some exceptions, they are so incomplete for the 1600s and 1700s.

The coast of Scotland can be seen from the Antrim Coast of Northern Ireland. That is how close they are. However, unless people had a reason to go to Scotland, they never did. Because of the geographical closeness, a reason for traveling back and forth were landlords shipping tenants as seasonal workers from estates in Ireland to estates in Scotland. Other purposes were business, religious, and educational. Presbyterians commonly received higher education in Scotland, yet not until the Irish Potato Famine (1845-1851) did enormous numbers of Scots-Irish, along with their Catholic neighbors, have a motive to immigrate en masse to Scotland. Keep in mind that most immigrations to Ulster from Scotland were in the 1600s and very early 1700s. Only in the 1800s were they from Ulster to Scotland.

Consistorial Courts of Ulster

County	Consistorial Courts
Antrim	Connor, Derry, Down, Dromore
Armagh	Armagh, Dromore
Cavan	Ardagh, Kilmore, Meath
Donegal	Clogher, Derry, Raphoe
Down	Connor, Down, Dromore, Newry & Mourne
Fermanagh	Clogher, Kilmore
Londonderry	Armagh, Connor, Derry
Monaghan	Clogher
Tyrone	Armagh, Clogher, Derry

Books detail the Scottish origins of Ulster individuals. Among them is the series *Scots-Irish Links* and *Later Scots-Irish Links*, by David Dobson. As important as the books are, remember that those documented are among the minority of Ulster-Scots. The research problem will typically always remain in tracing an ancestor from the United States to Ulster, not from Ulster to Scotland.

It must be stated that sometimes the children or grandchildren of the Scottish immigrant to Ulster were the immigrants to the United States, and they arrived in the United States with family stories about Scotland. Family sketches with their information are often found in old county or town histories.

Several websites can be used to study and explore Scottish history. They include Ancestry.com, FamilySearch.org, and Findmypast.com. Scotland is working to digitize and index historic records. The endeavor is ScotlandsPeople.gov.uk, the creation of the National Records of Scotland that is Scotland's national archive. Another principal website is ScotlandsPlaces.gov.uk, which is a partnership between the Historic Environment of Scotland, the National Records of Scotland, and the National Library of Scotland. The two Scottish websites are a one-stop shop for Scottish genealogy, although not even they have all documents. The main collections, however, are represented in the databases.

Outlining the records of Scotland are several primary instruction books. As with all reference books, they tend to be dated for Internet records and for where records are deposited. Still, a parish register is a parish register and a land record is a land record, and that discussion has not changed. Therefore, the following reference works are not for online sources but remain valid for the

discussion of what the record is and how to use it:

Cory, Kathleen B., *Tracing Your Scottish Ancestry*, 3rd ed. Baltimore, Maryland: Genealogical Publishing Co., 2004.

Durie, Bruce, *Scottish Genealogy*, 4th ed. Stroud, Gloucestershire, UK: The History Press, 2017.

Hamilton-Edwards, Gerald, *In Search of Scottish Ancestry*. Chichester, Sussex, UK: Phillimore & Co., 1972.

Irvine, Sherry, *Scottish Ancestry: Research Methods for Family Historians*, rev. ed. Provo, Utah: Ancestry 2003.

Jonas, Linda and Paul Milner, *A Genealogist's Guide to Discovering Your Scottish Ancestors: How to Find and Record Your Unique Heritage*. Cincinnati, Ohio: Betterway Books, 2002.

The National Archives of Scotland. *Tracing Your Scottish Ancestors: A Guide to Ancestry Research in the National Archives of Scotland*, 5th ed. The National Archives of Scotland and Birlinn Ltd., 2009.

Stewart, Alan, *My Ancestor was Scottish: A Guide to Sources for Family Historians*. London, UK: Society of Genealogists Enterprises, Ltd., 2012.

Figure 51: Circa. 1846, Original Nauvoo Temple, Nauvoo, Illinois. This was the second temple built by the followers of Joseph Smith, Jr. It was dedicated on 1 May 1846 by Orson Hyde. The original was later destroyed by fire and weather, but an exact replica was rebuilt and dedicated in 2002. (This work is in the public domain in its country of origin and other countries and areas where the copyright term is the author's life plus 100 years or fewer.)

Figure 52: Circa. 1842, Joseph Smith, Jr., founder of the Church of Jesus Christ of Latter-day Saints. (This work was published before 1 January 1925, and it is anonymous or pseudonymous due to unknown authorship. It is in the public domain in the United States as well as countries and areas where the copyright terms of anonymous or pseudonymous works are 95 years or fewer since publication.)

Chapter Fifteen

Special Strategy: The Latter-day Saint Connection

The Latter-day Saint movement and how it pertains to converts born in Ulster requires special attention. The reason to present it is that in its genealogies, an entire family's roots in Ulster may be preserved if a relative of the immigrant ancestor joined the Latter-day Saints. The situation is the same with the Quakers and Moravians, who, along with Latter-day Saints, continue to be exceptional record keepers.

Converts to the Latter-day Saints constructed records at practically all steps in their new religious lives. In fact, almost too many records were created instead of too few. To pursue the research strategy for these immigrants, the present chapter focuses on their context, history, and a few sources. To some extent, most of their lineages are already online on pedigree-linked databases.

The Latter-day Saint expression of faith is not Catholic, Protestant, or Orthodox because it is not derived from any of the traditional branches of Christianity. It considers itself Christian, but as with all new religious movements, its creed is complex. Views from the outside extend from Latter-day Saint churches not being Christian to their being new branches of Christianity or emerging new world religions. Regardless, built within the Latter-day Saint movement is a research strategy that, when effective, can identify Ulster origins even if the ancestor had no personal Mormon connections whatsoever.

The Latter-day Saint movement comprises varied denominations that see history and theology from vastly differing perspectives, ranging from survivalist polygamists living in compounds to LGBTQ groups in metropolitan areas and everything in between. However, only the two largest denominations are of concern to the study herein, although a historical mention of a third is made because it ties into the two. The largest denominations are the Church of Jesus Christ of Latter-day Saints (LDS), headquartered in Salt Lake City, Utah, and the Community of Christ, headquartered in Independence, Missouri. While the two denominations theologically are surprisingly dissimilar, they do share a history until at least 1846. Today, the Utah church has 16 million members, and the Missouri church has 250,000 members.

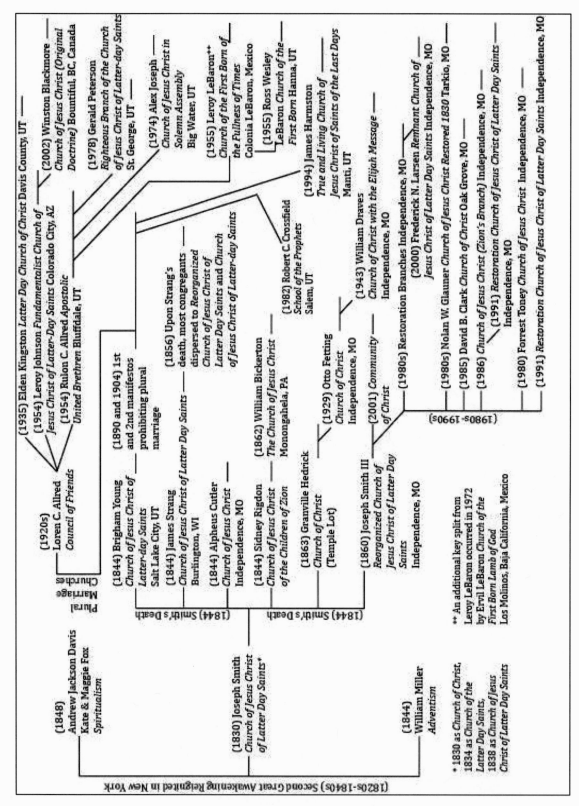

Figure 53: Select schisms of Joseph Smith's Church of Jesus Christ of Latter Day Saints, later the Church of Jesus Christ of Latter-day Saints.

To begin with, the word "Mormon" requires some further clarification to avoid misconceptions. It has been a tolerated term for most of the movement's history. "Mormon Church" is a title representing nothing, and "Mormon" was originally used as a prejudicial label, an empty reference point. Because it created confusion in the public's mind with the Utah church, the Community of Christ has always despised the name. The LDS Church in Utah tolerated it for most of the church's history and even used it as a branding term understood by everyone. In 2018, members were counseled by their prophet-president not to use it, but it remains embedded in the popular language of most countries and is definitely a precedent that is well known in discussions, books, and newspaper articles.

Background Information
What is commonly called the Mormon Church was founded by Joseph Smith (1804-1844) in Upstate New York in 1830. His place in American religious history remains both fascinating and controversial. One of the best, although not sole, academic books written about his life is Richard Lyman Bushman's *Joseph Smith: Rough Stone Rolling* (New York, New York: Knopf, 2005). Joseph Smith broke the monopoly on the Bible as supported by the evangelicals of his period by reinterpreting it and adding new scripture as canon. To Smith and the Latter-day Saints, the heavens were not closed, the Bible was not a closed canon, and God still spoke to them through prophets and apostles. Joseph Smith was the first of the restored prophets to act as God's spokesperson on earth, which tradition continues to this day.

Missionaries traveled the world with their message, accenting the doctrine that the heavens were open for all to receive their own revelations, promptings, inspirations, visions, and guidance dreams. The personal mysticism had a wide popularity not only on the frontiers of America but also in places where people were oppressed. It continues to appeal in the same manner, offering hope and meaning to the voiceless masses. In the nineteenth century, the message was especially well received in England, Scotland, Wales in the United Kingdom, Denmark, Sweden, Polynesia, and in some Native American tribes.

Converts were expected to immigrate and assemble with the rest of the Latter-day Saints in self-built communities that belonged to the larger Zion. The gathered became part of building the spiritual Kingdom of God and the physical Kingdom of God on Earth. The last Zion for the Utah church was founded in 1847, when Brigham Young and the pioneers settled in the Salt Lake Valley. From there, incoming members were assigned to colonies in other areas of the Intermountain West, forming distinct Mormon communities from southern Alberta to northern Mexico. Salt Lake City was the hub of the spider web of hundreds of colonies in Zion. To describe the process as less than epic and legendary would be to diminish it. The North American West from Alberta to northern Mexico owes much to the LDS-controlled and faith-based migration pattern. By the early twentieth century, however, Zion was reinterpreted to mean wherever the pure in heart dwell. It was more of a community of believers and state of being instead of a geographical locality. A future Zion will be built in Independence, Missouri.

The all-important research strategy being presented comes into focus at this point. The Mormon missionaries entered Ireland in 1840 and established mission bases in Belfast and Dublin with limited positive impact, yet they encountered scores of Ulster-Scots Protestants who had already immigrated to the urban industrialized jungles of Scotland and around the cities in Lancashire, England. There, they had a great deal of success because the Ulster-Scots Protestant families had already been uprooted once in search of a better life. Mormon missionaries had entered England in 1837, just seven years after the church was founded. Many individuals, often young single people or young families, converted and left their entire extended families behind as they immigrated to Zion. Their extended families did not convert or join them in the gathering, and so the church lives of the converts were documented in entirely new sets of records separate from the family members who did not join. Likely, LDS records will have the places of birth for the converts and their families.

To demonstrate a case of Irish immigrants converting to the LDS Church, the congregation (branch) in Glasgow, Scotland, serves as an example. The Glasgow LDS records show 1,240 converts from 1840 to 1851, of which 228 or 18% were from Ireland. Specific to the famine years of 1845-1847, one in every three converts to this Glasgow Branch was Irish.

LDS Temple Work and Theology

LDS theology from the Utah church perspective has to be regarded differently than that of other denominations rooted in Protestantism because of the idea of continuing revelation through the prophet, who also acts as the president of the church. The prophet, always a man, is seen as holding the "keys," thus allowing him to alter church doctrine when needed. As the needs of the church change and readiness of its membership progresses, the prophet-president receives the word from God, and revisions are appropriately placed. Most changes are considered minor, and even forgettable, but some major announcements have had long-term effects on the lives of the members for generations. According to the theology, as new knowledge builds upon the old, modifications are seen not as contradictions but as clarifications.

Among foremost changes in the Utah church were the various manifestos renouncing the practice, not the belief, in plural marriages. The first pronouncement banning plural marriages occurred in 1890 and paved the way for Utah statehood. The Second Manifesto was in 1904, and it officially banned the practice of contracting new marriages worldwide in the church. The two manifestos, along with later ones, radically transformed the very family structure and worldview of an entire region of North America. They also brought the church further into mainstream North American culture and defined which members were in good standing and which were not.

Another revelatory action was in 1978, when the long-established ban on people of African descent receiving priesthoods was lifted. The ban had been instituted by Brigham Young, not by Joseph Smith. The revoking of the ban instantly launched LDS missionary work for the entire world, along with the building of temples and the radical expansion of the genealogy program. Membership spiked throughout the Caribbean, sub-Sahara Africa, and Latin America. Today, most members are no longer of northern European descent.

From the LDS perspective, it would be challenging to write an evangelical-style systematic theology book outlining a particular understanding of biblical doctrine that can be debated and argued among theologians and ministers seeking truth and clarification. In contrast, the very nature of continued revelation sets the standard, becoming new scripture or quasi-scripture. Certain core doctrines cannot be altered, as an example, the mission of Jesus, whereas others remain to be questioned and reevaluated as needed.

Many works on the LDS book market address core teachings and are in an A-Z encyclopedic or dictionary formats. Among helpful works are:

Burton, Rulon T. *We Believe: Doctrines and Principles of the Church of Jesus Christ of Latter-day Saints*. Draper, Utah: Tabernacle Books, 1994.

Dahl, Larry E. and Donald Q. Cannon, eds. *Encyclopedia of Joseph Smith's*

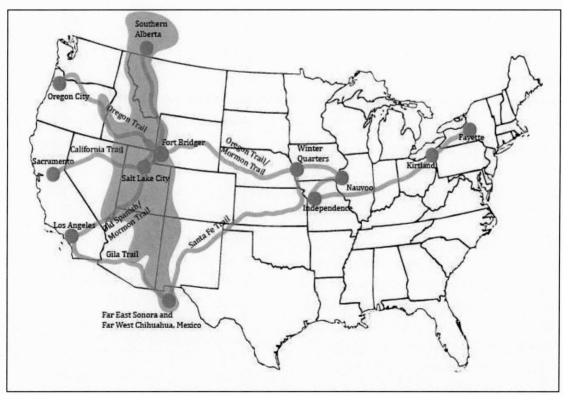

Figure 54: The Mormon Migration Routes and Primary 19th-Century Settlement Regions.

Teachings. Salt Lake City, Utah: Deseret Book, 1997, 2000.

Galbraith, Richard C. *Scriptural Teachings of the Prophet Joseph Smith*. Salt Lake City, Utah: Deseret Book Company, 1993.

Ludlow, Daniel H. *Encyclopedia of Mormonism*, 5 vols. New York, New York: Macmillan Library Reference, 1992.

Largey, Dennis L., ed. *Book of Mormon Reference Companion*. Salt Lake City, Utah: Deseret Book, 2003.

McConkie, Bruce R. *Mormon Doctrine*. Salt Lake City, Utah: Deseret Book, 1966.

McConkie, Joseph Fielding and Craig J. Ostler. *Revelations of the Restoration: A Commentary on the Doctrine and Covenants and other Modern Revelations*. Salt Lake City, Utah: Deseret Book, 2000.

Millet, Robert L., Camille Fronk Oslon, Andrew C. Skinner and Brent L. Top. *LDS Beliefs: A Doctrinal Reference*. Salt Lake City, Utah: Deseret Book, 2011.

Smith, Joseph Fielding. *Answers to Gospel Questions: The Classic Collection in One Volume*. Salt Lake City, Deseret Book, 1998.

As with any faith, the theology creates records. In the case of the LDS Church, the records have to include documenting baptisms for the dead or marriages for the dead that have been completed in the temple. They also include the sealings of individual families into units and the undertakings of individual endowments, the dates of which are only important to members keeping track of what temple work has been completed in their lineages. The temple ordinance dates are reflected on LDS family group sheets, which are unlike those produced for non-LDS family historians. Nonetheless, the essential vital information, such as dates and places of births, marriages, and deaths, is public.

In regard to membership records, the historic ones are open to the public for study, but to protect sensitive information, originals are not digitized or online. Much has been published about early members, though, and can be found in compilations and various academic studies. Mission records listing members, for example, the old Belfast and Dublin missions, can hold important specifics, as when their people emigrated and where they went. Not all moved to Utah, at least not at first. Excommunications from the church also are noted in mission records and in the memberships in the local congregations. Even if people were excommunicated or simply separated from the church, because they had been associated with it, they might have records of where they were born and their parents' names.

To round out the discussion on how LDS theology affects record-keeping practices, the reason for family history as practiced by the Utah church is needed for context. All practicing members are taught to research their family histories. Whether they do or not is another matter. The goal of members' research is "temple work." The temples are not church buildings but, rather, places where the veils between the world of the living and the world of the conscious dead are considered the thinnest. In LDS theology, the Spirit World is another dimension located on earth. In the temple, a living proxy stands on behalf of a deceased person, often a relative, and is baptized by submersion. Marriages for the living and the deceased are also performed in the temples, as are sealings of families into units for the eternities. Another ceremony for the living and the dead is the highly symbolic and esoteric endowment one.

All ordinances (rituals) are based upon genealogy, whether people submitted their personal lineages to the temple or whether the names were gathered through one of the controlled extraction programs of old records. Rituals such as baptisms, marriages, and sealings of family units must be performed by the correct church authorities, as restored by Joseph Smith. The rituals can be binding in the next life. All Christians and non-Christians alike who did not have the chance to accept the ordinances in this life through the restored authorities can do so after death by way of the temple work. The conscious dead are free to choose whether to accept or reject the proxy work. There is no compulsion. The preceding explanation is the simplified version of a quite multi-layered and complex after-life theology with the result being kingdom building in the eternities in an exalted deified state for the believer.

Discovering a Latter-day Saint Branch of the Family

The emphasis on genealogy in the Utah church coupled with the fact that so many Ulster-Scots did join and immigrate means that Ulster origins and parents' names may be within a church record—and may be the only place they are preserved. For example, if a convert born in 1820 joins the Latter-day Saints in 1845, being 25 years old, then his or her parents likely were born on either side of 1800 and their parents on either side of 1775, birth dates for the parents and grandparents being before most Protestant church records began in Ireland. Thus, if a Mormon convert leaves behind a record discussing the grandparents' generation, the lineage will be extended further back than one that could have been obtained using the majority of Irish records.

A Mormon branch of the family is usually discovered through connecting with a Latter-day Saint researcher on the Internet or finding a reference in a book or on a database of genealogies. Typically, the first clue is when a distant family line is found living in the western United States, especially in Arizona, Idaho, Nevada, Utah, and Wyoming. A branch of the family may also be in southern Alberta, centered around Cardston, Lethbridge, and Raymond because Mormons colonized that area of Canada after arriving from the United States. Latter-day Saints still remain a strong presence in southern Alberta. LDS memberships also extend to the northern Mexico states of Chihuahua and Sonora, where some of the Mormon colonies that survived the Mexican Revolution (1910-1920) can still be found. Evidence will be in one of the genealogy databases that are part of FamilySearch. To hear family historians discuss finding their "Mormon branch of the family" is familiar.

Sometimes, converts came into the Utah church through some of the strangest experiences. For example, in the article "William Taite of Downpatrick, Ireland, to Utah Territory via Scotland and India," Lola Sorensen recounts the journey of William Tait and the wide variety of records covering miscellaneous countries and continents she used to reconstruct his life history. William Tait was born in Downpatrick, County Down, on 3 November 1818, and he was Protestant. He was baptized into the LDS Church in 1841 in Glasgow, Scotland. William was in the British Army stationed in Poona, India, where in 1852, he met and married Elizabeth Xavier, a mixed-race Portuguese-Indian Catholic. She was born and christened in Colaba, India, in 1833. The couple had moved to southern Utah by at least 1860, and they lived in Cedar City, Iron County, for several decades. William died in 1896 in Cedar City, and Elizabeth died in 1914 in Enterprise, Washington County, Utah. During their time in Cedar City and through their participation in the ordinance work at the St. George Temple in southwest Utah, William left behind records of his parents, siblings, and cousins who never joined the LDS Church. He also left knowledge that his family had been in Downpatrick for 4 to 5 generations (*The Irish at Home and Abroad*, Vol. 2, No. 4 (1994/95), pp. 151-152).

The story of William Tait joining the Mormons in Scotland is not exceptional. The fact that as a Mormon in the British Army, he found himself in British India and met and married a mixed-race Portuguese-Indian woman is more unusual. What the two had in common with anyone living in the southern Utah town of Cedar City, besides religion, is beyond imagination. From the tropics of India to the deserts of Utah Territory was no small exploit, but, most importantly, he was involved in temple work and left behind knowledge of his ancestry and relatives at the St. George Temple, which was not a singular occurrence at all. The LDS Church records may be the only place in the world where the facts about his life were saved, including his records from Ireland, Scotland, the British Army, and British India. The descendants of William Tait's siblings or cousins who are now doing genealogy should be very interested in finding their "Mormon branch of the family!"

Three works about Irish Latter-day Saints from the Utah perspective can be helpful. The first is Brent A. Barlow's *History of the Church of Jesus Christ of Latter-day Saints in Ireland since 1840* (Thesis Paper presented to the Department of Graduate Studies in Religious Instruction, Brigham Young University, 1968). The second is a chapter by Barlow, "The Irish Experience," in V. Ben Bloxham, James R. Moss and Larry C. Porter, eds, *Truth Will Prevail: The Rise of the Church of Jesus Christ of Latter-day Saints in the British Isles 1837-1987* (Solihull, Warwick: The Church of Jesus Christ of Latter-day Saints, 1987): 299-331. The third appeared in the publication of the *Daughters of the Utah Pioneers*, "The Mormons from Ireland," Our Pioneer Heritage 13 (1970): 313-372. The DUP is a secular Salt Lake City based lineage society open to anyone who can trace his or her lineage back to someone who arrived in Utah

Territory before the completion of the Transcontinental Railroad in 1869.

Once a Mormon branch of the family has been discovered, comparing research and sorting through any contradictions is prudent. Proceed to understanding who the convert was, and what the original LDS records state about that person and his or her lineage. With the Utah church, frequently the problem is too many records instead of not enough.

Community of Christ (former RLDS Church)

A word about the Community of Christ is in order, a denomination that is today the second largest in the Latter-day Saint movement. Its strength is in the Midwest, headquartered at the historic Latter-day Saint center of Independence, Missouri. It is a record-keeping and historically minded denomination; however, it has little in common with the Utah church. The Community of Christ comprises Latter-day Saints who did not follow Brigham Young on the overland Mormon Trail to Utah from the church capital of Nauvoo, Illinois, as it was abandoned. They stayed in the Midwest and by 1860, under the leadership of Joseph Smith III, son of the founding prophet, established the Reorganized Church of Jesus Christ of Latter Day Saints (RLDS). It kept that name until 2001, when it changed to the Community of Christ, moving toward a trinitarian Liberal Protestant theology and away from its Latter-day Saint roots.

The early members have been documented in Harvey B. Black's six-volume work *Early Members of the Reorganized Church of Jesus Christ of Latter Day Saints* (Provo, Utah: Infobases, 1996), which has been made into a database by the same name on Ancestry.com. Many Scots-Irish are listed in the database of members. It is an excellent place to begin the research, afterward branching out into other record types, such as congregational records, church periodicals, and histories.

Figure 55: Joseph Smith III, one of several successors to Joseph Smith, Jr., and the first prophet/president of the Reorganized Church of Jesus Christ of Latter Day Saints (RLDS), now known as the Community of Christ. (This work is in the public domain in its country of origin and other countries and areas where the copyright term is the author's life plus 70 years or fewer.)

A couple of examples demonstrate the diversity of the group of converts to the RLDS Church from the Utah LDS Church. One is an early immigrant who never reached Utah, and the other is one who arrived in Utah but left.

The first is Richard Allen, Sr., born September 1821 in County Armagh, Ireland.

He immigrated first to Australia and there entered the LDS Church. His intentions were to join the Saints in Utah. He went as far as southern California, where he was baptized a member of the RLDS Church in 1867. He remained in California, attended the San Bernardino RLDS congregation, and died in California in August 1891 (Sources provided: RLDS Deceased Files/ Early Reorganization Minutes, 1852-1871, Book A, pp. 389, 568/ Saints' Herald Obituaries, 1891, p. 643/ Early Reorganization Minutes, 1872-1905, Book B/ Black, Membership of The Church of Jesus Christ of Latter *Day* Saints: 1830-1848, 49:114/ San Bernardino, California, RLDS Branch Records.)

The second case is that of John Teasdell (Teasdale) born August 1832 in Down, Ireland. He joined the LDS Church and moved to Utah. He was baptized in the RLDS Church in 1870 at Ogden, Utah. He left to settle in Coalville, Webster County, Iowa, where he lived for 20 years, dying there in March 1899 (Sources provided: Early Reorganization Minutes, 1852-1871, Book A, p. 634/ Early Reorganization Minutes, 1872-1905, Book B/ Early Reorganization Minutes, 1872-1905, Book C/ Saints' Herald Obituaries, 1899, p. 288.).

When studying massive biographical works, such as Black's database, it is important to know how history intersects with biography, placing the information into context, because it is outside the scope of any database in revealing the entire story. For example, a large segment of the RLDS Church when it was organized in 1860 was formerly of a historically important Midwest sect known as the Church of Jesus Christ of Latter Day Saints (Strangites). While Strangite is not part of the name of the church, it does help distinguish it from the Utah church by the same name. The rise and fall of the self-proclaimed prophet James Strang (1813-1856) is a topic that has fascinated scholars for decades. Two such works are Roger Van Noord's *King of Beaver Island: The Life and Assassination of James Jesse Strang* (Champaign, Illinois: University of Illinois Press, 1988) and Vickie Cleverley Speek's *God Has Made Us a Kingdom: James Strang and the Midwest Mormons* (Salt Lake City, Utah: Signature Books, 2006). Many such works, including chapters in books and journal articles, are dedicated to James Strang and his followers.

Founded by James Strang in 1844 soon after Joseph Smith's murder, Strang claimed the status of prophet over the movement. For those who did not align with Brigham Young or other claimants, Strang provided a viable alternative. Several thousand would follow him and establish their new kingdom home on Beaver Island, Michigan, where he was named King. Strang was assassinated in 1856. With the dispersal of the church from Beaver Island, most would align themselves with what became the RLDS Church, or they headed westward to Utah. In consequence, still another set of records for documenting ancestors can be examined, especially for those who initially rejected Brigham Young and the trek to the deserts of Utah. The Strangite newspapers, which basically are the church records, have been indexed in Frank J. Young's *Strangite Mormons: A*

Finding Aid (Vancouver, Washington: F. J. Young, 1996). About 100 Strangites remain today. Former Strangites can be interwoven into the lineages of members of both the LDS Church and the Community of Christ—and they predictably are.

In a twist of irony, the Strangites announced their belief and practice of plural marriages before Brigham Young did. They were practicing polygamy on Beaver Island, Michigan. Those who merged into the coalescing RLDS Church were joining a rabidly anti-polygamy camp of Latter-day Saints. Thus, the "don't ask and don't tell" policy was understood among the earliest RLDS membership. Facts such as this can be read into the texts of biographical works, as in Harvey B. Black's compilation, even if they are not stated explicitly. In studying early RLDS members, do not assume they did not practice polygamy! With the RLDS, not only does theology create records but also it keeps them from being created.

The Community of Christ never taught temple work for the dead. Its temples have an unrelated purpose and are used for gatherings and official meetings. The Community of Christ has had an active missionary program for its entire history. Based upon a message that did not include polygamy, genealogy, or temple work, it sent missionaries to Utah Territory by the 1860s and there gathered dissatisfied members of the Utah church. Not all in Utah were happy with the church-state theocracy under Brigham Young or with plural marriage. Among the converts from Utah were many born in Ireland, and after their conversion to

the RLDS Church, they either stayed in Utah or migrated elsewhere. Many went to California, another historical fact that can be read into biographical works if a context is known.

The Community of Christ and all Latter-day Saints share the theology of continuing revelation. Even though the core beliefs remain intact, for example, the mission of Jesus, other doctrines are open to further exploration, found in three central revelations that have altered its very face. The three principal changes are: building the long-promised temple in Independence, Missouri, which was decreed in 1984 and completed in 1994; granting women priesthoods in 1984; and discarding the lineage presidencies from Joseph Smith in 1996. By looking toward a trinitarian Liberal Protestantism as a model, the Community of Christ has moved forward beyond its Latter-day roots while retaining beneficial parts of its heritage. It no longer had to define itself in terms of what it was not, "Utah Mormons," but with the changes, many more traditional members separated and formed their own denominations and groups centered upon various claims to divine authority. Their new denominations and organizations continue today.

Some standard writings outline the Community of Christ beliefs and views of scripture. Several are classic works despite the major changes within the church:

Cheville, Roy A. *Scriptures from Ancient America: A Study of the Book of Mormon.* Independence, Missouri: Herald Publishing House, 1964.

Edwards, F. Henry. *The Edwards Commentary on the Doctrine and Covenants*. Independence, Missouri: Herald Publishing House, 1986.

Howard, Richard P. *Restoration Scriptures: A Study of Their Textual Development*. 2nd ed. Independence, Missouri: Herald House, 1969, 1995.

Tyree, Alan D. ed. *Exploring the Faith: A Series of Studies in the Faith of the Church Prepared by a Committee on Basic Beliefs*. Independence, Missouri: Herald House, 1987.

The Mormon Reformation (1856-1857) and California

Although some Utah LDS members would join the RLDS Church and migrate to California, their new church was not the only reason to go further west. Aside from the gold fields, which were especially attractive to young men in Utah, the turmoil surrounding the "Mormon Reformation" was another contributing factor, and, therefore, a few words about the Mormon Reformation and California are required.

Understand that many Latter-day Saints emigrated only to find life in the deserts of Utah under Brigham Young (1801-1877) intolerable or at least not what they expected. Many from Ireland, along with other European converts, arriving during the Mormon Reformation (Fall 1856 to Summer 1857) continued their journey to California. A favorite place of settlement was Sacramento, where most would merge into the larger society and lose all contact with the LDS Church. Descendants frequently rediscover their Latter-day Saint roots through genealogy. Polly Aird's article "'You Nasty Apostates, Clear Out': Reason for Disaffection in the Late 1850s" in *Journal of Mormon History*, 30, #2 (Fall 2004): 129-207 details the history of the traumatic time for the California-bound Latter-day Saints.

During the Mormon Reformation, the LDS Church consolidated power and recommitted its membership. It was a complex period in the history of the Intermountain West, directly influencing what people did and why they reacted in certain ways. One example is the infamous and still controversial Mountain Meadow Massacre (7-11 September 1857) in Southern Utah, a tragedy that alone shaped the general public's hostility and attitudes about Mormons for generations.

Before the completion of the Transcontinental Railroad in 1869, crossing the Great Plains for all emigrant parties was a traumatic experience. Sickness and death were commonplace, and all the overland trails, including the Mormon Trail, were littered with shallow graves. They were raided by American Indians, and if the emigrants were not properly prepared, they starved to death. The expedition in itself was a hostile ordeal for anyone, and in Utah, some emigrants simply met their limits and moved on to California. Remember that during the period, Utah was a church-state. It was a religious theocracy operating in isolation, far removed from political power in the eastern United States. Conflicts arose with the United States government, which was probably more concerned with the nation-within-a-nation, church-state theocracy than it was with polygamy. However, anti-polygamy laws became the precise tool used to rouse public disgust in the East and ultimately dismantle the Mormon Theocracy by 1890. It is easy to forget that when the Mormons arrived in Utah in 1847, they were in Mexico, having left the United States as religious refugees. The War of 1848 annexed into the expanding United States the entire region from Colorado to California. Once again, the Mormons had to deal with a government that was hostile toward them and their beliefs.

If research identifies a Mormon branch of the family and then loses it in the church records, California is the next place to look. Birthplaces and parents' names may be in the Latter-day Saint records regardless of how long people were associated with the church.

Repositories of Records
If a Latter-day Saint branch of the family is revealed, learning all that can be found from the church records, diaries, and histories documenting it is wise. Again, Latter-day Saint records may be the only source where Ulster birthplaces are preserved, and many from both the LDS Church and the Community of Christ are in the Family History Library. Some are online at FamilySearch.org, and others are deposited in the Special Collections of universities, for instance, the University of Utah or Utah State University. The Family History Library in Salt Lake City has a large group of the original records of the Utah church. The World Headquarters Library in Independence, Missouri, has ones for the Community of Christ as well as information on early Latter-day Saints. The library holdings of the secular society, Daughters of the Utah Pioneers, are also worth exploring.

Scholarly publications, such as the *Journal of Mormon History* published by the independent non-profit Mormon History Association, are filled with articles that mention individual members from across the theological spectrum of the Latter-day Saint movement. Such periodicals should not be ignored for gaining an understanding of the context of this complex expression of faith.

Further Reading

Church of Jesus Christ of Latter-day Saints References
Alexander, Thomas G. *Mormonism in Transition: A History of the Latter Day Saints, 1890-1930,* 3rd edition. Sandy, Utah: Greg Kofford Books, Inc., 2012.

Arrington, Leonard J. Brigham Young: American Moses. New York, New York: Knopf, 1987.

Arrington, Leonard J. *Great Basin Kingdom: An Economic History of the Latter Day Saints, 1830-1900,* new edition. Champaign, Illinois: University of Illinois Press, 2004.

Bushman, Richard Lyman. *Joseph Smith: Rough Stone Rolling.* New York, New York: Knopf, 2005.

Compton, Todd M. *In Sacred Loneliness: The Plural Wives of Joseph Smith.* Salt Lake City, Utah: Signature Books, 1997.

Flanders, Robert Bruce. *Nauvoo: Kingdom on the Mississippi.* Champaign, Illinois: University of Illinois Press, 1975.

Givens, Terryl L. *By the Hand of Mormon: The American Scripture that Launched a New World Religion.* Oxford, UK: Oxford University Press, 2003.

Stegner, Wallace. *The Gathering to Zion: The Story of the Mormon Trail.* Lincoln, Nebraska: University of Nebraska Press, 1992.

Van Wagoner, Richard S. *Mormon Polygamy: A History.* 2nd ed. Salt Lake City, Utah: Signature Books, 1989.

Community of Christ References
Bolton, Andrew, John Hamer, David Howlett, Lachlan Mackay and Barbara Walden. *In Pursuit of Peace: Community of Christ's Journey.* Independence, Missouri: Herald Publishing House, 2017.

Edwards, F. Henry. *The History of the Reorganized Church of Jesus Christ of Latter Day Saints,* 8 vols. Independence, Missouri: Herald Publishing House, 1973. (Eight volumes covering 1805 to 1946).

Launius, Roger D. *Joseph Smith III: Pragmatic Prophet.* Champaign, Illinois: University of Illinois Press, 1995.

Scherer, Mark A. *The Journey of a People,* 3 vols. Independence, Missouri: Community of Christ Seminary Press, 2013-2016. (Three volumes covering 1820 to 2015).

Figure 56: Manti Temple of the Church of Jesus Christ of Latter-day Saints, located in Manti, Utah, USA. Breaking ground in 1877, it was completed in 1888 and was the third temple completed after the Saints moved west. Photo courtesy of Dwight A. Radford.

Ulster

Chapter Sixteen

Special Strategy: Southeastern Native American Connection

The Scots-Irish and others from the British Isles intermarried or had common-law marriages with American Indians, and so by the removal period in the 1830s, some tribes had such strong extents of mixed-race (also termed mixed-blood) elements that tracing an ancestor is complicated. Many of the mixed-race families lost contact with their tribes, assimilating into either the white or free black American landscapes, while others stayed and continued to live in isolated clusters known in academic and genealogy circles as "tri-racial isolates." Still other mixed-race families remained with their tribes and were removed to what is now Oklahoma. The Scots-Irish and their descendants were parts of all of them, and so Native American heritage cannot

be defined by skin color. Moreover, the search for Ulster origins may take research into the Native American histories and genealogies even if no legend of native heritage is preserved in a family line.

A word needs to be added about the tri-racial isolates because the genesis of so many of their documented families is in colonial times, when the population of the American colonies was small and the segregation and slavery laws had not caught up to the actions of the people. The colonial governments were trying to decide what constituted a slave and for how long he or she could be held. It was a world in which humans being sold on the auction blocks in Baltimore or Charleston might have been directly off the ships from Scotland, England, Ireland, India (called East India Indians), or Africa, or they were Native Americans. Their religions included Catholic, Protestant, Islamic, Hindu, or Traditional. It was a United States history none of us in the modern Western world can begin to absorb.

In that 1600s era, an ancestor could have been an Irish Catholic indentured servant. It was one hundred years before the Scots-Irish migrated in massive numbers into the same geographical areas, and by then, the intermixing of the cultures and races had been progressing for a long time in the colonies. The tri-racial isolates, although important, and the Scots-Irish, who furthered the mixing process, are not the focus of the present study. The current chapter is centered on the mixed-blood descendants who remained with the tribes as well as those who stayed and integrated with the larger white culture. Because the topic is complex and new for most researchers, it requires attention.

Tribal membership is based upon a genealogy traced back to a key document, such as a tribal census or an already enrolled member. The original documented member in the 1830s, for instance, might have had a parent, grandparent, or earlier ancestor who was Scot-Irish. Today, published genealogies documenting the bi-racial or tri-racial families back to the immigrant are common, and so by researching a mixed-race lineage, the birthplace for an immigrant in Ulster can sometimes be found. The strategy is odd, maybe only alluded to in genealogy instruction books since the emphasis is on tracing the native lines and not the Europeans who intermarried with them. The research does not come without its singularities and internal logic as it advances.

Whites and the tribes had constant contact. The Caucasians included white traders, trappers, missionaries, farmers, government officials, members of the military, and the general frontier blazers. A good deal of white-native interaction occurred at the United States government's trading posts, sometimes referred to as factories, and regardless of the reasons, often led to intermarriages, common-law marriages, or other familial arrangements. The settlement patterns of the Scots-Irish on the frontiers brought them within reach or even within the native nations of the Southeast, and their unions included white men and white women. A white man who had business with the tribes could have had a tribal wife as well

as a white wife back home. If a white man had dealings with several tribes, he could easily have had a wife and children in each tribe. Marriages and relationships in such situations have to be evaluated according to the times and circumstances in which they occurred.

The discussion herein is on four of the five Southeastern tribes who were removed on the Trail of Tears, the Cherokee, Chickasaw, Choctaw, and Muscogee (Creek). The Seminole are not included because they share a distinctly different history from the others, and many of their early interactions were with freed or escaped slaves and people from the Caribbean. The Catawba of South Carolina, who were not removed, are also explored in this chapter because all Catawba have Scots-Irish ancestry. Statistics on the four of the five tribes removed on the Trail of Tears in the 1830s are found in the table on the next page.

The United States government documented those who were removed and relocated to Indian Territory (now Oklahoma) through censuses, muster rolls, and ration lists. When the native nations were broken up before removals, the government noted the ones who disposed of or stayed on their lands. It is a common misperception that all Native Americans left at the removals.

General Research Resources
The largest collections of records in tribal research are at the National Archives, the Oklahoma Historical Society, and the Family History Library, and are now coming online on Ancestry.com. Southeastern state archives also have collections

Trail of Tears Tribe Removal 1830s

Tribe	Removal Treaty	Year	Removed*	Years
Choctaw	Dancing Rabbit Creek	1830	12,500	1831-1836
Muscogee (Creek)	Cusseta	1832	19,600	1834-1837
Chickasaw	Pontotoc Creek	1832	4,000	1837-1847
Cherokee	New Echota	1835	22,000	1836-1838

*These numbers also include those who removed on their own.

about the local tribes in each of their areas. The Family History Library, Library of Congress, and the Allen County Public Library (Fort Wayne, Indiana) have the largest compilations of genealogies, family histories, and genealogical periodicals in the country, all of which can be used in Scots-Irish/Native American research.

A foundation for a nation-wide discussion of records and research strategies of Native American genealogy is Curt B. Witcher and George J. Nixon's chapter "Native American Research" in *The Source: A Guidebook to American Genealogy* (3rd ed), Loretto Dennis Szucs and Sandra Hargreaves Luebking, eds. (Provo, Utah: Ancestry, 2006): 777-837. For research into the earliest records for

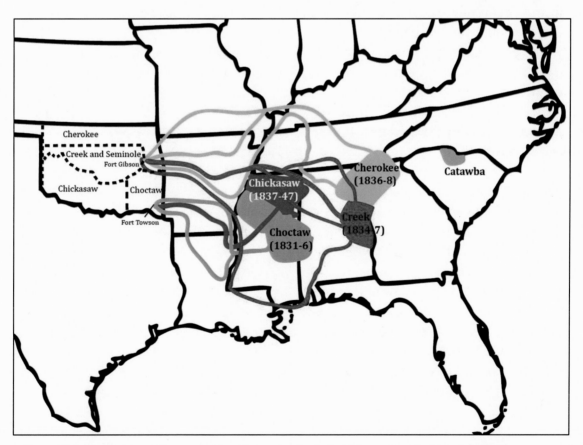

Figure 57: Removal routes of four main tribes likely to involve Scots-Irish as well as the Catawba tribe that was not removed. (The Seminoles are generally not pertinent to Scots-Irish research and are not represented here.)

the southern tribes, the standard textbook is Rachel Mills Lennon's *Tracing Ancestors Among the Five Civilized Tribes: Southeastern Indians Prior to Removal.* (Baltimore, Maryland: Genealogical Publishing Co., 2002). Her contemporary treatment of early Southeastern tribal research complements any general how-to reference work, article, or biographical compilation. Periodical Source Index (PerSI), an online periodical index to article titles locked away in thousands of genealogical journals worldwide, is often the only way to access the printed material and should not be overlooked. The database version of PerSI is available on the Findmypast.com website.

Because of the interest in mixed-race Native American research, some essential instructional genealogical articles and books should be consulted as groundwork, with comments added. Although dated, that is, written before the advent of the Internet and databases, they are still valid because the sources, strategies, and logic have not changed; only how to access records has:

Blumer, Thomas J. "Practical Pointers in Tracing Your Indian Ancestry in the Southeast," in *Journal of the Afro-American Historical and Genealogical Society* 13 #1-2 (1994): 67-82. (The well-thought-out article by Catawba specialist Thomas J. Blumer presents useful advice to the beginners who are trying to document a potential Indian line. His recommendation is to remain determined and learn about the tribe being researched.)

Byers, Paula K., ed. *Native American Genealogical Sourcebook.* Detroit, Michigan: Gale Research Co., 1995. (The general reference book is sound with sections on fundamental research methods, tribe specific sources, and state guides.)

Carter, Kent, "Wantabes and Outalucks: Searching for Indian Ancestors in Federal Records." *Chronicles of Oklahoma* 66 (1988): 99-104. (The iconic article outlines the limitations of Native American research and bluntly states that not all legends are true. While some subject matter does not apply to early mixed-race research, Carter's advice and research methods are solid, making the article timeless.)

Clark, Blue. *Indian Tribes of Oklahoma: A Guide.* Norman, Oklahoma: University of Oklahoma Press, 2009. (Written for a general audience, the work details the diverse tribes in Oklahoma and answers questions posed by the general public. It largely replaces Muriel H. Wright's classic work *A Guide to the Indian Tribes of Oklahoma.* Norman, Oklahoma: University of Oklahoma Press, 1951.)

Hill, Edward E. *Guide to Records in the National Archives of the United States Relating to American Indians.* Washington, D.C.: United States. Government Printing Office, 1981. (Dated but provides core insight into the nation-wide collection housed at the National Archives. It has long been a standard in any genealogical library.)

Martini, Don. *Southeastern Indian Notebook: A Biographical and Genealogical Guide to the Five Civilized Tribes, 1685-*

1865. Ripley, Mississippi: Ripley Printing Co., 1986. (The book presents short biographies, including many of mixed-race families and their European immigrant ancestors.)

Martini, Don. *The Southern Indians: A Biographical Guide to the Cherokee, Chickasaw, Choctaw and Creek Indians, 1700-1907*. Ripley, Mississippi: [s.n.], 1993. (A large reference work documenting the tribes, the tribal leaders, traders, intermarried whites, missionaries, and government agents in the Southeast and in Oklahoma.)

Martini, Don. *Who Was Who Among the Southern Tribes: A Genealogical Notebook, 1698-1907*. Falkner, Mississippi: D. Martini, 1998.

Pangburn, Richard. *Indian Blood: Finding Your Native American Ancestor*. 2 vols. Louisville, Kentucky: Butler Book Publishing, 1993-1994. (A collection of biographies of the Cherokee, Delaware, Seneca, and Shawnee tribes that includes information about the people who intermarried with them.)

Vann, Robert. "Indian Research: Researching Native American Ancestry," in *Valley Leaves* 37, #1 (September 2002): 5-8; 37 #2 (December 2002): 53-56; 37 #3 (March 2003): 107-109. (In the three-part article, Vann discusses American Indian genealogy using the Cherokee as an example. In his excellent primer on the topic, his advice is reasonable and comprehensible.)

Some biographical works are more detailed than others. Several focus on the immigrant, discussing the mixed-race children and native spouse. Others concentrate on one of the mixed-race children and perhaps mention the origins of the parents. Either way, they take the researcher into the ancestral line in question, typically citing sources and names from which research can proceed. Sometimes, knowing only where the family lived in Maryland, North Carolina, South Carolina, Pennsylvania, or Virginia before moving into the native nations can be a needed piece of evidence. Biographical compilations quite often divulge such details, even in passing. It is important to remember that the emphasis of the biographical and genealogical sketches is on native history and not necessarily on Ulster or any other European origins.

Examples of biographies loaded with clues are of the two Folsom brothers who settled among the Choctaw. The Folsoms are perhaps the largest of the Choctaw mixed-race families:

> Nathaniel Folsom (Choctaw). White; trader among the Choctaws; son of Israel Folsom; born Rowan County, North Carolina, May 17, 1756; settled among Choctaws, 1780s; died Mountain Fork, I.T., October 9, 1833; married Aiahniehih Ohoyo and her sister, nieces of Mingo Puscus; father of 24 children, including Molly (married Samuel Mitchell), David, Israel, Robert, Isaac, Elsie, Rhoda (married Peter P. Pitchlynn), McKee, Samuel, John, Sophia (married John Pitchlynn), Jacob, Daniel, and Peter.

> Ebenezer Folsom (Choctaw). White; brother of trader

Nathaniel Folsom; born 1765; lived among Choctaws until 1789, when he moved to Mobile; appointed Spanish interpreter to Choctaws, 1791; moved to Arkansas, 1804; married Sarah White Lewis, widow of Samuel Lewis; father of Michael Nathaniel, William, and Sophia (married John Pitchlynn).

(Don Martini's *The Southern Indians: A Biographical Guide to the Cherokee, Chickasaw, Choctaw, and Creek Indians, 1700-1907* (1993), pp. 105, 108.).

Nathaniel stayed with the tribe and removed to Indian Territory, where he died in 1833. He married two Choctaw sisters. His brother Ebenezer did not settle with the Choctaws in Indian Territory but went to Mobile and then to Arkansas with what appears to be his white family. If Ebenezer's family was tracing its genealogy, it would encounter the Choctaw branch through the brother Nathaniel. The Choctaw records could be pursued next for Nathaniel's life and family and continue back to Rowan County, North Carolina. The relevant suggestion in the case may be Rowan County. There, the search for Ulster origins can progress if the scores of Choctaw records and books already have not afforded the answer.

A typical area to address with research such as that of the Folsom family is whether any contemporary efforts would augment Martini's 1993 work. Another is whether the subject, the Folsom family in this discussion, was Scot or Scot-Irish. The latter issue must be resolved

because both ethnic groups were heavily involved with the Southeastern tribes.

General Research Strategies

A few basics are helpful when thinking in terms of mixed-race research to track back to where the Ulster immigrant intersects:

- A question to answer at the start of research is: Was the Scot-Irish ancestor in the right place at the right time to encounter a specific tribe? That's perhaps the most important inquiry in the research. It is imperative to remember that because an ancestor lived on Native American lands does not mean the tribe was still there. Consider the Georgia Land Lotteries. Eight times from 1805 to 1833, the state of Georgia held lotteries to distribute recently vacated Muscogee (Creek) and Cherokee lands. Through them, Georgia distributed three-fourths of the state to thousands of families and individuals. The typical settlers were white with no connection to the tribes, and so those settlers are not foremost candidates for mixed-race research. The geography may be right, but the timing is completely wrong.

- If the Ulster immigrant is known, but where in Ulster he or she lived is not known, start with the immigrant and learn more about his or her children and grandchildren. It is genealogy in reverse, tracing *forward,* learning about each successive generation. When a mixed-race branch of the family is identified, it is time to look at Native American sources. Of course, if it was the immigrant who married into the tribe, all subsequent branches are of mixed heritage. If it was one of the children of the immigrant who married into the tribe, addressing the issue of origins can yet be done. Knowledge of Ulster origins might have been preserved in the history of the mixed-race branch. Take into account that the geography and period have to be right for the approach to be successful.

- When it is known that a mixed-race family stayed with the tribe, research from the opposite direction. Look at all tribal records and genealogies working *back* to the immigrant (as with any other lineage research) instead of forward *from* the immigrant.

- Even though the ancestral branch of the family did not marry into a tribe, the ancestor might have had a brother or sister who did. The Ulster origins may be preserved through a mixed-blood branch. It is essential to always keep in mind that for contact between whites and a tribe to have occurred, the geography and time must be right.

- Having found the branch of the family that intermarried with natives, learn whether the

members removed with the tribe or stayed and, to use the crude term, "passed for white." Like African Americans, the American Indians had their own burdens to bear in a privileged white-dominated society. If persons could "pass for white," it was to their advantage to do so. Perhaps only a vague rumor of native heritage has survived in family lore, which is quite ordinary, especially for families with Southeastern roots.

- Determine whether a surname can be traced to a tribe or to more than one since the tribes intermarried, too. A published Indian roll or census may contain the surname. All tribes have rolls and censuses. Also do not forget that a white man might have had children by several women in several tribes.

- Always be aware that not all native people went westward. Many stayed in the eastern United States, and their descendants are there today. Native Americans can have black, white, or brown skin tones. Having blond hair and blue eyes does not mean someone does not have Native American ancestry any more than it does not for those with black skin and hair. Racial features and physical appearances cannot be used as guides, but DNA tests can be.

- The current trend is for mixed-race families in a given area to reconstruct and incorporate as a tribe. They then submit their genealogies and proof for either state or federal recognition. Alabama, North Carolina, and South Carolina have the largest numbers of reconstructed tribes, which are bi-racial and tri-racial in nature. Some tribes simply cannot connect to the required documentation to reorganize into acknowledged tribes. However, even if the petition is rejected, the genealogy generated in the process remains.

- Search for printed family histories and published genealogical works about the mixed-race branch. As a result of racial attitudes, many family histories published before approximately 1970 discuss mixed-race families without mentioning that they are of mixed heritage. With a little background knowledge and using their surnames, the periods, and their residences as a guide, it is possible to recognize multiracial families—and the lineages can be obvious even when the authors of the books hid them from the readers. The further back in time the research progresses, the greater the chance of finding published material. Native American research is a specialized pursuit and additionally can be directed at a specific time and a specific place.

The Scots-Irish and Tribal Intermarriage

The intermixing of Native Americans and the Scots-Irish occurred through violence as well as through co-existence. Using New England as a side example, it came by force. Beginning in 1690, the French and Indians began to push their way into New York and New England, raiding and kidnapping families for sale in New France (Quebec). Most of the raids were linked to the following wars: King William's War (1688-1697), Queen Ann's War (1702-1713), Lovewell's War (1721-1725), King George's War (1744-1748), and the French and Indian War (1754-1763). The raids continued until 1763, when France ceded its claim to what is now Canada. Many Scots-Irish were among those kidnapped and sold in Quebec. Ninety years of raids ravaged colonial New Hampshire, the home of so many early Scots-Irish settlers.

Tales about families captured, divided, and sold in Quebec have filled books because the topic has fascinated authors and scholars for decades. Some captives who, years later, made their way back to New England could barely speak English. Instead, their languages were French and tribal. Some had native or French spouses, had acquired French and native names, and returned as Roman Catholics! Emma Lewis Coleman's *New England Captives Carried to Canada Between 1672 and 1760 During the French and Indian Wars* (Portland, Maine: The Southworth Press, 1925) includes well-investigated stories of New England captives. It is a standard text for New England research, cited in many Scots-Irish family histories.

Most who intermarried outside of New England did not do so by force, kidnapping, or white slavery but through coexistence, particularly in the southeastern United States between the incoming Scots-Irish and the native tribes. Theda Perdu's *Mixed Blood Indians: Racial Construction in the Early South* (Athens, Georgia: University of Georgia Press, 1992) is an academic treatment of the interracial aspects of many of the tribes. Because the mixed-blood element within any of the tribes is so widespread, a comprehensive general history or tribal history should discuss it.

The incoming settlers, alongside their native friends and relatives, signed various Indian treaties. The United States government encouraged their cooperation and then used the local white men as interpreters and agents. The treaties have been published in Charles J. Kappler's *Indian Treaties: 1778-1883.* 2 vols (Washington D.C.: Government Print Office, 1904). The work is invaluable for mixed-race research and is commonly known as *Kappler's Treaties* in genealogy circles. *Kappler's Treaties* can be used to identify the areas where the mixed-race families lived, tribal designations, and family associations.

Another source, even if an odd one, for documenting whites and the tribes, especially Cherokee and Muscogee (Creek), is Dorothy Williams Potter's *Passports of Southeastern Pioneers, 1770-1823: Indian, Spanish and Other Land Passports for Tennessee, Kentucky, Georgia, Mississippi, Virginia, North and South Carolina* (Baltimore, Maryland: Genealogical Publishing Co., 1982, 1990).

Because tribal lands were considered foreign countries, passports were required to trade, collect debts, recover stolen horses or escaped slaves, or to simply pass through on the way to Spanish colonies. Passports were often obtained in Knoxville, Tennessee, which was on the northern edge before entering the Cherokee Nation.

Mixed-race families who left a tribe frequently moved deeper into the frontiers. The *Territorial Papers of the United States* (Washington D.C.: Government Printing Office, 1934-1962), in 26 volumes compiled and edited by Clarence Edwin Carter, is reliable for documenting their movements. As the families advanced into the frontiers, they would have lost all contact with the tribes and over the generations, blended into either the white or free black communities. Many free blacks were also pushing westward along with other Americans.

An example of the intermingling of Scots-Irish, Choctaw, and French cultures is:

> Cornelius McCurtain (Choctaw), white; son of Cornelius and Honoree Che McCurtain of Ireland; born 1747; married Margarite LeFleur (1760-1790), sister of Choctaw trader Louis LeFleur, at Mobile, November 24, 1778; witnesses were Jean Favre, George Troup, James McGillivray, and John McIntosh; received grant of 400 acres, January 6, 1794; filed claim for granted land, 1804; died Mobile, 1814 (Don Martini's *The Southern Indians: A*

Biographical Guide to the Cherokee, Chickasaw, Choctaw, and Creek Indians, 1700-1907 (1993), p. 196.).

Determining Mixed-Race Surnames

A simple way to discover whether an ancestor's surname is among the Cherokee, Chickasaw, Choctaw, Muscogee (Creek), Mississippi Choctaw, or the Eastern Cherokee is to consult two major Indian rolls, the Dawes Commission (1894-1914) and the Guion Miller Roll (1909). The massive collections of family data verified who qualified for tribal membership. Genealogists used the rolls to explore all kinds of native heritage questions.

The first major roll to consult is the records of the Dawes Commission, which began the United States government process of breaking up tribal nations in Oklahoma (Indian Territory) and allotting the lands to individual Indians. The original goals of the Dawes Commission were to change how the tribes owned land and to abolish tribal governments. Its function was expanded by 1896 to authorize a membership roll for the Cherokee, Chickasaw, Choctaw, Muscogee (Creek), and Seminole. Even today, membership in the Oklahoma tribes is based upon documenting descent from an ancestor enrolled through the Dawes Commission. An excellent guide to the history and use of the records is Kent Carter's *The Dawes Commission: And the Allotment of the Five Civilized Tribes, 1893-1914* (Orem, Utah: Ancestry Publishing, 1999).

The Dawes Commission source is important in mixed-race research because it contains the surnames in the Five Tribes and the Mississippi Choctaw. In the vast majority of the cases, Scots-Irish connections into the tribes were previous to the final 1838 removal, accounting for the large number of European surnames in the records. The Dawes Commission records can also reveal who stayed with a tribe or whether the surname crossed into different tribes. Researchers frequently are convinced they have native heritage, especially if their families spent time in the Oklahoma area. If a surname is not preserved in the Dawes Commission records, though, the assumption needs to be questioned further.

The Dawes Commission records are vast. Enrollments began in 1896, but because they were considered invalid, the process began again in 1898. The majority of people enrolled from 1898 to 1907, with a few others added in 1914. The final rolls consist of 101,000 names, which were only one-third of those who applied. Two-thirds of the applicants were rejected. The records also list the black Freedmen, slaves or descendants of slaves owned by the Five Tribes who were adopted into the tribes. The Freedmen intermarried or had children with the Native Americans, and so they, too, share Scot-Irish immigrant ancestors if they did not already have them. The Dawes Commission records are widely available and are online at Ancestry.com. The second important roll is the Guion Miller, a key document that is especially applicable to those who were not part of the removal process. However, it is not as straightforward as the Dawes Commission's—and for some of the most unsuspected reasons. The purpose of the Guion Miller Roll was to accept applications for membership in the Eastern Cherokee Nation, which is the Cherokee tribe that remained in western North Carolina. It is still there today. The list has preserved the surnames of those who might *not* have removed to Indian Territory, and its value is in the thousands of people who applied who might or might not have been Cherokee, inclusive of both accepted and rejected claims. The Guion Miller Roll is not merely a source for Cherokees; many mixed-race families with various tribal roots are included because they had nowhere else to apply at the time.

Between 1906 and 1909, some 45,940 applications were submitted from throughout the United States, Canada, and Mexico. The Guion Miller Roll lists an estimated 90,000 applicants, each of whom was required to trace lineage to someone in the 1835 Henderson Roll before the removal. Most applications were rejected because evidence was inadequate. Unless clearly fraudulent, the rejected applications still preserve the genealogies back to the 1835 period. They also provide insight into mixed-race families that were long separated from the tribes, merged into the white or black communities, or found themselves somewhere in between as tri-racial isolates. The Guion Miller Rolls are on Ancestry.com and the National Archives website.

Finding family surnames in either the Dawes Commission records or the Guion Miller Rolls is one step closer to looking for mixed-race genealogies. At the least, a listing is evidence that the family *thought* it was Native American even if a claim was rejected.

The Scots-Irish as Catawba

From the early days, the Catawba intermarried with Cherokees as well as with local white settlers, especially those of Scots-Irish and English descents. The treaties of Pine Hill (1760) and Augusta (1763) established a fifteen-square-mile reservation along the Catawba River in South Carolina near North Carolina. By 1760, Catawba lands had already been encroached upon by whites, mainly Scots-Irish migrating south from North Carolina. During the time, the Catawba began leasing their lands to the settlers. Through intermarriages and common-law arrangements, all modern-day Catawba have Scots-Irish ancestries. It is also not rare for white-Catawba blended families to have left the area in and around York County, South Carolina, losing all connections to the tribe.

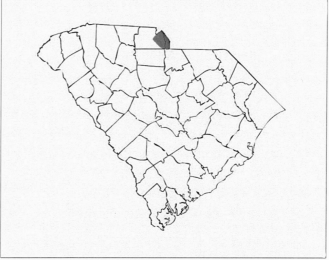

Figure 58: Eventual Catawba Reservation borders, encompassing York County (on the west) and Lancaster County (on the east).

That the Catawba were allowed to stay rather than be removed is somewhat unique in southern Native American history. For a brief time, the tribe joined the Cherokee in North Carolina. By 1847, however, most Catawba had returned to South Carolina. The Catawba Reservation near Rock Hill, York County, South Carolina, is recognized by both the State of South Carolina and the United States government.

Some special considerations will help the Catawba research process:

- The Catawba tended to use their European given names rather than their Catawba names beginning in the eighteenth century. A surname identified as European indicates that a white man married or had a child by a Catawba woman. A child from a common-law arrangement went by either the mother's name or the father's name. A Catawba mother might have had children with different last names.

- The Catawba historically tended to intermarry with the Scots-Irish rather than with the free-color population, resulting in a more bi-racial than tri-racial heritage.

- The tradition was to name a son after his father, and so two different men in the records could have the same name. A Catawba custom separated two people with the same name by attaching "Big" and "Little" before it to indicate that one is older than the other.

- Many Catawba joined and assimilated with the Eastern Cherokee Nation in North Carolina. Others joined and were granted citizenship with the Choctaw in the West in 1851.

- Until 1917, the matrilineal (mother's) line determined Catawba lineage. Children of a Catawba man and a white woman were not counted as Catawba. Because the Catawba did not benefit from this custom, it was altered.

- The average Catawba lineage extends to the late eighteenth or early nineteenth century. Yet, during this period, the Catawba were completely surrounded by the Scots-Irish who leased land in their reservation. The Scots-Irish portion of the lineage could extend further.

Catawba Surnames

The first documented European-Catawba surname was Brown, which dates to 1730. By 1780, 56% of Catawba men had surnames. All surnames came into being between 1730 and 1810, which reflects the time of white settlements in the Catawba area of South Carolina. The list of core surnames below was compiled from Ian Watson's work, the LDS Catawba Branch church registers (1885-1943), and the 1825 Rent Book:

Ayers, Blue, Brown, Bullen, Bunch, Canty, Chitner, Clinton,

Cook, Deloe, Dudgeon, Evans, Gandy, Garcia, George, Gordon, Harris, Hart, Head, Heart, Joe, Kegg, Kennedy, Morrison, Mursh, Nettles, New River, Otis, Owl, Patterson, Redhead, Robins, Robinson, Rooker, Sanders, Scott, Simmons, Stevens, Thomas, Thompson, Timms, Wade, Wahoo, Watts, White, Whitesides, Wiley, Williams.

An example of how the Europeans came into contact with the Catawba is illustrated in the sketch of the Brown family in Judy Canty Martin's history, *My Father's People: A Complete Genealogy of the Catawba Nation* ([S.l.]: J.C. Martin, 1999), p. 21:

> Patrick Brown, white trader, born around 1690, he was associated with his brother Thomas Brown and Alexander Kilpatrick. Patrick bought the tracts of Dr. Daniel Gibson and Henry Gignilliat and three hundred acres at the bend of Congaree Creek, the site of the old fort.
>
> Thomas Brown, white man of northern Irish origin, said to be the greatest Indian trader in the Nation. He was probably born around 1690; his will was dated December 4, 1745. He states William Brown, "My natural son born of a free Indian Woman of the Catawba Nation," and that William was 15 years old. In 1735, Thomas bought land between the Congaree and Wateree Rivers. Thomas served as

executor of Alexander Kilpatrick's will. After Thomas's death, George Haig served as his executor and took care of William. He was an Indian Agent as early as 1743 and died shortly thereafter.

Although this family biography did not list the Browns' place of birth in Ulster, it does extend the lineage far beyond what the Irish records state. Also, with names, dates, and sources, other records for the Brown family can now be explored to try to uncover a more exact place in Ulster. It is important not to overlook that the purpose of these types of books is not Ulster origins but, rather, Catawba genealogy. It is a tribal emphasis and not a European one. Logical questions based upon a prudent research strategy are:

- Although the above cited sketch does not list from where in Northern Ireland the Browns came, is there another source or family history that would? The reasoning is that this was so far back and the Browns are to this day such a prominent Catawba family that many other descendants or academics must be asking the same question.

- Do a thorough search of all Catawba histories for what they contain about the Browns. The family would have to be addressed in any thoroughly researched history book.

- What has been published on the Indian-White relations in South

Carolina? Check the works for references to the Browns.

- How accurate are the online pedigrees? Consult online databases and family sketches in the pedigrees on Ancestry.com, FamilySearch.org and MyHeritage.com for clues only. Never accept them as accurate unless documented. Unfortunately, most are not. The FamilySearch pedigrees and databases may be of special interest because most of the Catawba Nation converted to Mormonism in the 1880s. They may or may not be correct, but at least a religiously motivated genealogical interest is among church members.

- What is preserved at the South Carolina Department of Archives and History on the Brown family? Using the Catawba connection, weeding quickly through all the Brown families in the state should be easy.

- Was the Brown family Scot or Scot-Irish? The question should be asked of any mixed-race family. Regardless of what pedigrees or published family histories may state, never neglect the question. The Catawbas were surrounded by incoming Scots-Irish, and so the most likely answer is that the family was Ulster-Scot.

Continuing with the example of the Browns, perhaps Ian Watson put it into perspective when speaking of Thomas's mixed-race son William as the progenitor of this very large Catawba family today: "Interestingly, if we accepted that this William Brown was the progenitor of the Brown name among the Catawbas, it would call into question the fullbloodedness of many Catawbas of the late nineteenth and early twentieth century ..." (Ian Watson, *Catawba Indian Genealogy* (Geneseo, New York: Department of Anthropology, State University of New York at Geneseo, 1995, p. 19).

Catawba: Source Material and Genealogies

The two major repositories for Catawba records are the South Carolina Department of Archives and History (SCDAH) and the Family History Library. Much information is also on the Internet. Thomas J. Blumer's *Bibliography of the Catawba* provides an inventory of the vast amounts written about the tribe. Another valuable book, which details sources and strategies, is Ian M. Watson's *Catawba Indian Genealogy: A Report to the National Endowment for the Humanities* (1995).

Excellent instructions for documenting South Carolina tribes in the colonial period are in William L. McDowell's two-volume *Colonial Records of South Carolina: Documents Relating to Indian Affairs*. The first volume covers 1750 to 1754, and the second, 1754 to 1765.

A bibliography of Catawba resources by Robert H. MacKintosh, titled *Sources for Researching Catawba Indian Ancestry and History at the South Carolina Department of Archives* (Columbia, South Carolina: The South Carolina Department of Archives, 1993), supplies archives' reference numbers. Ian Watson's *Catawba Indian Genealogy* extracts primary evidence for tracing Catawba families and genealogical sketches for the prominent families.

Catawba: Census Records

The United States census enumerators did not count the people living on the Catawba reservation until 1880. Early censuses include:

25 February 1786: Petition of "Catawba Indians" in the South Carolina General Assembly Papers.

1849: List of Catawba Indians residing in the Cherokee Nation in Haywood County, North Carolina; in Greenville, Chester, and York districts in South Carolina; and also at the Echota Mission of the Methodist Episcopal Church and at Qualla Town, both in North Carolina.

1854 Census: B. S. Massey's *Report to the Governor of South Carolina on the Catawba Indians* (R. W. Gibbes, 1854) lists all adult Catawbas on the reservation receiving supplies.

1869-1883: The *Reports and Resolutions of the South Carolina General Assembly* contains a year-by-year report on the Catawbas, including the payment of allotments to each Catawba.

Catawba: Church Records

Beginning in 1884, the majority of the tribe converted to the Church of Jesus Christ of Latter-day Saints (Mormons or LDS). The LDS congregation located in Rock Hill was originally known as the Catawba Branch. Most Catawbas remain members of the LDS Church. The Catawba Branch (1885-1943) records are at the Family History Library. The membership registers were extracted and published in Pat Smith (White Buffalo Woman) and Dwight A. Radford's article "The Scots-Irish as Catawba" in *The Irish At Home and Abroad* 6, #3 (1999): 112-119. The LDS membership records are a foundation of Catawba research, although they are typically ignored by non-Catawba researchers, who simply mention the Mormon connection to the tribe or the social and educational benefits the tribe received from its association with the church.

Catawba: Land Records

Scots-Irish moved into Catawba lands in the 1750s and 1760s and settled close to their villages. To protect the Catawba from further white encroachment, the Treaty of Augusta (1763) established a 15-square-mile reservation of 144,000 acres, which is located in present-day Lancaster and York Counties, South Carolina. The Catawba Nation welcomed white settlement by granting leases of 99 years. The resultant lease books are an important genealogical source for early Catawba research. The leasing of the Catawba Reservation was historically unique.

The earliest lease book did not survive, but some legal actions concerning mortgages, depositions, sales of property, and gifts were recorded in the York County deed books. They assist in reconstructing early white settlements on Catawba lands. The deeds have been extracted in Elizabeth Whitman Schmidt's article "Occupants of Catawba Indian Land in York District, South Carolina Taken From York County Deed Books A B C D E F 1786-1807" in *SCMAR*, 13 (2) (1985):76-86. Both Catawba and white names are listed in the deeds.

Agents who supervised the process and kept books were appointed by the South Carolina General Assembly. The books contained the surveys, leases, and plats. They named Catawba heads of families who were allotted sections of the lands and were thus designated to receive the rent from each tract leased out. The records also have the names of the white lessees. By 1840, the Catawba Nation was settled by whites, and the lease system lost its original meaning. The Catawba ceded their lands to the State of South Carolina under the Treaty of Nation Ford. The lease records, called bundles, are at the South Carolina Department of Archives and History and have been transcribed by Douglas Summers Brown in "Catawba Land Records, 1795-1829" in *The South Carolina Historical Magazine*, 59 (2) (April 1958): 64-77; 59 (3) (July 1958): 171-176; 59 (4) (October 1958): 226-233. Louise Pettus's work *Leasing Away a Nation: The Legacy of Catawba Indian Land Leases* details the families who leased lands from the Catawba. It recounts the history of the Catawba Reservation from the Treaty of Augusta (1763) to the Nation Ford Treaty (1840) that ended the leasing process. It is a primary source for documenting Scots-Irish on the Catawba lands.

The Scots-Irish as Cherokees

From the 1770s, a strong connection existed between the Cherokee tribe and the Scots-Irish as well as with other Europeans. As waves of Scots-Irish settled on the frontiers of Alabama, Georgia, North Carolina, South Carolina, and Tennessee, they lived, traded, fought, and married the Cherokee. A few of the Ulster connections are the Adair, Dougherty, Ferguson, Finley, Franklin, Gaylord, Kyle, McCollough, McDonald, McDuffie, and McGill families. Millions of modern Americans have Cherokee heritage because so many mixed-race families left the tribe and never were removed. The Cherokee intermixing into the population at large, both white and black, also left an imprint of Native American heritage upon the popular imagination. One rule to remember in Cherokee research is that not all native heritages are Cherokee! Checking the geography and the surnames to ascertain whether the person being researched was Cherokee is important.

By the time of removal in 1838, the Cherokee had thoroughly assimilated white ways. They had adopted Christianity, printed a newspaper, established their own alphabet, held slaves, lived in towns as well as farms, and discarded the clan system in favor of a government patterned after that of the United States.

Because of the interest in the tribe, a wealth of published genealogical material and instruction books for tracing Cherokee ancestors can be located. Three helpful ones are:

Gormley, Myra Vanderpool. *Cherokee Connections*. Baltimore, Maryland: Genealogical Publishing Co., 1995, 2002.

McClure, Tony Mack. *Cherokee Proud: A Guide for Tracing and Honoring Your Cherokee Ancestors*. 2nd ed. Somerville, Tennessee: Chunannee Books, 1999.

Mooney, Tom. *Exploring Your Cherokee Ancestry: A Basic Genealogical Research Guide*. Tahlequah, Oklahoma: Cherokee National Historical Society, 1990.

Cherokee: Recognized and Unrecognized Tribes

Defining who exactly is a qualified Cherokee is complicated and convoluted. Three tribes are federally recognized: the Cherokee Nation of Oklahoma (Tahlequah, OK), the Eastern Band Cherokee Indians (Cherokee, NC), and the United Keetoowah Band of Oklahoma (Tahlequah, OK). Smaller tribes made up of mixed-race families have obtained state but not federal recognition. In addition, numerous ones have submitted genealogies in support of either state or federal claims for recognition, but their applications have been rejected or are still pending. Of importance is understanding which tribes are and are not state or federally recognized based upon their genealogies.

Applying for state and federal recognition is a long and complicated legal process that takes years. When an organization is not legally acknowledged as a tribe or perhaps has a pending petition, it generally means that the compiled history and submitted genealogy of the tribe do not meet either a state or a federal standard. It does not imply that the reorganized tribe is not of Cherokee heritage or that its genealogy is invalid. Whether a tribe is approved or not, a Scots-Irish connection is still typical. Some organizations, though, are indeed fraudulent and are termed "wannabes," which possibility especially needs to be considered among the Cherokee.

The Cherokee Nation of Oklahoma has placed an extensive list online of organizations *it* considers fabricated and fraudulent. The list includes state recognized tribes. Whereas many organizations are indeed fabricated, others simply cannot be documented to the required standard to be legally accepted as tribes. Sometimes, reconstructed tribes are too blended with the larger white society with insufficient historical paper trails to distinguish them as Cherokee. Again, the lineages submitted may be valid but not for the intended purposes. Four Cherokee tribes are recognized by the state of Alabama, two in Georgia, and one in South Carolina. The Bureau of Indian Affairs for each state has contact information for its tribes online.

An example of an unrecognized tribe on the suspect list from the Cherokee Nation of Oklahoma is the Chickamauga Cherokee Nation (White River Band and Sac River Band). The Chickamauga Cherokee claim to be the tribe from the tri-state area around Chattanooga, Tennessee, that moved westward decades before general removal and settled in what is today Arkansas and Missouri. It blended so thoroughly with the local white society that not until a group tried to reconstitute the tribe did many white families learn of their potential Cherokee heritage. The reorganized tribe submitted enrollments, but it has been denied

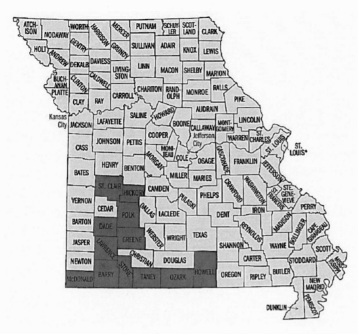

Figure 59: Primary counties where the core families of the White River Band of the unrecognized Chickamauga Cherokee reside in Missouri. Original state image courtesy of Aphis.usda.gov. No copyright implied.

Figure 60: Primary counties where the core families of the Sac River Band of unrecognized Chickamauga Cherokee reside in Arkansas. Original state image courtesy of Aphis.usda.gov. No copyright implied.

Continuing with the Chicka-mauga Cherokee example, the key to studying it is knowing that the core families of the Sac River Band in Arkansas are centered in Baxter, Benton, Fulton, Independence, Jackson, Johnson, Lawrence, Madison, Newton, Pope, Searcy, Sharp, Stone, and Woodruff Counties. The principal families of the White River Band in Missouri are centered in Barry, Dade, Greene, Hickory, Howell, McDonald, Lawrence, Ozark, Polk, St. Clair, Stone, and Taney Counties. In the areas, the core surnames are reconstructed as found in the enrollment pedigrees submitted. Even if the tribe failed to obtain state and federal acknowledgment, the genealogies are available in the search for Ulster origins. The Scots-Irish certainly are inter-mixed in the pedigrees in several places because the earliest Cherokee blended considerably into the white communities in the Arkansas and Missouri counties just named.

Cherokee: Research Considerations

The key to researching mixed-blood Cherokee genealogy is having a sense of the tribe's history and relating it to what is known about the family being researched. For instance, by the terms of the Treaty of New Echota (1835), the Cherokee would relinquish their lands. At

both state and federal recognition. Although rejected, the massive compilation of pedigrees from its process is at the Family History Library.

that time, Cherokee were living in what are today the following states and counties:

- **Alabama**: Blount, Cherokee, DeKalb, Etowah, Jackson, and Marshall

- **Georgia**: Cass, Catoosa, Chattooga, Cherokee, Bobb, Dade, Dawson, Fannin, Floyd, Forsyth, Gilmer, Gordon, Haralson, Lumpkin, Murray, Paulding, Pickins, Polk, Towns, Union, Walker, and Whitfield

- **North Carolina**: Cherokee, Clay, Graham, Macon, and Swain

- **Tennessee**: Bradley, Hamilton, Marion, Meigs, Monroe, and Polk

If ancestors lived in these general areas before removal, they could be associated with the tribe. If they arrived after the Cherokees were removed, the chance of having native heritage diminishes immensely after the 1830s. Use a thorough reference work on Cherokee history when preparing to search the records. Be alert to a few special situations:

- A mixed-race family, especially one that did not remove, was often recorded in the United States census as white, black, mulatto, or Indian. Mixed-heritage families moved westward and northward from the old Cherokee Nation, crossing the continent. Particular surnames are associated with the pre-removal period (pre-1838). While some of the families enrolled in either Oklahoma or North Carolina tribes, more lost all contact with both of them. The surname may be the first clue to mixed-race heritage.

- Terms such as "Black Dutch" and "Black Irish" were used by mixed-race families (mostly of Cherokee descent) to hide their Indian origin. It was the first step in the process of passing for white when a person's skin tone was darker than most in the community.

- Family descent from a "Cherokee Princess" is a familiar legend, one to be ignored because the Cherokees did not have princesses. It does not discredit the possibility of Cherokee descent but only the princess claim.

Cherokee: Published Family Genealogies

Knowing Cherokee surnames and the correct locality are aids in distinguishing Cherokee and non-Cherokee family histories with the same surname. Seek out compilations of families in a locality or publications on a subject such as white settlement. Six important works demonstrating locality and subject are:

Bell, George Morrison. *Genealogy of Old and New Cherokee Indian Families*. Bartlesville, Oklahoma: George Morrison Bell, 1972.

Shadburn, Don L. *Cherokee Planters in Georgia, 1832-1838: Historical Essays on*

Eleven Counties in the Old Cherokee Nation of Georgia. Roswell, Georgia: W. H. Wolfe Associates, 1990.

Shadburn, Don L. *Unhallowed Intrusion: A History of Cherokee Families in Forsyth County, Georgia*. Alpharetta, Georgia: WH Wolfe Associates, 1993.

Shadburn, Don L. *Upon Our Ruins: A Study in Cherokee History and Genealogy*. Cumming, Georgia: The Cottonpatch Press, 2012.

Starr, Emmet. *Old Families and Their Genealogy: History of the Cherokee Indians and Their Legends and Folklore*. 1921. Norman, Oklahoma: University of Oklahoma Foundation, 1968.

Warren, Mary B. *Whites Among the Cherokees - Georgia, 1828-1838*. Danielsville, Georgia: Heritage Papers, 1987.

George Morrison Bell's work traces the frontier-blazing Adair family, providing a model for Ulster research into origins. He began the family sketch with William Adair, "an Englishman" who originally settled in Kinhilt, County Antrim, in the late 1500s. His Adair family history is also an example of how convoluted a lineage can be as it proceeds from England to Ulster to Scotland and then to the American colonies. In Bell's presentation, he identified ancestors as Englishmen, Irishmen, and Scotsmen, depending on where they were born. While both accurate and inaccurate at the same time, it does cause one to linger in deliberating information. The portion of the lineage from Ulster to the Cherokee Nation is (Bell, p. 8-9):

THOMAS ADAIR - An Irishman, born ca 1679 in Genoch, Amtrim [sic] County, Ireland. He married in Scotland but no record of wife's name. He came to America in 1730 and is believed to have settled in Virginia or North Carolina. He died and was buried in that country. He was my fifth great-grandfather. He was the son of Alexander Adair.

JAMES ADAIR – A Scotsman, born in 1709 in Scotland. No record of wife's name. He came to America with his father in 1730 and settled in the Cherokee Nation East, Georgia, for he was living in Georgia in 1735. He was my fourth great-grandfather. He died and was buried in Georgia. He was a son of Thomas Adair.

JOHN ADAIR, 2nd – A Scotsman, born ca 1753. (1m) Mrs. Ga-ho-ga Foster, his (2m) was to Jennie Kilgore. He died in the Cherokee Nation East, Georgia, and was buried there, place unknown. He was the son of James Adair.

The Cherokee line comes through John Adair, 2nd and his first wife Ga-ho-ga. They had five mixed-race children born near Adairville, Barton County, Georgia. His second wife, Jennie Kilgore, was a white woman, and they had ten children near New Echota, Georgia. Through her, the non-native line, the Bell descends on the Adair line.

However, Don L. Shadburn has more current research on the Adair family, although he presented some of the same story that Bell did. In his work *Upon Our Ruins: A Study in Cherokee History and Genealogy* (2012), he wrote the following about the immigrant Thomas Adair:

> It is known from exhaustive research that John and Edward Adair's direct descent came from Alexander Adair and Margaret Agnew of County Antrim. Their son Thomas Adair was born about 1680 and died in 1755 at Duncan's Creek in Laurens County, South Carolina. He married in 1703 to Margaret Henart, a native of Port Patrick, Wigtown, Scotland, emigrated in 1730 to Chester County, Pennsylvania, and later moved into South Carolina (pp. 1-2).

Shadburn then documented the children of Thomas Adair and Margaret Henart and connected them and their Ulster spouses in footnotes to the branch of the family that settled in the Cherokee Nation. Shadburn added the following about Thomas's grandson John Adair, whose first wife, according to Bell, was Cherokee:

> JOHN ADAIR was born circa 1755 in County Antrim, Ireland, and died testate in November 1815 in Pendleton District, South

Carolina, soon after making his will...

> Adair first married about 1779 to half-blood wife, Mrs. Nancy Foster (born c.1754), sister of Dorcas Duncan (wife of Charles Gordon Duncan), daughters of John Lightfoot. Lightfoot, captain of a group of Virginia militia, was born about 1725 in Williamsburg, Virginia, and is believed to have been a son of Philip Lightfoot and a grandson of William Lightfoot of London, England. Captain Lightfoot was married by custom in the early 1750s to a woman whose Cherokee name may have been Gehoga (p. 4).

Not only did John Adair marry a Cherokee woman but also his first wife was mixed race, although she was English, rooted in Colonial Virginia. By consulting many different works and seeking out fully footnoted contemporary ones, one can build upon the other in the research process.

In the findings of Bell in 1972 and Shadburn in 2012, similarities and contradictions can be noted. Bell, in the family history of the Quaker Harlans, traced the lineage through the Cherokees into Pennsylvania, to Ulster, and then to England in the 1600s. In the Ulster to America to the Cherokee Nation portion of the family sketch are four generations listed as follows (Bell, 200-202):

> GEORGE HARLAN, 1st – an Englishman, born ca 1649 in Monkwearmouth County,

England. (m) Elizabeth Duck on September 17, 1678 in County of Armough [sic], Ireland. They came to America in 1687 and settled in Chester County, Pennsylvania. He was a Quaker. He died in July 1724 and was buried in Chester County. He was the son of James Harlan (p. 201).

EZEKIEL HARLAN, SR – Irish-English descent, born June 16, 1679 in the County of Down, Ireland. Came to America in 1687 with parents. (m) Rachel Buffington, ca 1706 in Chester County, Pennsylvania. He was a Quaker. He died and was buried in Chester County. Son of George, 1st and Elizabeth (Duck) Harlan.

EZEKIEL HARLAN, JR. – Irish-English descent, born May 19, 1707 in Chester County, Pennsylvania. (m) Hannah Osborn on October 23, 1724 in Chester County. He died and was buried in Chester County. He was the son of Ezekiel, Sr. and Rachel (Buffington) Harlan.

ELLIS HARLAN - Irish-English descent, born ca 1731 in Chester County, Pennsylvania. He went to the Cherokee Country and settled in McMinn County, Tennessee, and (m) Catherine

Kingfisher, a full blood Cherokee. He died and was buried in McMinn County. Son of Ezekiel and Hannah (Osborn) Harlan.

Of course, Monkwesarmouth is not a county but a city in Durham, England, and Armough is County Armagh, Ireland.

Cherokee: Early United States Government Rolls

The early Cherokee rolls include removal records (both voluntary and forced), muster rolls, rations, and censuses. The rolls taken for various reasons include both the Oklahoma and North Carolina tribes. The list below encompasses the rolls up to 1883.

Cherokee Emigration Rolls (1817-1838): A list of Cherokees who voluntarily removed. The United States government enticed removal by giving the Cherokee rifles, tobacco, kettles, blankets, and money.

Census of Cherokee (1835): Commonly called the Henderson Roll, a census of Cherokee living in Alabama, Georgia, North Carolina, and Tennessee. It was the main source for documenting Cherokee who were forcibly removed, and it has served as a basis for later enrollment in the Cherokee Nation.

Ration Books (1836-1838): Ration books from camps where the Cherokee were located before their removal to Indian Territory. Some were taken at New Echota, Georgia, and some at Camp

Clanwaugh near present-day Chattanooga, Tennessee. They have been published as *Cherokee Ration Books, 1836-1837-1838, New Echota* (Signal Mountain, Tennessee: Mountain Press, 1999).

Cherokee Muster Rolls (1838): A muster roll of a forced removal, accompanying the Henderson Roll. It is divided into columns: name of head of family and total number in family *or* number of males and females over or under 21.

Mullay Roll (1848): Roll for the Eastern Cherokee lists Cherokee who remained in North Carolina after the majority of the tribe removed under the 1835 Henderson Roll. It set aside funds for those wishing to migrate to Indian Territory.

Drennen Roll (1851): Also called the Immigrant Roll, a roll of Eastern Cherokee who settled in what is now Oklahoma after 1835. Many mixed-blood families had assimilated into the larger American society and removed on their own.

Siler Roll (1851): An Eastern Cherokee roll that determined the distribution of the money owed to tribal members under the 1835 Treaty. It is arranged by county in the states of Alabama, Georgia, North Carolina, and Tennessee.

Chapman Roll (1852): The roll listed per capita payment made to those named on the Siler Roll.

Tompkins Roll (1867): A census of Cherokees residing in Indian Territory listed by district with both the English and Cherokee names of every person. It includes the Freedmen Indices for 1867.

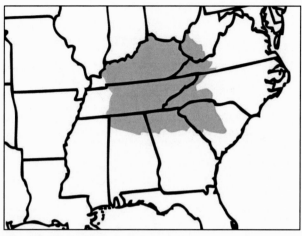

Figure 61: Original Cherokee claims before cessions and removal.

Swetland Roll (1869): Roll of the Eastern Cherokee in Georgia, North Carolina, and Tennessee.

Hester Roll (1883): A census taken between 1882 and 1884 of the Eastern Cherokee who resided east of the Mississippi River. It listed families in Alabama, Georgia, North Carolina, Tennessee, and elsewhere.

Cherokee: Church Records

Several early missions were among the Cherokee. The Congregational Church and Presbyterian Church ran the Brainerd Mission in what is today Chattanooga, Tennessee, through the American Board of Commissioners for Foreign Missions (ABCFM). The missionaries' journals described their own activities and Cherokee life and are transcribed in Joyce B. Phillips and Paul Gary Phillips's *The Brainerd Mission: A Mission to the Cherokees, 1817-1823* (Lincoln, Nebraska: University of Nebraska Press, 1998). Through the ABCFM missions, Christianity became more commonplace among the Cherokees.

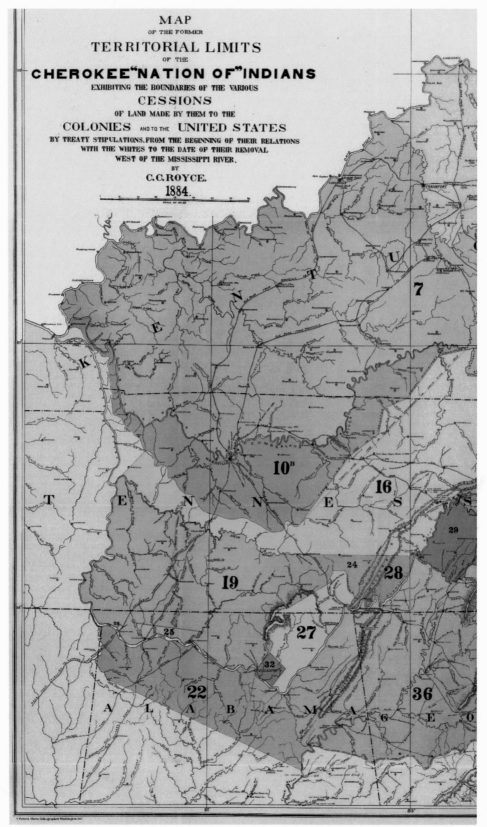

Figure 62a: 1884 Map by C.C. Royce showing the gradual depletion of Cherokee lands with each cession in numerical order. See legend on page 224 for detailed dates. ("Fifth annual report, plate VIII and plate IX.")

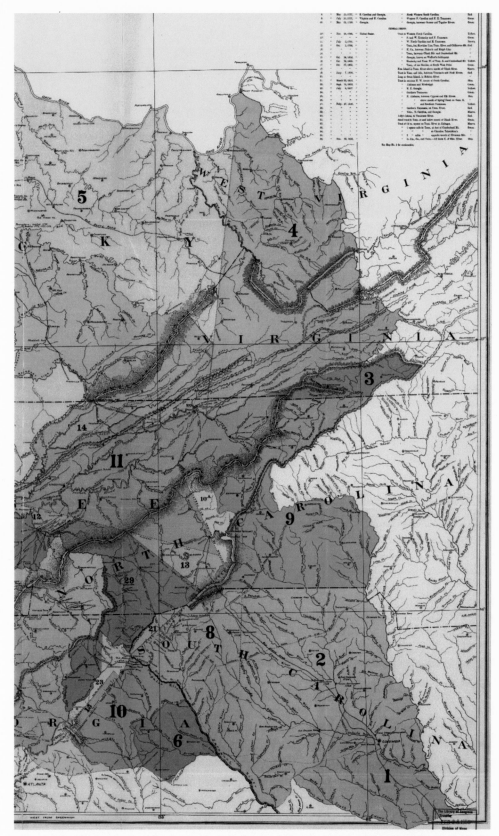

Figure 62b: 1884 Map showing the gradual depletion of Cherokee lands with each cession in numerical order. (Image from Library of Congress, Geography and Map Division. Public Domain, published before 1922)

NUMERIC AND CHRONOLOGIC SCHEDULE OF CHEROKEE CESSIONS.

COLONIAL PERIOD.

No.	Date and Designation of Treaty.	Description of Cession.	Color.
1.	Treaty of 1721 with Gov. Nicholson, of S. Carolina.	Tract in S. Carolina, between Santee and Saluda and Edisto Rivers.	Red.
2.	" Nov. 24, 1755, with Gov. Glenn, of S. Carolina.	" " " Wateree and Savannah Rivers.	Blue.
3.	" Oct. 14, 1768, " J. Stuart, British Supt. Indian Affairs.	" South Western Virginia.	Mauve.
4.	" Oct. 18, 1770, at Lochaber, South Carolina.	" Virginia, W. Virginia, N. E. Tenn., and E. end of Ky.	Red.
5.	" 1772, with Governor of Virginia.	" Virginia, West Virginia, and Eastern Kentucky.	Yellow.
6.	" June 1, 1773, " J. Stuart, British Supt. Ind. Affrs.	" Georgia, north of Broad River.	Mauve.
7.	" March 17, 1775, " Richard Henderson *et al.*	" Kentucky, Virginia, and Tennessee.	Blue.
8.	" May 20, 1777, " S. Carolina and Georgia.	" North Western South Carolina.	Red.
9.	" July 20, 1777, " Virginia and N. Carolina.	" Western N. Carolina and N. E. Tennessee.	Green.
10.	" May 31, 1783, " Georgia.	" Georgia, between Oconee and Tugaloo Rivers.	Green.

FEDERAL PERIOD.

No.	Date and Designation of Treaty.	Description of Cession.	Color.
10*.	" Nov. 28, 1785, " United States.	Tract in Western North Carolina.	Yellow.
10*.	" " " " "	" S. and W. Kentucky and N. Tennessee.	Green.
11.	" July 2, 1791, " "	" W. North Carolina and E. Tennessee.	Brown.
12.	" Oct. 2, 1798, " "	" Tenn., bet. Hawkins Line, Tenn. River, and Chilhowee Mt.	Red.
13.	" " " " "	" N. Ca., between Picken's and Meig's Line.	"
14.	" " " " "	" Tenn., between Clinch Riv. and Cumberland Mt.	"
15.	" Oct. 24, 1804, " "	" Georgia, known as Wafford's Settlement.	"
16.	" Oct. 25, 1805, " "	" Kentucky and Tenn. W. of Tenn. R. and Cumberland Mt.	Yellow.
17.	" Oct. 27, 1805, " "	" Tenn., of one Section, at South West Point.	Green.
18.	" " " " "	First Island in Tenn. River above mouth of Clinch River.	Mauve.
19.	" Jany. 7, 1806, " "	Tract in Tenn. and Ala., between Tennessee and Duck Rivers.	Red.
20.	" " " " "	Long or Great Island, in Holston River.	"
21.	" March 22, 1816, " "	Tract in extreme N. W. corner of South Carolina.	Blue.
22.	" Sept. 14, 1816, " "	" Alabama and Mississippi.	Green.
23.	" July 8, 1817, " "	" N. E. Georgia.	Yellow.
24.	" " " " "	" Southern Tennessee.	Green.
25.	" " " " "	" N. Alabama, between Cypress and Elk Rivers.	Blue.
26.	" " " " "	" " above mouth of Spring Creek on Tenn. R.	"
27.	" Feby. 27, 1819, " "	" " and Southern Tennessee.	Yellow.
28.	" " " " "	" Southern Tennessee, on Tenn. River.	Red.
29.	" " " " "	" Tenn., N. Carolina, and Georgia.	Mauve.
30.	" " " " "	Jolly's Island, in Tennessee River.	Red.
31.	" " " " "	Small tract in Tenn. at and below mouth of Clinch River.	Green.
32.	" " " " "	Tract of 12 m. square on Tenn. River in Alabama.	Mauve.
33.	" " " " "	" 1 square mile in Tenn., at foot of Cumberland Mt.	Green.
34.	" " " " "	" " " at Cherokee Talootiskee's.	"
35.	" " " " "	" 3 " miles " opposite mouth of Hiwassee Riv.	"
36.	" Dec. 29, 1835, " "	" in Ala., Ga., and Tenn.—All lands E. of Miss. River.	Blue.

Figure 63: Dates and descriptions for the maps found on pages 222-3, detailing the Cherokee cessions from their original land claims.

The most well-known and well-documented missions were those of the Moravian Church, which had missions among the Cherokee as early as 1737. Converts are mentioned in detail. The original records (written in both German and English) are at the Moravian Archives in Bethlehem, Pennsylvania, and are available elsewhere on microfilm. The mission and its records are detailed in *Guide to the Records of the Moravian Mission Among the Indians of North America from the Archives of the Moravian Church Bethlehem, Pennsylvania* (New Haven, Connecticut: Research Publications, 1970). A surname index to the collection is Carl John Fliegel's *Index to the Records of the Moravian Mission Among the Indians of North America* (Woodbridge, Connecticut: Research Publications, 1970).

Cherokee: Land Records

No one resource of early Cherokee land records covers the entire tribal nation before its removal. The following, though incomplete, are important. David Keith Hampton's *Cherokee Reservees* (Oklahoma City, Oklahoma: Baker Publishing Co., 1979) provides details of lands given to the Cherokees in Hamilton County, Tennessee. The book has the names of the applicants who settled their claims with the United States government in 1817, including families who received life reservations, persons who were compensated for reservations taken by the state of Georgia, and claimants for lost reservations.

Following the treaty of 1817, the United States Secretary of War deeded land to each of the Cherokee chiefs who had signed the treaty. Each tract was either in newly ceded lands or in older ones ceded through earlier treaties. Every chief was given 640 acres (one square mile) of land. Robert Armstrong was the surveyor of the lands in Alabama, North Carolina, and Tennessee. The surveyor's records for Georgia have not survived. Each survey and the accompanying plat have been published in James L. Douthat's *Robert Armstrong's Survey Book of Cherokee Lands: Lands Granted from Treaty of 27 February 1819* (Signal Mountain, Tennessee: Mountain Press, 1993). The published version displays over 100 plats of the reserved lands and has a full name index.

The Cherokee Agency in Tennessee was in operation until 1835. Its records have been transcribed in Marybelle W. Chase's *Records of the Cherokee Agency in Tennessee, 1801-1835* (Tulsa, Oklahoma: M.W. Chase, 1990), and they contain much genealogical information, such as lists of widows and orphans. They also include an 1819 listing of those who had originally enrolled for emigration but misunderstood the treaty and wanted to remain. The records can be used alongside others of the time.

One often overlooked source is the county land deeds. When mixed-race families who had received their reserves decided to move and sell their lands, the transactions would have been recorded in their local counties.

The Scots-Irish as Chickasaw

The Chickasaw Nation was located historically in northern Mississippi, northwestern Alabama, and in Tennessee and Kentucky west of the Tennessee River. At the time of removal, its lands had already been reduced to northern Mississippi and northwestern Alabama with the Tennessee line forming its northern border.

Because the Scots-Irish had contact with the Chickasaw, many mixed-race Chickasaw trace their ancestry back to Ulster. Some Chickasaw mixed-race family names whose roots are in Ireland include Berryhill, Graham, Herron, Lindsey, Mays, McCuthen, and Norwood. Their lineages are mixed with the Europeans as well as with the Cherokee and the Choctaw. Many Chickasaw remained in Mississippi after the tribe's removal, but others eventually returned from Indian Territory. Those who returned tended to assimilate into the larger white society. Today, large numbers of Mississippi residents in Chickasaw, Clay, Itawamba,

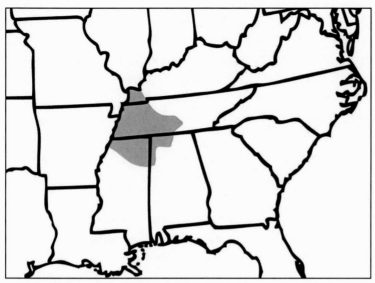

Figure 64: Original Chickasaw claims before cessions and removal.

LaFayette, Monroe, Pontotoc, Tisho-mingo, and Union Counties have mixed-race ancestries.

In Oklahoma, the Chickasaw Nation has a jurisdictional territory of 7,648 square miles in south-central Oklahoma. It covers all or part of the 13 counties of Bryan, Carter, Coal, Garvin, Grady, Jefferson, Johnston, Love, Marshall, McClain, Murray, Pontotoc, and Stephens.

When considering Chickasaw heritage, three important points about the tribe might be helpful in formulating a research strategy.

- Mixed-blood Chickasaw frequently stayed in Mississippi and Alabama. The families often used terms such as "Black Dutch" to hide their ethnic origin, but the term "Black Dutch" was more common among mixed-race Cherokee families. If the term survives in the family, make sure it is really

a Chickasaw family being researched and not a Cherokee family.

- Mixed-race Chickasaw generally used their European names instead of their native names; yet an accompanying Chickasaw name often may be found in the records of Alabama, Mississippi, and Oklahoma.

- Oft-repeated legends among mixed-race descendants in Mississippi are of family members who disappeared and were never heard from again or of family members who went to Oklahoma. Families that disappeared might have simply passed for white and deliberately blended into the larger society. Families that went to Oklahoma might have been those that did not, could not, or would not pass for white.

Chickasaw: Source Material and Genealogies

Anne Kelley Hoyt includes an extensive inventory of material in her *Bibliography of the Chickasaw*. The Tribal Library in Ada, Oklahoma, has a genealogist on staff to help with research. The Itawamba Historical Society in Mantachie, Mississippi, is a major genealogical library in the area and houses family files and published genealogies. *Itawamba Settlers*, published by the Itawamba Historical Society, and *The Northeast Mississippi Historical and Genealogical Society Quarterly* by the Northeast Mississippi

Historical and Genealogical Society in Tupelo are major regional journals that publish Chickasaw related articles and extracted records.

Chickasaw: Church Records

Thomas C. Stuart of the South Carolina Presbytery established a Presbyterian mission at Pontotoc, and E.T. Winston published a copy of Rev. Stuart's diary in *"Father" Stuart and the Monroe Mission*. The diary, which includes baptisms and minutes (1823 to 1838), has been extracted and posted on several websites.

Chickasaw: Early United States Government Rolls

The Chickasaw are documented in the following censuses or muster rolls that are widely available online:

1818: A census of 1818 that is part of the Chickasaw Nation Records collection at the Oklahoma Historical Society.

1837: A muster roll of the Chickasaw before they left Mississippi; it can be used with the 1839 Upshaw Roll.

Upshaw Roll (1839): A muster roll of the tribe after its arrival in Indian Territory.

1847: A census taken in Indian Territory.

Chickasaw Nation Records

The Chickasaw Nation Records, compiled by the tribe in Oklahoma, have early material relating to the original emigrants from Mississippi and Alabama. Among them are the 1818 census and an "Incompetent Record and List of Original Claimants" documenting payments between 1839 and 1849 to individual Chickasaw under the Treaty of 1834.

Chickasaw: Agency Records

Chickasaw Agency Records are titled "Letters Received by the Office of Indian Affairs, Chickasaw Agency, 1830-1835." In addition to the general correspondence, they have lists, for example, of Chickasaw who were members of exploring parties and of those who were named in treaties.

Chickasaw: Land Records

Under the Treaty of Pontotoc Creek (1832), the Chickasaw Nation ceded its lands in northern Mississippi and northwest Alabama to the United States government. Until the 1837 removal, its core settlement areas were in Monroe, Pontotoc, and Tishomingo Counties in Mississippi and Colbert, Franklin, and Marion Counties in northwest Alabama.

Under various treaties with the government, the Chickasaw agreed to abandon their Mississippi and Alabama lands when the tribal leaders found a suitable home west of the Mississippi River. In the meantime, according to provisions of the Treaty of 1834, the government supervised the division of tribal lands into temporary parcels for each family that expected to live on the allotment until the tribe moved west. Eventually, each allotment was sold by the family occupying it. Funds were to be used for the family's emigration and support once it was in Indian Territory. The allotments covered about one-third of the Chickasaw Nation. Background information on the process is in Mary Elizabeth Young's *Redskins, Ruffleshirts and Rednecks: Indian Allotments in Alabama and Mississippi, 1830-1860.*

After the allotments were surveyed in 1834, land companies, land speculators, and farmers wishing to purchase the allotments flooded into northern Mississippi. Settlers also swarmed to purchase Chickasaw lands that had not been allotted to individual Chickasaw. By the 1837 removal year, hostile white neighbors surrounded the Chickasaw. As a consequence, the Chickasaw are found in county land deeds selling their allotments. County deed records that include information on the sales of lands have been published. For example, the Itawamba County Historical Society in Mississippi has published Books 1 and 2 as Bob Frank's *Early Deeds of Itawamba County, Mississippi: 1836-39* (Mantachie, Mississippi: the Itawamba Historical Society, 2008), which compilations have general, slave, and Chickasaw indexes. Using them as a reference, the conclusion is that the whites who arrived later into Chickasaw lands are not good candidates for mixed-race connections.

Although most tribal members sold their land allotments and emigrated, some did not. Wealthy members traveled back and forth between Indian Territory and Mississippi to manage their business ventures. If a husband died, his property could have been placed under court-appointed guardianship, leaving his widow and children to become wards of the county and never emigrating. Other families assimilated into the white communities or periodically immigrated into Indian Territory until 1850. Further details are found in Arrell M. Gibson's *The Chickasaws*.

Even before their lands were sold on the market, land records were generated for the Chickasaw properties. To access them, first ascertain the legal description of the land (township, range, section). The description can be found in county deed books or in the Bureau of Land Management's General Land Office Records index (Glorecords) to land claims, which is online. The General Land Office records can be accessed by the name of the person (in the case of Chickasaw names, the spellings should not include hyphens) or by the land description (township, range, section).

Maps that were compiled about land as it was patented or allotted to individuals are known as Township Plat Maps. They illustrate entire townships and ranges on single maps with outlines of the boundaries of plots with the owners' names. Their value is in reconstructing entire neighborhoods. The Township Plat Maps for Chickasaw lands, organized by the lands' descriptions, are part of the Chickasaw Meridian. The treaty that called for the temporary allotments in Mississippi also applied to the eastern part of the Chickasaw Nation in what is now Colbert and Franklin Counties, Alabama. Margaret Matthews Cowart extracted the United States government tract books for the two counties. Alabama patents and Indian Allotments are also part of the General Land Office Records online index.

Chickasaw: Indian Reserve Files
The BLM's "Indian Reserve Files" (Record Group 49) are documents created in connection with special grants or reserves of land for individual Indians. The

collection, at the National Archives, concerns many tribes nationwide. Specific Chickasaw items include:

Box 2: Cancelled Chickasaw land patents, which were transfers of land patents to incoming white settlers.

Box 6: Certificates of orphan lands, which present the names of the incoming settlers and the names of the Chickasaw whose lands were purchased.

The Scots-Irish as Choctaw

Like other native peoples in the American Southeast, the Choctaw had family connections with Scots-Irish. Some Choctaw families with roots in Ulster are Folsom, Jones, McKee or McGee, McKinney, Perry, McCurtain, Walker, and Wall.

The Choctaw, whose ancestral lands included the lower two-thirds of Mississippi and western Alabama, was one of the largest tribes east of the Mississippi River. It was the first tribe to be selected by the United States government for removal to Indian Territory, and its rights were defined in the Treaty of Dancing Rabbit Creek (27 September 1830). Through the Treaty, the Choctaw ceded all its eastern lands and prepared for removal, but the treaty also allowed many Choctaw to stay in Mississippi.

The Choctaw who chose to stay were mostly congregated in the counties of Greene, Jasper, Kemper, Leake, Neshoba, Newton, Perry, and Scott. The Choctaw who remained in Mississippi did not readily assimilate into the community at large. Many retained some of their native culture. Some intermarried into the black or white communities, but most chose to become invisible. Learning from the experience of the Choctaw removal, the United States government developed policies under which other tribes later were removed. For further information on the removal, see Arthur H. DeRosier's *The Removal of the Choctaw Indians*.

The Choctaw tribes in Mississippi and Oklahoma are not the only Choctaw ones. State or federally recognized smaller Choctaw tribes in Alabama and Louisiana include the MOWA Choctaw Indians in Washington County, Alabama; the Jena Band of Choctaw of LaSalle and Catahoula Parishes, Louisiana; the United Houma Nation along the southeast coast of Louisiana in the parishes of Jefferson, Lafourche, and Plaquemines; the Biloxi-Chitimacha Choctaw Confederation of Muskogees in Lafourche and Terrebonne Parishes, Louisiana; and the Choctaw-Apache of Ebarb in western Sabine Parish, Louisiana.

Today, the judicial area of the Choctaw Nation consists of 11,000 square miles and covers all or part of fourteen Oklahoma counties: Atoka, Bryan, Coal, Choctaw, Haskell, Hughes, Johnston, Latimer, LeFlore, McCurtain, Pittsburg, Pontotoc, and Pushmataha. The Choctaw Nation is based in Durant, Oklahoma.

When formulating a research strategy to study Choctaw lineage, consider:

- The old Choctaw Nation in Mississippi was divided into districts that are often referenced in the records. The districts were formed in the early nineteenth century and were centered on the three major river systems: the Tombigbee in the East, the Pearl and Big Black in the West, and the Chickasawhay and Pascagoula in the South.

- Many Choctaw used native names rather than European names; others took first names as surnames. Therefore, surnames such as Amos, Betsey, Billy, Bob, Jack, Jim, John, Ned, Peter, Phillip, Thomas, and Tom appear among the Choctaw tribe today.

- Some Choctaw families have little personal information preserved resulting from the custom of "not calling the name of the dead."

- Historically, the maternal line of descent was the most important.

Choctaw: Source Material and Genealogies

The main repositories for Choctaw records are the National Archives, the Oklahoma Historical Society, the Mississippi Department of Archives and History, and the Family History Library. Because of the Choctaw's historic importance, many historical and cultural works were written about them. Samuel J. Wells's thesis "Choctaw Mixed-Bloods and the Advent of Removal" (Ph.D. Thesis, University of Southern Mississippi, August 1987) describes the history of the Choctaw mixed race from 1795 until the time of the Choctaw removal in 1830. Wells listed many mixed-race names and included charts for some of the more prominent families. Bibliographic material about

Choctaw sources can be found in Kidwell and Roberts's *The Choctaws: A Critical Bibliography*.

Choctaw: Church Records

The American Board of Commissioners for Foreign Missions (ABCFM), a joint effort between the Congregational Church and the Presbyterian Church, established missions among the Choctaw in Mississippi. The ABCFM missionaries moved with the tribe to Indian Territory, where they continued their work. The ABCFM Archives (1818-1859) are microfilmed. The Mississippi Department of Archives and History has a manuscript titled "Missionary Papers, no. 14, Notices of Choctaw Converts, 1830."

Choctaw: Early United States Government Rolls

The United States government took censuses of the Choctaw in preparation for their removal, and again once they arrived in Indian Territory. Most of them have been published or extracted on several websites. They are also available on microfilm.

Armstrong Roll (1830): A census of the Choctaw made at the time of the Treaty of Dancing Rabbit Creek in 1830.

Choctaw Emigrants to the West (1831, 1832): Not all of the Choctaw left at one time. During 1831 and 1832, most had been removed to five areas known as depots in southeast Oklahoma or in Fort Smith, Arkansas.

23 May 1855: "Roll of Eastern Choctaw Prepared by Douglas H. Cooper, U.S. Indian Agent, Choctaw Indian Agency,

Indian Territory, Alabama, Mississippi, and Louisiana, 1855" includes a register of Choctaw living in Jasper and Newton Counties, Mississippi; St. Tammany and Orleans Parishes, Louisiana; Mobile, Alabama (known as the Six Town Clan); and Neshoba County, Mississippi (Bogue Citto Clan).

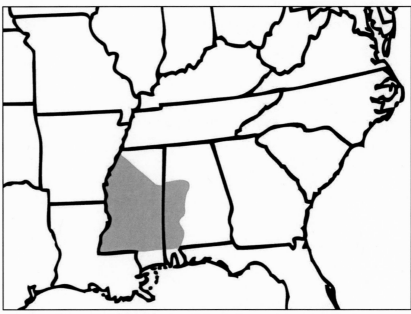

Figure 65: Original Choctaw Claims before cessions and removal.

Choctaw: Land Records

Since the Choctaw was the first tribe designated for removal by the United States government, the subject of land and the tribe are inseparable. Records of Choctaw lands can be found in a wide variety of sources.

Under the Treaty of Dancing Rabbit Creek, the Mississippi lands of the Choctaw were ceded to the United States government. The Treaty contained an article whereby any Choctaw who wished to stay in Mississippi could receive a reservation. Article 14 of the Treaty stated that the remaining Choctaw had to register with the Indian Agent in 1831. The registers can be found in the "Choctaw Nation Records."

Many Choctaw received scrips for lands that allowed the recipients to select public lands instead of assignments of specifically defined allotments. The selections were restricted to designated areas. For example, the scrips given under the

Treaty of Dancing Rabbit Creek had to be redeemed for lands in Mississippi, Louisiana, Alabama, or Arkansas. For background information regarding Choctaw lands, see Mary Elizabeth Young's *Redskins, Ruffleshirts and Rednecks: Indian Allotments in Alabama and Mississippi, 1830-1860*. Franklin L. Riley's "Choctaw Land Claims" in *Publications of the Mississippi Historical Society* (1904): 345-394 is an historical study of the Choctaw claims and the frauds and scandals arising from the terms of the Treaty of Dancing Rabbit Creek. Riley also describes efforts made by state and federal officials to resolve the claims.

Other land related sources that are Choctaw specific are:

American State Papers. The *American State Papers, Public Lands,* Volume 7, 1834-1835 has listings of Choctaw and Americans owning farms in the Choctaw Nation in Mississippi in 1830. They have the number of persons in each family, the size of the farm, its location, the quality of the land, and other information.

Choctaw Nation Records. Records concerning the Choctaw in both Mississippi and Oklahoma were filed with the Choctaw Nation in Oklahoma. "Choctaw Nation Records (1830-1899)" are located at the Indian Archives Division, Oklahoma Historical Society, and include:

- "Mississippi Choctaw Claimants under 14th Article" (Choctaw Volume 436), which contains the names of those making claims under the provisions of Article 14 of the Treaty of Dancing Rabbit Creek.

- "Lists of names of Choctaws to whom scrip was issued under the 14th Article of the Treaty of Dancing Rabbit Creek, prepared by the Indian Office for identification" (Choctaw Volume 437). The volume is a typescript of the Mississippi Choctaw claimants. Another version with some differing information is found in Choctaw Volume 437-2.

- "A list of Choctaw Heads of Families Claiming Lands under the 14th Article of the Treaty, Undated" (Choctaw Census Document 13592 - 1 H). An index to this material was created in 1876 (Choctaw - Census Document 13592 - 1 I).

- "Lists of Claimants under the Fourteenth Article of the Treaty of 1830, whose claims were allowed by Acts of Congress and approved" (Choctaw Volume 438). The volume has the register of Agent William Ward's Choctaw names and a "supplemental list of names of persons whose claims under the Fourteenth Article of the Treaty of 1830 were recommended by the Senate, or who appear on certain of Ward's lists."

- "A Copy of American State Papers, Public Lands, Volume 7, 1834-1835" (Choctaw Treaty of 1830 Document 24324). The volume begins with a list of captains in Nitachachee's District in 1830.

- "Application for Identification as Mississippi Choctaws, 1899" (Choctaw - Citizenship Document 13693). The material has testimony taken from 24 January through 10 February 1899, concerning the applications, a list of claimants with blood quanta shown, and the names and post office addresses of rejected families.

Indian Reserve File. A file of miscellaneous material pertaining to various tribes. All the material in the Indian Reserve File concerns lands. It is part of Record Group 49 of the Bureau of Land Management records at the National Archives. Within this file is: Box 8: Choctaw land (1842-1883), miscellaneous Choctaw letters 1809-1845), Choctaw orphan lands in Mississippi (1820-1840); and

Box 9: Choctaw orphan lands (1850-1900).

Choctaw: School Records

A Choctaw school was established in 1825 near Blue Springs and Georgetown in Scott County, Kentucky. Many prominent Choctaw families, especially those of mixed race, wanted to further their education; they sent their children to the Choctaw school or attended as adults. The Choctaw ended their association with the school in 1842. Names of the students were published as *List of Choctaw Students Attending Schools in the States*. The correspondence for the school has been transcribed and indexed in Joe R. Goss's *The Choctaw Academy: Official Correspondence, 1825-1841* (Conway, Arkansas: Oldbuck Press, 1992).

The Scots-Irish as Muscogee (Creek)

The Scots-Irish and other Europeans first came into Muscogee (Creek) country as traders. They or their descendants intermarried with the tribe located in what is modern-day Alabama, Georgia, and northern Florida. The Europeans referred to them as Creek, which is still used as a colloquial term. The proper name for the tribe is the Muscogee (Creek) Nation. Some tribal families with immigrant origins in Ireland are Carr, Crawford, Frazier, Kennard, Killam, MacFarlane, McClure, McComb, McConnell, McCoy, McGhee, McGillicuddy, McKillop, McKinney, Marshall, Robeson, Sample, Scroggins, and Watts.

Most of the Muscogee were removed from their native lands by the United States government starting in 1836.

Today, the Muscogee (Creek) Nation is located in east-central Oklahoma with its headquarters in Okmulgee, Oklahoma. The Nation covers all or parts of eleven counties: Creek, Hughes, Mayes, McIntosh, Muskogee, Okfuskee, Okmulgee, Rogers, Seminole, Tulsa, and Wagner.

The Muscogee (Creek) Nation in Oklahoma is the largest of the Creek tribes but certainly not the only one. The Poarch Band of Creek Indians, headquartered in Atmore, Escambia County, Alabama, is the only federally recognized tribe in that state. State recognized tribes include: Ma-Chis Lower Creek Indian Tribe headquartered at New Brockton, Coffee County, Alabama, and the Star Clan of Lower Muscogee Creek Indians, headquartered in Troy, Pike County, Alabama.

A branch of the tribe in Georgia has purchased the old Tama Town site, where they have reorganized its part of the tribe. It did not remove westward but blended into the white communities in Early and Grady Counties. The Lower Muskogee Creek Tribe is located in Whigham in modern day Grady County, Georgia. Membership is accepted into the tribe based on an unbroken lineage back to a Muscogee ancestor found on a treaty or a roll. Accordingly, the tribe has numerous genealogies, many of which trace back to a Scot-Irish immigrant.

Before proceeding with Muscogee research, take into account the following:

- Muscogee migrations and removals can be divided into three

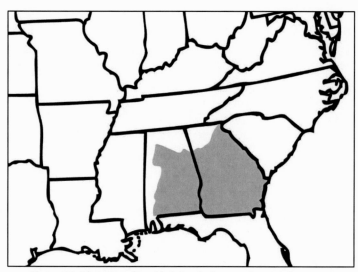

Figure 66: Muscogee (Creek) claims before cessions and removal.

family names. Both the native and European names were used throughout a person's life, and both also might have been used simultaneously in United States government records. The Muscogee was a matriarchal society, and so clan and tribal town affiliations and properties were passed through the mothers. If a father was white, the mixed-race children might have sought association with their mother's family rather than with their father's. Conversely, if a family was trying to "pass for white," it would have associated with the father's surname.

periods: 1) the "Old Settlers" who emigrated westward before 1833; 2) those who emigrated westward at their own expense between 1833 and 1840; and 3) those forcibly removed beginning in 1837. Different records document each of the three groups.

- The Muscogee Confederacy was composed of tribal towns, each of which was a centralized community. The complex political units were the underpinning of the Muscogee Confederacy. Tribal towns acted both independently and cooperatively as members of the confederacy. The Muscogee often named their new towns in Oklahoma after their old ones in the Southeast, especially those from eastern Alabama, thus offering a geographical link between the two places.

- Records often listed Muscogee men and women by tribal names in preference to their European

Muscogee (Creek): Published Source Material

Muscogee (Creek) family histories can be found at the Library of Congress, the Family History Library, the Oklahoma Historical Society, the Alabama Department of Archives and History, the Birmingham Public Library, and the Mobile Public Library. Three books written in the nineteenth century offer some insights about the tribe that can be found nowhere else: George Stiggins's *Creek Indian History: A Historical Narrative of the Genealogy, Traditions and Downfall of the Ispocoga or Creek Indian Tribe of Indians*, edited by Virginia Pounds Brown (Birmingham, Alabama: Birmingham Public Library Press, 1989); Thomas Woodward's, *Woodward's Reminiscences* of the Creek, or Muscogee Indians, Contained in Letters to Friends in Georgia and Alabama) (1859. Reprint, Birmingham, Alabama: Birmingham Book Exchange, 1939); and Benjamin Hawkins's *A Sketch of the Creek Country, in the Years 1798 and 1799, and Letters of Benjamin Hawkins, 1796-1806* (Spartanburg, South Carolina: Reprint Co., 1974).

Muscogee (Creek): Eastern Land Records

By the 1832 Treaty of Cusseta, the Muscogee ceded their lands east of the Mississippi River to the United States. Under the Treaty, a Muscogee could remove westward or stay on his or her lands and thus be absorbed into the white communities. All Muscogee who chose to stay were given titles to their individual lands after a five-year period. For background information, see Mary Elizabeth Young's *Redskins Ruffleshirts and Rednecks: Indian Allotments in Alabama and Mississippi, 1830-1860*.

After the 1832 census, the Muscogee lands were surveyed and sold either through the Montgomery Land Office or the Mardisville Land Office. A chapter in Marilyn Davis Barefield's book *Old Montgomery Land Office Records and Military Warrants (1834-1869)* (Birmingham, Alabama: Southern University Press, 1991) titled "Indian Deeds" concerns the records that were created when some Muscogee deeded their lands to white settlers. Barefield's other important work *The Old Mardisville, Lebanon & Centre Land Office Records & Military Warrants (1834-1860)* (Greenville, South Carolina: Southern Historical Press, 1990) documents lands sold from that

office. The modern-day counties covered by the land offices are:

> Montgomery Land Office:
> Autauga, Barbour, Bullock, Chambers, Coosa, Elmore, Lee, Lowndes, Macon, Montgomery, Russell, Talladega, and Tallapoosa.

> Mardisville Land Office:
> Cherokee, Clay, Cleburne, DeKalb, Etowah, Jackson, Marshall, Randolph, St. Clair, and Talladega.

The names of Muscogee and mixed-blood Muscogee, most of whom were removed but who were granted land patents, can be found in the BLM Tract Books, which are divided by land office and then by township, range, and section. Each Muscogee person is listed under the column of "Name of the Purchaser" by "Creek Treaty 1832," and the name is accompanied with the notation of "reserved for." Although the Muscogee in the BLM records never received the patents to their lands, the descriptions of the lands (townships, ranges, sections) place the families in specific locations. The researcher, therefore, can investigate neighbors, families, and relationships for mixed-blood descendants. The Tract Books are at the National Archives and are being scanned for its Glorecords website.

The records in "Creek Reservations Under the Treaty of March 24, 1832 (7 Stat. 366)" give access to the BLM Tract Books for exact surnames. These reservation records are part of the "Creek National Records" in the Indian Archives Division, Oklahoma Historical Society. The seven books cover

1832 to the 1870s and list the names of tribal members with legal descriptions of their Alabama lands. Each book is alphabetized by the first letter of the surname, then by the first letter of the given name, and then by the Muscogee town in Alabama where the person lived. After locating the description of the land (township, section, and range), the researcher can consult the BLM Tract Books. The process of selling off the Creek lands allowed the Alabama legislature to divide the Muscogee (Creek) Nation into the counties of Benton (named Calhoun in 1858), Chambers, Coosa, Macon, Randolph, Russell, Tallapoosa, and Talledega. All are on the Glorecords website.

The United States government maps of the Muscogee allotments show the individual allocations as squares with the name of each owner written in the square. With the maps, it is possible to reconstruct entire neighborhoods to search for interrelated families, many of whom were mixed race. Maps for the following counties with corresponding map numbers are part of Record Group 75, Records of the Bureau of Indian Affairs, Central Map File, at the National Archives: (#243) Chambers County-eastern Tallapoosa County; (#238) Russell County; (#241) Barbour County; and (#256) Macon County.

Muscogee (Creek): Early United States Government Rolls

The primary United States Government Rolls for the Muscogee (Creek) have been published or extracted on various websites.

Abbott and Parsons (1832): Also called the Upper Creek Roll, the census documents the Muscogee (Creek) Nation before removal.

Lower Creek Census (1832): The enumeration is of heads of families, the number of males, females, and slaves in each family, and the towns in which the families lived.

Old Settler Roll (1857): June 1857 census taken of the Muscogee in Indian Territory lists the heads of households and those in the households who had moved westward before 1833. The people and their descendants became eligible for funds under the Treaty of 7 August 1856.

Dunn Roll of Citizens (1867): Census of the Muscogee households in Indian Territory.

Stidham Roll (1886): The roll lists the claims of Muscogee who had moved westward at their own expense between 1830 and 1840.

Further Reading

General References
Debo, Angie. *And Still the Waters Run*. Princeton, New Jersey: Princeton University Press, 1940, 1973.

DeMarce, Virginia Easley. "Looking at Legends – Lumbee and Melungeon: Applied Genealogy and the Origins of Tri-Racial Isolates," in *National Genealogical Society Quarterly* 81 (March 1993): 24-45.

DeMarce, Virginia Easley. "Verry Slitly Mixt": Tri-Racial Isolate Families of the Upper South - A Genealogical Study" in

National Genealogical Society Quarterly 80 (March 1992): 5-35.

Foreman, Grant. *Indian Removal: The Emigration of the Five Civilized Tribes of Indians*. Norman, Oklahoma: University of Oklahoma Press, 1953.

Hudson, Charles. *The Southeastern Indians*. Knoxville, Tennessee: University of Tennessee Press, 1976.

Swanton, John R. *The Indian Tribes of North America*. Reprint, Baltimore, Maryland: Genealogical Publishing Co., 2007.

Walton-Raji, Angela Y. *Black Indian Genealogy: African-American Ancestors Among the Five Civilized Tribes*. Westminster, Maryland: Heritage Books, 2007.

Young, Mary Elizabeth. *Redskins, Ruffleshirts and Rednecks: Indian Allotments in Alabama and Mississippi, 1830-1860*. Ann Arbor, MI: University Microfilms International, 1989.

Catawba References

Blumer, Thomas J. *Bibliography of the Catawba*. Metuchen, New Jersey: Scarecrow Press, 1987.

Blumer, Thomas J. *Catawba Nation: Treasures in History*. Charleston, South Carolina: History Press, 2007.

Brown, Douglas Summers. *The Catawba Indians: The People of the River*. Columbia, South Carolina: The University of South Carolina Press, 1966.

Hudson, Charles M. *The Catawba Nation*. Athens, Georgia: University of Georgia Press, 2007.

McDowell, William J. *Colonial Records of South Carolina: Documents Relating to Indian Affairs, May 21, 1750-August 7, 1754*. Columbia, South Carolina: South Carolina Archives Department, 1958.

McDowell, William J. *Colonial Records of South Carolina: Documents Relating to Indian Affairs, 1754-1765*. Columbia, South Carolina: University of South Carolina Press, 1970.

Merrell, James H. *The Indians' New World: Catawbas and Their Neighbors from European Contact Through the Era of Removal*. Chapel Hill, North Carolina: University of North Carolina Press, 1989.

Pettus, Louise. *Leasing Away a Nation: The Legacy of Catawba Indian Land Leases*. Columbia, South Carolina: Palmetto Conservation Foundation, 2005.

Watson, Ian M. *Catawba Indian Genealogy*. Geneseo, New York: Department of Anthropology, State University of New York at Geneseo, 1995.

Watson, Ian M. *Catawba Indian Genealogy: A Report to the National Endowment for the Humanities*. Rochester, New York: by author, 1986.

Cherokee References

Anderson, William L. *Cherokee Removal: Before and After*. Athens, Georgia: University of Georgia Press, 1992.

Anderson, William L. *A Guide to Cherokee Documents in Foreign Archives*. Metuchen, New Jersey: Scarecrow Press, 1983.

Conley, Robert J. *A Cherokee Encyclopedia*. Albuquerque, New Mexico: University of New Mexico Press, 2007.

Conley, Robert J. *The Cherokee Nation: A History*. Albuquerque, New Mexico: University of New Mexico Press, 2008.

Ehle, John. *Trail of Tears: The Rise and Fall of the Cherokee Nation*. New York, New York: Doubleday, 1989.

McLoughlin, William G. *After the Trail of Tears: The Cherokees' Struggle for Sovereignty, 1839-1880*. Chapel Hill, North Carolina: University of North Carolina Press, 1994.

McLoughlin, William G. *Cherokee Renascence in the New Republic*. Princeton, New Jersey: Princeton University Press, 1992.

Perdue, Theda. *The Cherokee Removal: A Brief History with Documents*. Boston, Massachusetts: Bedford/St. Martin's Press, 2004.

Perdue, Theda and Michael Green. *The Cherokee Nation and the Trail of Tears*. New York, New York: Viking Adult, 2007.

Rogers, Mary Evelyn. *A Brief History of the Cherokees, 1540-1906*. Baltimore, Maryland: Gateway Press, 1986.

Woodward, Grace Steele. *The Cherokees*. Norman, Oklahoma: University of Oklahoma Press, 1982.

Chickasaw References
Cowart, Margaret Matthews. *Old Land Records of Colbert County, Alabama: A Comparison of 2 Copies of the Government Tractbook for Colbert County, Alabama*. Huntsville, Alabama: M. M. Cowart, 1985.

Cowart, Margaret Matthews. *Old Land Records of Franklin County, Alabama: A Comparison of 4 Copies of the Government Tractbook for Present-day Franklin County, Alabama*. Huntsville, Alabama: M. M. Cowart, 1986.

Gibson, Arrell M. *The Chickasaws*. Norman, Oklahoma: University of Oklahoma, 1971.

Hoyt, Anne Kelley. *Bibliography of the Chickasaw*. Metchen, New Jersey: Scarecrow Press, 1987.

Morgan, Phillip Carroll. *Chickasaw Renaissance*. Norman, Oklahoma: University of Oklahoma Press, 2009.

Swanton, John Reed. *Chickasaw Society and Religion*. Lincoln, Nebraska: University of Nebraska Press, 2006.

Winston, E.T. *Story of Pontotoc: The Chickasaws*. Pontotoc, Mississippi: Pontotoc Progress Print, 1931.

Choctaw References
Akers, Donna. *Living in the Land of Death: The Choctaw Nation, 1830-1860*.

East Lansing, Michigan: Michigan State University Press, 2004.

Debo, Angie. *The Rise and Fall of the Choctaw Republic.* 2d ed. Norman, Oklahoma: University of Oklahoma Press, 1961.

DeRosier, Arthur H. *The Removal of the Choctaw Indians.* Knoxville, Tennessee: The University of Tennessee Press, 1970.

Galloway, Patricia Kay. *Choctaw Genesis.* Lincoln, Nebraska: University of Nebraska Press, 1998.

Kidwell, Clara Sue. *Choctaw and Missionaries in Mississippi, 1818-1918.* Norman, Oklahoma: University of Oklahoma Press, 1995.

Kidwell, Clara Sue. *The Choctaws in Oklahoma: From Tribe to Nation, 1855-1970.* Norman, Oklahoma: University of Oklahoma Press, 2007.

Kidwell, Clara Sue and Charles Roberts. *The Choctaws: A Critical Bibliography.* Bloomington, Indiana: Indiana University Press, 1980.

McKee, Jesse O. and Jon A. Schlenker. *The Choctaws: Cultural Evolution of a Native American Tribe.* Jackson, Mississippi: University Press of Mississippi, 1980.

O'Brien, Greg. *Choctaws in a Revolutionary Age, 1750-1830.* Lincoln, Nebraska: University of Nebraska Press, 2005.

O'Brien, Greg, ed. *Pre-Removal Choctaw History: Exploring New Paths.* Norman, Oklahoma: University of Oklahoma Press, 2008.

Reeves, Carolyn Keller. *The Choctaw Before Removal.* Jackson, Mississippi: University Press of Mississippi, 1985.

Wells, Samuel J. and Roseanna Tubby. *After Removal: The Choctaw in Mississippi.* Jackson, Mississippi: University Press of Mississippi, 1986.

Muscogee (Creek) References

Corkran, David H. *The Creek Frontier, 1540-1783.* Norman, Oklahoma: University of Oklahoma Press, 1967.

Debo, Angie. *The Road to Disappearance.* Norman: Oklahoma: University of Oklahoma Press, 1967.

Ethridge, Robbie. *Creek Country: The Creek Indians and Their World, 1796-1816.* Chapel Hill, North Carolina: University of North Carolina Press, 2003.

Harris, Walter A. *Here the Creeks Sat Down.* Macon, Georgia: J.W. Burke, 1958.

Saunt, Claudio. *A New Order of Things: Property, Power and the Transformation of the Creek Indians, 1733-1816.* New York, New York: Cambridge University Press, 1999.

Swanton, John Reed. *Early History of the Creek Indians and Their Neighbors.* Washington D.C.: Government Printing Office, 1922.

ARTICLES

OF THE ASSOCIATED LOYALISTS,

UNDER THE HONOURABLE BOARD OF DIRECTORS.

HIS Majesty having been graciously pleased to approve of a Plan for the Purpose of employing the Zeal of his faithful Subjects in North America, in annoying the Sea Coasts of the revolted Provinces, and distressing their Trade, either in Co-operation with His Majesty's Land and Sea Forces, or by making Diversions in their Favour, when they are carrying on Operations in other Parts; and for that Purpose has been also pleased to nominate a Number of Gentlemen as a Board of Directors for the Conduct and Management of said Business. And his Excellency Sir Henry Clinton, K. B. and Commander in Chief, having issued a Commission constituting their Excellencies William Franklin, Esquire, Governor of New Jersey, and Josiah Martin, Esquire, Governor of North Carolina, and Timothy Ruggles, Daniel Coxe, George Duncan Ludlow, Edward Lutwyche, George Rome, George Leonard, Anthony Stewart, and Robert Alexander, Esquires, a Board of Directors for the Purposes aforesaid, with Powers to embody and associate all such Persons as may be willing to act under their Orders, and, with his Approbation, to plan and direct any Enterprize they may think expedient.

Wherefore, in Order more effectually to obtain the important Ends of this Establishment, We the Subscribers, do hereby agree to be subject to the following Rules and Regulations, and bind ourselves for the true Observance of the same to the Board of Directors, and to each other, upon that Principle of Honor and good Faith which ought to regulate the Conduct of every loyal Subject and honest Associator.

First, That we will be subject to and strictly obey all such Rules and Orders as shall, from Time to Time, be established and ordained by the Board of Directors for the Regulation and good Government of this Association; And that We will, at all Times, yield a chearful and ready Obedience to all Officers who shall, on the Recommendation of the Board, be commissioned by the Commander in Chief, and conform ourselves, in every Respect, to that orderly Conduct and good Discipline so essentially necessary for our personal Security and the Success of every Enterprize. But, as it is not our Intention, while We become Adventurers in this Undertaking, and by our Exertions provide for ourselves and Families, as well as aid His Majesty's Arms, to be bound for an unlimited Time, or viewed in the Light of enlisted Soldiers, it is hereby provided, that if any of us should in future chuse to withdraw from this Association, We shall be at full Liberty so to do: Previous, however, to a Dismission, the Person desiring the same, shall give at least three Months Notice in Writing of his Intentions to the Board of Directors, or to his Commanding Officer, to be reported to the Board; and, after the Expiration of the Term, he shall receive a full Discharge, unless actually engaged on any Enterprize, and in that Case as soon as the same shall be compleated.

Secondly, For the equitable Distribution of any Captures that may be made by the Associators, and as an Inducement to behave with Courage and Perseverance on all Occasions of Duty, and as it is our Wish, that no quiet inoffensive Inhabitant or other innocent Person without the Lines shall suffer by this Establishment, and our Determination that all Excesses, Barbarities or Irregularities, contrary to the acknowledged Laws of War as practised by civilized Nations, shall be avoided, and that compleat Retribution may take place whenever any such Inhabitant shall suffer Injury, We agree that Ten per Cent. of the nett Proceeds of all Captures shall first be appropriated as a Retribution Fund for satisfying such Claimants who may, in the Opinion of the Commander in Chief, or of the Board, on a full Enquiry, be entitled to Compensation: Provided the Reservation of this Sum, or any Part thereof, shall not exceed the Term of Six Months after our Return from an Expedition; at the Expiration of which Term, the same, or such Part thereof as shall remain on hand, shall be equally divided among the Captors. We do also agree, that a further Sum of Ten per Cent. of the nett Proceeds of all Captures shall be reserved and set apart as a Charity Fund for the Relief and Support of any who may be sick, wounded, maimed, or otherwise disabled in the Service, and for the Maintenance of Widows or Orphans belonging to the Association; an Account of the Disposition of which shall be always open to the Inspection of the Associators. And also that another Reservation of Five per Cent. shall be assigned as a Reward to such Officers, who, by their judicious or spirited Conduct, shall merit particular Distinction. The Application and Distribution of the said two last mentioned Funds, are submitted entirely to the Judgment and Direction of the Board. The Remainder to be equally divided amongst all the Associators concerned in the Enterprize without Regard to Rank or Station.

But, *Thirdly,* If any Effects should happen to be taken from any loyal, quiet, or inoffensive Inhabitant, and distributed, (for which Compensation shall not have been made as above directed) the Amount of the same shall, when ordered by the Commander in Chief of his Majesty's Land Forces, be repaid from future Captures.

Fourthly, If in the Prosecution of an Enterprize under the Authority of the Board, it should be the Misfortune of any of us to be taken Prisoner, or killed by the Enemy; in the first Case the Person so taken, and in the latter his legal Representative, shall nevertheless receive as full a Share as the other Associators concerned in the Enterprize: As shall also all others, who may by Accident, be rendered incapable of acting, after setting out with the Party. And whenever Circumstances shall render an Exemption from a particular Service proper or expedient, the same shall be in Course granted by the Commanding Officer, on Application; in which Case the Person so excused, shall not be entitled to a Share or Proportion of the Benefits arising from that Expedition.

Fifthly, And as the many Advantages attending this Association can only be obtained by a regular Behaviour, and the Privileges in Favour of the Associators secured by the strictest Obedience to the lawful Commands of those in Authority, We do most willingly consent and agree that such Courts, composed of our own Officers, as may be appointed for the Purpose by the Board, shall be held whenever the irregular, disobedient, or disorderly Behaviour of any Individual may render them necessary. The Proceedings to be conducted according to Justice and Equity; and, in Case of Guilt, the Punishment directed (not extending beyond Fine or Expulsion, according to the Nature of the Offence) to be subject to the Revision and Mitigation of the Board, on Appeal by the Person deeming himself aggrieved.

Lastly, To all and every of these Articles We give our most hearty Assent, and respectively engage Ourselves to, and

enroll under

whom we hereby acknowledge our Commanding Officer for the Purposes above written.

Figure 67: Articles of the Associated Loyalist, 1781. (Image from Library of Congress, Rare Book and Special Collections Division, Ephemera Collection. Public Domain, published before 1922.)

Ulster

Chapter Seventeen

Special Strategy: United Empire Loyalist

As a result of the American Revolution, the United States was formed, shattering its domination by the British Empire and impelling the growth of what is today Canada. The two nations were created at different times, but the roots of their development were in the American Revolution. **The present chapter focuses on the Ulster-Scots people in what became the United States who remained loyal to the Crown and who were exiled to what is now Canada.** It does not concern British troops in British North America or British soldiers who did not return to their countries after the war ended but, instead, settled in Canada.

The families cast out from the newly independent United States, a segment of the population termed Loyalists or Tories, provide an important strategy in the research of Scots-Irish immigrant origins. Although the logic of the tactic is straightforward, it does require some explanation because many researchers will find it unfamiliar. For example, yes, most Scots-Irish did indeed fight in droves for the American cause and incurred hardships because of it. They went on to forge the United States. But Scots-Irish also fought for the British cause and struggled greatly as Loyalists. Like other wars that involved the United States, family allegiances were often split along political lines. From the Canadian perspective of history, those who suffered were heroes and nation builders just as much as their American counterparts were. A great deal of interest is current in both countries about who the Loyalists were and what they contributed to the progress of the nation of Canada.

Probably the main focus in traditional Loyalist research is determining where the Loyalists resided in the United States before their exiles. For this study, it is taken one step further, to where in Ulster the Loyalists who came to America before the Revolutionary War were born. There is no master list of all Loyalists, but information about them can be found in numerous places and documents. Published books and databases are essential tools in organizing a viable strategy because many resources may be brought under one search, which can yield new results to an old search.

Once the Loyalists were expelled to the British colonies in modern Canada, often with only the clothes on their backs, they had to reconstruct their lives, furnishing

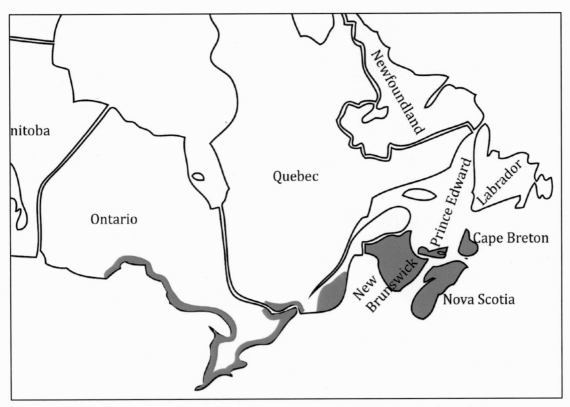

Figure 68: American Loyalist settlement areas in present-day provinces of Canada.

a new set of records that may list birthplaces. To limit a family's Revolutionary War service to the American cause is to ignore that a sibling or parents might have thought differently and supported the British—same family, same Ulster origins, just on opposing sides of the war. The expulsion of the Loyalists from the United States is largely forgotten in United States history but remains instrumental in understanding the settlement and improvement of Canada. With the arriving exiles, new colonies were framed in British North America, such as New Brunswick from Nova Scotia in 1784 and Quebec's splitting into Lower Canada (Quebec) and Upper Canada (Ontario) in 1791.

Although the labels Loyalists and Tories are often used in history books and in manuscripts, another term was invented

later. They were dubbed United Empire Loyalists by the Canadians, often abbreviated UEL. The designation described the incoming loyal British during and after the Revolutionary War, when the name Canadian was not in general use except for the First Nations tribes. (For United States researchers, "First Nations" is the Canadian name for Native Americans.)

The Loyalists were a significant part of the settlement and advancement of Canada. Canadians with Loyalist lines are not uncommon, which means they also tie into the same lines that their United States relatives are trying to research. For Ulster ancestors, the goal is the same, to identify where in Ulster families originated. The large amount of records produced by generations of Canadian researchers may hold those keys for

Americans, and the generations of American researchers may have the solutions for the Canadians.

Several reference works can be helpful in learning more about Canadian research. Typically, but not always, they are provincial-based research manuals written by Canadian genealogists. All should include information on tracing Loyalist ancestors. Even if instruction books are dated, the information on the records themselves remains valid. The only changes are the records having been digitized for a database or perhaps the relocations of copies of microfilms. For the provinces from Ontario eastward and all of Canada, the following are solid references:

Baglole, Harry. *Exploring Island History: A Guide to the Historical Resources of Prince Edward Island*. Belfast, Prince Edward Island: Ragweed Press, 1977.

Bunnell, Paul J. *Research Guide to Loyalist Ancestors: A Directory of Archives, Manuscripts, Published and Electronic Sources*. Westminster, Maryland: Heritage Books, 2006.

Cox, Kenneth G. *A Call to the Colours: Tracing Your Canadian Military Ancestors*. Toronto, Ontario: Dundurn Press, 2011.
Douglas, Althea. *Finding Your Ancestors in English Quebec*. Toronto, Ontario: Heritage Productions, 2001.

Douglas, Althea. *Finding Your Ancestors in New Brunswick*. Toronto, Ontario: Heritage Productions, 2002.

Fellows, Robert F. *Starting a Family History Project in New Brunswick, Canada*. Fredericton, New Brunswick: Provincial Archives of New Brunswick, [199-].

Irvine, Sherry and Dave Obee. *Finding Your Canadian Ancestors: A Beginner's Guide*. Provo, Utah: Ancestry Publishing, 2007.

Jones, Orlo. *Family History in Prince Edward Island: A Genealogical Research Guide*. [S.l.]: Prince Edward Island Heritage Foundation, 1981.

Merriman, Brenda Dougall. *Genealogy in Ontario: Searching the Records*. Toronto, Ontario: Ontario Genealogical Society, 2013.

Merriman, Brenda Dougall. *United Empire Loyalists: A Guide to Tracing Loyalists Ancestors in Upper Canada*. Campbellville, Ontario: Global Heritage Press, 2006.

Punch, Terrence M. *Genealogical Research in Nova Scotia*. 4th ed. Halifax, Nova Scotia: Nimbus Pub., 1998.

Punch, Terrence M. and George F. Sanborn, Jr. *Genealogist's Handbook for Atlantic Canada Research*. 2nd ed. Boston, Massachusetts: New England Historic Genealogical Society, 1997.

Taylor, Ryan. *The Canadian Sourcebook*. Ottawa, Ontario: Canadian Library Association, 2004.

Quebec has a somewhat separate history from the rest of Canada, but it has a definable Protestant minority population and a Loyalist heritage. Despite the differing pasts, the major genealogical instruction book for Loyalists is in the part of old Quebec, Upper Canada, that is now Ontario. Brenda Dougall Merriman's *United Empire Loyalists: A Guide to Tracing Loyalists Ancestors in Upper Canada* (2006) can be consulted for general principles, particularly as they apply to Ontario. It lists record groups that pertain to all the regions where Loyalists settled.

Two other works have become standards in the genealogy field. Both Brenda Dougall Merriman's *Genealogy in Ontario: Searching the Records* (2013), now in its fifth edition, and Terrence M. Punch's *Genealogist's Handbook for Atlantic Canada Research* (1997) are second to none. Genealogists on both sides of the border use the two books as necessary guides.

The research strategy is as valid in reverse for Canadians. In the search for Ulster origins, Canadians can look to those who fought for the Americans during the war for clues just as Americans can look to the Loyalists for clues.

Several websites can assist with Loyalist research. Noteworthy is the Héritage website, Heritage.canadiana.ca, which has digitized microfilm mainly from the Library & Archives Canada. The best way to find relevant material is to use "Loyalist" as the keyword in the general search. This site also has some early church registers from the Maritimes and Ontario that include Loyalists. Another major website is the "Genealogy & Family History" section of the Library & Archives Canada website, bac-lac.gc.ca. Look for

the category of "Topics" and then "Loyalists" as a subject heading.

The Rise of the Loyalists

Loyalists came from all economic backgrounds and classes of the population in the colonies that became the United States. Other than political, another reason for remaining loyal to the Crown was monetary because many families depended on England for their livelihoods. Newer immigrants also tended to support the Crown. Beyond their defense of Britain, the groups of people, from all walks of life, had little in common. As in any revolt, who became a Loyalist or a rebel depends on the perspective of who backed the losing side, although that is a simplification of a multi-level topic. According to the United Empire Loyalist Association of Canada (UELAC) website, the uniting thread might have been the people's conviction that too much democracy would lead to mob rule. Historians have deduced that up to 250,000 people in the Thirteen Colonies opposed the Revolution.

Areas in the Thirteen Colonies were controlled by Loyalists, and others were under the command of the Revolutionaries. Regardless, the people in the opposition party were more or less treated the same in all districts. They were not allowed to vote, sell land, be involved in legal matters, or work in certain professions.

In locales in the hands of the Revolutionaries, Committees of Safety were set up that acted as shadow governments. Their job was to harass Loyalists. In British-held areas, about 50 Loyalist regiments were formed during the war. Banishments from the Thirteen Colonies began as early as 1775 by way of the Committees of Safety, but the main ones occurred with the signing of the Treaty of Paris in 1783 that recognized the independence of the United States. With it, a massive expulsion of Loyalists began, and an estimated 70,000, at the least, fled at that time. Those who wished to remain in British North America had several options, the colonies of Nova Scotia (present-day Maritimes Provinces) and Quebec (present-day Ontario and Quebec) or the Caribbean for those in East Florida. They could go to Great Britain as well.

Consider that upon their exiles, the families were going far away, to some areas that were already populated and to some that were not. Many left with nothing. They also were among the first settlers and founders of new communities.

The first shipload of Loyalists arrived in Nova Scotia in 1776. By 1783, approximately 50,000 Loyalist refugees were in New York alone, and more than 30,000 of them left for Nova Scotia. They did not mix well with the established settlers, and the Loyalists petitioned the government for a separate colony along the St. John's River Valley and on St. John's Island (modern Prince Edward Island) and Cape Breton Island. Their request was granted in 1784, and New Brunswick was born with a population that was 90% Loyalists.

In the original colony of Quebec, some Loyalists established residences in the area that became Quebec; however, the majority settled in what became Ontario. Most were members of the disbanded Loyalists Regiments and made their homes along the St. Lawrence River upstream from Montreal and along the north shore of Lake Ontario. To compensate them for their losses, the government granted them free lands. Grants were given to the heads of households by military ranks, then dispensed to wives and children. They were colonized by ethnic group and religion. In 1791, the British Government passed the Canada Act that divided Quebec into Upper Canada (Ontario) and Lower Canada (Quebec).

The Loyalists' distrust of republicanism and mob rule contributed to Canadian nation building, influencing how the country emerged in a non-violent way. Their loyalty to the British Crown and their aversion to the United States allowed them to shape a viable and independent North American country.

Who is a Loyalist and Who is Not?

The definition of what constitutes a Loyalist may seem obvious, but Brenda Dougall Merriman in her Ontario textbook chapter "Who is a Loyalist?" in *United Empire Loyalists: A Guide to Tracing Loyalists Ancestors in Upper Canada* (2006), pp. 7-18 points out that even in Canadian history, classifications have varied. Several names and their descriptions are still in use while others are seldom heard today. In her research, she noticed that some terms, often debated, can overlap one another. Her conclusions about the people going into what is now Canada during the Loyalist period can be condensed as follows:

- Pre-Loyalist: The term has no meaning because it generally refers to settlements before the Revolutionary War. People have used the name when they mean "planter" settlers who arrived from Britain or New England and settled in what is now New Brunswick. In other words, there are no Pre-Loyalists in the sense that the label has been used.

- First-Loyalists: Refugees who arrived before the Revolutionary War ended.

- Maritime Loyalists: Settlers who arrived in Nova Scotia, Prince Edward Island, and New Brunswick (when it was created) during or after the war and applied for land grants.

- Associated Loyalists: Refugees who arrived by the thousands from New York City and settled in Nova Scotia, along with a few in Quebec.

- Treasury Loyalists: British and American colonists who went to England during or after the war. They received pensions and financial aid through the Treasury.

- Late Loyalists: Also known as Simcoe Loyalists, they were the refugees who went to Upper Canada (Ontario) in the 1790s after Governor Simcoe invited Loyalists to settle.

- Black Loyalists: A large group of African Americans who fled to Nova Scotia on the promise of freedom. To avoid prejudice, about half left for the colony of Sierra Leone in Africa.

- Florida Loyalists: Also known as St. Augustine Loyalists, they differed from other kinds of Loyalists. East Florida (St. Augustine) and West Florida (Pensacola) were British colonies from 1763 to 1783, but in 1781, the Spanish drove out the British. They went as refugees to Nova Scotia.

- American Loyalists: Also called Loyal Americans, they were usually what most people think of as Loyalists, often combining all the others with them.

Knowing the terms can be helpful because each of the group migrations to what is now Canada and what became of them has a distinct history. The names will uncover books and sources that treat them specifically.

Brenda Dougall Merriman also tackles the opposite question about who were not Loyalists, which she sees as more complicated than researchers often think it is. Although not labeled, as in the first list, they were groups of settlers during the same period. The following list summarizes her research about them:

- Soldiers of the regular British Army were not Loyalists. They were hired and paid to fight for the King. They include soldiers from the German areas of Europe.

- Quakers (Society of Friends), Mennonites, and other religious non-combatants were not typically considered Loyalists. However, categorizing them is not clear-cut because many of the pacifists bore hardships for their religious beliefs.

- Women traditionally were not considered Loyalists. Although they were not soldiers, they did protect their homes and families. Many widows applied for benefits based upon their husbands' losses or service. Women considered Loyalists are becoming more familiar.

- Men of French or British descent who lived in the colonies, such as Nova Scotia or Quebec, who did not rebel but who participated in the war effort were not considered Loyalists. The reasoning is that they did not sustain losses or destructions of properties, nor were they exiled. Although many did defend their homes, they were still behind the lines. While they are considered claimants, their children were not, as was the case with Loyalist settlers.

Each of the groups of men, women, and children generated its own history, which may lead to published histories and documents.

Claims for Losses

One set of records constructed specifically about Loyalists was the Claims for Losses, made through the Commissioners of American Loyalist Claims. The requests were for losses of personal and real estate in former colonial residences. If their applications were approved, some amounts of compensations were granted. The Commission was first set up in 1783. While more than 100,000 Loyalists fled what became the United States, only about 2,000 applied for claims through the Commission.

Although barely representing the scope of the Loyalist settlers in Canada, the records yielded some valuable information about those who applied. The database "UK, American Loyalist Claims, 1776-1835" on Ancestry.com indexes Audit Office (AO) 12 and AO 13. The original records are at the National Archives, Kew, England. Birthplaces often are not in the sequence of records. Digital images accompany the index.

The records are also indexed in a series of books by Peter Wilson Coldham. One is *American Loyalist Claims: Abstracted from the Public Record Office, Audit Office Series 13, Bundles 1-35 & 37* (Washington, D.C.: National Genealogical Society Bookstore, 1980-). For his work *American Migrations, 1765-1799: The Lives, Times, and Families of Colonial Americans Who Remained Loyal to the British Crown Before, During and After the Revolutionary War, as Related in their Own Words and through Their Correspondence* (Baltimore, Maryland: Genealogical Publishing Co., 2000), he obtained documentation from AO 12 and AO 13 to reconstruct the family stories. Even if a claim was rejected, the supporting reports, usually in AO 13, restore many personal facts about the applicants or the families. The latter book by Coldham has been digitized as the database "American (Loyalist) Migrations, 1765-1799" on Ancestry.com. Records are also digitized on FamilySearch.org.

Church Records

A major source for documenting Loyalist Ulster-Scots is church records. The registers for marriages or burials may have birthplaces, just as they may in the United States. Until they are searched, the content of any entry cannot be known. Even if it is indexed in a database, viewing a copy of the original is advised because the indexers might not have entered all the information, such as parents' names or birthplaces. When seeking Canadian church registers, a few principal points to remember are:

- The historically known Episcopal Church in the United States is historically the Church of England in Canada. It is today called the Anglican Church. Congregations are parishes that are grouped into dioceses.

- The United Church of Canada was instituted in 1925 through a merger of the majority of the Methodist Church, Canada; the Congregational Union of Ontario and Quebec; about 70% of the Presbyterian Church in Canada; and the Association of Local Union Churches (mostly in the Prairie Provinces). The Canadian Conference of the Evangelical United Brethren Church joined in 1968. The United Church of Canada is a mainline Protestant denomination and the largest Protestant denomination in the country. The union of the churches affects records.

- A Loyalist could have arrived in Canada as an Anglican (Church of England), Presbyterian, Congregationalist, Methodist, or Baptist. As revivals spread throughout Canada, denominational loyalties might have changed, which is not much different than for people in the United States except for the refugee statuses.

- The first Irish Methodist congregations were not in Ireland but were in what is now the United States and Canada beginning in the 1760s. In Canada, they started in modern Ontario and spread from there. Methodism did not emerge from the Church of Ireland to become its own denomination until 1817/8. Thus, Irish Methodism was in Canada before, during, and after the arrival of the Loyalists.

One fundamental set of registers to consult for Quebec is the "Drouin Collection" database on Ancestry.com that is "Quebec, Canada, Vital and Church Records (Drouin Collection), 1621-1968." In Quebec, most vital records of births, marriages, and deaths were copies of church registers. No full civil registrations on the January 1994, and so second copies of church registers from all denominations provincial basis were instituted until 1 January 1994, and so second copies of

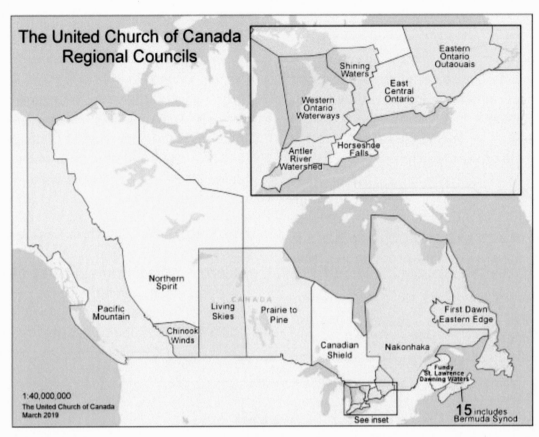

Figure 69: Regional Council jurisdictions of The United Church of Canada as of March 2019. Image courtesy of The United Church of Canada.

church registers from all denominations from throughout Quebec were sent every year to each church's local courthouse. In the 1940s, they were microfilmed by the Institut Généalogique Drouin, becoming popularly known in genealogy circles as the "Drouin Collection."

Obviously, in Quebec, most of the "Drouin Collection" consists of Roman Catholic registers, but it includes all denominations, making it a prime Protestant source for researching incoming Scots-Irish to what is now Quebec. The collection includes births/baptisms, marriages, death/burials, and other records, such as admissions' registers.

Outside of Quebec, church registers are not gathered into one database as the "Drouin Collection" is, but major databases have been compiled. Copies of many Protestant records are available at the Family History Library, and its collections and databases should not be ignored. Other church registers have been part of provincial microfilming or digitization programs. One example is Prince Edward Island. Its "PARO [Public Archives Record Office] Collections Database" includes church records from all denominations beginning in the 1770s.

Researchers may not realize that church registers are hidden under terms such as vital records, which could also include later civil registration of births, marriages, and deaths. The databases may be duplicated on FamilySearch.org or Ancestry.com. Therefore, before undertaking a long and tedious search for a needed Presbyterian record, checking online databases first is prudent. Also compare it to what is on the provincial websites. A website search always brings up the provincial archives.

Records for each denomination are housed in a central archive or series of archives. The United Church of Canada Archives in Toronto holds large collections of church registers, biographical files and periodicals, and personal papers from the Regional Councils, former five Conferences of London, Toronto, Hamilton, Bay of Quinte, and Manitou—all in

Ontario. It is the main archive but not the only one. Several research guides are also on the United Church of Canada Archives website, including "Genealogy Research: United Church of Canada Records," which focuses on the Ontario collections. The United Church of Canada Archives website has links to Conference and Presbytery websites, from where additional services can be obtained in locating records.

The Presbyterian Church in Canada Archives serves the entire country. It retains church registers, biographical files, private papers, and reference books helpful to family historians. On its website is "Guide to Genealogical Sources at the Presbyterian Church in Canada Archives."

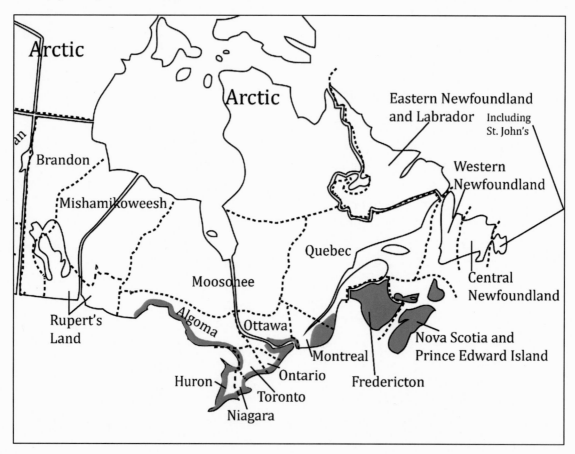

Figure 70: Anglican Diocesan Map for the eastern Provinces, including the settlement regions of American Loyalists.

The work quickly notes that documents from Presbyterian congregations who merged with the United Church of Canada in 1925 are now in United Church records, not Presbyterian records, including the pre-1925 registers. The archive is actively encouraging member congregations to have their records microfilmed or digitized by the archive.

Each Anglican Church of Canada diocese has its own archive that is responsible for collecting and preserving the historical documents from its geographical area, including parish registers. If the diocese to which a parish belonged or where someone lived is not known, the General Synod Archives in Toronto can assist in directing inquiries.

Many Anglican parish registers have been microfilmed or digitized and are at provincial or diocesan archives. The Family History Library has some of the church registers, often now digitized. Many parish histories have been published and can be found at several archives. The Family History Library has a large collection of them.

Plentiful Anglican registers have also been published in various periodicals in North America. Periodical Source Index (PerSI) on the Findmypast.com website is the best way to access their extractions. Aside from parish register extracts, articles detailing the tombstones in the parish cemeteries may be useful in the search for Ulster origins.

The Baptists, although they were perhaps not as numerous among the Loyalists as were other denominations, were still present. Nevertheless, it probably is safer to

state that many Loyalists or their descendants joined Baptist congregations in what became the United States and Canada. They did not arrive from Ulster to the colonies as Baptists.

Baptist history in Canada is as convoluted as it is in the United States because of the various kinds of Baptists, some of which join a like-minded convention, ministry, or association. The Baptist tradition dates back to the 1760s in Nova Scotia, before the Loyalists arrived. Baptists also entered in the waves of Loyalists from the United States, and, consequently, it is an important and historic denomination. The largest is the Canadian Baptist Ministries (CBM) headquartered in Mississauga, Ontario, which is a federation of four Baptist denominations: Canadian Baptists of Ontario and Quebec, Canadian Baptists of Western Canada, the Convention of Atlantic Baptist Churches, and Union d'Églises baptistes francophones du Canada. In addition, Regular Baptists, General Baptists, Freewill Baptists, Reformed Baptist, Free Baptist, Landmark Baptists, Evangelical Baptists, National Baptists, and independent Baptists are congregations that belong to none of the larger organizations. Baptist congregations are free to join or withdraw from any larger federations.

One place to begin the search for Baptist records is the Canadian Baptist Archives at McMasters Divinity College in Hamilton, Ontario. It currently possesses the largest collection of Baptist records in Canada with emphasis on Central Canada (Ontario and Quebec). The Canadian Baptist Historical Society is also at

McMasters Divinity College. The Atlantic Baptist Archive at Acadia University, Wolfville, Nova Scotia, collects for the eastern Canadian provinces. It has archival material from the 1700s and early 1800s, but most of its collection covers the late 1800s and afterward.

Records of value may consist of memberships, transfers in and out of congregations, and perhaps obituaries for ministers or prominent members in denominational periodicals or newspapers. All have potential.

United Empire Loyalist Association of Canada

Founded in 1897, the United Empire Loyalist Association of Canada (UELAC) is a lineage society headquartered in Toronto. The UELAC has branches for each geographical region throughout Canada and serves scattered members around the world, especially in Australia, New Zealand, and the United States. The UELAC estimates that 1 in 10 Canadians have a Loyalist ancestor.

The UELAC not only functions as a lineage society but also as a preservation and historical organization. In many ways, its purpose is similar to the National Society, Daughters of the American Revolution (NSDAR) in the United States. Both organizations are notable for preserving genealogies and history. Resources generated by organizations such as the UELAC and the NSDAR are essential parts of any family historian's documentation of an ancestor from the Revolutionary period of North American history.

To begin with, as with any lineage society, joining and participating in the stated organizational goals have requirements that for the UELAC, as stated on its website, include:

- Either male or female, a resident of the American colonies as of 19 April 1775, and joined the Royal Standard before the Treaty of Separation of 1783, or otherwise demonstrated loyalty to the Crown, and settled in territory remaining under the rule of the Crown; or

- a soldier who served in an American Loyalist Regiment and was disbanded in Canada; or

- a member of the Six Nations of either the Grand River or the Bay of Quinte Reserve who is descended from one whose migration was similar to that of other Loyalists.

The website states that membership in the UELAC provides no special status in Canadian society, although many members choose to place the letters UE after their name.

On the UELAC website is a "Loyalist Directory," which includes basic information on Loyalists with sources cited. It is not a comprehensive treatment of those listed, but it provides enough to identify the people, sometimes from where they came in the United States, as well as birthplaces. Birthplaces are not always noted, but knowing they were Loyalists initiates further exploration about them. The database can be viewed alphabetically. The search is straightforward because a register of all persons by surnames can be studied for clues. Moreover, the directory and the UELAC website can be manipulated in many different ways for more detailed information.

The UELAC website also has a broad search feature, wherein terms like "Antrim" can be entered as the keyword without using a surname. If the family being researched is known to have emigrated from County Antrim, all others from Antrim can be studied with the strategy. If they all came from a particular town or state in the United States, a significant pattern might have just been discovered. With the approach, more detailed biographies of Loyalists can be viewed on the website if they are posted, some of which are several pages long. The keyword also reveals applications that provide more details on the Loyalists in Canada, the United States, and Ireland.

In yet another approach, if a keyword is "North Carolina" with no surname, wherever North Carolina appears will be listed. It allows the inclusion of Loyalists from their homes in the United States, some of whom might have known one another before their exiles and perhaps in Ulster. The search can be narrowed further by "Cumberland Co., North Carolina" but becomes a bit more difficult because Cumberland Counties in Canada will come up, too.

Such a database not only seeks to identify Ulster birthplaces but also expands the search for others from the same area of Ulster or from the United States who might have been relatives or friends from

Ulster. Success depends on how much is known ahead of time and how effective the search engines are on a site.

The UELAC website has links to Canadian libraries and organizations with Loyalist collections as well. It notes that many of the provincial genealogy societies, such as the New Brunswick Genealogical Society, have their own collections. Links to various websites and databases are listed on the UELAC website.

The UELAC database can be used even if no record from the American side indicates that a Loyalist was in the family. Do not exclude the possibility of discovering one or more Loyalist forebears. By manipulating the database with surnames only or geographical place names in the United States, an unexpected Loyalist relative may be discovered, the first indication of such. Whether the person was a sibling or a cousin, within reason, he or she would have been from the same place in Ulster, making the UELAC website indispensable and applicable with or without prior knowledge of a Loyalist family member.

Among the research papers, applications, histories, and links, the UELAC website is one of the first places to pursue a Loyalist in the family. It is by no means the end of the search, nor do they have all things Loyalists since there is no complete listing of Loyalists in exile.

Published Books and Databases

As a result of the importance of Loyalists in Canadian research, a vast library of books and databases with details about the families and from where they came has developed. Some references concentrate on the lives of the Loyalists in the United States and their exiles to Canada. Therefore, not all books focus on where someone was born. Other works seek to explore the entire biography of a person from his or her origins, to immigration to the American colonies, and through life in Canada after exile. Documenting Loyalists has been undertaken by both historians and genealogists in Canada and the United States because the subject has been a source of fascination on both sides of the border. For many family researchers, depending on perspective and how they have been taught to view history, Loyalist relatives may or may not engender immense pride.

Because of the war and the flight to Canada (or elsewhere), almost any sources for the period are valid for identifying Loyalists. A land record claim can be as valuable as a military list. Foremost is the time in question. What resources can provide evidence for a Loyalist family before, during, and after it left the United States for refuge when it resettled in Canada? A more wide-ranging database, such as a land grant index, includes Loyalists by default because they were among the first settlers. The same could be stated for church or court records.

Such types of records and compilations are often digitized or made into databases on Ancestry.com and FamilySearch.org. The list below has been taken from their catalogues because most researchers on both sides of the border begin searches in the two websites before visiting archives or libraries in either country. The list represents only a selection of what has actually been published on the Canadian and American markets, but it, at the least, demonstrates to people new to Loyalist research the types of works that are available. The list from the FamilySearch catalog is astonishing, and its collection is not complete here. Be aware that provincial and state libraries and archives have additional published material on the Loyalists. The library of the UELAC is a major research center as well. Some general works, and databases from both countries are:

General

Ancestry.com. *The Old United Empire Loyalists List* [database online]. Provo, Utah: Ancestry.com Operations Inc, 2008.

Ancestry.com. *United Empire Loyalists, Part I* [database online]. Provo, Utah: Ancestry.com Operations Inc, 2008.

Ancestry.com. *United Empire Loyalists, Part II* [database online]. Provo, Utah: Ancestry.com Operations Inc, 2008.

Ancestry.com. *UK, American Loyalist Claims, 1776-1835* [database online]. Provo, Utah: Ancestry.com Operations, Inc., 2013.

Bunnell, Paul J. *The New Loyalist Index.* 7 vols. Bowie, Maryland: Heritage Books Inc. 1989-1998; Milford, New Hampshire: P J. Bunnell, 2005-2008.

Clark, Murtie June. *Loyalists in the Southern Campaign of the Revolutionary War.* 3 vols. Baltimore, Maryland: Genealogical Publishing Co., 1981.

Coke, Daniel Parker, Hugh Edward Egerton. *The Royal Commission on the Losses and Services of American Loyalists, 1783 to 1785: Being the Notes of Mr. Daniel Parker Coke, M.P., one of the Commissioners During that Period.* New York, New York: Lenox Hill Pub., 1971.

Coldham, Peter Wilson; Sally Lou (Mick) Haigh, ed. *American Loyalist Claims: Abstracted from the Public Record Office, Audit Office Series 13, Bundles 1-35 & 37.* Washington, D.C.: National Genealogical Society Bookstore, 1980-.

Dornfest, Walter T. *Military Loyalists of the American Revolution: Officers and Regiments, 1775-1783.* Jefferson, North Carolina: McFarland & Co., 2011.

Fryer, Mary Beacock and William A. Smy. *Rolls of the Provincial (Loyalist) Corps., Canadian Command, American Revolutionary Period.* Toronto, Ontario: Dundurn Press, 1981.

Hall, Jerry Hunter. *British, German, and Loyalist Officers in the American Revolution.* Magna, Utah: J. Hall, 1990.

Hayward, George H. *Loyalist Officers, 1782/83.* Fredericton, New Brunswick: G. H. Hayward, 1993.

Palmer Gregory, Lorenzo Sabine. *Biographical Sketches of Loyalists of the American Revolution.* Westport, Connecticut: Meckler Publishing, 1984.

Sabine, Lorenzo. *The American Loyalists, or, Biographical Sketches of Adherents to the British Crown in the War of the Revolution.* Boston, Massachusetts: C. C.

Little and J. Brown, 1847.   (This title is also known as *Biographical Sketches of Adherents to the British Crown in the War of the Revolution.*)

United Empire Loyalists' Association of Canada. Toronto Branch. *Loyalist Lineages of Canada, 1783-1983.* Agincourt, Ontario: Generation Press, 1984-1991.

Canada

New Brunswick

Holmes, Theodore C. *Loyalists to Canada: The 1783 Settlement of Quakers and Others at Passamaquoddy.* Camden, Maine: Picton Press, 1992.

Wright, Esther Clark. *The Loyalists of New Brunswick.* Fredericton, New Brunswick: [s.n.], 1955.

Nova Scotia

Ancestry.com. *Nova Scotia, Canada, Land Petitions, 1765-1800* [database online]. Provo, Utah: Ancestry.com Operations, Inc., 2012.

Gilroy, Marion, Daniel Cobb Harvey. *Loyalists and Land Settlement in Nova Scotia.* Baltimore, Maryland: Clearfield Co., 1990.

Ontario

Chadwick, Edward Marion. *Ontarian Families: Genealogies of Upper Empire Loyalists and Other Pioneer Families of Upper Canada.* 2 vols. Toronto, Canada: Rolph Smith & Co, 1894-1898.

Crowder, Norman K. *Early Ontario Settlers: A Source Book.* Baltimore, Maryland: Genealogical Publishing Co., 1993. (This is an Ancestry.com database.)

Fitzgerald, E. Keith. *Loyalist Lists: Over 2000 Loyalist Names and Families from the Haldimand Papers*. Toronto, Ontario: Ontario Genealogical Society, 1984.

Fitzgerald, E. Keith. *Ontario People, 1796-1803*. Baltimore, Maryland: Genealogical Publishing Co., 1993.

Fraser, Alexander. *United Empire Loyalists: Enquiry into the Losses and Services in Consequence of their Loyalty: Evidence in the Canadian Claims*. 2 vols. Baltimore, Maryland: Genealogical Publishing Co., 1994.

Pathfinder Genealogical Services. *Loyalist Children of Upper Canada: A Collection of Names: Sources, Ontario Archives*. St. Catharines, Ontario: Pathfinder Genealogical Services, 2000.

Potter-MacKinnon. *While the Women Only Wept: Loyalist Refugee Women*. Montreal, Quebec: McGill-Queens's University Press, 1993.

Reid, William D. *The Loyalists in Ontario: The Sons and Daughters of the American Loyalists of Upper Canada*. Baltimore, Maryland: Genealogical Publishing Co., 1994, 1973.

Rubincam, Milton. The Old United Empire Loyalist List. Baltimore, Maryland: Genealogical Publishing Co., 1976. (This work is also known as *Centennial of the Settlement of Upper Canada by the United Empire Loyalists, 1784-1884*.)

Smart, Susan, ed. *Index to the Upper Canada Land Books*. 9 vols. Toronto, Ontario: Ontario Genealogical Society, 2001-2005.

Wright, Barbaranne. *UE Loyalists & Military claimants of Upper Canada: registered warrants and fiats, 1798-1865*. St. Catharines, Ontario: Pathfinder Genealogical Services, 2001.

Prince Edward Island

Jones, Orlo and Doris Halsam. *An Island Refuge: Loyalist and Disbanded Troops on the Island of Saint John*. [S.l.]: Abegweit Branch of the United Empire Loyalist Association of Canada, 1983.

Quebec

Fitzgerald, E. Keith. *Loyalist Lists: Over 2000 Loyalist Names and Families from the Haldimand Papers*. Toronto, Ontario: Ontario Genealogical Society, 1984.

United Empire Loyalists' Association of Canada. Sir John Johnson Centennial Branch. *The Loyalists of the Eastern Townships of Quebec*. Stanbridge East, Quebec: Sir John Johnson Centennial Branch U.E.L., 1984.

Watt, Gavin K. *Loyalist Refugees: Non-Military Refugees in Quebec 1776-1784*. Milton, Ontario: Global Heritage Press, 2014.

United Empire Loyalists' Association of Canada. Heritage Branch (Montreal). *The Loyalists of Quebec, 1774-1825: A Forgotten History*. Saint-Lambert, Québec: Heritage Branch, United Empire Loyalists' Association of Canada, 1989.

United States

Connecticut

Siebert, W. H. *The Refugee Loyalists of Connecticut*. Pawtucket, Rhode Island: Quintin Publications, 199?.

Tyler, John W. Connecticut Loyalists: An Analysis of Loyalist Land Confiscations in Greenwich, Stamford and Norwalk. New Orleans, Louisiana: Polyanthos, 1977.

Delaware
Hancock, Howard Bell. *The Delaware Loyalists.* Wilmington, Delaware: Delaware Historical Society, 1940.

Florida
Clark, Murtie June. *Loyalists in the Southern Campaign of the Revolutionary War.* 3 vols. Baltimore, Maryland: Genealogical Publishing Co., 1981. (Volume 1 includes Florida.)

DeVille, Winston. *Mississippi Valley Mélange: A Connection of Notes and Documents for the Genealogy and History of the Province of Louisiana and the Territory of Orleans.* 6 vols. Baton Rouge, Louisiana: Provincial Press, 2009. (Volume 3 discusses the Loyalist military in colonial Mississippi in 1779.)

Siebert, Wilbur Henry. *Loyalists in East Florida, 1774 to 1785: The Most Important Documents Pertaining Thereto.* DeLand, Florida: Florida State Historical Society, 1929.

Georgia
Clark, Murtie June. *Loyalists in the Southern Campaign of the Revolutionary War.* 3 vols. Baltimore, Maryland: Genealogical Publishing Co., 1981. (Volume 1 includes Georgia.)

Louisiana
Clark, Murtie June. *Loyalists in the Southern Campaign of the*

Revolutionary War. 3 vols. Baltimore, Maryland: Genealogical Publishing Co., 1981. (Volume 1 includes Louisiana.)

Maryland
Clark, Murtie June. *Loyalists in the Southern Campaign of the Revolutionary War.* 3 vols. Baltimore, Maryland: Genealogical Publishing Co., 1981. (Volume 2 includes Maryland.)

New, M. Christopher. *Maryland Loyalists in the American Revolution.* Centreville, Maryland: Tidewater, 1996.

Massachusetts
Jones, E. Alfred. *The Loyalists of Massachusetts: Their Memorials, Petitions and Claims.* Baltimore, Maryland: Clearfield Co., 1995.

Maas, David E. *Divided Hearts, Massachusetts Loyalists, 1765-1790: A Biographical Directory.* [S.l.]: Society of Colonial Wars in the Commonwealth of Massachusetts, 1980.

Stark, James Henry. The Loyalists of Massachusetts and the Other Side of the American Revolution. Boston, Massachusetts: James H. Stark, 1910.

Mississippi
Clark, Murtie June. *Loyalists in the Southern Campaign of the Revolutionary War.* 3 vols. Baltimore, Maryland: Genealogical Publishing Co., 1981. (Volume 1 includes Mississippi.)

DeVille, Winston. *Mississippi Valley Mélange: A Connection of Notes and Documents for the Genealogy and History of the Province of Louisiana and the*

Territory of Orleans. 6 vols. Baton Rouge, Louisiana: Provincial Press, 2009. (Volume 3 discusses the Loyalist military in colonial Mississippi in 1779.)

New Hampshire
Siebert, Wilbur Henry. *The Loyalist Refugees of New Hampshire*. Columbus, Ohio: Ohio State University, 1916.

New Jersey
Jones, E. Alfred. *The Loyalists of New Jersey, Their Memorials, Petitions, Claims, etc. from English Records*. Newark, New Jersey: New Jersey Historical Society, 1927.

Stryker, William S. *"The New Jersey Volunteers" (Loyalists) in the Revolutionary War*. Trenton, New Jersey: Naar Day & Naar, 1887.

New York
Ancestry.com. *New York, Sales of Loyalist Land, 1762-1830* [database online]. Provo, Utah: 2013. (This database does not include the Southern District, which included the New York City area, Suffolk and Westchester counties.)

Burleigh, Herbert Clarence. *Confiscations, Albany, Charlotte, and Tyron Counties, New York*. Toronto, Ontario: United Empire Loyalists' Association of Canada, 1970.

Burleigh, Herbert Clarence. *New York State – Confiscations of Loyalists*. [Toronto, Ontario: United Empire Loyalists' Association of Canada, 1970.

Flick, Alexander Clarence. *Loyalism in New York During the American Revolution*. New York: Columbia University Press, 1901.

Hulslander, Laura Penny. *New York Loyalist Confiscations*. Alexandria, Virginia: Sleeper, 1995.

Ptak, Diane Snyder. *The American Loyalists: Origins and Nominal Lists*. Albany, New York: D. S. Ptak, 1993.

Randlet, Philip. *The New York Loyalists*. Knoxville, Tennessee: University of Tennessee Press, 1986.

Yoshpe, Harry Beller. *The Disposition of Loyalist Estates in the Southern District of the State of New York*. New York, New York: Columbia University, 1939.

North Carolina
Clark, Murtie June. *Loyalists in the Southern Campaign of the Revolutionary War*. 3 vols. Baltimore, Maryland: Genealogical Publishing Co., 1981. (Volume 1 includes North Carolina.)

DeMond, Robert O. *The Loyalists in North Carolina During the Revolution*. Baltimore, Maryland: Genealogical Publishing Company, 1979. (This is an Ancestry.com database.)

Pruitt, Albert Bruce *Abstract of Sales of Confiscated Loyalists Land and Property in North Carolina*. Rocky Mount, North Carolina: A. B. Pruitt, 1989.

Pennsylvania
Clark, Murtie June. *Loyalists in the Southern Campaign of the Revolutionary War*. 3 vols. Baltimore, Maryland:

Genealogical Publishing Co., 1981. (Volume 2 includes Pennsylvania.)

Williams, Mildred C. *Loyalists, Outlaws, Aiders, Abettors, "Attained Traitors" of Bucks County, Pennsylvania*. Newtown, Pennsylvania: Witt-Britt Books, 1988.

South Carolina

Clark, Murtie June. *Loyalists in the Southern Campaign of the Revolutionary War*. 3 vols. Baltimore, Maryland: Genealogical Publishing Co., 1981. (Volume 1 includes South Carolina.)

Lambert, Robert Stansbury. *South Carolina Loyalists in the American Revolution*. Columbia, South Carolina: University of South Carolina Press, 1987.

Moss, Bobby Gilmer. *The Loyalists in the Siege of Fort Ninety Six*. Blacksburg, South Carolina: Scotia-Hibernia Press, 1999.

Vermont

Burleigh, Herbert Clarence. *Sequestrations, Confiscations and Sale of Estates: State Papers of Vermont*. Toronto, Ontario: United Empire Loyalists' Association of Canada, 1970.

Virginia

Clark, Murtie June. *Loyalists in the Southern Campaign of the Revolutionary War*. 3 vols. Baltimore, Maryland: Genealogical Publishing Co., 1981. (Volume 2 includes Virginia.)

INDEX